WHY TESOL?

THEORIES AND ISSUES IN TEACHING ENGLISH TO SPEAKERS OF OTHER LANGUAGES IN K–12 CLASSROOMS
Third Edition

Eileen N. Whelan Ariza

Carmen A. Morales-Jones

Noorchaya Yahya

Hanizah Zainuddin

Florida Atlantic University
Boca Raton. Florida

KENDALL/HUNT PUBLISHING COMPANY
4050 Westmark Drive Dubuque, Iowa 52002

Book Team

Chairman and Chief Executive Officer   Mark C. Falb
Senior Vice President, College Division   Thomas W. Gantz
Director of National Book Program   Paul B. Carty
Editorial Development Manager   Georgia Botsford
Developmental Editor   Lynne Rogers
Vice President, Production and Manufacturing   Alfred C. Grisanti
Assistant Vice President, Production Services   Christine E. O'Brien
Project Coordinator   Angela Puls
Permissions Editor   Elizabeth Roberts
Designer   Jenifer Chapman
Managing Editor, College Field   Paul Gormley
Acquisitions Editor, College Field   Marla Swartz

Dedication

We wish to dedicate this book to all the children who, for many reasons, migrate to the United States and become English language learners in our schools. It is our strong belief that they deserve the most qualified teachers possible. This book is our contribution to the training of teachers who will make a positive difference in the lives of these children, who in turn will significantly influence the future of this great nation.

The Authors

Contents

PART FOUR: A Knowledge Base in Assessment and Evaluation   189

PART FIVE: Teachers' Reflections   225

Foreword

As cultural and linguistic diversity has increased in classrooms across North America and in other parts of the world, it has become clear that the knowledge base required to effectively teach in these classrooms must include specialized information about second language development and its relationship to academic success. It is a pleasure to write a foreword for a book that articulates this expanding knowledge base in a clear, accessible, and comprehensive manner.

This book is particularly timely in view of the increased concern about accountability in our schools. The requirement in states such as Florida, that all teachers of English language learners obtain appropriate qualifications to prepare them to teach these students effectively, reflects this concern for accountability. We still, however, face many challenges in implementing appropriate educational reforms that create effective and equitable learning environments for culturally and linguistically diverse students. Among these challenges are the following:

○ Ensuring that statewide assessment mandates are valid and realistic for English learners, in addition to students for whom English is their first language (L1);
○ Providing appropriate instructional support for English learners, not only in the early stages of learning conversational English, but also in the longer process of catching up in academic aspects of English;
○ Building flexibility into instruction and assessment provisions that recognizes the diversity among English learners and avoids slotting these students into a "one-size-fits-all" school system intended for "generic" monolingual, monocultural, English L1 students;
○ Ensuring that special education assessment procedures are valid for English learners so that these students are not over-represented in categories such as "learning disability" or "communicative disorder" as has happened in the past;
○ Providing encouragement and opportunities for students to continue to develop their home language ability, as this is the foundation upon which we construct English academic development.

Because issues related to immigration and increasing diversity have been controversial, it is not surprising that there are many misconceptions regarding the language and academic development of bilingual students. For example, students are often assumed to have overcome the "language barrier" when they have acquired the ability to converse relatively fluently in English. We know, in fact, that it can take much longer (five or more years) for students to bridge the gap in academic aspects of English.

Similarly, students' first languages are still frequently seen as either irrelevant or detrimental to their academic progress. Nothing could be further from the truth. For more than thirty years, research has shown that bilingual students who continue to develop their L1 as they acquire English experience linguistic advantages such as increased awareness of how language works and how to use language effectively. As one example, students from Spanish-speaking backgrounds have a significant potential advantage in gaining access to the low-frequency Latin- and Greek-based lexicon of academic English, since most of these words have cognates in Spanish. The word *encuentro* in Spanish is a cognate of the English word encounter, which is much less frequently used than its Anglo-Saxon derived synonym *meet*. As students progress through the grades and learn ever more complex concepts in science, math, and social studies, the proportion of low-frequency Latin- and Greek-derived vocabulary that they must learn increases dramatically. Spanish-speaking students' L1 can be a significant advantage in this process. If we are aware of these extensive L1/L2 linkages, we can help students to search for cognate connections in texts, thereby increasing their ability to infer the meanings of unknown words.

This volume is clearly not intended as a recipe book for implementing appropriate instruction for English-language learners. There are no recipes or formulas that can be applied to every student or situation. Rather, the intent is to provide educators with the information necessary to make informed and skillful decisions regarding the school policies and instructional practices that are likely to be effective in addressing the learning needs of a very diverse group of students. This implies that we must see ourselves individually and collectively as researchers who are learning from our own experiences in teaching bilingual students. Our goal should be not only to implement a knowledge base, but also to contribute to it.

In order to apply the existing knowledge base to our own unique context, and to contribute to the expansion and refinement of this knowledge base, we must engage in a collective problem-posing and problem-solving process. What approaches have worked for us in the past? What strategies are in place in our schools for involving parents and the community? Are there ideas that have been implemented elsewhere that might improve our practice in this and other areas? Do we, as a school faculty, have a consistent set of beliefs and assumptions about language and literacy teaching for bilingual students? If not, how can we discuss and resolve inconsistencies so that students are not confused by very different instructional strategies from one year or classroom to the next? What accommodations and/or instructional strategies might be helpful to enable English learners to succeed on state-mandated assessments, despite the fact that they may be required to undergo these assessments long before they have had time to catch up academically in English?

There are no easy answers to many of these questions, but we are much more likely to pursue reasonable directions if we are discussing the issues within our own faculty, drawing on our collective experience, and brainstorming possible solutions. In other words, every school can benefit from articulating a language policy—a set of beliefs and practices about language learning and academic achievement that have been formulated specifically with the students we teach in mind. Such a policy should be sensitive, both to the unique situation of our students (and faculty) and the general knowledge base that exists from research and theory. The present volume provides an excellent starting point to understanding the knowledge base that already exists. As educators, we should see ourselves as adding to this knowledge base as a result of our individual and collective actions to implement the best possible instruction for all our students.

In conclusion, it is common these days to hear policymakers and school administrators talk of the school as a learning institution. In doing so they usually try to imply not only that schools are institutions where pupils are engaged in learning, but also that the school itself must continue to learn from its own collective experiences if it is to adapt to the changing cultural, economic, technological, and global challenges of the twenty-first century. As educators, we are in the vanguard of this learning process when we welcome new students and families into our society. We have to learn from our own experiences—our successes and failures—if we are to implement effective instruction and contribute significantly to the knowledge base regarding the education of linguistically and culturally diverse students.

Jim Cummins
The University of Toronto

Preface

AUDIENCE AND PURPOSE

We have written *WHY TESOL? Theories and Issues in Teaching English to Speakers of Other Languages in K–12 Classrooms*, to provide current and prospective teachers who have English language learners in their classrooms with a knowledge base in the field of teaching English as a second/new language (TESOL). Today, more than ever, when teachers enter their classrooms they encounter a diversity in the student body that brings richness, and at the same time challenges, that teachers must address. The intent of this book is to provide an in-depth theoretical background for teachers as they try to address the needs of English language learners in their classrooms.

In *WHY TESOL? Theories and Issues* we provide:

○ National statistics that help clarify the global nature of our American society in this twenty-first century
○ An historical perspective on the laws that have influenced the teaching of second language learners in today's schools
○ A description of a variety of English as a second/new language (ESL/ENL) programs
○ A profile of English language learners and the needs they bring to today's classrooms
○ An analysis and explanation of the nature of language and first or native language acquisition
○ A discussion of second language theories and models
○ A look at assessment and relevant issues as they relate to English language learners

ORGANIZATION

WHY TESOL?, third edition, has five parts. Part One develops an essential knowledge base for readers. It describes the legal rights of English language learners (ELLs) and gives an historical overview of the laws that have had an impact on what is being done today to address the needs of ELLs in America. Part One also provides a clear classification of English as a second/new language (ESL/ENL) programs available throughout the United States, as well as a discussion of factors that affect the design of these programs. Lastly, Part One offers a profile of English language learners in the United States.

Part Two provides a basic grounding in the core areas of linguistics: phonology, morphology, syntax, pragmatics, discourse, and other related areas, such as non-verbal communication, dialectal variation, English language development, and World Englishes. This section is not intended to be an exhaustive study on the language system, rather it attempts to get the reader's "feet wet" when it comes to the nature of the English language. Such an understanding of how language works and what it means to know a language will help the reader understand the complexities involved in acquiring a language. This section begins with a general introduction of the universals across languages. Despite the linguistic divergence of the world's languages, human languages are remarkably similar in many ways. All languages share the same common properties and components, such as phonology, morphology, syntax, and semantics which make up the grammar of a language and make human communication possible. Part Two then provides a description of the sound systems of a language, including all the possible sound sequences and constraints, and discusses why certain sounds are difficult for foreign speakers to produce. Next, it introduces concepts related to the process of word creation within a language, and how we learn to recognize words or non-words in a language. It also examines how we recognize and form grammatical sentences and interpret potential ambiguities within a sentence, and highlights potential difficulties that second language learners may have with English sentences. A chapter is also devoted to a discussion of how speakers arrive at meanings of words and sentences in their native language and how this process is filtered through the experience, culture, and worldview of the speakers.

The second half of this section looks at a number of related issues. It examines how speakers use language to carry out specific linguistic and social tasks and how the context of a language event influences meaning. It also describes differences in nonverbal communication across cultures and how these differences may result in misunderstandings between native and non-native speakers. Cross-cultural conversational and rhetorical patterns are also discussed with implications for teachers to facilitate second language learners' communicative abilities in their target language. Part Two then discusses how variation in human languages is influenced by factors related to socioeconomic status, region, and ethnicity, and takes a brief look at the sociolinguistic and linguistic profiles of the different varieties of English used around the world.

Finally, the section ends with a brief overview of the historical development of the English language, how language families are established based on lexical similarities between languages, and the influence of other languages on English as demonstrated by extensive loan words in English.

Part Three contains first and second language theories and applications. Issues discussed focus on first and second/new language processes with the developmental milestones in first and second language learning compared from a linguistic perspective. The non-linguistic factors affecting second language acquisition, such as age, personality, cognitive factors, socio-cultural factors, motivation, and learning environment, are also discussed. Another section explains the complexity of the second language acquisition process through first language acquisition theories such as the behaviorist, innatist, cognitivist, social interactionist, and brain-based approaches. It also discusses second language acquisition theories and models such as Krashen's Monitor Model, Cummins' Second Language Framework, Selinker's Interlanguage Theory, McLaughlin's Attention-Processing Model, and Bialystok's Analysis/Automatic Processing Model. Strategies and styles in language learning such as Gardner's Multiple Intelligence Model, Cognitive Academic Language Learning Approach (CALLA), and second language communication strategies are also explored. Sources of error and error treatment are discussed to help teachers understand the difficulty learners experience when learning a new language. The development of methodologies in foreign language teaching and ESL teaching is traced, starting with the more traditional methods, such as the Grammar Translation Method, to the later approaches, such as the Natural Approach, and the Whole Language Approach. The section ends with a chapter that argues the significance of meeting the needs of second language learners.

Part Four of this book addresses the importance of teachers being accountable for effective teaching. This is especially important when we assess students who are learning English, and we are expected to grade them regardless of their proficiency levels. How do teachers make sure that they are testing academic content as opposed to language proficiency? This topic is thoroughly explored, as it is important to understanding the appropriateness of standardized tests versus alternative assessments when determining the success of instruction and learning for second language learners. Finally, the laws governing testing and assessment are examined so teachers can see how legal issues affect their daily planning, grading, and implementing proper administrative procedures in accordance with fairness and the law.

Part Five is a short section in which a new teacher and an experienced teacher share their classroom experiences. They tell how they adapt themselves and their teaching strategies to better measure the academic successes of the second language learners in their mainstream classrooms.

FEATURES

WHY TESOL? contains the following pedagogical features designed to make the material accessible and lasting for the reader:

○ Because it is believed that readers should have an idea of what the chapters will be addressing, each chapter presents the "Key Issues" discussed in the chapter.
○ Each chapter opens with a "real life" scenario intended to capture the essence of the chapter. The reader can later go back to this scenario and consider the content of the chapter and how it was reflected in the opening scenario.
○ In our effort to help the reader acquire the most essential knowledge base, each chapter ends with a list of key "Points to Remember."

To help the reader reflect on and apply the knowledge acquired from each chapter, a separate CD workbook has been developed. For each chapter, there are a series of "Challenge Sheets" containing exercises/ questions/research assignments to be completed after reading the chapter. Instructors using this book as a text for an ESOL class may require students to complete these sheets to be turned in as part of their written assignments.

Glossary of Terms

At the back of *WHY TESOL?*, an in-depth definition of key acronyms employed throughout the book has been included. In addition, key terms have been listed and defined for quick reference.

SOME POINTS FOR CLARIFICATION

Typically, English learners speak a primary language other than English at home. English learners vary in their proficiency in their primary languages, as well as in English. Beginners to intermediates in English are often referred to as limited English proficient (LEP), a term that is used in federal legislation and other official documents (Peregoy & Boyle, 2005). In this book the terms English language learners, English learners, second language learners, non-native speakers of English, language minority students, and language enriched pupils will be used synonymously to refer to students who are in the process of acquiring English as a new language and whose primary language is not English. (Refer to Glossary of Terms for further clarification.)

Acknowledgments

At this point we would like to talk about Jim Cummins. Dr. Cummins' research on BICS (Basic Interpersonal Communication Skills) or social language, and CALP (Cognitive Academic Language Proficiency), or academic language provided an academic epiphany in the field of TESOL. When we first read his research, it made us exhale with relieved understanding as we had finally found a name to apply to the phenomenon occurring in our schools that showed English language learners speaking perfect English while failing academically. This research is valuable information we can relay to our pre-service and practicing teachers as it arms them with a knowledgeable answer when confused educators ask, "Why is this child in ESL/ENL? He speaks perfect English!", as the child fails dismally. With this knowledge in their cache, teachers are able to apply powerful strategies for potent classroom instruction.

We wish to thank Dr. Cummins for taking the time to read this manuscript, and for writing the foreword. It gives us great personal pleasure and professional satisfaction to know an individual of his stature endorses the work we are doing, as we prepare teachers to graduate with TESOL competency ready to teach linguistically, ethnically, and culturally diverse students in the classrooms of today, and of the future.

Eileen N. Whelan Ariza, Ed.D.
Carmen A. Morales-Jones, Ph.D.
Noorchaya Yahya, Ph.D.
Hanizah Zainuddin, Ph.D.
Florida Atlantic University
Boca Raton, Florida

Writing a book can be a delightful torture that lasts for years, as life goes on around you. Deadlines loom as your family and friends wait patiently for you to finish that one last word or thought, before it escapes you forever. Papers, articles, books, and references are strewn about the house and office with wild abandon. Neatness, such as it was, becomes an elusive goal. But although I write alone, I cannot do it alone. I write for pleasure, as my incredible children, Stefani and Nico, take a temporary back seat, but they always show their pride in my work. I am deeply grateful to them and they are the loves of my life. I dedicated this book to them.

I also could not have completed this project without the help of Renee Zelden, a whiz at administrative details and organization. She has an incredible eye, noticed things I overlooked, and helped me make my work a success. Thank you, Renee; you and your lovely mom, Janice Zelden, have proved to be unforgettable additions to my universe.

My mother, Nancy Whelan, I thank as well, because she always told me I could be anything I wanted to be. She was the one who told me: "go travel, see the world . . ." and "Bring any of your friends home . . . I don't care where they are from, or what color, or faith they are . . ." and "Why don't you learn Spanish," which led me to my life and career today. Awesome woman that she is, she made the first cross-cultural leap in the family by having the audacity to be an Anglo Protestant who married an Irish Catholic bar owner in the 1940's—a radical move!

Eileen N. Whelan Ariza
Associate Professor of TESOL
Florida Atlantic University
Boca Raton, Florida, Spring 2006

I wish to thank my loving husband, Charlie, for his continued support and endless encouragement. He, who so willingly and unselfishly has shared me with my writing throughout the entire revision process of this book and especially during my first year of retirement, deserves my heartfelt thanks. "How blessed I am to have such a caring and loving presence in my life."

Carmen A. Morales-Jones,
Professor
Florida Atlantic University
Boca Raton, Florida, Spring 2006

I would like to thank my three sons, Shafiq, Abdullah, and Abdul, for being so understanding and patient. My gratitude goes to Suzzane St. Aubin and others who helped me through the writing of this manuscript.

Noorchaya Yahya, Associate Professor
Florida Atlantic University
Port St. Lucie, Florida, Spring 2006

I am deeply indebted to my husband and two children who have been so patient with me and especially forgiving for the many hours and weekends that I have spent finishing this manuscript.

Hani Zainuddin, Associate Professor
Florida Atlantic University
Boca Raton, Florida, Spring 2006

The authors would like to thank the very talented Marci Maher for creating the cover design, the cartoon illustrations, and for offering her perspective as a new teacher facing classroom realities. Her creativity is only limited by the universal problem of mutual time constraints.

In addition, we want to thank Betty Lacayo, a veteran teacher of ESOL students, who is an expert on literacy-based curriculum in St. Lucie County, for sharing her insights with us, and thanks also go to Bianca Swanson for sharing her rubric (which was a class assignment).

Finally, to all the educators trying to become ESOL endorsed, thank you for making the effort to learn how to successfully teach the delightfully diverse English language learners.

The Authors

About the Authors

Eileen N. Whelan Ariza received her Ed.D. in Multilingual/Multicultural Education from the University of Massachusetts, Amherst, and her MAT in TESOL, Spanish as a Second Language, and her Bilingual/Multicultural Endorsement from the School of International Training in Brattleboro, Vermont. A Teaching Fellow for many years at Harvard University's English Language Institute, she is now an associate professor of TESOL in Florida Atlantic University's teacher education program, where she prepares both prospective and current teachers in the undergraduate and graduate programs for Florida's mandated ESOL endorsement. Ariza has spent time in more than 70 countries, and has taught English as a foreign and second language in eight countries to students ranging from preschoolers to the elderly. Her primary research interests are in ESOL, both in the United States and overseas, cross-cultural communication, and preparation of mainstream teachers with English learners in their classroom.

Carmen A. Morales-Jones received her Ph.D. in Curriculum and Integrative Studies from Florida State University, Tallahassee, in 1975. Her career encompasses the teaching of ESL and French at the Laboratory School of the University of Puerto Rico, as well as teacher training at Florida Atlantic University in the area of language acquisition (language arts for elementary education majors, foreign languages for foreign language majors, and English as a new language for elementary pre-service teachers and in-service teachers). Currently, she is on phased retirement after having served as a professor of education at Florida Atlantic University for thirty years. She teaches and supervises student teachers and interns in the spring semesters. Her research interests are in the areas of teacher training, English language acquisition, and foreign language teaching.

Noorchaya Yahya received her Ph.D. in rhetoric and linguistics from Indiana University of Pennsylvania. Currently, she is an associate professor at Florida Atlantic University, where she teaches TESOL methods courses. She has taught ESL for more than ten years at institutions of higher learning both inside and outside of the United States. She is currently involved in the training of pre-service teachers for ESOL endorsement and in-service teachers for ESOL certification in Florida. Her research interests lie in the areas of second language writing, teacher education, and second language acquisition.

Hanizah Zainuddin received her Ph.D. from Indiana University, Bloomington, Indiana in 1995 and is currently an associate professor of TESOL at Florida Atlantic University, Boca Raton. Her areas of interest include second language writing, contrastive rhetoric, teacher education, family literacy, the potentials offered by learner stories in bridging intergenerational relationships between immigrant adults and their "Americanized" children, and the sociocultural adaptations of indigenous and immigrant populations in the United States. She also has extensive experience teaching English as a second language to adults and adolescents inside and outside of the United States. She is currently involved in a project to develop a curriculum that reflects the issues and needs for English language use of Mayan adults from Guatemala who are currently residing in the United States.

Part One

A KNOWLEDGE BASE FOR SECOND LANGUAGE TEACHING

Chapter 1

Why TESOL?
Diversity in America

Key Issues

- ○ Immigration patterns in the United States
- ○ Effects of immigration patterns in today's schools
- ○ Increases in the percentage of English Language Learners (ELLs) during the last decade
- ○ Demographics pertaining to ELLs in the United States
- ○ Multilingual diversity in today's schools in America
- ○ Challenges United States schools face in the twenty-first century

SCENARIO

It is the first day of "pre-planning," the beginning of a new school year at Golden Gate School. Mr. Quintana has just received his homeroom class roster. He is preparing to develop his seating chart. He has names such as "Nancy," "Paul," "Mike," and "Sherry." He also has "Guillermo," "Leonor," "Paolo," "Ceceile" and "Dergenise."

Mr. Quintana is eager to learn more about the composition of his class, especially his students' ethnic backgrounds and English language proficiencies. He discovers that Guillermo, Leonor, Paolo, Ceceile, and Dergenise have all been identified as limited English proficient (ELLs). Guillermo and Leonor recently arrived from Venezuela and do not speak any English; Paolo came from Brazil and attended Golden Gate last year. He speaks some English. Ceceile and Dergenise came from Haiti and have been in the United States for six months. They, too, have attended Golden Gate, but only for one semester. All of these students are limited in their proficiency in the English language. The rest of Mr. Quintana's class is composed of native speakers of English.

Mr. Quintana enjoys having the English language learners in his class, because he feels they add a new dimension to the teaching/learning exchange in his classroom. He also embraces with enthusiasm the new challenges these students bring. Mr. Quintana says: "This is why I became a teacher; these are the challenges that keep me growing and current in my profession."

IMMIGRATION: EDUCATIONAL CHALLENGES

In the great sweep of American history, immigration has proven to be a positive influence for the United States. The diversity that immigrants have brought, and continue to bring, is an asset to the American way of life. These contributions are not only evident in the performing arts, literature, religion, and scientific research, but in the areas of international business and economic growth as well. As immigrants have settled in areas ranging from sleepy towns to vibrant international metropolises, they have had a significant impact on the development of this country. The diversity immigrants bring with them is also an asset in educational settings. One of the greatest assets is the opportunity afforded to develop a global perspective so necessary in this twenty-first century. Global independence is a thing of the past; global interdependence is inevitable.

It is a reality, though, that despite its positive effects, immigration also means an increase in the numbers of students as well as a shift in the composition of the student body. These diverse students who contribute such great richness of cultural heritage to our schools, classrooms, and communities also bring considerable challenges (Schall, 1995). In addition to the need to learn English, these students need extra academic instruction, since many come to this country with limited schooling, forcing schools to make major adjustments to accommodate their needs. Today, with more and more newcomers coming into an already frail educational system, our schools are being overwhelmed. As the 1950's baby boomers age, their children's children are entering into their prime child-bearing years. The echo effect can be seen as school enrollments around the country expand (Cortez, 2003). Schools that are already struggling with the strains of these high enrollments, are also dealing with an influx of students who need special services if they are to be served adequately. Bilingual education/two-way and one-way developmental including content ESL have been found to be the most successful programs (Thomas & Collier, 2001).

Shifts in Student Populations

Based on the most recent survey results (2003–2004), it is estimated that 5,044,361 English language learners (ELLs) are enrolled in public schools (pre-K through grade 12). This number represents approximately 10 percent of the total public school enrollment, and an approximately 68.7 percent increase over the reported 1997–1998 public school enrollment.

Estimates indicate that the ELL population is growing at a rate of 9.3 percent per year. The ELL count for 2000–2001 was 4,584,048, 1.6 percent greater than the number reported for 1999–2000 (4,416,580), and has continued an upward trend over the past several years. Since 1997–1998, yearly increases in the number of ELLs have ranged from 8.0 percent in 1999–2000 to almost 10 percent in 2001–2002.

TABLE 1.1

Trends in ELL Enrollment 1997–1998 to 2002–2003

Year	ELL Enrollment	% ELL Change from Prior Year
1997–1998	3,470,268	—
1998–1999	3,540,673	19.8%
1999–2000	4,416,580	18.0%
2000–2001	4,584,940	9.6%
2001–2002	4,747,763	9.7%
2002–2003	5,044,361	9.4%

Source: Adapted from U.S. Department of Education, Office of English Language Acquisition, Language Enhancement and Academic Achievement www.ncela.gwu.edu/policy/states/index.htm.

From 1997–1998 to 2002–2003, the reported overall number of ELLs has increased by 46.5 percent (Table 1.1). In these six years, only nine states reported decreases in ELL enrollment, while twenty-five states reported increases greater than 30 percent. The following thirteen states have reported increases of 50 percent or more:

California, Georgia, Idaho, Indiana, Kentucky, Minnesota, Missouri, New Jersey, North Carolina, Pennsylvania, South Carolina, Wisconsin, and

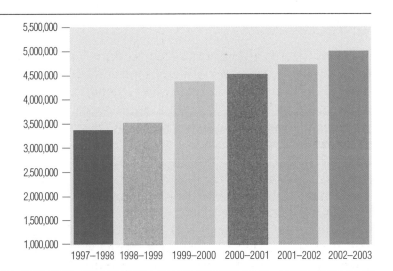

Limited English Proficient Student Enrollment, United States

1997–1998	3,470,268
1998–1999	3,540,673
1999–2000	4,416,580
2000–2001	4,584,948
2001–2002	4,747,763
2002–2003	5,044,361

FIGURE 1.1 ELL Enrollment, 1997–1998 to 2002–2003

Source: Adapted from National Clearing House of English Language Acquisition (NCELA) Report. Retrieved (2005) from www.ncela.gwu.edu/policy/states/index.htm

Washington. The greatest increases have been in Wisconsin (75%), North Carolina (84%), South Carolina (127.6%), and Georgia (210.1%). From 1990 to 1997, fifteen states reported an increase of 10 percent or more in their ELL populations. In the last six years (1997–2003), thirty-one states have reported increases of 10 percent or more. These figures indicate that the immigrant influx is becoming more widespread throughout the United States and not concentrated in a few states as it has been in the past.

Estimates indicate that the ELL population is growing at a rate nine times faster than the general school population (refer to Figure 1.1 and Table 1.1). Thus there is no evidence that the ELL population will diminish in the near future.

States with the largest general population and school enrollments tend to be the states with the largest enrollment of ELLs as well. California leads the rankings with 1,511,646 ELLs, followed by Texas (570,022), Florida (254,211), and New York (239,097). (Table 1.2) In the year 1996–1997 the cumulative percentages represented by these states indicated that approximately two-thirds of the ELL enrollment was in four states: California, Texas, Florida, and New York. (National Clearing House for Bilingual Education, 1996) As Table 1.2 indicates, the cumulative percentages of these four states has decreased to 53.4 percent, clearly showing that the immigrant population is settling in other states as well.

TABLE 1.2

States with Highest Percentage of ELL Enrollment, 2003–2004

Rank	State	Enrollment	% of National Enrollment	Cumulative
1	California	1,598,535	31.6%	31.6%
2	Texas	660,707	13.0%	44.6%
3	Florida	282,066	5.0%	49.6%
4	New York	191,992	3.8%	53.4%

Source: Ibid, adapted

Student Body Profile

Table 1.3 shows the twenty most common language groups among ELL students as weighted to be nationally representative (Hopstock and Stephenson, 2003). The report revealed that the Spanish speaking group continues to be the largest, representing 76.9 percent of the total ELL population. This percent shows an increase of approximately 4 percent from a decade ago. Vietnamese and Hmong continue to be the second and third largest language groups represented in the ELL

TABLE 1.3

ELL Population Distribution by Language Group (2002–2003)

Language Group	No. of ELL Students	Percent ELL Students
Spanish	2,963,256	76
Vietnamese	90,659	2.4
Hmong	68,892	1.8
Korean	47,427	1.2
Arabic	44,681	1.2
Haitian-Creole	43,137	1.1
Cantonese	36,942	1.0
Tagalog	35,495	0.9
Russian	33,860	0.9
Navajo	33,622	0.9
Khmer	28,910	0.8
Portuguese	24,684	0.6
Urdu	24,092	0.6
Chinese (Unspecified; not Mandarin)	22,255	0.5
Mandarin	18,097	0.5
Japanese	14,950	0.4
Punjabi	14,502	0.4
Serbo-Croatian	14,220	0.4
Bengali	14,056	0.4
Laotian	13,778	0.3

Source: Hopstock and Stephenson, 2003, Report for the U.S. Department of Education, Office of English Language Acquisition, Language, Enhancement, and Academic Achievement for Limited English Proficient Students (OELA). Retrieved (2005) from http://www.ncela.gwu.edu/stats/2 nation.htm

population in the United States. In 1993, the Haitian-Creole language was number eleven on the list, yet as indicated by the figures in Table 1.3, this group has moved up to number six; the Arabic language was number twelve, and it has moved up to number five. There are five new language groups that now appear among the twenty most common. These are Khmer (#11), Urdu (#13), Punjabi (#16), Serbo-Croatian (#18), and Bengali (#19). The following language groups are no longer represented among the top twenty: Cambodian (formerly #5), Armenian (formerly #15), Farsi (formerly #18), Hindi (formerly #19), and Polish (formerly #20). Thus, it appears that the immigrant population in the United States is changing.

In Florida (the third leading state in ELL population) the trend has shifted from the national trend during the last decade. Although Spanish, consistent with the national trend, remains the language spoken by the majority of ELLs in Florida, the number of Haitian-Creole speakers is eleven times greater than the national figure. The percent of Portuguese speakers in Florida is also larger than the percent reported nationwide. The percentages reported in Figure 1.2 are consistent with those reported a decade ago. Data provided by the Florida Department of Education Automated Information Database Surveys (2000–2001), indicate that Florida's ELL come from 257 different countries of national origin and speak 207 languages. However, only thirteen countries account for 90 percent of the state's ELL population (see Table 1.4).

Of the thirteen countries that account for 90 percent of the ELLs in Florida, ten are Spanish-speaking countries. Thus, Spanish is the language spoken by the majority of the ELLs in Florida.

Data from Table 1.4 and Figure 1.2 clearly show how closely Florida compares with the national trend regarding Spanish, the native language spoken by the majority of ELLs: nationwide, 76 percent, Florida 71.31 percent.

A Student Population at Risk

According to a report from the Intercultural Development Research Association (Cortez, 2003), there are notable changes in the demographic profiles of

Native Language	% of Total ELLs
Spanish	76
Haitian-Creole	12
Portuguese	2.0
French	1.0
Vietnamese	1.0
Arabic	1.0
Chinese (Unspecified; not Mandarin)	1.0
Russian	1.0

FIGURE 1.2 Native Languages Spoken by ELLs in Florida (2000–2001)

Source: U.S. Department of Education Survey of the States' Limited English Proficient Students and Available Educational Programs and Services. Retrieved (2005) from http://www.ncela.gwu.edu/stats/3 by state.htm

TABLE 1.4

Countries Contributing More Than One Percent of the ELL Population in Florida

Country of National Origin	% of Total ELLs	Language Spoken
United States*	48.79	Varied
Cuba	7.48	Spanish
Haiti	6.41	Haitian-Creole/ French Creole
Colombia	5.87	Spanish
Mexico	5.44	Spanish
Puerto Rico	5.11	Spanish
Venezuela	2.49	Spanish
Brazil	2.04	Portuguese
Nicaragua	1.65	Spanish
Peru	1.42	Spanish
Argentina	1.14	Spanish
Honduras	1.14	Spanish
Dominican Republic	1.11	Spanish

*Born to immigrant families or Native Americans

school age children in the United States in more and more states. Around the country, Hispanic students are the fastest growing group. The U.S. Census Bureau estimates that the nation's Hispanic population has grown by 60 percent in the last fifteen years. Although the majority of the country's Hispanic population is concentrated in a few states (California, Texas, Florida, New York, Illinois, New Jersey, Arizona, and New Mexico), many other states are also experiencing significant growth. The following are among the states with the greatest percentage increases in their Hispanic population: North Carolina (394%), Arkansas (337%), Georgia (300%), Tennessee (278%), Nevada (217%), South Carolina (211%), Alabama (208%), Kentucky (173%), Minnesota (166%), and Nebraska (155%).

This growing trend has serious implications for many aspects of public school education. According to Kindler (2002), ELLs represent 9.6% of all students enrolled in public schools in the United States. Unfortunately the majority continues to be at risk in today's social institutions.

As of July 2002, there were 819,000 migrant children nationwide (Gibson, 2003). These children are among the most disadvantaged in the United States due to the combined effects of poverty, poor nutrition and health care, high absenteeism from school, and family mobility. The best and most recent studies of school completion rates estimate that only about half receive a high school diploma. Although drop-out rates vary across national-origin groups, students of Mexican descent, for example, drop out at a rate of at least double that of the national average (Ruiz de Velasco et al., 2000).

It is important to understand that all ELLs are not alike. Among immigrant students, some ELLs have strong academic preparation and for the most part only need English language development so that they can continue to grow academically. These students can transfer their academic knowledge to the subjects they are taking in the United States. Other immigrant students arrive with limited formal schooling, perhaps due to war or the isolated location of their homes (August, 2002). According to Ruiz de Velasco and Fix (2000), 20 percent of all ELLs at the high school level and 12 percent at the middle school level have missed two or more years of schooling since age six. Among Hispanic students ages 15–17 who are newcomers, more than one-third are enrolled below grade level (Jamieson, Curry, and Martinez, 2001). These students are not literate in their native language and have significant gaps in their educational backgrounds; they often need additional time to become accustomed to school routines and expectations.

Schools also enroll students who have been born and raised in the United States but who speak a language other than English at home. While most of these acquire English during their elementary school years, some, nonetheless, reach secondary levels having never mastered literacy in English or in their home language.

What Schools Must Do to Meet the Needs of English Language Learners

○ Have high expectations for the academic achievement of all students.
○ Have high levels of parental involvement.
○ Have strong instructional and organizational leadership.
○ Value the students' home languages and cultures.
○ Have school leadership that makes ELLs a priority.
○ Provide outreach and communication in the parents' home language.
○ Provide staff development to train and assist teachers and other staff for effective service to ELLs.
○ Develop class schedules that include ELLs in classes with English speaking students.
○ Make placement decisions on the basis of adequate assessment and consultation.
○ Develop programs that address multicultural concerns (both social and academic) (Romo, 1993).
○ Provide dual language or bilingual programs when at all possible.
○ Ensure that academic programs for ELLs are strong and meet their academic needs.

How Can Teachers Nurture, Celebrate and Challenge Their English Language Learners?

- ○ Study their cultures.
- ○ Develop cultural units of instruction.
- ○ Familiarize themselves with their students' backgrounds.
- ○ Engage all students in sharing life stories.
- ○ Enlist the aid of bilingual students without teachers abdicating their responsibility of providing comprehensible input.
- ○ Set up mentor pairs.
- ○ Involve English language learners in all classroom activities.
- ○ Recruit native speaking volunteers from the community.
- ○ Develop volunteer programs to involve high school bilingual students as tutors for elementary school children.
- ○ Develop recognition awards to instill a sense of self-worth in bilingual volunteers (Vaznaugh, 1995).
- ○ Involve parents in classroom activities.

FINANCIAL CHALLENGES IN THE TWENTY-FIRST CENTURY

To address and meet the needs of the fast-growing English language learner population, adequate, upfront funding to support the educational expenditures is crucial. As ELLs continue to enroll, far more programs and services need to be provided to serve them adequately: curricular changes that take a multicultural student body into account, initial assessment and placement services, systems to assess on-going language proficiency, "newcomer" programs, year-round school calendars, cultural sensitivity training, parent outreach, and partnerships with community agencies and organizations. New physical facilities and equipment are also needed. Generally, the need for these services and facilities is most acute in urban school districts, which already have the largest populations and school enrollments. These large, urban districts are least likely to have the resources to provide for the special needs of their growing ELL school population. Thus, federal funds channeled to school districts need to be substantial to serve the needs of their diverse student bodies (Stewart, 1994), as costs for specially designed programs to meet the needs of English language learners are very high. Not only must school districts face this challenge, but teachers must be partners in this endeavor as well. With all forces joined in pursuit of a common goal, successful English language learners are on the horizon.

Points to Remember

✓ Immigration into the United States shows no sign of abating.

✓ Immigration brings richness as well as challenges.

✓ Providing for the English language learners is one of school districts' greatest challenges.

✓ ELLs speak many different languages; Spanish is the language spoken by the majority of ELLs in the United States.

✓ The dropout rate among Hispanics is a national problem; it is 50% greater than the national average.

✓ Although large numbers of ELLs are concentrated in a few states; the growth of ELL populations is becoming widespread throughout the United States.

✓ Thirty-one states have reported increases of 10% or more in their ELL populations.

✓ School systems, as well as all teachers, are responsible for the success of the ELLs academic growth.

Chapter 2

Legal Rights of English Language Learners (ELLs) in the United States: An Historical Overview

Key Issues

○ Laws that protect the Constitutional Rights of ELLs

○ Court cases that have had a major impact in the education of ELLs

○ Defining Limited English Proficiency and Limited English Proficient

○ The Florida Consent Decree

SCENARIO

Domingo and Elia Rodriquez have recently arrived in the United States from the Dominican Republic. They are not proficient in English and worry about their three children, who they will be enrolling in school today. The couple is not familiar with the school system, and thus feel that their children will have much difficulty studying in English because they do not speak it at home. Domingo and Elia are also worried about how they will communicate with school officials.

When they arrived at the school, much to their surprise, there was a Spanish-speaking interpreter who helped them enroll the children. In addition, they were assured that the children could receive instruction in the school's ESOL "pull out program" from a trained ESOL teacher who also happened to be bilingual (Spanish/English), or they could elect to have their children placed in a dual language program, also available at this school. In this dual language program, their children would receive instruction in two languages: English and Spanish. Their children would have as peers English speaking students as well as other Spanish speaking students. This program requires parents to elect to have their children participate in it. Domingo and Elia were very impressed with the school, and were relieved to find out that their children would be given assistance while developing English language proficiency.

THE UNITED STATES CONSTITUTION

AMENDMENT 1, THE CONSTITUTION OF THE UNITED STATES, ADOPTED IN 1791

Congress shall make no law . . . abridging freedom of speech . . .

AMENDMENT 14, THE CONSTITUTION OF THE UNITED STATES, ADOPTED IN 1868

No state shall make or enforce any law which shall abridge the privileges or immunities of citizens of the United States; nor shall any state deprive any person of life, liberty, or property, without due process of law; nor deny to any person within its jurisdiction the equal protection of the laws.

FEDERAL LAWS

In 1970, the Office of Civil Rights informed school districts with more than five percent national-origin minority children that they had to take affirmative steps to rectify these students' language "deficiencies." This memo mandated that districts offer some type of special language instruction for ELL students (Diaz-Rico & Weed, 1995). The federal courts began to enforce Title VI of the Civil Rights Act which outlaws discrimination in federally supported programs. In *Serna* v. *Portales Municipal Schools*, a 1972 case, a federal judge ordered native language instruction as part of a desegregation plan.

LANDMARK CASE

The failure of the San Francisco school system to provide English language instruction to approximately 1,800 students of Chinese ancestry who did not speak English, or to provide them with other adequate instructional procedure, denied them a meaningful opportunity to participate in the public educational system. Thus, this neglect violated Section 601 of the 1964 Civil Rights Act which banned discrimination based "on the ground of race, color, or national origin," in "any program or activity receiving federal financial assistance," and the implementation of the regulations from the Department of Health, Education, and Welfare. This resulted in the landmark case *Lau* v. *Nichols.*

The 1974 case made it extraordinarily clear that a student may not be denied equal access to basic subject instruction or to any program offered by an educational entity because of that student's limited English proficiency. There is not a prescribed threshold of English competency that a student must reach before receiving curricular and extracurricular offerings for which such a student is qualified, irrespective of English proficiency.

OTHER RELEVANT CASES

Castañeda v. *Pickard,* 1981

Castañeda v. *Pickard* was a class-action complaint brought against the Raymondville Independent School District in Texas. This complaint alleged that the district's educational policies discriminated against Mexican-American students by failing to implement adequate instruction to overcome the linguistic barriers that prevented their equal participation in the district's educational program. In defining "adequate instruction," the court provided the criteria by which a school system's program for ELL students could be deemed appropriate to the needs of those students.

These criteria are:

1. Whether the program is based on sound educational theory; that is, one accepted as sound by experts in the field.
2. Whether the program provides adequate resources and personnel to effectively implement the educational theory adopted by the school system.
3. Whether the school system adequately monitors the effectiveness of the program and takes appropriate actions to modify the program as necessary (Garcia, B., 1995).

Plyler v. *Doe,* United States Supreme Court, 1982

Plyler v. *Doe,* a 1982 District Court class-action suit, was filed on behalf of school-aged Mexican children in Smith County, Texas who could not establish that they had been legally admitted into the United States. The action complained of the exclusion of these children from the public schools of the Tyler Independent School District 2.

The appellants argued that because of their immigration status as undocumented aliens, they are not "persons within the jurisdiction" of the State of Texas, and therefore, they had no right to equal protection under Texas law. This argument was rejected by the Court of Appeals. It was reiterated that whatever the status under the immigration laws, an alien is surely a "person" in any ordinary sense of that term. Aliens, even aliens whose presence in this country is unlawful, have long been recognized as "persons" and are guaranteed due process of law by the Fifth and Fourteenth Amendments (ibid).

After making extensive findings of fact, the District Court held that illegal aliens were entitled to the protection of the equal protection clause of the Fourteenth Amendment, and that the Texas statute violated the clause. Thus, the Texas statute withholding funds from local school districts for the education of children not legally admitted into the United States, and authorizing districts to deny enrollment to such children, violated this clause. On appeal, the United States Supreme Court affirmed such violation (ibid).

FLORIDA EDUCATIONAL EQUITY ACT, 1984

Discrimination on the basis of race, national origin, sex, handicap, or marital status against a student or an employee in the State system of public education is prohibited. No person in this state shall . . . be excluded from participation in, be denied benefits of, or be subjected to discrimination under any education program or activity, or in any employment conditions or practices, conducted by a public educational institution which receives or benefits from federal or state financial assistance.

All public education classes shall be available to all students without regard to race, national origin, sex, handicap, or marital status; however, this is not intended to eliminate the provision of programs designed to meet the needs of students with limited proficiency in English or exceptional education students.

Although the Constitutional rights of English language learners (ELLs) have long been established, further clarification is needed to ensure that all states respect these rights and provide the access to instruction that ELLs are guaranteed under the United States Constitution.

Even identifying ELLs has been a difficult task. There is no federally mandated definition of limited English proficiency. While the federal Bilingual

TABLE 2.1

**Criteria Most Often Used by SEAs to Identify ELLs
(1994–95; N = 47)**

Criteria	States Using Criteria	% SEAs Responding to Question
Non-English Language Background	34	72.0
Difficulty with English Language (speak, understand, read, write)	23	49.0
Percentile Cutoff on Standardized Test	10	21.0
Local Determination	9	19.0
Other	14	30.0

Source: National Clearing House for Bilingual Education, 1996.

Education Act includes an operational definition of limited English proficiency, determination of ELL (limited English proficient) status depends largely on state and local agencies. The lack of a mandated uniform definition of limited English proficiency has led to a wide range of identification procedures to determine eligibility for services across states, districts, and schools. It also leads to inconsistent reporting of information on ELLs within and across states. As a result, states are found non-compliant in court cases for not providing the mandated and necessary services to all ELLs.

In 1994–1995, of forty-seven state education agencies (SEAs) who responded to the question on ELL definition and criteria, eight reported having used the federal ELL definition; an additional fifteen SEAs included all of the Title VII criteria, without citing the definition itself. Thirty-four used "non-English language background" as the criterion; twenty-three used "difficulties with English speaking, reading, writing, and understanding," and twenty used both (see Table 2.1).

The federal definition of "limited English proficiency" is found in Section 7501 of the Bilingual Education Act, Title VII of the Elementary and Secondary Education Act as amended in the Improving America's Schools Act of 1994. See the box below.

Improving America's Schools Act of 1994
Title VII

**"PART E—GENERAL PROVISIONS
"SEC. 7501. DEFINITIONS;
REGULATIONS.**

"Except as otherwise provided for purposes of this title—

"(8) Limited English proficiency and limited English proficient.—The terms 'limited English proficiency' and 'limited English proficient', when used with reference to an individual, mean an individual—

"(A) who—
"(i) was not born in the United States or whose native language is a language other than English and comes from an environment where a language other than English is dominant; or "(ii) is a Native American or Alaska Native or who is a native resident of the outlying areas and comes from an environment where a language other than English has had a significant impact on such individual's level of English language proficiency; or "(iii) is migratory and whose native language is other than English and comes from an environment where a language other than English is dominant; and "(B) who has sufficient difficulty speaking, reading, writing, or understanding the English language and whose difficulties may deny such individuals the opportunity to learn successfully in classrooms where the language of instruction is English, or to participate fully in our society.

Source: National Clearing House for Bilingual Education, 1996.

The Florida Consent Decree

***League of United Latin American Citizens
(LULAC) et al. v. State Board of Education,*** **United States Court of the Southern District, Florida 1990.**

Like similar laws in other states, the Florida Consent Decree addresses the civil rights of English language learners. Foremost among those civil rights is equal access to all education programs. It does not grant ELLs any new rights. It simply provides a structure for compliance with the following federal and state laws regarding the education of ELLs:

○ Title VI and VII of the Civil Rights Act of 1964
○ Office of Civil Rights Memorandum (Standards for Title VI Compliance) of May, 1970
○ Section 504 of the Rehabilitation Act, 1973
○ Requirements based on the Supreme Court decision in *Lau* v. *Nichols,* 1974
○ Equal Education Opportunities Act, 1974
○ Requirement of Vocational Education Guidelines, 1979
○ Requirements based on the Fifth Circuit Court decision in *Castañeda* v. *Pickard,* 1981
○ Requirements based on the Supreme Court decision in *Plyler* v. *Doe,* 1982
○ Americans with Disabilities Act (PL 94-142)
○ Florida Education Equity Act, 1984

In providing the framework for compliance with the above jurisprudence regarding the rights of ELLs to equal access to educational programs, the Consent Decree ensures the delivery of the comprehensible instruction to which these students are entitled.

The Florida Consent Decree addresses six broad areas. These are listed below with a synopsis of each area.

○ **Section I: Identification and Assessment**
Synopsis: All students with limited English proficiency must be properly identified and assessed to ensure the provision of appropriate services. The Consent Decree details the procedures for placement of students in the English for Speakers of Other Languages (ESOL) program, their exit from the program, and the monitoring of students who have exited the program.

○ **Section II: Equal Access to Appropriate Programming**
Synopsis: All ELL students enrolled in Florida public schools are entitled to programming appropriate to their level of English proficiency, their level of academic achievement, and to any special needs they may have. ELL students shall have equal access to appropriate English language instruction, as well as instruction in basic subject areas that is understandable to the students, given their respective level of English proficiency, and equal and comparable in amount, scope, sequence, and quality to that provided to English proficient (or non-ELL) students.

○ **Section III: Equal Access to Appropriate Categorical and Other Programs for ELL Students**
Synopsis: ELL students are entitled to equal access to all programs appropriate to their academic needs, such as compensatory, exceptional, adult, vocational, or early childhood education programs, as well as dropout prevention programs and other support services, regardless of their level of English proficiency.

○ **Section IV: Personnel**
Synopsis: This section details the certificate coverage and inservice training teachers must have to be qualified to instruct ESOL students. Teachers may obtain the necessary training through university course work or through school district-provided inservice training. The Consent Decree details specific requirements for ESOL certification and inservice training and sets standards for personnel delivering ESOL instruction.

As a result of the Florida Consent Decree, all Florida teachers are required to have training in the field of ESOL commensurate with what they teach. At a minimum, this training must involve three university credit hours (or sixty inservice points). The break-down is as follows:

Elementary, English, Exceptional Education teachers	15 credits (or 300 inservice points)
Secondary Teachers (except English teachers) and Administrators	3 credits (or 60 inservice points)
Secondary Content Area Teachers	3 credits (or 18 inservice points)

Media Specialists/
  Guidance Counselors
  Art, Music, P.E.,
  Foreign Language,
  Social Psychologists,
  Voc. Ed. Teachers,   3 credits
  Pre-K   (or 18 inservice points)

A state-approved ESOL Endorsement program consists of fifteen credit hours which may be broken down as follows:

Methods of Teaching ESOL
Curriculum Development in ESOL
Testing and Evaluation in ESOL
Applied Linguistics and TESOL
Multicultural Education

○ **Section V: Monitoring Issues**
Synopsis: The Florida Department of Education is charged with the monitoring of local school districts to ensure compliance with the provisions of the Consent Decree pursuant to federal and state law and regulations, including Section 229.565, Florida Statutes (Educational Evaluation Procedures) and Section 228.2001, Florida Statutes (Florida Educational Equity Act). This monitoring is to be carried out by the Office of Multicultural Student Language Education (OMSLE), Division of Public Schools, Florida Department of Education.

○ **Section VI: Outcome Measures**
Synopsis: The Florida Department of Education is required to develop an evaluation process to address equal access and program effectiveness. This evaluation system shall collect and analyze data regarding the progress of ELL students and include comparisons between the ELL population and the non-ELL population regarding retention rates, graduation rates, dropout rates, grade point averages, and state assessment scores.
(Florida Department of Education, 1990)

Undergraduate/Graduate Teacher Preparation ESOL Infused Programs
Graduates from state approved programs that lead to initial teacher certification, are able to qualify for the ESOL endorsement without having to complete the required five courses as listed in Section V, if they complete a state approved ESOL infused program. In these infused programs some of the required TESOL competencies are infused in the methods courses and students complete two or three ESOL specific courses.

The No Child Left Behind Act of 2001

On January 8, 2002, President Bush signed into law the No Child Left Behind Act (NCLB). No Child Left Behind is a comprehensive plan to reform schools, change school culture, empower parents, and improve education. NCLB applies to all children who attend public schools including children with disabilities as well as children who traditionally have been excluded, such as minorities, immigrants, and English language learners.

NCLB requires annual testing of reading and math skills. Beginning with the 2005–2006 school year, students in grades 3–8 must be tested in each grade and at least once for those students in grades 10–12. In 2007–2008, NCLB will also include testing of science skills and knowledge. This will require students to be tested in science at least once in grades 3–5, 6–9, and 10–12.
(U.S. Department of Education, 2005. Retrieved from http://www.ed.gov/nclb/accountability/index.htlm.)

PRESIDENT BUSH OFFERED THIS ADVICE TO PARENTS:

"We know that every child can learn. Now is the time to ensure that every child does learn. As parents, you are your children's first teachers and their strongest advocates. You have a critical role to play in how you raise your children and in how you work for meaningful and accurate accountability in their schools. Too many children are segregated in schools without standards, shuffled from grade to grade . . . This is discrimination, pure and simple.

Some say it is unfair to hold disadvantaged children to rigorous standards. I say it is discrimination to require anything less. It is a soft bigotry of low expectations."

President George W. Bush

Under the NCLB Act's accountability provisions, states must describe how they will close the achievement gap and make sure all students, including those who are disadvantaged, achieve academic proficiency. They must produce annual state and school district report cards that inform parents and communities about state and school progress. Schools that do not make progress must provide supplemental services, such as free tutoring or after school assistance and take corrective actions. If, after five years, they are still not making adequate yearly progress (AYP), they must make dramatic changes to the way the schools are run. (Ibid)

Local Freedom

Under NCLB, states and school districts have unprecedented flexibility in how they use federal education funds, in exchange for greater accountability results.

It is possible for most school districts to transfer up to 50 percent of the funds they receive under the Improving Teacher Quality State Grants, Educational Technology, Innovative Programs, and Safe and Drug-Free Schools programs to any of these programs or to their Title I programs, without separate approval. This allows school districts to use funds for their particular needs, such as hiring new teachers, increasing teacher pay, and improving teacher training and professional development. Similarly, the law's consolidation of bilingual education programs gives states and districts more control in planning programs to benefit all English language learners.

Proven Methods

No Child Left Behind puts special emphasis on determining what educational programs and practices have been proven effective through rigorous scientific research. Federal funding is targeted to support these programs and teaching methods that work to improve student learning and achievement. (Ibid)

Choices for Parents

> "... School choice is part of the strategy to give every child an excellent education ..."
>
> U.S. Secretary of Education Margaret Spellings

The No Child Left Behind Act provides new education options for many families. This federal law allows parents to choose other public schools or take advantage of free tutoring if their child attends a school that needs improvement. Also, parents can choose another public school if the school their child attends is unsafe. The law also supports the growth of more independent charter schools, funds some services for children in private schools, and provides certain protections for home schooling parents. Finally it requires that states and local school districts provide information to help parents make informed educational choices for their children. (Ibid)

NCLB and ELL Classification

The rapid growth of ELLs in the United States demands consistent and accurate measurement of their academic progress and determination of the areas where they need the most assistance. Accordingly, NCLB has mandated inclusion of these students in national and state assessments using reliable and valid measures (Abedi, 2004). Unfortunately, criteria for identifying ELLs are not uniform across the nation. This is problematic since there is not a national definition of limited English proficiency.

NCLB provides an operational definition of limited English proficiency (NCLB, 2002). According to this definition:

> The term "limited English proficient," when used with respect to an individual, means an individual
> (A) who is aged 3 through 21;
> (B) who is enrolled or preparing to enroll in an elementary school or secondary school;
> (C) (i) who was not born in the United States or whose native language is a language other than English;

(ii) (I) who is a Native American or Alaska Native, or native resident of the outlying areas; and

(II) who comes from an environment where a language other than English has had a significant impact on the individual's level of English language proficiency; or

(iii) who is migratory, whose native language is a language other than English, and who comes from an environment where a language other than English is dominant; and

(D) whose difficulties in speaking, reading, writing, or understanding the English language may be sufficient to deny the individual

(i) the ability to meet the State's proficient level of achievement on State assessments;

(ii) the ability to successfully achieve in classrooms where the language of instruction is English; or

(iii) The opportunity to participate fully in society

(Abedi, 2004)

NCLB and ELLs

While the NCLB definition of ELL seems to be operationally defined, different states, school districts, and schools may interpret these criteria differently. (Ibid)

Based on the inclusion instructions described in NCLB, the National Assessment of Educational Progress (NAEP) excludes ELLs who have received reading or mathematics instruction primarily in English for fewer than three school years and cannot demonstrate their knowledge of reading or mathematics in English even with the accommodations permitted by NCLB/NAEP. However, the high rate of transience in schools with large numbers of ELLs may cause inaccuracy in reporting the number of years in English-only classes for these students.

Two other problems are the type of assessment instruments being employed to judge ELLs' ability to demonstrate their knowledge, and the fact that the reporting of the students' ability may be inaccurate since it may be subjective.

A provision of NCLB allowing states to test ELLs in their native language for up to three years (or five on a case-by-case basis) appears to add a measure of flexibility to the system. In reality, it does not. Native-language assessments are often unavailable and are rarely aligned with state standards. Some are merely translations from English-language tests, a procedure that is considered invalid due to the fact that, among other things, the difficulty of vocabulary tends to differ across languages (August and Hakuta, 1997). In addition, native language tests are inappropriate for ELLs who often have limited literacy development in their native language.

It is fair to say that existing instruments for assessing the academic achievement of ELLs, whose validity and reliability are questionable at best, cannot be counted on to generate meaningful information for accountability purposes. Yet, state plans approved under NCLB rely heavily on such achievement tests. (NABE, 2004)

No Accountability without Reasonable Expectations

In NCLB's accountability system, the ELL subgroup itself is a problematic construct. This is a highly diverse population in terms of socioeconomic status, linguistic and cultural background, level of English proficiency, amount of prior education, and instructional programs experience. It is also a highly fluid population, as newcomers often enter programs speaking little English and others leave after being reclassified as fully proficient in English when in actuality they are not. A common exit criterion is the 36th percentile in English reading/language arts. In other words, ELLs are *defined* by their low achievement level. When they have acquired minimal English proficiency, they exit the subgroup and their scores are no longer counted in the computation of adequate yearly progress (AYP). So it is not merely unrealistic—it is a mathematical impossibility—for the ELL subgroup to "hold schools accountable" for failing to achieve the impossible. Indeed, lumping virtually all schools with significant ELL enrollments in the same "needs improvement" category would defeat the purpose of accountability.

Another difficulty in setting reasonable AYP targets is the variability in the time it takes children to acquire a second language, especially the kind of language needed for success in school. Research has shown that students in bilingual and English as a second language (ESL) programs require five to seven years to achieve grade-level academic achievement (Crawford, 2004).

Points to Remember

✓ The United States Constitution protects the rights of all who live in the United States.

✓ All legal and illegal aliens are protected under federal laws.

✓ There have been numerous court cases that have resulted in clarification of peoples' rights in the United States.

✓ *Lau* v. *Nichols* is considered the landmark case that served as the catalyst that forced districts to provide adequate educational opportunities for ELL students in the United States.

✓ *Lau* v. *Nichols* clarified what is meant by "equal access" under the law.

✓ There is no federally mandated definition of limited English proficiency. This causes serious problems, especially when trying to identify English language learners and make decisions about programs to serve them.

✓ The Florida Consent Decree is an agreement between the Florida State Board of Education and a coalition of eight groups represented by Multicultural Education, Training, and Advocacy, Inc. (META).

✓ The Florida Consent Decree provides a structure for compliance with all the jurisprudence insuring the rights of ELL students in Florida, and equality in educational opportunities as afforded to all native-English-speaking students.

✓ As a result of the Florida Consent Decree, all teachers must receive some type of training in teaching English as a second language.

✓ NCLB requires annual testing of all students, 2005–2007 in reading and mathematics; 2007–2008 and thereafter in reading, mathematics, and science.

✓ NCLB places ELLs at a testing disadvantage.

Chapter 3

Description of ESL/ENL Programs from A to Z

Key Issues

- Classification of English as a Second/New Language (ESL/ENL) Programs
- Factors affecting the design of ESL/ENL programs
- A case for bilingual education
- Fallacies regarding bilingual education
- Why not bilingual education in the twenty-first century?

SCENARIO

A group of Chinese educators has come to south Florida to learn more about the educational system. As part of their experience they visit a number of schools in several counties.

As they enter one classroom, this is what they hear:

Teacher: *"Hoy tenemos unos visitantes de China que vienen a observar nuestros programas. ¿Cómo podemos darles la bienvenida?* (Translation: "Today we have some visitors from China who are here to observe our programs. How could we welcome them?")

Students: *"Buenos días y bienvenidos a nuestra escuela."*

Teacher: "The students have said: 'Good morning and welcome to our school.'"

In the afternoon these same students have all their subjects in English.

English language learners are no longer isolated cases in the nation's schools today. Names such as "Maria," "Pedro," "Kuzumi," "Rashid," or "Jacques" are swelling the rosters of public schools, sitting side by side with Mary and William. Close to 5 million ELLs resided in the United States in 2003–2004, an increase of approximately 1.5 million students since 1996–1997 (National Clearing House of English Language Acquisition, 2003). Over 460 languages are represented in U.S. schools on any given day. As the number of ELLs grows and language diversity increases, districts around the country have tried to implement effective academic programs to meet the needs of students who lack the English language skills necessary to succeed in English-only classrooms.

No federal laws exist that mandate a specific type of program to serve the needs of ELLs. However, legislation provides funding and support for services for them. In addition, federal court decisions have focused primarily on civil rights for non-English speakers supporting their entitlement to services that offer equal educational opportunity to all ELLs (Kindler, 2002).

Educational Programs for ELLs

The great majority of ELLs are being served by some program designed to meet their needs in school. Regardless of its design, the minimal goal of each program must be to provide each student with the English skills necessary to function successfully in an academic setting. In a survey conducted in 1996–1997 (SEA Survey, 1996–1997), approximately 84 percent of ELLs (public schools only) were enrolled in some type of program designed to meet their needs. The report also claimed that over 400,000 ELLs enrolled in public schools were not being served by any type of special program in accordance with their needs (National Clearing House for Bilingual Education, 1996–1997). As a result of the Supreme Court decision *Lau* v. *Nichols* (Collier & Thomas, 1996), this practice is now illegal in the United States.

HOW ARE ENGLISH AS A SECOND/NEW LANGUAGE (ESL/ENL) PROGRAMS CLASSIFIED?

There are numerous program models for ELLs in the United States. They range from programs that provide most support in the native language (L1) to those that emphasize the second language (L2). The next few pages give a description of existing program models.

Immersion Bilingual Programs

Immersion bilingual programs provide academic instruction through both L1 and L2 for grades K–12 and originally were developed for language majority students in Canada and used as a model for two-way bilingual education in the United States. Two-way bilingual programs are those programs where language majority students, as well as language minority students, are both being taught in two languages, i.e. bilingually. The goal is for both student populations to become bilingual.

Early total immersion (in the United States, often referred as the 90-10 model, or the Eastman model in California)

> Grades K–1: 90 percent of academic instruction through L1 language

> Grade 2: One hour of academic instruction through L2 language added

> Grade 3: Two hours of academic instruction through L2 language added

> Grades 4–5 or 6: Academic instruction half of day through each language

> Grades 6 or 7–12: 60 percent of academic instruction through L2 language and 40 percent through L1 language

Partial-immersion (in the United States, the 50-50 model)

> Grades K–5 or 6: Academic instruction half of day through each language (L1 and L2)

> Grades 6 or 7–12: 60 percent of academic instruction through L2 language and 40 percent through L1 language

Two-Way Developmental Bilingual Programs/ Dual Language Programs

Language majority and language minority students are schooled together in the same bilingual class with many variations possible, including immersion bilingual education and late-exit bilingual education.

Late-Exit or Maintenance Bilingual Programs

Academic instruction is given for half a day in each language for grades K–6. Originally, this type of program was developed for grades K–12, but this model has rarely been implemented beyond elementary school in the United States. Theoretically, the goal is to maintain the native language of the second language learners; however, this goal is unattainable if the program ceases in sixth grade.

Early-Exit or Transitional Bilingual Programs

Academic instruction is provided for half of the day in each language, with gradual transition to all L2 language instruction in approximately two–three years. The goal is not bilingualism, the goal is to provide academic instruction in the native language until the student has acquired "enough" English to function in the mainstream "English only" classroom. It is known that it takes more than three years to acquire a second language (Cummins, 1981). Thus, this type program is ineffective in providing for the language development needs of the English language learner.

English as a Second/New Language (ESL/ENL) or English to Speakers of Other Languages (ESOL) Instruction, with No Instruction through the Minority Language (ibid).

Structured Immersion Programs

These programs may be offered either in elementary or secondary schools. Immersion programs include, in varying degrees, development of language skills and content area instruction in English. No structured ESL component is included, since content area instruction is based on the notion of "comprehensible input" in which the teacher uses second language acquisition strategies, including sheltered English. In these programs, teachers are usually bilingual; students may address them in their native language, although the teacher will generally respond in English.

Sheltered English or Content-Based Programs

Programs that are used primarily in secondary schools. In these content classes, ELLs from different backgrounds, who usually have intermediate English proficiency, come together to receive content instruction especially designed to provide "comprehensible input." A trained ESL teacher who is not necessarily bilingual provides the instruction. Sheltered English or content-based programs may parallel virtually all mainstream academic curricular offerings or may consist of only one or two subjects.

ESL/ENL or ESOL Pull-Out Programs

These programs are generally used in elementary schools. The student is "pulled-out" of the regular classroom for special instruction in English as a second language (ESL). Instruction is conducted by a trained ESL teacher who employs second language acquisition techniques. Students may receive instruction primarily in English (language arts), science, and social studies, but not necessarily exclusively in these subjects. Subject areas may vary from district to district. Students from different minority language backgrounds are grouped together. Teachers may or may not be bilingual. These programs vary anywhere from thirty minutes a day to half a day.

ESL/ENL or ESOL Taught as a Subject

This approach is generally used in middle or high schools. The students receive ESL instruction during a regular class period. Students generally receive credit for this course, taken in a departmentalized setting. Students may be grouped according to their level of English proficiency.

Submersion

No instructional support is provided by trained specialists. This is not a program model. It is illegal in the United States not to provide the adequate support needed by ELLs.

Table 3.1 summarizes the information discussed in the previous paragraphs. Although bilingualism appears as the linguistic goal for the late-exit or developmental bilingual education, this goal is unattainable if this type of program is only provided at the elementary school level. Thus, although the goal is bilingualism, in reality, it may not be achieved unless students continue to be taught in both languages through high school.

WHAT FACTORS AFFECT THE DESIGN OF ESL PROGRAMS?

District Demographics

Some districts have large, relatively stable populations of ELLs from a single language or cultural background. Others have large groups of ELLs representing several language backgrounds. Still other districts may experience a sudden increase in the number of ELLs from a given group: the number of Vietnamese, Hmong, Cubans, Haitians, and Guatemalans in many districts has increased significantly in direct response to social and political changes in these students' countries of origin. Some districts have very small numbers of ELLs from many different language groups, while others report more than one hundred language groups with very few students from each scattered across grade levels and schools, i.e., some districts in South Florida are beginning to enroll small numbers of students whose native language is Russian. The characteristics of these populations, including the numbers and kinds of students per language group, the size of language groups and the mobility of their members, as well as geographic and grade distribution of students influence the type of ESL instructional program design that a district needs to develop.

TABLE 3.1

Characteristics of the Major Program Models for English Language Learners

Language(s) of Instruction	Typical Program Names	Native Language of ELLs	Language of Content Instruction	Language Arts Instruction	Linguistic Goal of Program
English and the native language	• Two-way Bilingual Education • Bilingual Immersion, or • Dual Language Immersion	Ideally, 50% English-Speaking and 50% ELL sharing same native language	Both English and the native language	English and the native language	Bilingualism
	• Late-exit or • Developmental Bilingual Education	All students speak the same native language	Both, at first, mostly the native language is used. Instruction through English increases as students gain proficiency	English and the native language	Bilingualism
	• Early-exit or • Transitional Bilingual Education	All students speak the same native language	Both at the beginning, with quick progression to all or most instruction through English	English; Native language skills are developed only to assist transition to English	English acquisition; rapid transfer into English-only classroom
English	• Sheltered English, • Structured Immersion, or • Content-based ESL	Students can share the same native language or be from different language backgrounds	English adapted to the students' proficiency level, and supplemented by gestures and visual aids	English	English acquisition
	• Pull-out ESL/ENL	Students can share the same native language or be from different language backgrounds; students may be grouped with all ages and grade levels	English adapted to the students' proficiency level, and supplemented by gestures and visual aids	English; students leave their English-only classroom to spend part of their day receiving ESL instruction	English acquisition

Source: Zelasko & Antonez 2000 in DiCerbo, National Clearing House for Bilingual Education: Framing Effective Practice, 2000. (With some adaptations)

Individual Student Characteristics

Some ELLs enter U.S. schools with strong academic preparation in their native language. They have attended schools in their own country, have learned to read and write well in their native language, and are at comparable (or better) levels as native English speakers of the same grade level and age. Others may not have such extensive academic preparation. Due to social, economic, or cultural factors, their schooling may have been interrupted or nonexistent. This means some students at every age level come with little or no exposure to reading and writing, and may be unable to do even basic mathematical computations. Thus, designing an instructional program to serve students of such diverse needs becomes an increasingly complex task.

District Resources

The capability of individual districts to provide human and material resources greatly influences the type of program that is developed to serve ELLs. Availability of resources varies from district to district. Some have trained ESL personnel to staff schools as need arises, while others have to scramble to find someone who can work with a few students on a volunteer basis. Some districts can draw upon a large stable community group for bilingual personnel to staff immersion bilingual programs; others must look beyond the local area.

Some districts are experiencing declining enrollments, freeing up classroom space to allow magnet schools or resource centers to flourish where ELLs from several schools come together at one centrally located school. Other districts are bursting at the seams, making it almost impossible just to find classroom space to house an ESL program.

IS THERE ONE IDEAL PROGRAM TO BEST MEET THE NEEDS OF THE ELLS?

The design of any ESL/ENL program must take so many factors into account that it becomes a complex task to determine which type of program would be best in any given set of circumstances. It can be said that the best program is one which:

❍ is tailored to meet the linguistic, academic, and affective needs of students;
❍ provides English language learners with the instruction necessary to allow them to progress through school at a rate commensurate to their native English-speaking peers;
❍ makes the best use of district and community resources.

However, because researchers have made considerable advances in the fields of psycholinguistics, second language acquisition, bilingual pedagogy,

and multicultural education, today we know a great deal more about the challenges faced by English language learners and about promising strategies for overcoming them.

A CASE FOR BILINGUAL EDUCATION

Meta-analysis, an objective method that weighs numerous variables in each study under review, has yielded positive findings about bilingual education (Greene, 1998 in Crawford, 1998). A comprehensive review of research regarding the use of first and second languages in education was carried out for the World Bank (Dutcher, 1994 in Tucker, 1999). The following are among the conclusions drawn from this study:

❍ Individuals most easily develop literacy skills in a familiar language.
❍ Individuals most easily develop cognitive skills and master content material when they are taught in a familiar language.
❍ The best predictor of cognitive/academic language development in a second language is the level of development of cognitive/academic language proficiency in the first language.
❍ If the goal is to ultimately help the student develop the highest possible degree of content mastery and second language proficiency, time spent instructing the student in a familiar language is a wise investment.
❍ Development of the mother tongue promotes cognitive development and serves as a basis for learning the second language.

Although there is much to be learned about the contexts and strategies that facilitate transfer across languages, the fact that transfer of academic concepts already mastered occurs from one language to another is not a topic of debate. The work of Hakuta (1986; 1997a) and his colleagues provides clear evidence that a student who acquires basic literacy or mathematical concepts in one language can transfer this knowledge easily to a second language. The literature is abundant with examples confirming the importance of nurturing the student's native language. Gonzalez (1998), in particular, writes about the need to develop the basic functions of literacy, mathematical concepts, and scientific discourse in the first language to the fullest extent possible, while facilitating the transfer to the second language. Learning time spent in well-designed bilingual programs is time well spent. Knowledge and skills acquired in the native language—literacy in particular—are transferable to the second language. They do not need to be relearned in English (Krashen, 1996; Cummins, 1992). Thus, there is no reason to rush ELLs into the mainstream before they are ready (Crawford, 1998).

Research over the past few decades has determined that, despite appearances, it takes anywhere from five to seven years to develop cognitive academic language proficiency (CALP) or academic language. Often the English language learner is quick to develop basic interpersonal communication skills (BICS) or social language used on the playground or to communicate simple needs, yet they are nowhere ready to employ the cognitively demanding decontextualized language used for academic pursuits; this takes much longer to acquire (Cummins, 1981; Thomas & Collier, 2001).

Bilingual education programs that emphasize a gradual transition to English and offer native language instruction in declining amounts over time provide continuity in the ELLs' cognitive growth and lay a foundation for academic success in the second language (ibid).

If bilingual education appears to be the most effective model in teaching ELLs, then, why is it not the most widely employed? Research on the effectiveness of bilingual education still remains a dispute. This, due to the fact that program evaluation studies, featuring appropriate comparison groups and random assignment of subjects or controls for pre-existing differences are extremely difficult to design. Moreover, there is considerable variation among the methods employed, the schools, the students, and the communities being compared. While numerous studies have documented the benefits of bilingual programs, much of this research has faced methodological criticisms, as noted by an expert panel of the National Research Council (August and Hakuta, 1997a).

One of the most commonly alluded to fallacies about bilingual education is that it is far more costly than English language instruction. All programs serving English language learners require additional staff, training, instructional materials, and administration; thus, they cost a little more than regular programs for native English speakers, yet, in most cases the difference is minimal. A study commissioned by the California legislature examined a variety of well-implemented program models and found no budgetary advantage for English-only approaches. The incremental cost was approximately the same each year ($175–$214) for bilingual and English immersion programs, as compared with $1,198 for English as a second language (ESL) pull-out programs. The reason was simple: pull-out programs require supplemental teachers, whereas in-class bilingual approaches do not (Chambers & Parrish, 1992). Although this is the case, ESL pull-out programs remain the model of choice for many school districts. This could be attributed to the diversity in the English language learner population, the shortage of bilingual teachers, or the lack of expertise in bilingual methodologies. Nevertheless, a consensus of applied linguists (Crawford, 1998) recognizes that the following propositions have strong empirical support:

○ Native-language instruction does not retard the acquisition of English.
○ Well-developed skills in the native language are associated with high levels of academic achievement.
○ Bilingualism is a valuable skill for the individuals and for the country.

Bilingual education was adopted by numerous school districts in the 1960s and 1970s to remedy practices that denied English language learners equal educational opportunities. Yet, it was hardly an innovative idea. There is a long bilingual tradition in the United States in which minority language schooling has played a central, yet largely forgotten, role.

Points to Remember

✓ There are numerous program models for providing meaningful education for ELLs.

✓ Research indicates the bilingual program model seems to be the most effective for learning a second language.

✓ The myth about the exorbitant cost of bilingual programs is untrue.

✓ Bilingual programs are less costly than "ESL pull-out" programs.

✓ There are factors such as demographics, ELLs' student body characteristics, and district resources which affect the type of program model employed in schools today.

✓ Program models range from 90 percent use of the L1 to 100 percent use of the L2.

✓ It has been found that the use of L1 provides for cognitive development which later transfers to the L2.

✓ There is no question that concepts and knowledge acquired in the L1 transfer to the L2.

✓ Well-developed bilingual education programs are the ideal programs for ELLs.

Chapter 4

The English Language Learner

Key Issues

○ Characteristics of ELLs

○ Factors affecting the ELL's perception of self and overt behavior

○ A challenge for twenty-first century teachers

SCENARIO

A few years ago, a professor decided to try something different with her elementary education majors at Florida Atlantic University. She began the introduction to her TESOL class in Spanish rather than English. She made no effort to make the input comprehensible. Three of the students understood Spanish and were able to follow along; the rest of the students sat in disbelief, shocked by what was happening. When she concluded this short episode, she projected the following on the overhead screen:

> Please take out a piece of paper and capture in writing your impressions of what just happened; describe your feelings, your thoughts. We will discuss your comments in a few minutes.

The professor gave the students a few minutes to write and then discussed their feelings. The consensus was that they felt "stupid," shy, confused, and frustrated, because they could not follow along. At first, some thought they might have entered the wrong classroom and began to leave, but when the professor wrote TSL 4080 on the board they realized they were in the right room and began to feel anxious. Although they thought that she would certainly not be teaching the entire semester in Spanish (Florida Atlantic University would not allow that, or was it possible that this could be for real?), they were feeling inadequate while the episode was taking place—not a good feeling.

This strategy worked, since for the first time, these students were able to experience how English language learners feel in mainstream classrooms. It also helped the students realize that they, as future teachers, will be the ones who will make a profound impact in their English language learners' lives.

In the last six years, the number of non-English speaking students in American schools has increased over 46.5 percent. Spanish language speakers have increased by 60 percent since 1990 (Cortez, 2003) and the Asian population has increased between 48 percent and 72 percent.* (U.S. Census Bureau, 2002) There are notable changes in the demographic profiles of school-age children. In more and more states around the country, Latino students are reflecting the fastest growing subgroup, often accounting for a substantial proportion of enrollment increases. This growing national trend has serious implications for many aspects of public school education. States that are slow to recognize these, do so at their students' peril (Cortez, 2003).

ELL PROFILE

At first, newcomer ELLs may seem excited about being in a new country, a new neighborhood, and a new school. The newness of it all creates a sense of adventure, but soon, reality sets in. They may feel

*The range is due to whether they are counted as Asian alone (45%) or in combination with groups from the Far East, Southeast Asia, or the Indian sub-continent (72%).

lonely, missing family members and friends. They may feel "stupid" because of the language barrier, or angry, since they did not ask to be brought to this country. Many do not understand why they are in this new environment. All they know is that they do not understand what surrounds them. They do know that before coming to this country, they could communicate their basic needs and wants; they could laugh and joke; they had friends; now they are surrounded by sounds and words that are incomprehensible.

They sit in school, trying to make sense of the world in which they are immersed, without much success. Their limited English proficiency does not allow them to participate in what takes place in the classroom, and they may feel intimidated when they observe their native-English-language peers effortlessly involved in the lessons they find so confusing.

In addition, ELLs are intimidated when required to interact with school personnel such as teachers, aides, the school principal, cafeteria workers, and guidance counselors, who seem to have such a command of the language they are unable to speak.

These students enter U.S. schools with a tremendous language and conceptual development gap when compared with their native English language peers. The lack of conceptual development stems from the fact that many concepts are neither present in these students' cultures nor part of the everyday culture of their families. Consequently, some experiences from home may never get named at school and certain experiences at school cannot be taken home (Perke, 1991 in Horbury & Cattrell, 1997). The learning within each realm is experienced in separate, non-interchangeable domains.

At times, ELLs may feel embarrassed about their own heritage. Some do not want to be seen with their parents, sensing that their ways are different from those of the majority culture. Often their parents do not speak English, which from the newcomer's perspective only compounds their problems.

Some educators believe English language learners have short attention spans. Do they really? It is very difficult to remain on task and be attentive when the input received is totally incomprehensible. Their short attention spans are not innate, but rather a normal reaction to the classroom situation they are encountering. Others describe these students as shy; this is normally the result of being in an environment where they are unable to interact. When these students are observed in mainstream classrooms, they appear quiet and withdrawn; however, when they are observed in their ESOL (pull-out) classrooms surrounded by other English language learners, the difference is remarkable. In this environment, among peers who speak their language or who are at their same level of English language proficiency, they are eagerly and actively involved in the teaching/learning situation. Additionally, teachers must keep in mind that learning a new language and trying to perform cognitive tasks within that new language is exhausting. For that reason the English language learner child may show physical symptoms of fatigue and actually sleep in the classroom.

Diverse origins, values, capabilities, and needs characterize the ELL teacher's clientele. Some language minority students have never been to school, despite their advanced age. Some have parents who value education for all their children; others have parents who believe schooling is worthwhile for males only, and who perceive the school as only a protective holding tank for daughters until they are marriageable. Some parents send their children to school on a regular basis; others keep them home often to look after younger siblings or to serve as interpreters for them (Fleming, 1993).

It is a reality that many English language learners eventually learn to accept their new challenges and develop a sense of comfort in their new environment. If they are in schools where their English language development is taken seriously and ESOL programs are available to them, these students will develop the English language proficiency needed to succeed and remain in school (Ross, 1995). Others, unfortunately, become frustrated and, if not provided the necessary aid, will stop trying, eventually leading them to drop out of school as soon as they become of age.

Research indicates that language minority students who enter school with positive self-esteem lose confidence in themselves as a result of the lower expectations they encounter in school (Morse, 1989 in Martinez et al., 1994; Hakuta, 2001). It is not known if low self-esteem causes low academic achievement or if low academic achievement causes low self-esteem. A study of migrant farm workers' children compared high and low academic achievers and their responses regarding their memory of having a "bad" teacher ("one who would not go out of the way to help them"). It was found that 40 percent of low achievers reported having had a "bad" teacher while only 10 percent of high achievers reported having had a "bad" teacher. Although this study cannot be used as conclusive data to describe the total U.S. migrant student population, it is important. Perhaps low achievers have teachers whose mistreatment affected their self-esteem, and as a result, their school performance (Martinez et al., 1994; Gonzalez and Padilla, 1997; Osterman, 2000).

Several million recent immigrants reside in the United States, and according to a recent survey, more than three and a half million are school-age children (Hoffman, 2000). Many of these immigrants settle in urban areas because of family contacts or job opportunities; however, scattered across the country are thousands of children from a variety of ethnic groups who do not attend school in either suburban or rural areas. As reflected in the cities, the bulk of the language minority students in nonmetropolitan areas represent immigrant groups. As of the early 1990s, schools were enrolling ELLs from three main regions: Southeast Asia, eastern Europe, and Latin America (including Mexico and the Caribbean).

A study conducted among students from migrant farm worker families in Florida (Martinez et al., 1994) reported the following:

❍ Of the eighty-four students interviewed, 61 percent were born in the United States and 39 percent in Mexico.
❍ Seventy-five percent had worked or were working in the fields.
❍ Despite legislation to keep children out of the fields, children as young as six were still working in the fields.
❍ Fifty percent of those working in the fields did not have a favorite crop and almost 40 percent could not think of a least favorite crop.

❍ Eighty-two percent reported Spanish as the primary language spoken at home.
❍ Of the 82 percent who spoke Spanish at home, 40 percent of the fathers and 43 percent of the mothers were non-English speakers.
❍ Fifty-eight percent reported that when they missed school it was so that they could be translators for their parents, 25 percent watched over younger siblings, and 7 percent worked.
❍ Thirty-three percent needed glasses to see well; of these, only a little over one-half had received glasses.
❍ Ninety-six percent reported they liked school; 42 percent that they liked to learn; 21 percent that it was "fun"; 16 percent that it was a way to "improve their way of life."
❍ Eighty-nine percent reported that they could remember a teacher who had gone out of the way to do something for them.
❍ Thirty-eight percent reported they could remember a teacher who had not gone out of the way to do something for them.
❍ A significant relationship was found between self-esteem and grade level, with high school students having the highest self-esteem levels and elementary the lowest.
❍ A sharp decrease in self-esteem occurs at grade 8, at which point many migrant students drop out of school.
❍ A significant relationship was also found between self-esteem and reading ability, with poor readers reporting significantly lower self-esteem than good readers.

Not all English language learners come from migrant families. Some are in the United States on international exchanges or as international students; they are sons and daughters of wealthy families who want their children to learn English for the status and the professional opportunities it affords. These students tend to be bright and academically oriented—top-notch students who are highly literate in their native language. Their parents value education. Many of these students attend private schools and thus do not pose a financial burden to the public schools' budgets. These students' needs are usually met by private tutors paid by their parents, or provided by the private schools which they attend and where the costs of these tutors is encompassed in the tuition their parents pay. International students are usually in the United States on a transitory basis; many of whom are here without their parents, in boarding schools. These students are in school from the beginning of the school year, and unless there is an extenuating circumstance, until the last day. They are involved in extracurricular activities and they excel at most of their undertakings.

Researchers (Olsen and Jaramillo,1999; Ruiz de Velasco et al., 2000; Freeman and Freeman, 2004), have identified three types of ELLs: long-term English language learners, recent arrivals with limited or interrupted formal schooling, and recent arrivals with adequate schooling. Long-term English language learners are those who have attended United States schools for several years; they speak English and are often no longer classified as ELL, but still struggle academically. These students have mastered social language but are lacking academic language/vocabulary. Recent arrivals with limited or interrupted formal schooling are those ELLs who arrive in the United States many times in the middle of the school year and possess limited academic knowledge in their native language due to limited or interrupted schooling. These students have very little or no social language, thus they need to develop academic and social language as well. Those students who are recent arrivals with adequate schooling do not have the social language, however, they do possess academic language and academic content knowledge in their native language (L1). As their English language develops, they are able to draw on this background knowledge and catch up with their classmates.

Generation 1.5

There is another large group of ELLs, a relatively new phenomenon, that has been identified as Generation 1.5. These students are in a complex situation in terms of coming to the United States, with whom they identify, and how they label themselves. Much of this stems from their in-between position in terms of their language development and literacy. These students are in the middle of two generations of immigrants (Figure 4.1).

These 1.5ers come to the United States when they are young; it could be before school age, or during elementary or high school age, thus, they could be partially foreign-educated and partially U.S.-educated. These students may develop a strange pattern of language use, they may be English-dominant, they may be home-language dominant, and they may identify with one language, but are actually more proficient in the other. For these reasons, these ELLs are considered in between and in the Generation 1.5 category.

How can Generation 1.5 students be identified? In reality, these 1.5ers cannot be identified by the number of years they have been in the United States, nor by the number of years of schooling either in their L1 or in English. These students can only be identified by asking questions such as: What does their language look like? What do their life experiences look like? How do they label or identify themselves? The boundaries for identifying 1.5ers are not clearly defined. Much depends on factors such as those in the questions posed.

There are other groups of ELLs that can also be identified as Generation 1.5ers:

"Immigrants from U.S. territories", e.g., Puerto Rico

"Parachute Kids"—those who come to the United States usually from Asia, alone, to live with extended family members and who attend K–12 schools

1st Generation	Generation 1.5	2nd Generation
Adult Immigrant Foreign Born	Childhood Immigrant Foreign Born	Children of Immigrants U.S. Born
Foreign Educated	Partially Foreign Educated	U.S. Educated
L1 Dominant	Partially U.S. Educated: L1 or English Dominant	English Dominant

FIGURE 4.1 Generation 1.5

Source: Adapted from Roberge, M.M. (2000)

"Native-born, non-native English speakers—these are U.S. born students from linguistics enclave communities (very little exposure to English)*

"Transnationals"—those students who have complex patterns of back and forth migration

Many of today's classrooms are microcosms of the global situation experienced in the United States in the present times. Teachers, like diplomats, must be prepared to deal with the constant variation and change that this reality imposes on them. Teachers must learn to provide for the needs of this varied student population of native speakers of English, as well as English language learners who come with an array of differences that need to be addressed.

*There is also a phenomenon being seen in college more and more—U.S.-born, non-native speakers of English. These students have been schooled in the United States, yet have lived in enclave communities in non-literate families and have had very little exposure to English outside of school. Most of their interactions outside of class time are in another language.

Points to Remember

✓ The school/classroom environment has a tremendous impact on ELLs' retention and success.

✓ Non-speakers of English feel intimidated when surrounded by input that is not comprehensible.

✓ There is great diversity among English language learners enrolled in the public/private schools of America today.

✓ More than two million of the immigrants in the United States are school-age children.

✓ Most English language learners come from three main regions: Southeast Asia, eastern Europe and Latin America (including Mexico and the Caribbean).

✓ In the agricultural areas of the United States, immigrant children are still found working in the fields.

✓ Many immigrant children serve as interpreters for their parents.

✓ Teachers are legally accountable for providing a comparable education for non-native English speakers.

✓ Teachers have a tremendous impact on the success or failure of their students, especially their ELLs.

✓ Teachers "going out of their way" to reach English language learners positively influence these students' self-esteem.

✓ There are three types of ELLs: long-term English language learners, recent arrivals with limited or interrupted formal schooling, and recent arrivals with adequate schooling.

✓ Generation 1.5 is a recent phenomenon of ELLs who are attending U.S. schools today.

Part Two

A KNOWLEDGE BASE
FOR LINGUISTIC SYSTEMS

Chapter 5

Human Language

Key Issues

- ○ All languages are equal from a linguistic point of view
- ○ Constraints within phonemic sequences
- ○ Universal facts about human language

SCENARIO

In the Introduction to Linguistics class, Dr. Cruz asks her students the following questions:

Dr. Cruz: *Who can tell me how many spoken languages there are in the world?*

Kim: *Five thousand?*

James: *Ten thousand?*

Dr. Cruz: *Good guesses. There are 6800 spoken languages in the world of which less than a thousand have written forms.*

Dr. Cruz: *What features do all languages share?*

Dr. Cruz lists the features on the board as students contribute their answers.

Linguistically speaking, no language is superior to another. All languages in the world have grammars, although it is not unusual to hear the remark that some languages have no grammar. Because all human languages are spoken, they must have sounds and sound systems, words and word-order systems, and word meanings. English has 14 vowels and Spanish has five vowels; Walbiri (an aboriginal language of Australia) has a more flexible word order than English, but this difference does not make Spanish or Walbiri inferior to the English language.

All languages have constraints within their phonemic sequence, the permissible way in which phonemes can be combined. In English, there are no words that begin with the nasalized /ŋ/ sounds like the end of /siŋ/, but in Malay, this sound is in the initial position as in the word /ŋantuk/ (sleepy). In Spanish, the /sp/ cluster only appears medially, therefore it is common to hear Spanish speakers say /estop/ or /especial/ for *stop* and *special*. These languages and a vast majority of other languages share a similar word order pattern, i.e., the subject precedes the object. In addition, although Spanish and English may inflect nouns for plurals and Haitian Creole and Spanish inflect nouns for gender, all three languages use the inflectional system to mark

different grammatical categories. Thus, even though Spanish, English, and Haitian Creole languages may seem very different from one another, they all share a number of universal features in their grammar. Many grammatical categories and rules within languages of the world are universal. Chomsky termed this concept as universal grammar (UG). The intricacies within UG perplex linguists and they continue to have an ongoing fascination with linguistic analysis as it reflects the structure and organization of the human mind.

Michael Krauss (Stephens, 1993), a professor of linguistics at the University of Alaska, reported that there are 6,000 dialects, plus or minus 10 percent, still spoken in today's world.

What are some of the universal properties of human language? Diaz-Rico and Weed (1993: 55) offer some universal facts about human language:

○ Language exists wherever humans exist. The main purpose of language is communication.

○ Every normal child, regardless of creed, geographical, or socio-economic background, is capable of acquiring any language to which he or she is exposed. Language is culturally transmitted; it is not biologically transmitted. An adopted

Cambodian child in an American family will grow up to speak American English because he is exposed to the American language and culture.

○ All human languages use a limited set of sounds and gestures to form meaningful sound combinations in words found in unlimited sets of possible sentences. For example, in how many ways can you say this sentence—*President Bush's Gallup poll rating is on a decline because of the war in Iraq?* You can say *Because of the war in Iraq, President Bush's Gallup poll rating is on a decline,* or *Bush's rating is decreasing because of the war in Iraq,* or *People are unhappy with President Bush's decision on the war in Iraq.* These are a few ways to communicate this idea and there are a dozen other ways. This property is called productivity. In contrast, animal language does not have this characteristic. A cicada has four fixed sounds, not three or two, and a vervet monkey has 36 signals, not 35 or 37. Animal language has this aspect of permanency, and the animals cannot change their system of communication.

○ All languages have properties to refer to past time, the ability to negate, use question forms, issue commands, and so on. This property of human language is called displacement. In contrast, animal language does not have this characteristic. For example, bees use the sophisticated "waggle" dance to direct each other to the location of the nectar, but bees cannot tell each other how sweet and wonderful the nectar was yesterday and that it will be better tomorrow. Only human language has this enabling property: people can talk about historical events and plan for what to do in the future.

○ All languages are dynamic; they undergo changes through time. Just listen to the words teenagers use nowadays. They love *surfing* the net; they like *cool* things, they visit each other's *cribs.* The original meanings of these words are completely changed.

○ Human language has the property of discreteness, i.e., it has distinct sounds. Even though some languages have sounds that others may not have, for example, /p/ and /b/ sounds are not distinguishable for Arabic speakers, they are distinct sounds to the English speakers because *parking* and *barking* are two different words.

What important factors should teachers of ELL know about language to be effective in the classroom?

○ Knowing that the purpose of language is communication and it is learned through use (Pinnel and Fountas, 1998), teachers will set a stage for a conducive learning environment in the classroom where ELLs are encouraged to take risks when communicating with one another.

○ Knowing that language is culturally transmitted, and people speak the same way as the people around them speak, teachers should embrace the varieties of English that their students bring into the classroom. But at the same time, teachers will impart and promote the use of standard English, which is the prevalent dialect in the academic circle. For the ELL whose family members do not speak English, it is vital that they are immersed in an environment where they can actively participate in learning English. Teachers need to involve these students in their lessons even though the ELL are at the beginning level of English language proficiency.

○ Knowing that human language has the characteristic of displacement—the property that enables humans to use language for a variety of functions: talk about past, present and future events, issue commands, ask questions, seek permission, express condolences, make a factual statement, disagree with others, etc., teachers need to understand language from the psycholinguistic and sociolinguistic sense.

What are the components of the human language system? All human languages have phonology, the sound system; morphology, the system in which words are built; syntax, the system of how words are arranged in sentences; semantics, the system of word meanings; and pragmatics, the system of how language is used in society.

Within the field of phonology, teachers of ELL, who are aware that not all languages possess the same distinct sounds, will understand and appreciate the non-native pronunciation of English words that their students produce.

In morphology, teachers who have the knowledge of morphemes across cultures will tolerate ELLs' incorrect usage of comparative or superlative adjectives of English such as more pretty or more good for prettier or better because they understand that their ELL transfer their L1 morphological rules when using English morphemes.

For syntax, one of the many pieces of information that teachers will have is that the arrangement of words in a sentence is not universal. For example, English sentences are arranged in Subject Verb Object order; whereas, Korean sentences have the Subject Object Verb word order pattern. Irish has yet another word order pattern—VSO. With this knowledge, teachers can be more effective in their use of appropriate strategies when teaching literacy skills.

How does knowing semantics help teachers? The field of semantics deals with meanings of words. There are many categories of words; the parts of speech such as nouns, adjectives, verbs, adverbs, and so forth, is one category and here are some others: Homonyms—words that sound the same but have different meanings (*bat, bank*), homophones—words that have the same sound but are spelled differently and have different meanings (*meat, meet*), homographs—words that are spelled the same but sound different (*read, read*); synonyms, antonyms, compound words, idioms. ELLs find the learning of idioms more challenging as idioms are complex. The phrase *go break a leg* has a non-literal meaning which often times confuses ELLs. These examples illustrate the complexity of the semantic system.

The nuances of the English language or any other language is mostly apparent in the pragmatic system. The pragmatic system involves social conventions of the speech community. For example, in the United States, the phrases speakers use to close a conversation are several: *See you later, have a nice day, bye, take care, we should go to lunch some time,* etc. Some of these phrases such as *we should have lunch some time*, or *see you later* are ostentatious in nature. ELLs who are new to the language and its social conventions may misunderstand these greetings and expect the speakers to follow through with them. Many miscommunications occur because of the limited understanding of pragmatics and teachers can ease their students' adjustment to the new language and culture by comparing their knowledge of the pragmatics of the English language system to the pragmatics of their students' native language system.

Points to Remember

✓ Linguistically speaking, no language is superior to another.

✓ All languages have constraints within their phonemic sequence.

✓ Grammatical categories and rules in many languages are universal.

✓ Every normal child is capable of acquiring his or her native language.

✓ Languages undergo changes through time.

Chapter 6

Phonology

Key Issues

- ○ The sound system of a language
- ○ Transfer of the first language's phonological rules to a second language
- ○ Distinctive sounds that make a difference
- ○ Permissible arrangements of sounds within a language
- ○ Problematic sound distinctions
- ○ Pitch, stress, tones, and relaxed pronunciation

Three English Language Learners (ELLs) were standing on a mountaintop. One said, "It's windy," and the other responded, "No, it's Thursday." The third student chimed in, "Yes, let's go and get a drink!"

What phonological explanations can you offer for the above conversational miscommunication?

Now examine the production of sounds in English phonology in the following sentences.

1. Say the word *fan*. How is the first sound of this word produced? The /f/ sound is produced by putting the top teeth and the bottom lip together, and blowing air between them.
2. Say the word *were*. This whole word is produced with one continuous motion of the vocal tract (lungs, tongue, lips, and so on), yet we perceive the production of this word as three separate speech sounds, /w-e-r/.
3. The words *hoe, sew, so,* and *dough* all have the same vowel, even though the vowel is spelled differently in each.
4. The sounds /**m**/ and /**b**/ are alike in that they are both produced by pursing the lips; /b/ and /g/ are different in that /g/ is not produced with the lips.
5. The vowel sound in the word *fad* is longer than the same vowel sound as in *fat*.

Example one shows that humans use the vocal tract to produce speech sounds. Example two represents the fact that words are psychologically viewed as a series of discreet units called segments, even though, physically, they are produced with one continuous motion. Example three displays the fact that a single segment can be spelled in a variety of ways because sound and letter correspondence in English is inconsistent; therefore, the phonemic alphabet is used in place of the English alphabet so that each symbol represents one sound. Example four shows the fact that smaller units called distinctive features are contained within each segment. Thus, /m/ and /b/ have the same distinctive feature; i.e., they are labial sounds because they are produced using both lips, whereas /b/ and /g/ do not share the same distinctive feature. Substituting /m/ in the word *bat* will result in a different meaning. Five illustrates that the same vowel /a/ can be lengthened in one context but shortened in another. Thus, the same vowel /a/ is pronounced differently in different contexts—long in *fad* but short in *fat*. Examples one through five are phonological in nature. In other words, the production of these sounds is governed by underlying phonological rules within the English sound system.

WHAT IS PHONOLOGY?

Phonology is the study of the sound system of a language. It also deals with the rules that govern pronunciation and studies the function and patterning of the sounds of a language.

There are some sounds and sound combinations in English that are not heard or differentiated by non-native speakers, who may have difficulty in producing them. The sounds of English that are mispronounced by non-native speakers oftentimes become a source for jokes and laughter in stand-up comedy. Examine the following dialogue.

Non-native speaker: *Hey, can you pass me the flying pan?*

Native speaker: *I'm sorry. You want what? A frying pan?*

In Chinese, the /r/ sound is not found in unit sound clusters such as /fr/, as in *fried*, or /wr/, as in *wrong*, or /spr/, as in *spring*. Most Chinese speakers of English have difficulty with the pronunciation of /wr/, /fr/, and /str/ sound clusters. Native Chinese speakers who are beginning learners of English will pronounce the words *spring*, *fried*, and *strawberry* as /spliŋ/, /fleyd/, and /stlɔbɛli/. Moreover, because in English not all sounds have one-to-one correspondence of sound and orthography, non-native speakers often are unsure of the correct English pronunciation, and thus transfer L1 phonological rules to L2, thereby mispronouncing words in English. For instance, the word *occupy* with the letter *c* in the middle is pronounced with the /k/ sound. However, in the word *proceed*, the letter *c* in the middle position does not take the sound /k/, but instead the sound /s/.

When these isolated mispronunciations occur in sentences that contain other words from which the listener can guess the meanings, communication is not hindered. However, frequent mispronunciations alongside heavily accented words can be major obstacles in communication.

Why are non-native speakers unable to pronounce native sounds of a language as shown in the examples above? Native speakers of any language are generally exposed only to the sounds of their language from birth; they only hear and use the sounds of their native language. Although linguists purport that when a baby is born, he or she has the capacity to hear all the sounds of any language in the world, they also state that as children grow up they will only have formed the connections in the brain for their native language sounds. Because other sounds are not heard or reinforced, connections for these sounds are not formed and will die away. This is why non-native speakers of any language may have difficulty in producing the sounds of a target language they are learning.

DESCRIPTION AND ARTICULATION OF CONSONANTS AND VOWELS

The earlier scenarios of non-native speakers encountering difficulties in producing English sounds can be further understood when we examine the sounds that make up a language, called phonemes, and minimal pairs. Phonemes are distinctive sound units that "make a difference" when sounds form words. Minimal pairs are words that differ by only one phoneme. Examples of minimal pairs in English are /pɪn/ *pin* and /bɪn/ *bin*; /stet/ *state* and /sted/ *staid*; /tɛn/ *ten* and /dɛn/ *den*. In Chinese, /ti/ and /di/ are minimal pairs, the former meaning *tears* and the latter *earth*; in Malay *sayang* and *dayang*, the former meaning *love* and the latter *princess's maids*. While in English, /p/ and /b/ sounds are distinguishable, they are not in Arabic. Arab speakers will say *barking lot* instead of *parking lot*, and *bile* instead of *pile*. English speakers are unable to say the word *nyamuk* (mosquitoes) as the Malays do, because English does not have nasalized sounds in word initial position. The /b/ and /v/ sounds are indistinguishable for some Spanish speakers when /v/ occurs in a medial position; therefore, some Spanish speakers who attempt to say /baklava/ will substitute the /v/ with a /b/ sound in the third syllable, producing /baklaba/ instead.

PHONOTACTIC CONSTRAINTS

In studying phonology it is important to note that each language has permissible ways in which phonemes can be arranged. This permissible arrangement is called phonemic sequence. Each language allows only specific sound combinations at initial, mid, or final positions. In English, there can be a single sound in a word such as *oh* or multiple consonants can occur successively in final position in a word such as *texts* /tɛksts/—CVCCCC, three consonants can occur successively in initial position such as in words like /sprɪŋ/ *spring* and /strɪŋ/ *string*—CCCVC. It becomes more complicated when there are only permissible combinations in consonant clusters; for instance, in English there is a word *draft* but not *sraft*, /dr/ is a consonant cluster in English whereas /sr/ is not. In Spanish, it is permissible to have the *s* cluster such as /sp/ occur in mid position, as in the word *español*, but never in initial position. This may explain why Spanish native speakers may say *espoiled* for *spoiled* or *espace* for *space* when speaking English.

How can we help non-native speakers of English with their difficulty in producing words with initial and final consonant clusters that are permitted in English? The most troublesome initial consonant clusters for the largest number of non-native English speakers seem to be those consisting of an initial /s/ followed by one or more other consonants. This large group includes /sf/, /sk/, /sl/, /sm/, /sn/, /sp/, /st/, and /sw/. To compound the problem for non-native speakers of English is the three-consonant clusters at the initial position of words such as /striŋ/ *string* and /skræp/ *scrape* and /skwɛr/ *square*. The above examples of initial consonant clusters violate the phonotactic rules of a number of languages, such as Chinese, Japanese, and Iranian.

Two- and three-consonant clusters in word final position also pose a problem for non-native speakers of English. Let us examine some of these sound combinations in the following words: /lb/ *bulb*, /gd/ *tagged*, /nd/ *cleaned*, /vd/ *lived*, /lf/ *self*, /rvd/ *carved*, /mps/ *camps*, /ŋks/ *links*.

Prator and Robinett (1985) suggest two ways of making clusters easier for non-native English speakers to pronounce. First is the process of phonetic syllabication and second is the omission of consonants. Phonetic syllabication can occur when a word ends in a consonant sound and the following word begins with a vowel as in the sequences *has it* /haezɪt/, *hide 'em* /haydəm/, and *give up* /gɪvəp/. In these examples, it is suggested that the final consonant of the first word be pronounced at the beginning of the second word: /hǽ-zɪt/, /háy-dəm/, /gɪ-v́əp/. In the same way, the last consonant of a final cluster can be moved forward and pronounced with the vowel of the following word. *Find out* can become /fayn-dáwt/, *Sixth Avenue* /sɪks-ǽvənyuw/, and *changed address* can become /čeynǰ-dədrés/. Two-consonant clusters are thus reduced to single consonants, three-consonant clusters to two-conso-

nant clusters, and four-consonant clusters to easier, three-consonant clusters. Proper use of phonetic syllabication can not only facilitate a student's pronunciation, it can also do much to make his or her English sound more authentic. The second way to make consonant clusters more pronounceable is simply to omit one of the consonant sounds. Native speakers of English do this more often than they realize: for example, many commonly pronounce *arctic* as /ártɪk/, omitting the first c. Probably everyone omits the difficult p in *raspberry*, which is normally pronounced /rǽzbɛ́rɪ/. Such omissions happen most frequently and are least noticeable in final three-consonant clusters when the middle consonant (the sound that is omitted), is a voiceless stop: *acts* /aekts/ becomes /aeks/, *lifts* /lɪfts/ becomes /lifs/, *asked* /æskt/ becomes /aest/. These are some ways to assist non-native speakers of English to overcome their problems with the pronunciation of words with initial and final consonant clusters.

Phonemes can be classified into two main categories: consonants and vowels. The third category of sounds that resemble both consonants and vowels is called semivowels. Consonants are made when the airflow is partially or completely obstructed in the mouth by the placement of the tongue and the positioning of the lips. Voiced and voiceless consonants are differentiated by the vibration felt when the larynx is touched. For example, /s/ does not produce any vibrations, while the production of /z/ produces vibration of the vocal folds (muscles). English consonants can be recognized by three modifications to the airstream: the place of articulation of the consonants, the manner in which the airstream is blocked, and voicing. Refer to Figure 6.1 (pg. 45) for places and manner of articulation for consonants. Refer to Table 6.1 (pg. 45) for consonant symbols and sample words. In the production of vowels, the airflow in the vocal tract is not blocked. English has fourteen vowels and five diphthongs. Diphthongs are two vowels that make up one phoneme. Vowels can be described using these characteristics: height, tongue advancement, lip rounding, tense (long)/lax (short). Look at Figure 6.2 (pg. 46) for symbols, and Table 6.2 for sample words for vowels and diphthongs. For example, us-

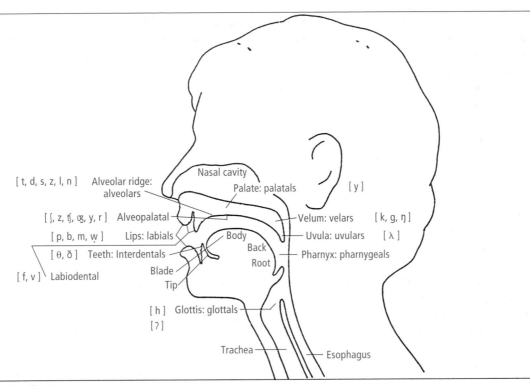

FIGURE 6.1 Places of articulation are listed, followed by a term used to describe sounds made at each place. Areas of the tongue are also provided.

TABLE 6.1

The International Phonetic Alphabet Symbols for American English Phonemes

Symbol	Sample Words	Symbol	Sample Words
Stops		*Affricate*	
[p]	pot, top, staple	[tʃ]	choke, batch, catching
[b]	bet, globe, dabble	[dʒ]	judge, cojole, page
[t]	tip, pat, staple		
[d]	dense, body, guard	*Nasals*	
[k]	can't, chemistry, kick	[m]	moose, comb, coming
[g]	garden, again, get	[n]	nine, banner, snow
[ʔ]	uh-oh	[ŋ]	sing, wringer, prong
	button, mitten (in some dialects)		
		Liquids	
Fricatives		[l]	leaf, hill, piling
[f]	fan, coffee, enough	[r]	ran, terrain, stare
[v]	van, dove, gravel	[ɽ] flap	written, bitter, liter
[θ] theta	through, teeth, ether		
[ð] epsilon	the, either, leather	*Glides*	
[s]	sweet, bask, fuss	[w] voiced	witch, worm, with
[z]	zip, design, kisses	[j]	exhume, yoke, lawyer
[ʃ]	shred, bashful, mesh	[ʍ]	what, whale, white (in some dialects)
[ʒ]	measure, vision, casualty		
[h]	who, cohort, ugh		

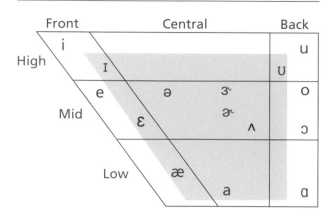

FIGURE 6.2 The vowel quadrilateral. Non-colored: tense vowel. Colored: lax vowels

TABLE 6.2

The Different Sounds of English Vowels in Sample Words

Symbol	Sample Words
Vowels	
[i]	beat, we, believe, people
[ɪ]	bit, injury, business
[e]	bait, reign, great, they
[ɛ]	bet, reception, says, guest, bury
[æ]	bat, laugh, anger, rally
[u]	boot, who, sewer, through
[ʊ]	put, foot, butcher, could
[o]	boat, beau, grow, though, over
[ɔ]	bought, caught, wrong, stalk
[a]	pot, father, far, car
[ʌ]	but, tough, another
[ə]	among, focus, sofa
[ʒ]	bird, her, stir
Diphthongs	
[au]	how
[ai]	tie
[ɔɪ]	boy
[eɪ]	bake
[oʊ]	rose

ing the vowel characteristics, let us describe the vowel /e/. Refer to Figure 6.2:

/e/ Description

Height: high-mid

Advancement: front

Lip rounding: retracted

Tense/lax tense

The information on the manner and place of articulation that phonologists provide is important for teachers of non-native speakers of English.

For example, some consonants in English are pronounced with a stronger release of air, such as the /p/ in *pin*. A lighted match placed close to the lips would be put out. However, there is less aspiration in the /sp/ cluster in *spin*. Nevertheless, aspiration is not a distinctive phoneme in English. Some languages may not produce this sound in the same manner that English does. For example, aspiration is a distinctive feature of the Khmer language—[pʰa]: *father* and [pa]: *silk cloth*. Likewise, when the place of articulation is changed even slightly, the word may not sound correct. For instance, pronounce the word *tin*. Now, move your tongue as far back as you can and pronounce this word again. Continue to place your tongue at different positions and pronounce the same word. What do you notice? In some languages, consonants are pronounced in a more forward position than in English, while in others, the places of articulation are further back in the mouth. The difference in the place of articulation contributes to one of the many qualities that make up "foreign accents." Tables 6.3 and 6.4 (pg. 47) contain examples of sounds that may pose problems for non-native English speakers, as well as some sounds in different languages that native English speakers have difficulty producing.

Spanish Speakers of English

Spanish and English differ in their phonemic system, both in terms of vowels and of consonants. English has fourteen vowel sounds and five diphthongs approximately, and Spanish has only five vowels. Because of this Spanish speakers of English will always experience difficulty with vowel production due to interference. For example, the word *pick* will be pronounced as /pik/, because /ɪ/ is nonexistent in Spanish. Other examples are *bake, tack, good, hope*. In *bake,* vowel /ei/—/e/; in *tack,* /ae/ —/a/; in *good,*

TABLE 6.3

Problematic Sound Distinctions in English for Spanish and Haitian-Creole Speakers

The first sound is the problem sound; the second is the substituted sound.

Consonant	Spanish	Haitian Creole
v/b	X	
θ/s (theta)	X	X
ʃ/tʃ	X	X
j/dʒ	X	
dʒ/j	X	
s/z	X	
θ/z (theta)		X
ð/d (epsilon)	X	
m/ŋ	X	
n/ŋ	X	X
w/g	X	
r/w		X

TABLE 6.4

Problem English Vowel Contrasts for Spanish Speakers

English	Problem Contrast	Spanish
/e/—ate /ʌ/—after	A	/a/—pluma (pen)
/i/—even or /ɛ/—every	E	/ɛ/—enero (January)
/aɪ/—ice or /ɪ/—sick	I	/i/—libro (book)
/o/—open or /ʊ/— move	O	/o/—blanco(a) (white)
/ju/—use or /ʌ/—under	U	/u/—nuevo(a)

/ʊ/—/u/, in *hope*, /ou/—/o/. Not all vowel productions are caused by interference, for instance, the word *feet*, Spanish speakers say *fit*, the substitution of /i/ for /ɛ/ is not caused by interference (Perez,

1994). Other similar examples are in words such as *men* (/ɛ/—/ae/), *room* (/u/—/ʊ/), *and some* (/ʌ/—/a/).

Some examples of common consonant interference are: with, /wit/; those, /douz/; vine, /baɪn/; shoe, /tʃu/, yes, /jɛs/. Refer to Table 6.5 for more examples of Spanish-influenced English vowel and consonant productions.

TABLE 6.5

Common Spanish-Influenced English Vowel and Consonant Productions

English Word	Spanish-Influenced English Transcription	Phonological Pattern	English Word	Spanish-Influenced English Transcription	Phonological Pattern
Vowel Articulations			*Consonant Articulations*		
lid	/lid/	ɪ → i	think	/tiŋk/	θ → t stopping
need	/nɪd/	i → ɪ	them	/dɛm/	ð → d stopping
mate	/met/ (will sound similar to /ɛ/	eɪ → e	vase	/bes/	v → b stopping
late	/lɛt/	eɪ → ɛ	you	/dʒu/	j → dʒ affrication of a glide
tennis	/teɪnɪs/	ɛ → eɪ	sheep	/tʃip/	ʃ → tʃ affrication of a fricative
dead	/dæd/	ɛ → æ			
bag	/bɑg/ or /bɛg/	æ → ɑ or ɛ	choose	/ʃuz/	tʃ → ʃ deaffrication
look	/luk/	ʊ → u	just	/jʌst/	dʒ → j deaffrication
pool	/pʊl/	u → ʊ	zoo	/su/	consonant devoicing
boat	/bot/ (will sound similar to /ɔ/	ou → o	was	/wʌs/	consonant devoicing
bug	/bɑg/ or /bag/	ʌ → ɑ or a	spot	/əspat/ or /ɛspat/	epenthesis of /ə/
word	/wɛrd/	ɝ → ɛr	leaks	/lik/	reduction of word-final consonant clusters

Source: Adapted from Penfield & Ornstein-Galicia, 1985; Perez, 1994; Wise, 1957.

Asian Speakers of English

Tables 6.6 and 6.7 summarize common consonant and vowel productions spoken by Asians/Pacific Islanders (Mandarin Chinese, Cantonese, Vietnamese, Korean, Japanese, and Pilipino). Several Asian languages are tone languages and intonation is considered phonemic since each tone has a different meaning. In contrast, intonation in English conveys the speaker's mood or intent, statement or question. There are fewer words that end with consonants in Mandarin Chinese and Cantonese than in English, so Asian speakers of English will delete the final consonants of English words as they are just transferring their L1 rule to English—applying a no-consonant-endings rule as in their L1. Another important difference between English and most Asian languages is the issue of grammatical rules and phonology.

In Chinese, each printed character is only one syllable in length, therefore Chinese speakers of English may pronounce multisyllabic words syllable by syllable in a telegraphic, or faltering, manner (Small, 2005).

TABLE 6.6

Common Consonant Productions for English Phonemes, as Spoken by Chinese, Vietnamese, Korean, Japanese, and Pilipino Speakers (Mandarin and Cantonese dialects of Chinese are shown separately)

Intended Phoneme		Observed Phoneme					
		Cantonese	Mandarin	Vietnamese	Korean	Japanese	Pilipino
Fricatives	θ	s, f	s, f	s		s, z	t
	ð	d	z, d		ʤ	z, j	d
	ʃ	s		s, t	s		s
	ʒ					ʤ, ʃ	d, ds
	f	~		p		h	p
	v	f, w	f, w		b, p	b	b
	z	s		s	s	dz, ʤ, s	s
Affricates	tʃ		ʃ	s, t, ʃ	t		ts
	ʤ	z		ʒ			ds
Liquids	r	l	l	z	l		
	l		r	n	r	r	

Source: Adapted from Baker, 1982; Cheng, 1987a, 1987b, 1994; and Shen, 1962.

TABLE 6.7

Some Common Vowel Productions in Asian/Pacific Influenced English

Chinese	○ æ → e or ɛ; ɛ → e; ɪ → i; ɔ → o; ʊ → u; ʌ → ɑ
	○ /ə/ is added to consonant clusters
Vietnamese	○ ɪ → i; æ → ʌ; ʊ → u
Korean	○ problems with the production of /i/, ɪ, u, and /ɔ/
Japanese	○ epenthesis of the vowels /ə/ or /u/ to the ends of syllables and words. (Most Japanese words end in an open syllable.)
	○ ɪ → i; æ, a or ə → ɑ; ɚ → ɑ; ʊ → u; ʌ → æ; eɪ → e; æ → ɛ
Pilipino	○ tensing of lax vowels, i.e., ɪ → i; ʊ → u; ɔ → o

Source: Adapted from Baker, 1982; Cheng, 1987a, 1987b, 1994.

Arabic Speakers of English

Unlike English that has 14 vowel sounds and five diphthongs, Arabic has only three vowels, /i/, /a/, and /u/, in short and long forms. The diphthongs in Arabic are /ei/ and /eu/. Several English consonants do not exist in Arabic, such as the stops /p/ and /g/, the fricatives /v/ and /ʒ/, and the nasal /ŋ/ (*Handbook of the International Phonetic Association, 1999*). Also in Arabic, there are no two or three consonant clusters at the beginning of the word, so that is why Arabic speakers of English will pronounce the word *scream* and *street* as /sikrim/ and /sitrit/—adding a vowel between consonants. Sometimes, Arabic speakers will also pronounce silent letters in English since Arabic alphabet is phonemic. For example the words *knot, could,* and *lamb* will be pronounced as /knɔt/, /kuld/, /laemb/. In English, the /c/ can take on different sounds depending on the surrounding sounds, for example, in the words *city, proceed, proclaim,* /c/ is pronounced as /s/, /s/, /k/. For Arabic speakers of English, they may pronounce the word *city* as /kiti/ and the word *soccer* as /sɔsə/.

Table 6.8 summarizes common Arabic-influenced English vowel and consonant productions.

Other problems learners of English have are demonstrated by words that have allophones, i.e., sound variants of the phonemes.

Say these words and note how the /t/ is pronounced in each word.

bottle	(ʔ glottal, t,)
kitten	(ɾ, flap)
stop	(non-aspirated)
top	(aspirated)
hunter	(/t/ is not pronounced in some regional dialects)

PITCH, STRESS, AND RELAXED PRONUNCIATION PATTERNS

Other sound qualities like pitch and stress are also important in the formation of sounds. In English, pitch and stress are important in distinguishing meaning within a sentence. For instance, "José is going to the movies," as a statement is said with a falling pitch, but when it is used as a question, the pitch rises at the end. Intonation is the rising and falling pitch in a language that does not change word meaning, but changes the function of a sentence. Patterns of intonation in English are said to resemble waves, with the crest of the wave over those syllables with the greatest stress. Intonation acts very much like punctuation in a sentence; emo-

TABLE 6.8

Common Arabic-Influenced English Vowel and Consonant Productions

English Word	Arabic-Influenced English Transcription	Phonological Pattern	English Word	Arabic-Influenced English Transcription	Phonological Pattern
Vowel Articulations			*Consonant Articulations*		
brought	/bot/	ɔ → o	party	/bartɪ/	p → b
bit	/bet/	ɪ → e	very	/fɛrɪ/	v → f
because	/bikuz/	ʌ → u	thin	/sɪn/	θ → s
cup	/kæp/	ʌ → æ	lesion	/liʃən/	ʒ → ʃ
set	/sæt/	ɛ → æ	witch	/wɪʃ/	tʃ → ʃ
bread	/brid/	ɛ → i	Jim	/ʃɪm/	ʤ → ʃ
note	/nat/	o → a	bathe	/bez/	ð → z
			think	/θɪnk/	o → t
			scream	/sikrim/	epenthesis of i

Source: Adapted from Altaha, 1995; Baker, 1982; Power, 2003b.

tions such as anger and impatience are signaled by intonation patterns. However, there are many languages that use pitch in individual syllables to contrast meaning; these languages are called tonal languages. There are more than 1,000 tonal languages in Africa alone. Chinese, Thai, and Burmese are also tonal languages, as are many Native American languages (Fromkin-Rodman, 1983). In Mandarin Chinese, the sound /ma/ when used with four different tones produces four different meanings: *horse*, *mother*, *hemp*, and *scold*. The word /mai/ can mean buy or sell.

Like pitch, stress also modifies the meaning of words. In English, stress indicates the part of speech of a particular word. Look at the following examples:

Where would you put the stress on the word used in both sentences?

1a. Carol's conduct at the party was the talk of the town.
1b. Carol will conduct a popular orchestra at the opening ceremony.
2a. McCoy is the meanest rebel in the group.
2b. McCoy and Kazaski rebel against the top members of the organization.

Can you figure out the rule for stress placement in the above examples?

Word stress at the sentence level can also change the intended meaning within a sentence. For example,

H/e did that? (Who did that?)

He d/id that? (Did he do that?)

He did th/at? (What did he do?)

Each statement asks a different question depending on which word is stressed.

Native speakers are seldom taught the explicit phonological rules in their native language, yet they know them. Speakers of any language have different styles of speaking: formal to informal to casual. In English, casual or relaxed speech has three forms in the pronunciation of words: (a) contrac-

tions, (b) "dropping" of sounds, and (c) changing of sounds. Examine the following examples of these three categories.

A. Contractions
   1. *Who'd do that?* (Who would do that?)
   2. *We've been there.* (We have been there.)

B. "Dropping" of sounds
   1. *Eat 'em.* (Eat them.)
   2. *She's changin' her clothes.* (changing)

C. Changing of sounds

In English, changing of sounds occurs when the final sound of one word and the beginning sound of the following word combine to make a third sound. Examples are:

1. *Did you do it?* (j → ʤ) or
2. *Is your brother home?* (j → ʒ)

APPLYING PHONOLOGY IN THE CLASSROOMS

How do teachers apply these phonological concepts when teaching ELL? Understanding that phonemes are individual units of sound in words is having phonological awareness (PA). Skills within PA are concept of spoken word, rhyme, syllables, phonemes, and phoneme manipulation. Children become fluent readers by learning to manipulate these sounds. Phonemic awareness falls under the umbrella of phonological awareness though phonemic awareness and phonological awareness are used interchangeably. Research has shown that phonemic awareness is the best single predictor of reading ability in kindergarten, followed by knowledge of letter names and kindergarten teacher predictions (ʤonc, 2000). Phonemic awareness is the first component of effective reading instruction (ʤonc, 2000). children need solid phonemic awareness training in order for phonics instruction to be effective (Blevins, 1997).

Using the following sample activities, children are taught the following PA skills (ʤonc, 2000):

- **Concept of spoken word** (sentence segmentation):
The ability to distinguish words in a sentence. Example: *Juan likes oranges.* (three words) Teachers can use counters (edible ones make cleaning up easier) when teaching this concept. Determine the number of words in the sentences that will be read to students. Give students five counters if you are reading sentences with three to five words. Ask students to lay the counters on their desk and push them up when they hear the words in the sentences. So, for the above example, students will push up three counters. Sentence segmentation is an important skill to teach ELL because, being new to the sounds of English, the words in the sentence may sound as one long word to them.

- **Rhyme:**
The ability to recognize rhyme, complete rhyme, and produce rhyme. Example: *Does hall rhyme with ball?* The teaching of this concept brings in the knowledge of minimal pairs—substituting the phoneme /h/ in /hall/ with /b/ changes the word meaning. An activity for this skill is to distribute two tongue depressors to the students. Have students draw a happy face on one and a sad face on the other. Call the happy face "Happy Harry" and the sad face "Sad Sandy." Read to the children some words with minimal pairs that rhyme and some words that do not rhyme. When they hear the rhyming words, children will hold up "Happy Harry" and when they hear ones that do not, they will hold up "Sad Sandy." Some possible word sets are: *bet-get, go-me, fan-pan, cake-take, gold-back, big-dig, dust-must.* This is a good way to find out if ELL students can hear and are able to distinguish sounds. As was mentioned earlier in the chapter, some Arab speakers of English do not make a distinction between /b/ and /p/, and some Spanish speakers do not distinguish /v/ and /b/; therefore, this will be a good assessment activity.

- **Syllables:**
The ability to blend, segment, and delete syllables. The activity for the teaching of this concept is to ask students to clap the word parts, for example, use their names, Claudia (two claps), John (one clap). Learning about syllables is a prerequisite for ELLs to put stress correctly on words. This particular activity will help the Chinese speakers of English whose L1 has one syllable per character.

- **Phonemes:**
The ability to recognize problematic sounds for ELL. Chinese speakers of English have a difficult time pronouncing consonant clusters such as /spr/ and /fr/, and Spanish speakers have difficulty with /ʃ/, /j/, /ʤ/. An example activity is making digraphs useful by using cross-checking meaning. Write a sentence with /s/ words and compare that to a sentence with a word /spr/. *Chen is sad. Hua is high-spirited.* For Spanish speakers who substitute /t/ for /θ/, use the same activity—*Maria thinks Anna is pretty. Francisco talks a lot.*

Teachers who possess knowledge of phonology will understand the difficulties faced by English Language Learners (ELLs) in producing English consonant and vowel sounds that are nonexistent in their language. They will not be overly frustrated about students' errors or insist on frequently correcting their students' mispronunciations and misspellings. Instead, they will focus on the problem sounds that ELLs have by using their knowledge of the place and manner of articulation of English sounds to demonstrate to students how these sounds are produced.

✓ Phonology is the study of the sound system of a language. It deals with the rules that govern pronunciation.

✓ Children growing up in their first language environment have formed only the connections in the brain for their native sounds.

✓ In phonology it is important to note that each language has permissible ways in which phonemes can be arranged. This permissible arrangement is called *phonemic sequence.*

✓ Phonemes can be classified into two main categories: consonants and vowels.

✓ Pitch and stress are important in distinguishing meaning within a sentence in English.

✓ Tonal languages use pitch as individual syllables to contrast meaning.

✓ Speakers of any language have different styles of speaking: from formal, to informal, to casual. In English, casual or relaxed speech takes three forms in the pronunciation of words: (a) contractions, (b) "dropping" of sounds, and (c) changing of sounds.

Chapter 7

Morphology

Key Issues

- ○ The internal structures of words
- ○ Word categories: function and lexical
- ○ Free and bound morphemes
- ○ Word formation: derivation and inflection
- ○ Morphemes across languages

SCENARIO

The following scenario involves the conversational exchange between a Spanish speaker and a pre-service teacher:

Teacher: *Where did you go, Alberto?*

Student: *I wented to Disney World.*

Teacher: *Oh, you went to Disney World.*

Student: *Gea*

Teacher: *Who did you go with?*

Student: *The brother of my father taked—tooked—me dere.*

Teacher: *Oh, you mean your uncle?*

Student: *Gea.*

Teacher: *Which rides do you like best?*

Student: *I like two ride. I like the Espace Mountin more better than the Esplash Mountin because it is the more long.*

What errors do you notice in the student's production?

WHAT IS MORPHOLOGY?

The above scenario illustrates that words have internal structures that non-native speakers have to learn. Morphology, a study of word formation, deals with the internal structure of words within a language. Before we go further in the study of morphology, let us begin by looking at what we know about the structure of words in English.

a) Words like *strongest* can be divided into two parts (i.e., *strong -est*), each of which has a meaning.

b) The word *female* has a meaning in and of itself, the word *in* does not. Rather, *in* indicates a relationship between two meaningful expressions (e.g., *The female in the room*).

[handwritten annotation: common form of a word but NOT a word in itself]

c) The form *milk* can stand alone as a word, the form *-es* cannot.

d) *Sickly* is a word, *sickestly* is not.

e) *e-mail* is a shortened form of *electronic mail.*

In any language, words can be divided into two broad categories: function and lexical. Function words are pronouns, such as *you, he,* and *she;* conjunctions are words such as *and, if,* and *because;* determiners are words such as *a, the,* and *an.* In the lexical category are words such as nouns (N) *table, chalk, iron,* and *flower;* verbs (V), such as *write, draw, drink,* and *sit;* adjectives (Adj.), such as *yellow, beautiful, skinny,* and *hand-crafted;* and finally adverbs (Adv.), such as *slowly, smoothly, fast,* and *greedily.*

The minimal meaningful units in a language are called morphemes. Morphemes, more traditionally referred to as linguistic signs, are arbitrary. This means that the connection between the sign and its meaning is purely conventional; it does not originate in some property of the object it stands for. For instance, there is nothing about the sound of the word *hair* that has anything to do with hair. It is just as appropriate to use the word *riah* to refer to this entity, or in French, *cheveux,* or in Spanish, *pelo.* The minimal meaningful units of language are not words, but arbitrary signs or morphemes.

FREE AND BOUND MORPHEMES

Let us look at the word *players*. This word has three meaningful units: *play, -er,* and *-s.* The word *players* is a free form morpheme because it can stand on its own and can occur in different positions in a sentence. In contrast, the units *-er* and *-s* do not count as words because they cannot stand on their own, nor are their positions flexible. These are bound morphemes.

There are two basic types of words in human language: simple and complex. Simple words cannot be broken down into smaller meaningful units, whereas complex words can be broken down to identifiable and meaningful components. The word *frogs* is made up of the form *frog* and the plural marker *-s,* neither of which can be divided into smaller morphemes. While many English words consist of only one morpheme, others can contain two, three, or more (see Table 7.1).

Complex words, like sentences, have internal structure. Let us take the word *industrialization*; the word *industry* is a free morpheme because it can stand on its own, while the other morphemes (*-ion, -al, -iz, -ation*) are bound morphemes, i.e, they have to be attached to free morphemes.

WORD FORMATION

New words are continuously being created in human languages. The lexical category is open in the sense that other words can be formed from lexical words. The two most common word formations are derivation and inflection. Derivation is the process by which another word is formed from a root word, usually through the addition of an affix. Derivation creates a new word by changing the category and/or the meaning of the base to which it applies. The derivational affix *-er,* for instance, in the word *waiter* combines with a verb (*wait*) to create a noun with the meaning *"one who does the action."*

Virtually all languages have contrasts such as singular and plural, and past and present. These contrasts are often marked by a morphological process called inflection. Inflection modifies a word's form to mark the grammatical categories to which it belongs. For instance, the inflectional affix *-s* in *boys* does not change the grammatical category (N) to which it belongs, and the inflectional *-ed* in the word *worked* does not change the grammatical category (V) to which the word *work* belongs. Refer to Tables 7.1.A, B, and C.

TABLE 7.1.

Words Consisting of One or More Morphemes

One morpheme	Two	Three	More than three
Or			
Girl	Girls		
Play	Player	Players	
Hospital	Hospital-ize	Hospital-iz-ation	Hospital-iz-ation-s
Gentle	Gentle-man	Gentle-man-ly	Gentle-man-li-ness

TABLE 7.1.A

Inflectional Categories and Affixes of English

Word class to which inflection applies	Inflectional category	Regular affix used to express category
Nouns	Number	*-s, -es:* table/table*s*, box/box*es*
	Possessive	*-'s, -':* the dog*'s* paw, James*'* bag
Verbs	Third person singular present	*-s, -es:* it hail*s*, Karen dance*s*, the river gurgl*es*
	Past tense	*-ed:* walk/walk*ed*
	Perfect aspect	*-ed:* paint/paint*ed* (has *painted*) (past participle)
	Progressive or continuous aspect	*-ing:* jump/jump*ing*, write/writ*ing* (present participle)
Adjectives	Comparative (comparing two items)	*-er:* short/short*er*
	Superlative (comparing three or more items)	*-est:* tall/tall*est*

Source: http://cla.calpoly.edu

Regular and Irregular Inflectional Morphology

TABLE 7.1.B

Type of irregularity	Noun plurals	Verbs: past tense	Verbs: past participle
Unusual suffix	ox*en*, syllab*i*, antenn*ae*		tak*en*, see*n*, fall*en*, eat*en*
Change of stem vowel	foot/f*ee*t, mouse/m*i*ce	run/r*a*n, come/c*a*me, flee/fl*e*d, meet/m*e*t, fly/fl*ew*, stick/st*u*ck, get/g*o*t, break/br*o*ke	swim/sw*u*m, sing/s*u*ng
Change of stem vowel with unusual suffix	brother/br*e*thr*en*	feel/f*e*l*t*, kneel/kn*el*t	write/wr*itten*, do/d*one*, break/br*oken*, fly/fl*own*
Change in base/stem form (sometimes with unusual suffix)		send/sen*t*, bend/ben*t*, think/th*ought*, teach/t*aught*, buy/b*ought*	send/sen*t*, bend/ben*t*, think/th*ought*, teach/t*aught*, buy/b*ought*
Zero-marking (no suffix, no stem change)	deer, sheep, moose, fish	hit, beat	hit, beaten, come

More ways inflection can be irregular:

Suppletion (instead of a suffix, the whole word changes):

be - am - are - is - was - were - been

go - went - gone

good - better - best

bad - worse - worst

some - more - most

Syntactic marking (added meanings are indicated by a separate word rather than marking with a suffix or change to the base):

Future of verbs: *will* go, *will* eat, *will* fight, etc.

Comparative/superlative of adjectives: *more* intelligent, *more* expensive, etc.; *most* intelligent, *most* expensive, etc.

English Derivational Morphology

Below is a sample of some English derivational *affixes*. This is only a sample; there are far more affixes than are presented here.

TABLE 7.1.C

Some Derivational Affixes of English

Affix	Class(es) of word to which affix applies	Nature of change in meaning	Examples
Prefix 'non-'	Noun Adjective	Negation/opposite	Noun: *non*-starter Adjective: *non*-partisan
Suffix '-ity'	Adjective	Changes to noun	electric/electric*ity* obese/obes*ity*
Prefix 'un-'	Verb Adjective	Reverses action opposite quality	tie/*un*tie, fasten/*un*fasten clear/*un*clear, safe/*un*safe
Suffix '-ous'	Noun	Changes to adjective	fame/fam*ous*, glamor/glamor*ous*
Prefix 're-'	Verb	Repeat action	tie/*re*tie, write/*re*write
Suffix '-able'	Verb	Changes to adjective; means 'can undergo action of verb'	print/print*able*, drink/drink*able*

Source: http://cla.calpoly.edu

In forming derivational morphemes in English, some words follow a hierarchical order. An example is the word *systematic*: the suffix *ic* is added to the root word *system*, yielding the meaning having a system, and when the prefix *un* is added to *systematic*, it means not having a system. However, the suffix *un* cannot be added to the root word, *system*, first because *unsystem* is a nonsense word. On the other hand, there are some derivational morphemes that do not follow this order. Either the prefix or the suffix can be added to the root word first. For instance, examine the word *unhappiness* which has three morphemes: *un, happy, ness*. Adding *un* first, to the base word *happy*, yields the meaning *not happy*, then adding the suffix *ness* to *unhappy* yields this meaning—*the state of not being happy*. This same meaning can be attained by building the word in another way. Adding the suffix *ness* to the base word, *happy*, will produce the meaning, *the state of being happy*. Now add the prefix *un* to the word

happiness. This will produce the antonym of the word, *happiness*, and produce the meaning, *the state of not being happy*.

As Table 7.2 illustrates, the English plural has three distinct pronunciations. The plurals of the first column are pronounced with the /s/ of sew, while those of the second column have the sound /z/ in zoo. The plurals of the third column are pronounced with a vowel followed by a /z/. This vowel is called a "schwa" and is written as /ə/. Therefore the three alternative pronunciations of the plural are /-s/, /-z/, and /-əz/.

English speakers are not free to select any form of plural that they happen to fancy, but must make their choice according to the final sound of the word to which it is attached. Words that end in "voiceless" consonants, including /p,t,k/ and some others, require /-s/ as their plural. Words that end in vowels or in "voiced" consonants, including /b,d,g,r/ and some others, require /-z/. Words ending in /s/,

TABLE 7.2

Allomorphs

Taps		Cobs		Hisses	
Mitts		Lids		Buzzes	
Backs	+ /s/	Lads	+ /z/	Crutches	+ /ə z/
Baths		Lathes		Judges	
Puffs		Doves		Wishes	

the /tʃ/ sound of church, and a few other consonants, require /-əz/. These three forms of the plural suffix differ in pronunciation, but they are all varieties of the "same" suffix. The individual forms /s/, /z/, and /-əz/ are said to constitute three allomorphs of the plural morpheme.

Selection among the forms of English verb suffixes follows a principle that is similar to those of selection among plural forms. Let us look at some of the past tense forms.

Present	Past
Walk	Walked /-t/
Beg	Begged /-d/
Chat	Chatted /-əd/

Can you predict the rule for the use of the three allomorphs above?

Other word formations are:

Term	Process	Examples
Compounding	Combine two words	blackbird, doghouse, mailbox
Clipping	Shortening of word	bike, condo, prep
Acronyms	Coining a new word from the first letters of other words	AIDS, NASA, FAU
Blends	Mixing two words and creating a new word	brunch, telethon
Onomatopoeia	Sound-like words	bow-wow, cock-a-doodle-doo
Backformation	A cut-off suffix with the base used as root	resurrect, enthuse
Brand names	Brand names become common words	Xerox, Kleenex
Borrowing	A word is taken from another language	hummus, wok, macho

---

MORPHEMES ACROSS LANGUAGES

In some languages other than English, free and bound morphemes do not have the same status. For instance, in Hare (an Athapascan language spoken in Canada's Northwest Territories), words that indicate body parts are always bound to a morpheme designating a possessor. The word *sefi* (which means *my head)* is made up of two units connected together; it can never be broken up into two morphemes: *se, *fi. Likewise, the word *nebe,* meaning *your belly,* is never spoken or written as just *be (O'Grady, 1989).

Just as there are free forms in English that are bound in other languages, there are bound forms in English that are free in other languages. Past tense, for example, is expressed by a bound morpheme in English (usually—ed), but in Mandarin Chinese it is expressed by a free form *le.* Consider the following sentences:

1. *Ta haek le cha.*
   He drank past tea. (He drank tea.)

2. *Ta haek cha le.*
   He drank tea.

The past tense marker in Mandarin /le/ is not attached to the verb haek since it can be separated from it by the direct object. The knowledge teachers acquire about morphology can help them understand why certain errors are made by non-native speakers of English.

In Spanish, the plural ending must show gender and article agreement, e.g., *amiga* (feminine) and *amigo* (masculine).

la amiga	*las amigas*
el amigo	*los amigos*
el amigo mío	*la amiga mía*
los amigos míos	*las amigas mías*

Another morphological problem for Spanish speakers has to do with the use of morphemes -er and -est. In Spanish, the comparatives and the superlatives are formed with *more* and *the most*. For example, prettier will be more pretty. Spanish speakers may also experience difficulty in using prepositions such as in, on, and at because in Spanish these three prepositions are collapsed into one (*en*). So, Spanish speakers may say *The book is in the floor* instead of *The book is on the floor*. Another form of interference in English Spanish speakers encounter is the *be* verb to express state of being or age. In Spanish, the verb *have* is utilized to express these concepts. For example, *I have ten years* instead of *I am ten years old*.

In Spanish, nouns are gender marked. For example, *table* is *mesa,* a feminine form, and *book* is *libro,* a masculine form. Articles preceding and adjectives following these noun forms must also agree in gender and number with the nouns, as in the following examples:

What changes do you notice in sentence two?

1. *El libro rojo está en la mesa pequeña.*
   The book red is on the table small.

2. *Los libros rojos están en la mesa pequeña.*
   The books red are on the table small.

Spanish, by contrast, inflects its nouns for number and gender, but not for possession (which is signalled by placing the particle *de* between the possessed item and the possessor, as in *la casa de mi madre*, *the house of my mother*. Spanish has far

TABLE 7.3

Spanish Inflectional Categories and Affixes

Word class to which inflection applies	Inflectional category	Regular affix used to express category
Nouns	Number	'-*s*' mano/mano*s* 'hand/hands'
	Gender	'-*a*' Fem., '-*o*' Masc. herman*a*/herman*o* 'sister/brother'

Source: http://cla.calpoly.edu

more inflectional categories—and affixes to mark them—for verbs than does English. Refer to Table 7.3 for Spanish inflectional morphemes.

Haitian speakers of English may leave out the plural -*s* marker in English because in Haitian Creole the plural is marked by a free morpheme, *yo*. The definite article in Haitian Creole appears after the noun and it takes on different forms according to the noun that precedes it. It can also occur at the end of a string of words, so Haitian children, when speaking English, may leave the definite article out altogether. Pronouns in Haitian Creole are invariant. The same form is used for I/me/my, they/them/their, etc. Meaning in this case is determined by word order; if it occurs before the verb, it is the subject. If it occurs after the verb, it is an object. Moreover, the Haitian Creole pronouns do not denote gender. One form is used for he/she/it and the corresponding forms. For this reason, Haitian children may tend to use the pronoun *he* when referring to females or inanimate objects. Another interference problem that Haitian children learning English may encounter is the use of the morpheme *be*. In sentences that describe states of being or location, no verb is utilized in Haitian Creole where the verb be would be used in English. For example: *I sick* instead of *I am sick*.

Another interesting difference between English and Haitian morphemes is in the verb tenses. In Haitian Creole, verb forms are invariant. Tense is indicated by particles placed before the verb. For instance, examine the following forms of the verb *speak*:

map pale—I am speaking

pale—spoke

a pale—will speak

te pale—have spoken

MORPHOLOGY APPLICATION IN THE CLASSROOM

Teachers may use the knowledge of morphology in this chapter to teach common suffixes, prefixes, and root words. A sample activity to teach a common prefix *re-* follows (Cunningham, 1995):

Write nine words that begin with *re-* on index cards. Use three words in which *re* means back, three words in which *re* means again, and three words in which *re* is just the first syllable and has no apparent meaning. Examples of words are:

rebound	redo	record
return	replay	refuse
replace	rework	reveal

Words are placed randomly on the board using magnets. Ask students what they notice about these words. Once students notice that these words begin with *re*, ask them to categorize these words under these labels: *re* for again, *re* for back, and *re* for just the first syllable.

A similar activity can be used for teaching suffix. On the board, draw three columns and write different suffixes such as *-er, -able, -ation* in each column. Ask students to do the same on a piece of paper. Model the activity by demonstrating the sample word, *import*. The root word *import* becomes *importer, importable,* and *importation.* Explain that the root word, which is a verb, becomes a noun when *-er* is added—the person that imports items, *import* (v) becomes *importable*, an adjective—things that can be imported, and *importation* is a noun, the act of importing. Then list other root words such as *present, adore, invite, restore, quote,* and *interpret* and ask students to fill in the columns.

A third activity that utilizes spelling skills also involves knowledge of morphemes. It is a hands-on activity. Choose 10–15 letters, vowels, and consonants and write them on a sheet of paper. For example, the letters are a, a, o, o, i, i, m, n, l, s, y, t, p, h, k. Students are asked to cut these letters and manipulate them to make words and write them on a piece of paper. Rules such as letters can only be used once or as many times as needed can be given to the students. This can be a game played in teams. Teachers with the linguistic knowledge of morphemes will find the teaching of digraphs, prefixes, suffixes, and parts of speech much easier.

Points to Remember

✓ Morphology is the study of word formation that deals with the internal structure of words within a language.

✓ There are two types of morphemes: free and bound.

✓ In English, free morphemes are flexible in terms of their word order positions in a sentence, whereas bound morphemes cannot stand alone as an intelligible word.

✓ Teachers with knowledge of morphemes across languages will better understand why non-native speakers of English make errors in speech and writing.

Chapter 8

Syntax

Key Issues

- Word order in a language — Syntax
- Lexical categories, linearity, and constituents
- Ambiguity: lexical and syntactical
- Word order across languages

SCENARIO

The following dialogue takes place between a teacher and her student, who meet while shopping.

Teacher: *Hi, Amir. What are you doing here?*

Amir: *Hello, Mrs. Thomas. I come to get another soccer shoe.*

Teacher: *Are you playing on the school team?*

Amir: *No, I just like to play soccer. If we practice sports, we will enjoy together.*

Teacher: *Yes, exercise is good. Do you have a favorite team?*

Amir: *Yes, I like very much Bundesliga team. In Bundesliga, have good methods to train their players.*

What do you observe about the student's sentences? Do they follow the pattern of English sentences? Why or why not?

Before we further discuss the concepts related to syntax, let us examine the following sentences and make some observations about the structure of phrases, clauses, and sentences:

1. The phrase *the smallest car* is acceptable English, *theest small car* is not.
2. The phrase *the small car* is acceptable English, the phrase *small the car* is not.
3. The phrase *chocolate cakes and pies* has two possible interpretations.
4. The interrogative *What is she doing?* is acceptable in English, *what she is doing?* is not.
5. The sentence *The palace was built in 1856* is acceptable English, *The palace has built in 1856* is not.
6. The sentence *I do not have any money* is acceptable English, *I not have any money* is not.
7. The sentence *Mary is planning to swim* is acceptable English, *Mary is planning will swim* is not.

Sentence one illustrates that words in a language are divided into parts of speech.

Sentence two illustrates that words in phrases move from left to right.

Sentence three illustrates that words in phrases are grouped into coherent and meaningful units (hierarchical structure).

Sentences four to six illustrate that sentence structures are related by transformations.

Sentence seven illustrates that there are constraints that limit transformation of sentences.

LEXICAL CATEGORIES, LINEARITY, AND CONSTITUENTS

Words within a language are organized into different categories according to their behavior. The four major lexical categories are: noun (N), verb (V), adjective (Adj.), and adverb (Adv.). Minor lexical categories include determiner (Det.), auxiliary verb (Aux.), preposition (P.), pronoun (Pro.), and conjunction (C). Words also belong to phrasal categories. These categories include noun phrases, verb phrases, adjective phrases, and adverb phrases. Each of the phrasal categories contains at least one lexical category of the same basic type—in other words, a noun phrase contains at least one noun. For example, the phrase *the cowardly attacker fled* contains the NP *the cowardly attacker,* which in turn contains the N *attacker.*

Words in English cannot appear in a random order. Phrase structure (PS) rules involve the codification of principles by which words are arranged. What is the word order pattern in the following sentence?

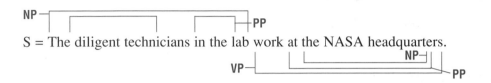

S = The diligent technicians in the lab work at the NASA headquarters.

In the above sentence there is a linear order in which words are strung. There are three large constituents (coherent groupings of morphemes): Noun phrase (NP), verb phrase (VP), and prepositional phrase (PP). In the above sentence, the NP is *The diligent technicians in the lab.* But within the large NP, there is a smaller constituent, the PP *in the lab.* Similarly, the PP *at the NASA headquarters* contains another smaller constituent, i.e., the NP *the NASA headquarters.* Constituents are, therefore, the building blocks of a sentence. The ways to test for constituents are:

1. Ability to stand as an answer to a question— Who works at the NASA headquarters? Where do they work?
2. Substitute pronoun form—They
3. Movement—At the NASA headquarters, the diligent technicians work.

Constituency is observed in the early language acquisition stage by both first and second language speakers. Teachers should not, therefore, ask students to answer in complete sentences; what is more significant is teaching students to string words into coherent groupings.

SYNTACTICAL AND LEXICAL AMBIGUITY

Constituents are extremely important in interpreting ambiguous sentences, sentences which contain two or more possible meanings. For instance, consider the phrase *Japanese culinary professor.* Any native English speaker may find this phrase ambiguous: it can mean either a professor of Japanese culinary arts or a culinary arts professor who is Japanese. This ambiguity is not caused by the lexical items, because none of the words contains more than one meaning. In examining the phrase Japanese culinary professor, we can group the words in two different constituents: (1) Japanese culinary; (2) culinary professor. In (1), the adjective Japanese describes culinary whereas in (2), culinary professor is a constituent modified by the adjective Japanese. In other words, the professor who teaches culinary arts is from Japan. Another example of a syntactically ambiguous sentence is *They are baking apples.* If the constituent has *baking* as a modifier that modifies apples, the sentence means the apples are specially for baking or cooking, but if the constituent includes *they are baking* in which *are baking* is a verb (present continuous tense), the sentence means some people are in the act of baking apples.

Another form of ambiguity arises when a word has two or more possible meanings. This is called lexical ambiguity. Consider these sentences:

Juan is sitting on a trunk.
Claudia is waiting for Juan at the bank.
Ms. Jimenez caught the bat.

[handwritten annotations: trunk — elephant, luggage, tree; bank — $, water; bat — animal, sports]

The word *trunk* has several meanings: trunk of a car, tree trunk, elephant's trunk, or storage trunk; the word *bank* has more than one meaning—financial institution, river bank; the word *bat* means baseball bat or an animal.

In school, students are taught to differentiate between active and passive sentences. From the linguistic perspective, an active sentence such as *The pitcher threw the ball in the field* has one meaning and one deep structure, but can be represented by several surface structures—Who threw the ball in the field? or The ball was thrown by the pitcher in the field. Whichever way the sentences are formed, the meaning of the sentence remains unambiguous: *The pitcher threw the ball in the field.* When a sentence has more than one meaning or deep structure, such as the sentence: *He is a Japanese culinary professor*, it is said to be an ambiguous sentence. The sentences *He is a Japanese culinary professor* and *Juan is sitting on a trunk* have one surface structure and two deep structures because both sentences have more than one meaning.

In English, several processes are involved in transforming sentences. Examine the following sentences and identify the general rule for the sentence transformation:

Affirmative	**Negative**
1. She was sleepy.	She wasn't sleepy.
2. John can play the piano.	John can't play the piano.
3. Mr. Tan has two cars.	Mr. Tan does not have two cars.
4. Helen borrowed Kathy's book.	Helen did not borrow Kathy's book.

In sentences 1 and 2, negation can be made by inserting *not* next to the auxiliary verbs (was and can). However, the above step cannot be used to negate the third and fourth sentences. In 3, *Mr. Tan has not two* cars is ungrammatical and so is 4, *Helen borrowed not Kathy's book.* To negate both sentences, several steps have to be taken. First, the verb *do* has to be used, and then we need to ensure that the verb agrees with the subject. In 3, *does* is used because it is a singular verb form which agrees with the singular subject—Mr. Tan. Next, *not* is then attached to *does*. In 4, *do* takes the past tense form and becomes *did*, because the affirmative sentence is in past tense.

A common difficulty non-native speakers of English encounter is the transformation of sentences to question forms. Look at the following questions:

1. Has the boy talked to the girl?
2. Is the girl talking to the boy?
3. Does the boy like the girl?
4. Did that lady chase those boys?
5. Didn't the manager fire the clerk?

Sentence 1 can be easily accounted for by moving the first word of the auxiliary to the beginning of the sentence, in front of the initial Noun Phrase. Thus *Has the boy talked to the girl* seems to be derived from *The boy has talked to the girl* by the movement of *has*. Similarly, sentence 2 is derived by moving the auxiliary *is* to the beginning of the sentence, in front of the Noun Phrase. Thus, *Is the girl talking to the boy* is derived from *The girl is talking to the boy* by the movement of *is*.

A more difficult transformation is the one that involves no auxiliary at all. The sentence *The boy likes the girl* has no auxiliary, and so it has nothing to move to the front in order to make a question. If a sentence like this is to be transformed into a question, *do*, *does*, or *did* as a kind of dummy auxiliary must be added. It seems that English questions need some sort of auxiliary to move to the front of the sentence and, if nothing else is available, a form of *do* will have to be supplied. There are several steps that must be considered in selecting the forms of *do*. First, the form of *do* must agree with the verb tense; second, it has to agree with the subject. Therefore, in the transformation of the sentence *The boy likes* the girl to the question *Does the boy like the girl?*, these steps must be followed:

1. Choosing *does* over *did*, or *do* because of its singular subject (the boy) and present verb tense (likes).
2. Insert *does* at the beginning of the sentence.
3. Use the root form of the verb in the question (*like*).

Passive sentences involve even more radical movements than questions. Consider a sentence such as *The mouse is chased by the cat.* This sentence can be derived from the active sentence *The cat chases the mouse*, but to get from the active to the passive, several changes are needed:

1. The old object (*the mouse*) moves to the beginning of the sentence.
2. The old subject (*the cat*) moves to the end of the sentence, picks up the preposition *by,* and forms a prepositional phrase. This prepositional phrase can be dropped.
3. Another word (*is* in this example) has to be added to the auxiliary.
4. The verb (*chase*) takes an *-ed* suffix.

WORD ORDER ACROSS LANGUAGES

Examine the set of sentences in each language and determine the dominant word order pattern in each. Is it Subject, Verb, Object (SVO); Subject, Object, Verb (SOV); or Verb, Subject, Object (VSO)?

Korean

Chun ku chayt poata.
Chun that book see (Chun sees that book).
Chun Bob-hako malhata.
Chun Bob with speak (Chun speaks with Bob).

Selayarese (a language of Indonesia)

Laallei doe Injo I Baso
Take money the Baso (Baso took the money).
Lataroi doe Injo ri lamari injo I Baso
Put money the in cupboard the Baso (Baso put the money in a cupboard).

Unlike English, in Selayarese VP begins the sentence.

French

Marie a mangé une orange.
Marie ate an orange.
Henri a une fleur rose.
Henri has a flower pink.

Irish

Is drafur Sean.
Hit brother Sean (Sean's brother hit him).

What difficulties would these speakers have in learning English syntax?

Spanish has a different form of negation than does English. In Spanish, the word *no* is placed before the first verb in the sentence. For example:

Juan tiene un televisor.	*Juan no tiene un televisor.*
(Juan has a television.)	(Juan no has a television.)

In Spanish, the adjectives usually follow nouns and always agree in gender and number. For example: *He lives in a house yellow* instead of *He lives in a yellow house.* Questions in Spanish have an upside down question mark at the beginning and a right side-up question mark at the end. Some examples are *¿Donde vives? (Where do you live?)* and *¿Como te llamas? (What is your name?).* The same declarative sentence can be used for question forms in Spanish. The question mark at the beginning and voice inflection will signal to the readers and/or speakers that that is a question.

In French/Haitian Creole, questions are formed by simply inserting the question phrase before the affirmative statement. For example:

Elizabeth is on vacation. *¿Est-que Elizabeth est en vacances?*

How can teachers use knowledge about syntax to help their students learn the English language?

Such knowledge gives teachers insight into how words are ordered in other languages. While English is an SVO, languages like Korean and Japanese are SOV, and Irish is VSO. Teachers who understand this will not dismiss syntactic errors made by nonnative learners of English as mere errors, but will understand that these errors result from a systematic application of their native language system when functioning in English. These teachers will then, for instance, focus more on the teaching of adjectives in context to reinforce students' visualization of the position of adjectives in English sentences. They will also recognize the need to teach step-by-step transformation of English sentences and focus on structures that are unavailable in the students' native language.

The following is a sample activity on teaching English syntax:

Students work with word cards to build sentences. Words cards are divided into part-of-speech categories: Nouns (he, she, John, school); Verbs (is, are, likes, jumps, walks), Adjectives (pretty, short, big, fat), Prepositions (in, on, to, under), and Articles (a, the). Teachers stack these word cards in their categories and students choose these word cards and arrange them in a correct English sentence order. For instance, from the above word card list, students can make sentences: *John is big. She likes school. He walks to school.* Students can work in groups in this activity. This is a good way for teachers to assess and observe ELLs' comprehension and application of English syntactic rules. What other sentence making activities can you think of?

Points to Remember

✓ Syntax is the study of how words are ordered within a sentence.

✓ There is a linear order in which words are strung in a sentence. Constituents are coherent groupings of morphemes, the building blocks in a sentence.

✓ There are two types of ambiguity: structural and lexical. A sentence that has one surface structure and two deep structures is an ambiguous sentence.

✓ Not all languages have the same word order as English (SVO)—Korean is SOV and Irish is VSO.

Chapter 9

Semantics

Key Issues

- ○ Semantic concepts that show relationships in meaning between words
- ○ Semantic concepts that show differences in meaning between sentences
- ○ Cross-cultural differences in expressions and meaning
- ○ How word meanings affect ESL learners' comprehension

SCENARIO

Read the following passage and determine what you need to know in order to comprehend it (Glover & et al. 1990).

Death of Piggo

The girl sat looking at her piggybank. "Old friend," she thought, "this hurts me." A tear rolled down her cheek. She hesitated, then picked up her tap shoe by the toe and raised her arm. Crash! Pieces of Piggo—that was the bank's name—rained in all directions. She closed her eyes for a moment to block out the sight. Then she began to do what she had to do.

The previous passage seems like a fairly simple narrative containing simple sentence constructions and common vocabulary; it centers around a topic familiar to most of us—piggybanks. So, let us start with what we know about piggybanks. We know that piggybanks may have the following characteristics:

1. representations of pigs,
2. a place to put money (coins) in,
3. smaller than real pigs,
4. made of plastic or material that can be shattered by dropping or a direct blow,
5. have a slot to put money in.

Now, the list of piggybank characteristics may be longer, but the point is that there is nothing in the passage that gives an overall description of a piggybank. Nevertheless, we know how it looks, its size, and value, by drawing from our life experience. In addition, other words in the passage add to our mental representation of the piggybank. For example, we know that a tap shoe can cause the piggybank to break, thereby suggesting its brittle composition. Once the bank is shattered in small pieces, it can no longer take its original form; hence, the implied death imagery, which sets the tone of the passage and allows the reader to understand the emotions experienced by the girl.

It seems that understanding the passage requires more than just knowing the meaning of specific words. In fact, we must fill in some information from our world knowledge and understanding of the relationship between words in a single discourse to fully comprehend the passage. You will also notice that words like death and rained are used in a figurative sense, a sense other than their usual meanings; in short, words may have emotive or connotative meanings. What this passage reveals is that the meaning of words involves drawing upon various kinds of knowledge, including the literal and figurative sense of words, real-world knowledge, and the relationship between words. Even a short and fairly simple passage, such as the piggybank story, may be difficult for first language learners who have not yet developed an awareness of the special connotative meanings of words and the real world knowledge necessary to comprehend what they read. Comprehension breakdown can be more serious for second language learners, who do not have proficiency in the new language, or the cultural knowledge necessary for text interpretation.

WHAT IS MEANING?

Before we probe further into the specifics of each contribution to meaning, let us consider the following examples and discuss how we determine meaning for each.

1. The word *bank* has more than one meaning in English. The word *seashore* does not.
2. The word *bachelor* can mean both single or unmarried.
3. The words *sofa* and *chair* seem to be closer in meaning than the words *sofa* and *ottoman*.
4. In the sentence *Rachael Ray is the mogul of home cooking in under 30 minutes,* and the phrase *Rachael Ray and the mogul of home cooking in under 30 minutes* refer to the same person, but do not mean the same thing at all.
5. If someone were to ask you to name a mammal, would you think of a whale before a dog or a cat?
6. The statement *The trash isn't out yet, dear* can mean more than one thing, depending on the context of its utterance.
7. The statements *A diamond is a semi-precious stone* and *Limestone is a semi-precious stone* are both false for different reasons.
8. The sentence *The dog chased the mouse* is more plausible than the reverse, *The mouse chased the dog.*

Our observations in sentences 1–8 indicate that there are certain facts that an explanation of meaning must address. Assuming that these phenomena are rule-governed like many other linguistic instances, we will present some concepts and principles that partially explain these phenomena, based on the current research in the field.

Semantics is the study of the meaning of words, phrases, and sentences. Two sources that have contributed to the study of meaning are linguistics and philosophy. While linguistics primarily addresses the core meaning or sense of individual linguistic expressions, philosophy looks at how we derive meaning from sentences by examining the references and truth conditions of each. Unfortunately, meaning is a highly complex and multifaceted phenomenon which must take into account a vast array of different facts. However, it is possible to highlight some of the key theories and principles that

have been developed to account for meaning. In our discussion, we will divide the study of semantics into three areas:

1. the semantic relationship between words,
2. the semantic relationship between words and syntactic structures,
3. language as an expression of culture and worldview.

SEMANTIC RELATIONSHIPS BETWEEN WORDS

One method linguists have used to determine the sense or meaning of words involves analyzing the semantic features that comprise words. This method of analysis is called lexical decomposition. Let us consider the words man, woman, boy, and girl. How do we know that man and boy or woman and girl are more closely related than boy and girl? We know this because man and boy are similar in that they both refer to males while woman and girl refer to females. Similarly, we know that sleep and awake constitute a contradiction.

Other types of semantic relationships between words are synonymy, antonymy, entailment, referent, extension, and prototype. Synonymy involves different words bearing the same meaning. For example, the words sofa and couch or attack and charge share similar meanings, although these words do not have exactly the same meaning in all cases. However, we consider these words to be synonymous because of the degree of overlap between them, as illustrated in Figure 9.1.

Antonyms, on the contrary, are words that are opposite in meaning. Pairs of words such as complete and incomplete, dead and alive, open and closed are examples of words that have contradictory relationships and share no middle ground. On the other hand, gradable antonyms are pairs of words that stand on the opposite ends of a continuum; for example, hot and cold, big and small, and tall and short are opposites on a scale. Liquids can be warm instead of hot or cold; a person can be either tall or short, and so forth. Words like above

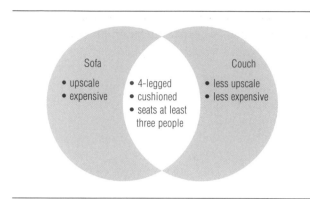

FIGURE 9.1

and under, doctor and patient are examples of converse antonyms which do not represent extremes on a physical dimension, but rather two items in a symmetrical relationship.

Entailment is when the meaning of a word is logically related to previous meanings. For example, a piglet must also have the properties of a pig. On the other hand, if it is not a pig, it cannot be a piglet. The partial semantic breakdown of piglet could be illustrated as:

piglet

pig

young

Meanings can also be determined by the reference of the linguistic expression. For example, if you point to a particular bus and say "That bus is taking the children to the zoo," then the referent for the expression *That bus* refers to the bus you are pointing to. When a child includes kittens, cats, tigers, lions, and leopards as examples of cats, the child is extending the referring expression to refer to entities that can be considered the set of all cats. This semantic process is known as extension and is similar to overgeneralization. When a child names a cat or a dog as an example of a pet, the child is including a prototype or a typical member of the set of all potential referents that refer to pets. Consider the following riddle: What has a face with numbers and makes a ticking sound? If you answer a watch

or clock, your answer is based on a list of characteristics of a prototype clock or watch.

SEMANTIC RELATIONSHIP BETWEEN WORDS AND SYNTACTIC STRUCTURES

Another area that semantics investigates is whether the sum of word meanings helps us get the meaning of the whole. In other words, can we derive meaning by stringing word meanings together? Consider the following sentences:

1. The little boy ate a cookie.
2. The cookie a little boy ate.*
3. The teacher read the book to the children.
4. The children read the book to the teacher.
5. The book was read to the children by the teacher.

Sentence one makes sense to us, but sentence two has no meaning at all, although the same words are used. Meanwhile, sentences three and four are not exactly the same, although they are formed from the same words. These sentences demonstrate that word order in a phrase provides meaning in a sentence; however, word order alone cannot help determine the meaning of a phrase, as exemplified in sentence five. Although sentence five does not have the same word order or the exact same words found in sentence three, we know that these two sentences have identical meanings. In other words, sentences three and five have identical deep structures. These examples illustrate that word order and syntactic structures help determine word meanings and the meaning of a sentence.

The relationship between grammatical structure and semantics can also be seen in sentences where words and phrases can be combined in two different ways, giving rise to two possible meanings; this is known as structural ambiguity (refer to section on syntax). Take the sentence *We need more humorous Bill Cosby episodes*. If *more* modifies the phrase

*represents ungrammatical sentence.

humorous Bill Cosby episodes, then the sentence refers to a need for more Bill Cosby episodes that are funny. But if the adjective phrase *more humorous* modifies the noun phrase *Bill Cosby episodes,* then the sentence suggests that the episodes must include more humor.

Another form of ambiguity arises when a word has more than one meaning that can only be determined by its context. This can be seen in homonyms that are common in terms of pronunciation, and sometimes have the same spelling, but are different in terms of meaning. For example, the sentence *The coach is full* is lexically ambiguous because the word *coach* can refer to a *carriage* or a *person.* Other examples include *bank* /bæŋk/ which could mean *a financial institution* or *the river bank, pot* /pat/ could refer to *drugs* or *a flowerpot,* and *bear* and *bare* could refer to *giving birth* or *without covering or protection.* Heteronyms, which are words that are spelled the same but pronounced differently and have different meanings, can potentially be lexically ambiguous. Without hearing the oral word and knowing the context, ELLs may have difficulty figuring out the exact meaning for the word. Some examples of heteronyms which may pose difficulties for English language learners are *sow* which could refer to *a female pig* or to *plant seeds* and *bow* which could refer to *bow and arrow, bending your head* or *body, or the front end of the boat.* Second language learners may find words with multiple denotative meanings difficult to process and understand without sufficient context and the opportunity to hear and see the words visually.

We also determine meaning based on the truth conditions of the words in a sentence, as in the following examples:

1. Pearl S. Buck, the famous American author, was ten years old when she went to West Virginia and realized that she belonged to two worlds: China and the United States.
2. Ruth did not return the books to the library.

In both sentences (1) and (2), truth or falsity cannot be determined by simply inspecting the words in the sentences. Rather, the truth or falsity of these statements depends on our knowledge of Pearl Buck from previous encounters or our consulting of reliable sources to verify the information.

LANGUAGE AS AN EXPRESSION OF CULTURE AND WORLDVIEW

Just as word order and syntactic structures are important to meaning, word meanings are also defined by individual and cultural experiences. Since word meanings often represent a speaker's reality, there is a degree to which these meanings are culturally bound. This is reflected in words that contain connotative or non-literal meanings, an area that is sometimes most challenging for the fluent, non-native speaker. Let us consider the following two sentences: *The lady is leaving the store* and *The chick is leaving the store.* Although the subject in both these sentences refers to a female adult, the second sentence runs the risk of sounding overly informal, sexist, and discriminatory.

Other examples such as *She is slim* versus *She is thin,* and *He is obstinate* versus *He is stubborn* demonstrate the emotive connotation embedded in words considered to be synonyms. Even though the pair of words share similar meanings, *slim* and *stubborn* are generally considered to be more acceptable than their counterparts. Emotional meanings can also be found in words used to refer to groups of people. For example, the word *Inuit,* the plural form of *inuk* meaning "person," is preferred over Eskimos because the word Eskimos literally means "eaters of raw fish" and thereby is considered insulting (Flexner & Sokhanov 1997). Hence, you can see that no two words can mean exactly the same thing in all cases. Connotative meanings convey our attitudes toward others as well as how we think about ourselves and our worldview. Second language learners not only have to process and translate meanings already familiar to another language, but also make new associations of these meanings with the correct context.

Another case that demonstrates how language is an integral part of culture is the use of idioms. Idioms or idiomatic phrases have a fixed meaning that cannot be inferred from the meanings of the individual words. While all languages contain many such expressions, speakers must learn the meanings and use specified by the culture from which they originate. Some examples of English idioms are as follows:

Knock it off

Bite your tongue

Give you a piece of my mind

Life is not a bed of roses

(to) build castles in the air

The lion's share

Give-and-take

(to) give someone a cold shoulder

How will the second language learner interpret the preceding and other idiomatic expressions such as *birds of a feather flock together*, the *iron curtain*, the *Cold War*, *the early bird catches the worm*, *he kicked the bucket*, *it is raining cats and dogs* and many other idiomatic expressions? To interpret idioms successfully, the student has to learn the special meanings of these expressions as if learning a new word. Often, success in acquiring idioms requires both exposure to and contact with native speakers of the language over an extended period of time, as well as an understanding of how words are sometimes used metaphorically to mean something beyond the linguistic expression.

By extension, subtle differences in meanings that we attach to words are directly related to our experience. Residents of Florida and those who live along the Atlantic coast of the United States have a rich vocabulary for describing hurricane conditions, just as Inuits and skiers have many words for different kinds of snow. These rich vocabularies involve concepts important to the particular speaker. To residents of geographical areas of the United States and parts of the world where hurricanes are not a naturally occurring phenomenon, the word hurricane may simply suggest an intense tropical storm that has the potential to cause massive destruction. The Nuu-chah-nulth people of the west coast of Vancouver Island, Canada have an enormous trove

of words relating to salmon, because they also not only make a living from the sea, but they also have salmon as a diet staple. Some of these words are displayed in Table 9.1.

As you can see from the table, the Nuu-chah-nulth not only have different words for different types of salmon, but also words describing the age of salmon because the life stage of the fish indicates "availability, edibility, and palatability which could not be described by using the word salmon" (Comrie and et al., 141). The average person would not make this degree of distinction among salmon other than to recognize that there are probably Atlantic salmon, farm-raised salmon, and Pacific salmon.

Other examples of culturally bound meanings are demonstrated in the way speakers use metaphors. George Lakoff and Mark Johnson (1980: 3) state that "[T]he way we think, what we experience, and what we do every day is very much a matter of metaphor." Metaphors, broadly defined, involve a process of looking for similarities in otherwise dis-

TABLE 9.1

Words for Types of Salmon	
cuẃit	"coho salmon"
hinku·ʔas	"dog salmon"
hu-pin	"salmon trout"
kωih̥nin	"old salmon"
sa-cin	"young spring salmon"

Salmon-Related Activities	
Camuqωa	"salmon roe boiling"
ḥuqstim	"salmon-drying pole"
λlḥata	"salmon jump as in spawning"
ʕaḥa	"salmon go upstream"

Words for Salmon Parts	
cu.ṗi	"fatback cut of salmon"
ċipuk	"salmon eggs"
ʕawin	"salmon head"

Source: Comrie et al., 1996: 141

similar things for the purpose of being critical, creative, or analytical. In other words, metaphors help us analyze, categorize, and make sense of our world in order to recreate, extend, and provide new meanings for our experiences. Benjamin Whorf (1956) proposes that cultures differ in the way they categorize and assign significance and that metaphors assist us in understanding how a culture represents a concept. For example, in American culture, time words are found in many expressions, such as the following:

Time is money.

Time is a valuable commodity.

Time is gold.

Time waits for no man, so make hay while the sun shines.

Time heals all wounds.

You're running out of time.

Use your time wisely while it is in your hand.

Time is on our side.

Although some of these expressions may sound trite now, we continue to use them because we attach personal meanings to them. More importantly, the kinds of language used to represent specific concepts also reveal something about what is important or unimportant to a culture. If we look at the time expressions above, we sense that humanity's relationship with time is an ambivalent one. While time is perceived as a conduit for our success, it can also be perceived as working against us, as indicated in expressions such as *time is running out, time is not on our side*, *time waits for no man*, and so forth.

Can you think of other expressions about time found in English and other languages? Compare the meanings for each. Are there differences in the way Americans and speakers of other languages view time?

Another example that illustrates a rich distinction between languages is the use of formal and informal second person pronouns. The *vous/tu* contrast in French and Haitian Creole, the Spanish *usted/tú*, and the *anda/awak* contrast in Malay are ways in which speakers show politeness. The Korean and Japanese languages, however, show politeness by adding a prefix to the verb. The following Japanese sentence illustrates how the prefix *masu-* is added to the verb to show politeness (Comrie et al., 55):

Taroo-ga	*sono*	*tegami-o*	*yomu-masu.*
SUBJ	that	OBJ	reads

Taroo reads that letter.

On the contrary, Spanish speakers display respect for authority and people of higher social status than themselves by using specific titles preceding a man or a woman's first name such as Doña Carmen and Don Charlie. There are also cultures that use honorific terms such as uncle/auntie and brother/sister with the addressee's name to address acquaintances, close friends, or relatives older than the speaker in order to be polite. For example, in Malay it is not unusual for a speaker to say *Kak nak pergi ke mana?* (Older sister, where do you want to go?) when asking directions of a complete stranger on the street, if the speaker perceives the addressee to be older than he or she is. This is not to suggest that politeness is not an issue for English speakers. Rather, the examples above underscore the importance of the age of speaker and addressee in accordance with religious and cultural principles of respect for elders and the different ways in which speakers would use language to express their cultural values.

To be a fully proficient language user in the target language, English language learners must understand words, sentences, and their meanings. This can be quite a daunting process when they do not know the meaning of words and the morphemes that compose them, and how the meanings of words combine into phrase and sentence meanings in the target language. The process can become even more difficult when the meaning of an expression in the target language is not very obvious or requires special knowledge that is not available to them. Here are some tips that classroom teachers may find useful in helping English language learners improve on their comprehension:

○ Highlight and explain cultural meanings behind words and idiomatic expressions used by English speakers.

○ Teach English language learners how to make inferences about the meanings of words by looking at other words surrounding the word in question. In addition, present the oral and visual form of lexically ambiguous homonyms and heteronyms to help them make more accurate predictions of word meanings.

○ Refrain from using unfamiliar and/or uncommon idiomatic expressions in English when speaking with new English learners. This will help learners to focus their attention on words that carry important messages they need to know before they can produce a reasonably intelligible response.

○ Invite learners to share cultural expressions from their native language. English-speaking students will gain insights about the newcomer, develop an understanding of the struggles associated in learning a new culture and language, and acquire an appreciation of another culture and language.

○ Encourage students to talk about words they hear, read, say, and write in English. This may help teachers to correct any misperception that their students may have about the new words. Additionally, teachers may learn about the different symbols and responses that influence how their English learners think and comprehend English words. In the meantime, students also gain a better understanding of the appropri-

ate forms of language used in the American mainstream culture and ultimately heighten their confidence in communicating with other English speakers.

○ Use graphic organizers such as Venn diagrams, semantic webs, and semantic feature analysis tables to help students create associations between words and concepts.

○ Activate prior knowledge of words and concepts by inviting English learners to brainstorm English words familiar to them that are associated with a topic of study. In doing so, teachers may be able to determine whether their students have a similar or relevant experience needed for comprehension, sending, and receiving messages. In addition, teachers could fill in any vocabulary gaps by using role-playing, concrete manipulatives, or physical demonstration activities to build the relevant experiences that learners will need.

○ Use paraphrasing as a strategy to facilitate and monitor learners' comprehension of word and sentence meanings. Show new English language learners how to paraphrase and encourage them to paraphrase sentences they find interesting and/or unusual as they are expanding their English vocabulary. At the same time, they improve their skills in writing a variety of sentences—a hallmark of good writing.

○ Teach students how to use the dictionary to find meanings of English words, phrases, and sentences that illustrate how words are used. Using sentences from the dictionary as a model, encourage students to develop their own sentences by using new words they have learned.

✓ The study of semantics reveals that the nature of meaning is a highly complex and multifaceted phenomenon. To give a satisfactory account of meaning, a wide variety of facts must be considered.

✓ Concepts such as synonymy, antonymy, entailment, referent, extension, and prototype enable native speakers of a language to recognize that certain meanings follow from certain other meanings and to infer and extend new meanings to a finite set of words.

✓ Word order and syntactic structures also help speakers determine the meaning of a phrase or sentence. This close relationship between grammatical structure and semantics is evident in structurally ambiguous sentences. Lexical ambiguity arises when words have multiple denotative or connotative meanings depending on the situational context. The truth or falsity of a sentence is also determined by some extralinguistic factors—in this case, real-world knowledge.

✓ Native speakers of a language recognize that words reflect concepts that are important in a culture, as we have seen in considering idioms and metaphors. Words hold special meanings for specific individuals as a result of their experience.

✓ Second language learners must have the appropriate cultural knowledge to process language that contains special connotative meanings, idiomatic expressions, and ambiguous sentences, as well as the relevant real-world knowledge to comprehend messages in a second language.

✓ Teachers must carefully scan materials and their oral instructions for any special or non-literal use of words that require special knowledge of the target culture on the part of the beginning ESL learner.

Chapter 10

Pragmatics

Key Issues

- ○ How context influences language use
- ○ How speech acts perform functions
- ○ Direct and indirect speech acts
- ○ Social rules in conversation: Grice's cooperative principles
- ○ Cross-cultural pragmatic rules

SCENARIO

Consider the following scenario described in Harste et al., *Language Stories and Literacy Lessons* (1984):

A pastor called all the children in his Congregational church and began his sermon as part of a regular worship service:

"Children, I'm thinking of something that is about five or six inches high; that scampers across the ground; that can climb trees; that lives in either a nest in the tree or makes its home in a hollowed-out portion of a tree's trunk. The thing I'm thinking about gathers nuts and stores them in winter; it is sometimes brown and sometimes gray; it has a big bushy tail. Who can tell me what I'm thinking of?"

Robert replied: "Well, ordinarily I'd think it was a squirrel, but I suppose you want me to say it was Jesus."

Do you think Robert's response is appropriate?

In the previous chapter, we defined semantics as the study of the meanings of words and sentences by examining their individual meanings and how they are combined to make larger meanings. We also included grammar as a component of semantics; however, to fully understand the meaning of an utterance we must also understand the context in which it is uttered. Pragmatics is the study of how people use language within a context and why people use language in a particular way.

In the previous scenario, the children knew they were in church and must display proper church behavior. For a moment, they remained silent, until Robert, age six, finally raised his hand. The pastor was relieved and asked Robert if he knew what he was describing. Although Robert appeared unsure, his response was not entirely inappropriate—rather it underscores the point that meaning is more than just a semantic interpretation of an utterance. In fact, Robert demonstrates sensitivity to his surroundings and the person he is addressing; he knows that context affects the way he responds.

What exactly is context? In pragmatics, context can be divided into four subparts: physical, epistemic, linguistic, and social. Physical context refers to where the conversation takes place, what objects are present, and what actions are taking place. Epistemic context refers to background knowledge shared by the speakers and the listeners. Linguistic context refers to things that were said previous to the utterances under consideration. And, finally, social context refers to the social relationship and setting of the speakers and listeners.

Now let us consider how these concepts apply in Robert's situation. Robert realizes that squirrels are not the sort of thing normally talked about in a church setting (physical context) although he knows the pastor is describing a squirrel (linguistic context). He thus concludes that the pastor is expecting him to say "Jesus" since they are in church (epistemic context). He also knows that he has to behave and show proper respect for the pastor (social context); hence he phrases his response politely (linguistic context).

Do you think Robert would adjust his response under a different set of circumstances? How would he respond to the same question if it were asked at school or by his friends or family?

DIRECT AND INDIRECT SPEECH ACTS

We will begin our discussion by describing some of the fundamental patterns of human interaction, and then proceed to how these patterns of interaction vary from culture to culture.

Speech Acts

In 1955 the British philosopher John Austin pointed out that we can use language not only to say things, but to perform an act, which makes language useful to us. This act is referred to as a *speech act*. Each speech act or event involves a locutionary act (i.e., the act of saying something) and illocutionary act (the act of doing something). For example, if a mother says to her child, *"You have to get up early tomorrow,"* the locutionary act provides a description of what is said, which in this case is the referring expression *you* and the proposition *have to get up early tomorrow.* On the other hand, the illocutionary force of that statement tells us what the speaker does with that statement. In this case, the mother's statement could be interpreted as an order or as an assertion. We can use language to perform a variety of functions: to convey or request information, to give orders, to make requests, to give a warning or advise, to deny a claim, and so on. Speech acts that perform their functions in a direct and literal manner are called direct speech acts. Examine the following sentences:

1. *Little John has a red truck.*
2. *Who switched off the light?*
3. *Stand there.*
4. *Please stand in line.*
5. *Stop talking or you'll have to go in time out.*
6. *Be careful, the plate is hot.*
7. *You should go to bed early if you don't want to miss the bus tomorrow morning.*
8. *I did not let the cat in the house.*

These sentences suggest that we can do many things with language. The following types of speech acts are significant because of the special syntactic structures used in marking them:

TABLE 10.1

Sentence type	Speech act	Function
Declarative	assertion denial	conveys information claims information is true or false
Interrogative	question	elicits information
Imperative	orders	gets others to behave in certain ways

Source: Language Files, 1994

To identify speech acts, we must also consider whether the action to be performed is situationally appropriate. Consider the following scenario: if a young child says to an adult, *"I'm going to drive you to work,"* we would not expect the child to perform the action, because we know the child is below legal driving age. In other words, for a speech act to be correctly performed, it must satisfy the felicity conditions associated with the act. Felicity conditions are based on (1) the participant's beliefs about the speaker's and listener's state of mind and capacities to carry out the action, and (2) whether speakers and listeners recognize the speech act to be appropriate, given the context and purpose.

It is easier for a listener to interpret a speaker's message if the speech acts are performed directly. However, this is not typically the case, as speakers may be indirect for face-saving purposes, to show politeness to other participants, to maintain secrecy, and so forth. Indirect speech acts are not performed in a direct, literal manner; i.e., what the speaker intends is quite different from what is literally said. If a mother says to a child, *"It's quite late for you to watch television right now,"* we know that the mother's statement cannot be literally interpreted to mean that the child can do something else but watch television, or that it is getting late. Rather, we interpret the mother's message as an indirect order to go to bed. Therefore, her statement is not a direct speech act of assertion, but an indirect speech act of ordering. We can also identify indirect speech acts by considering the responses they arouse. Indirect speech acts evoke a response to an utterance different from the response the literal meaning would arouse, as the following question suggests: *Could you pass me the salt?* If the question is directed at a hearer having a meal with the speaker, the response *"yes"* or *"no"* would be inappropriate. To assume this, the hearer must interpret the speaker's utterance as more of a request than a question.

GRICE'S CONVERSATIONAL MAXIMS

As noted in the previous section, indirect speech acts perform an action in an indirect, non-literal manner. In his article "Logic and Conversation," the philosopher H.P. Grice (1975) refers to this implied statement or proposition as implicature. For example, a student asks a teacher, *"Mrs. Smith, can we bring one favorite toy with us on the trip to the zoo?"* and the teacher responds, *"Not if you don't want to get it dirty."* The teacher's utterance raises an implicature that there is a risk that the toy may be damaged, since the group will be outdoors and moving about. Although the teacher's implicature is not part of her utterance, we can nevertheless draw the inference that this is why the teacher believes bringing a toy is a bad idea. In other words, implicatures are contextually dependent.

To understand how speakers and listeners use and interpret implicatures, we need to examine how they are used in conversations. Just as there are phonological and grammatical rules that govern language use, there are social rules that govern conversations. These rules inform participants about what to expect in a conversation and determine whether or not the conversation will serve the participants' goals. Grice proposes that participants in a conversation generally agree to cooperate with one another. He maintains that conversations are governed by four cooperative principles or conversational maxims. When speakers intentionally violate the maxims to convey an unstated proposition, they are,

in Grice's terms, flouting the maxim. Speakers may flout for various reasons. The four maxims that regulate conversations are discussed below.

A. Maxim of Quantity

1. Make your contribution as informative as is required.
2. Do not make your contribution more informative than is required.

Consider the following scenarios:

Jane asks her roommate, Sarah, when she walks into the kitchen of their apartment:

Jane: *What are you cooking?*

Sarah: *Lunch.*

Jane: *Something smells good. What are you making?*

In Jane's view, Sarah's response violates the maxim of quantity because what is implied in the question that she asked is what food is being prepared. If Sarah does not give a specific answer that satisfies Jane, Jane may come to the conclusion that her roommate may not be in the mood to talk or that she is more concerned about having food and not what food they will have for lunch. When speakers violate a maxim intentionally, they are flouting. The listener, on the other hand, must interpret the speaker's flout by inferring a reason for the response.

Another example of when a speaker might be obeying this maxim of quantity is illustrated in the following dialogue:

Jorge: *So what do you think of Sherman?*

Jacob: *Well, I call Sherman a "Jack of all trades." You see, in high school he spent his summers working as a lifeguard at a youth camp. He didn't really like the job, though. So when he finished high school, he worked part-time at a zoo. He . . .*

Jorge: *Hey, too much over share! I just want to know if we should hire him.*

Notice that Jorge was obeying the maxim of quantity. Obviously, he wanted Jacob to supply him information that he didn't know already about Sherman. On the contrary, Jacob's long answer may serve the purpose of ironing out any doubts that he felt Jorge might have about Sherman's ability. Contrary to what Sarah did in Scenario 1, Jacob has provided too much information. While both Sarah and Jacob flouted for different reasons, their responses have violated the principles embedded in the maxim of quantity.

B. Maxim of Quality

1. Say what you believe to be true.
2. Make a claim based on sufficient evidence.

The principles behind the maxim of quality provide us with some degree of confidence in the messages we deliver and receive. If people did not adhere to these two rules, we would have no knowledge as to whether someone is telling the truth or lying, and language would be useless to us. Of course, people have differing views on what they consider to be good evidence for their views. Nevertheless, we often assume that speakers are obeying this maxim and evaluate what others say based on this assumption. When the expectation for truthfulness is violated, a speaker in a conversation may flout this expectation in order to avoid sounding too confrontational or sarcastic, as the following conversation between two teenagers will illustrate:

Kim: *Hey, guess what? I received an email from the President of the United States yesterday.*
Jenny: *Oh yeah, and the First Lady sent me an invitation to their daughter's wedding.*

Do you think Jenny and Kim are telling the truth? What reasons might Jenny have for saying something that might be patently false? From the above dialogue, the implicature raised by Jenny's remark indicates that she did not believe that Kim was telling the truth. Instead of telling Kim directly that the information she has given is false, Jenny chose to say it indirectly by making a statement that is quite unbelievable. In this case, Jenny has flouted the maxim of quality as a way to express sarcasm or disbelief.

Consider another example:

Rishel: *I need someone who can make a chocolate cake for our picnic.*
JoAnn: *I can make my mom's famous chocolate cake.*

Later at the picnic, Rishel was disappointed with the result as illustrated in the following exchange:

Rishel: *I thought you said you could make a chocolate cake.*
Joann: *I thought I could.*

Why was Rishel disappointed? It is evident that Rishel may have inferred that Joann can make a chocolate cake because she had made it before. This inference may be invalid because Joann may have said this based on the fact that she has seen her mother bake her wonderful chocolate cake so many times in the past and assumed that she knew all she needed to know to make it. Rishel's disappointment illustrates her assumption (that Joann was telling the truth as conveyed in the *can*) was not met.

C. Maxim of Relevance

1. Be relevant.

This maxim assumes that speakers will obey the orderliness of conversations and refrain from making random topic shifts. Consider the first conversation between a mother and her 3-year-old son:

Mother: *Finish your food, Sam.*
Sam: *I want to play with my car.*
Mother: *Yes, you can play with your car after you finish your food.*
Sam: *I have [a] yellow car, green car, blue car, red car . . .*

Sam flouts the maxim of relevance because what he says is not relevant to what his mother has said. His statement raises an implicature. His mother would likely draw the inference that Sam is no longer interested in his food.

The importance of orderliness of conversation is again illustrated in the second example (Language Files, 1994):

Hayam: *Do you think Suher is dating that new kid, Jack?*

Marwan: *Well, she walks to school with him and sits with him during school lunch every day. She also appears at every school function that Jack attends.*

Hayam: *Aha . . . I thought so!*

Hayam may assume that what Marwan has said is relevant if she infers that Suher is dating Jack. But, if Marwan knew that Suher is frequently seen to be with Jack because she is returning a favor to an old friend, who happens to be Jack's best friend, then what Marwan said would have been misleading. Despite what Marwan knows or does not know, it is clear that speakers generally assume that people will not make random topic shifts as a way to maintain orderliness in communication.

D. Maxim of Manner

1. Avoid vague expressions.
2. Avoid ambiguous expressions.
3. Do not be excessively wordy.

These maxims are especially important for teachers to note because they concern the way we regulate conversations by expecting that speakers will avoid using jargon or expressions listeners cannot be expected to know. This maxim also stresses the need for messages to be delivered in a clear and concise manner. Consider the following statement:

Campbell's soup is the best because it has one-third less salt.

To challenge this claim, one might ask if this brand of soup is better because it has one-third less salt than what it used to have or because it has less salt than the soups of its competitors. We challenge this claim because its tends to implicate a lot using open-ended comparatives that imply multiple meanings, thereby making it ambiguous. Designed to convey the superiority of a product, these types of open-ended comparatives are abundant in the language of advertising. Here are a few examples (Schrank, http://sunset.backbone.olemiss.edu/~egjbp/comp/ad-claims.html):

"Anacin: Twice as much of the pain reliever doctors recommend most." (Twice as much of what pain reliever?)

"Supergloss does it with more color, more shine, more sizzle, more!"

"Coffee-mate gives coffee more body, more flavor."

"You can be sure if it's Westinghouse." (Be sure of what?)

"Scott makes it better for you."

Equally important to consider is how this maxim of manner may be applied in the way different cultures use language. Consider the following conversation between two friends:

Larry: *Did you like the movie, Hiroshi?*

Hiroshi: *Yeah, it was interesting. I liked the music a lot.*

Hiroshi's response might be considered vague and confusing by North Americans because no comment is made about the movie other than to comment on the music. The speaker may intentionally flout to avoid hurting a friend who has a high opinion of the movie. His indirectness reflects an attempt to preserve the dignity, feelings, and "face" of his friend, which is an important style of interaction of most East Asian cultures such as the Japanese, Korean, Thai, Chinese, and Malaysian, as well as Mexican culture (Samovar and Porter, 2004). While most Americans try to avoid vagueness and ambiguity and get directly to the point, Asians' and Mexicans' indirect approach to communication reflects the emphasis on protecting and maintaining the social harmony of the collective group. For many Americans, the immediate effect (the intended message) is a major goal of communication, whereas Asians generally do not want to be responsible for causing someone to feel shame. Even when negative messages are intended, Asians prefer the use of indirect language. In the Chinese culture, the most powerful insult is delivered when the words have the power to affect the conscience of the person being insulted or causing one to lose sleep. These differences make one thing very clear, though. North Americans' use of direct language may be viewed by most Asians and Mexicans as harsh and rude.

CROSS-CULTURAL PRAGMATICS

Pragmatics maintains that language is embedded in a cultural context; social rules governing language use may vary from culture to culture. For example, the Western or American greeting *"How are you?"* may be misconstrued by listeners from a different culture as a question which obligates the listener to impart extensive information, when, in fact, a simple response such as *"fine, thanks,"* *"good,"* or *"O.K."* would suffice. In some cultures, greetings may be signalled by the use of words that may be viewed as irrelevant, inappropriate, or meaningless by speakers of other languages. One form of Chinese greeting, *"Have you eaten?"* which is commonly used as a conversational opener, may strike Anglo speakers as odd, but, for a culture whose traditional history dates back to times when famine was common due to natural disasters, pestilence, and overpopulation, the priority given to food consumption in this greeting is a sign of prosperity. Hence, when one is greeted by a question related to whether one has eaten or not, the implicature of the question is that the speaker hopes that the person being addressed will have a prosperous life.

Similarly, the Malay language *"Where are you from?"* or *Where are you going?"* is a socially appropriate conversational opener, particularly among young, urban Malaysians. The question may raise several implicatures depending on the context. One implicature is that time is a valuable commodity in the increasingly fast-paced life of upwardly mobile Malaysians; the evoked response will help speakers and listeners gauge how much time should be invested in the conversation. Another implicature is that mobility is a sign of economic prosperity.

Another example of culture being manifested through language can be seen in how speakers vary in their strategies of responding to compliments. Those from Asian cultures, which tend to emphasize group over individual strength or success, may not know how to behave in an appropriate way in response to an English-speaker's compliment. Observe how the non-native speaker of Chinese background responds to a compliment given by a native speaker:

Native speaker: *That was the best roast duck I've ever tasted.*

Non-native speaker: *Thank you, but my mother and grandmother make more delicious roast duck.*

As you may conclude, *thank you* would have been a sufficient response. But in cultures that value group and team effort as being instrumental to individual success, it is not surprising to hear speakers respond to compliments in the same way as in the above dialogue. When speakers transfer social rules from their native language to another language, the result may be confusion and misunderstanding on the listeners' part. Second language learners must learn these pragmatic rules if they want to communicate effectively with native speakers. This process may take time.

Just as larger social contexts have bearing on how speakers use language to serve their purpose, there are also many social conventions that govern language behaviors in any classroom. For example, a student new to an American classroom would interpret the teacher's question *"What do you think?"* differently from his or her American counterparts. American students would generally interpret the teacher's question as one that seeks individual opinion. However, the new language learner may interpret the question as seeking confirmation of the teacher's opinions or views as a mark of respect for elders or for those in authority. This may lead the teacher to believe that the new student is unable to think or reason well. Diaz-Rico and Weed (1995) illustrate that when an American teacher asks a student who is sitting at her seat, *"Are you finished with your work?"* the implicature of the question is that the student should be self-directed and not waste time doing nothing once she is finished. However, in some cultures, students may expect the teacher to praise them for completing their work early. Differences in cultural values and how they are displayed may be sources of difficulties for second language learners who are new to American classrooms.

It goes without saying that the rules and uses of language reflect the values of a culture. As the previous examples illustrate, certain rules in a foreign language that appear to be arbitrary and meaningless to non-native speakers may appear to be quite logical to native speakers. Because language reflects many of the deep structure values of a culture, teachers of new English language learners must not simply assume that their students speak and think in the same way as those in the mainstream English culture and that the only thing needed is to teach them labels and expressions in English. To help new English learners understand English language expressions, teachers must present the rules and symbols of language in context and make culture a component of their English language instruction as much as possible. Here are some tips that teachers may find useful when teaching new English language learners about English pragmatics:

○ Use scenarios, case studies, cultural capsules in reading, writing, and discussions to highlight how speakers use language within a context and how culture may influence why speakers use language in particular ways.

○ Use direct and literal statements as much as possible to avoid confusion.

○ Provide models of different forms of classroom discourse and turn them into lessons on language and culture. Teachers could model how students should address their American teachers, what they would say to greet their peers and teachers, how to request information and permission from their teachers, how to express disagreements in class, and so on.

○ Suspend making negative judgments about the new English learners when they appear to say something that seemed confusing or awkward to you at first. Chances are that these learners may be transferring their cultural norms and native language patterns when communicating in English. Teachers should try to find out what they are trying to say by probing and asking confirmation questions such as "Do you mean to say . . . or . . .?" or ask them to elaborate, or explain by examples or acting out.

○ Encourage new English language learners to interact with their peers and teachers as much as possible. This allows them to learn the meanings of current words and expressions frequently used by native speakers in everyday communication.

✓ Pragmatics is the study of how people use language within a context and why people use language in a particular way.

✓ In pragmatics, context can be divided into four subparts: physical, epistemic, linguistic, and social.

✓ We can use language not only to say things (locutionary act), but also to perform an act (illocutionary act). This is referred to as a speech act.

✓ Speech acts that perform their functions in a direct and literal manner are called direct speech acts. For example, *Heidi has a ball*.

✓ Indirect speech acts are not performed in a direct, literal manner, i.e., what the speaker intends is quite different from what is literally said. For example, the statement *It is cold in here* raises an implicature; it could be interpreted as a request to turn up the thermostat.

✓ There are four conversational maxims that regulate conversation and help us understand how speakers and listeners use and interpret implicatures. These four maxims relate to quantity, quality, relevance, and manner of utterance. When speakers violate (flout) one or more of these maxims, their utterance raises an implicature. Because ESL learners may have a tougher time interpreting indirect or implied statements, teachers must be clear and concise in giving instructions or making statements to the students.

✓ Since language is embedded in a cultural context, social rules governing its use vary from culture to culture. For example, cultures may use different sets of social rules for the act of greeting or complimenting. When ESL speakers transfer social rules from their first to their second language, the result may be a communication breakdown. They must learn the pragmatic rules of the target culture if they are to communicate well with native speakers.

✓ There are also many social conventions that govern language behaviors in any classroom. ESL learners who are new to the American classroom need to learn the appropriate rules for doing things, or risk being misunderstood or misjudged by their English-speaking peers.

✓ Teachers need to teach ESL learners culturally acceptable classroom behaviors through simulated role plays and by going over classroom routines with new learners of English.

Chapter 11

Non-Verbal Communication

Key Issues

○ Different aspects of "silent language"

○ Cross-cultural differences in gestures, eye contact, space, and touch

○ Misunderstandings due to differences in non-verbal communication

SCENARIOS

What can you conclude is the main source of the cross-cultural misunderstandings between the participants in each scenario?

NON-VERBAL COMMUNICATION STRATEGIES

So far we have explored how language allows us to express our ideas and readily communicate information to one another, but in some types of communication, a great deal of information is conveyed non-verbally by using our faces, our bodies, and our sense of personal space. Non-verbal communication is defined as way of expressing feelings or meaning without using words.

In this section we will discuss the various aspects of non-verbal communication and point out how they vary from culture to culture, just as verbal language varies. Oftentimes, these non-verbal differences can be a source of confusion for individuals new to a culture. For example, looking someone in the eye may be acceptable in one culture but inappropriate in another. To accurately interpret each culture's particular style of communication, we need to understand the various aspects of the culture's "silent language."

Gestures

Every language and culture employs gestures or body movements that carry meaning. Just as there are verbal labels that convey different meanings across languages, there are also gestures that are not universal in meaning. Some gestures may convey meanings considered inappropriate or taboo in some cultures or languages. For example, the U.S. hitch-hiking signal is considered taboo in New Zealand and Australia. The hand signal with the outstretched arm and the palm facing down to show the height of a child is considered insulting in Colombia, as it is used only to show the height of an animal. The height of a person will be shown with the hand flipped up. The American gesture for "O.K." is a symbol for money in Japan and is considered obscene in several Latin American cultures. Latin American newspapers took delight in publishing a picture of President Nixon giving the O.K. symbol with both hands which is a vulgar symbol of infidelity in Latin American cultures (Reid, 1993; Leki, 1995). The goodbye gesture (open hand raised, shake from left to right and vice-versa) is considered insulting in Turkey, as it signals that someone is mentally unstable. While signs made with crossed fingers often signal a close bond between two people in the United States, the same signal is considered insulting in Paraguay and some Latin American cultures.

Space

In "high contact" cultures such as Arab, Latin American, and Greek, people are usually comfortable standing closer together than are Americans when talking. However, in "low-contact" cultures such as those found in Northern Europe and North America, people usually stand farther apart when talking. Typically, the distance between people in North America should be at least an arm's length or up to six feet, depending on the social relationship between the speakers and the situational context. For many mainstream Americans, this area of personal space may only be violated if speakers are close friends or family members. A stranger who violates this personal space will be viewed as confrontational and aggressive. Even in a crowded elevator, Americans generally signal the boundaries of their personal space by maintaining minimal eye contact or positioning themselves so they are not facing each other. A sensitive teacher must understand how students use personal space in their respective cultures and try to help them understand

how these norms are displayed in the American culture context.

It is also important to note that individual personalities and gender differences may influence people's use of personal space. Individuals who are more introverted may prefer to maintain a greater distance than those who are extroverted. Generally, individuals of the same gender will tolerate less distance between them than they will allow a person of the opposite sex. Whether personalities, culture, or context determine the messages we send non-verbally through the use of bodily space, it is clear that a violaton of the proxemics rule can cause discomfort to certain individuals.

Eye Contact

It is commonly accepted that, in certain situations, insufficient or excessive eye contact may cause cross-cultural misunderstanding. In North America, speakers must maintain some eye contact—sometimes accompanied by a smile—to show a level of interest in and attention to a speaker or listener. Failure to maintain sufficient eye contact may have negative consequences; speakers may be viewed as being inattentive, uninterested, or sometimes dishonest.

Speakers from east Asia, Mexico, and Latin American countries, however, will view some eye contact as a sign of disrespect for older and authority figures. In the Hispanic culture, for example, children are discouraged from looking at the adult in the eye when being reprimanded. In fact, children are expected to display shame or remorse by bowing their head when they are punished for misbehaving. Children from Spanish and Asian backgrounds may be given corporal punishment if they look at the adult in the eye.

Teachers who are not aware of this fact sometimes make false assumptions about non-native speakers who do not maintain eye contact. Unfortunately, the expression "Never trust a person who can't look you in the eye" resonates all too clearly in some teachers' impressions of new English language learners.

Touch

Interestingly, every culture sets out rules for when touching is tolerable or intolerable. The right to touch depends on various factors, such as the person's gender, social hierarchy, and the relationship between individuals. But how these rules are carried out varies from culture to culture, as well as from subculture to subculture. For example, African-Americans are more prone to touching than Caucasian Americans; however, Americans of any race generally find opposite-sex touch more tolerable in certain circumstances than people from the Mediterranean or the Far East. In some cultures, the right to touch increases as one moves up the social ladder; typically, a person of higher rank may touch a subordinate. Individuals who wish to interact with members of a different culture must learn to observe these rules or risk offending the other parties involved. Likewise, teaches must be sensitive to how their body language may demonstrate their attitudes toward diversity. Teachers who learn and employ cross-cultural skills will be able to build a classroom climate of respect and value for all students, regardless of their native origins—a climate which will have a great impact on student success.

Points to Remember

✓ Just as we use language to communicate, we also convey meaning through non-verbal means.

✓ Different aspects of non-verbal communication include how speakers use space, gestures, touch, and eye contact.

✓ Meanings assigned to gestures are not always universal across cultures. Some gestures are considered taboo in one culture, but not in another.

✓ High-contact cultures allow more bodily contact between speakers, while low-contact cultures define certain boundaries for personal and public space, depending on the level of intimacy, familiarity, gender differences between speakers, and the formality of the setting.

✓ In some cultures, eye contact between speakers must be maintained, whereas in others, eye contact is considered rude and confrontational, especially if displayed by a younger speaker toward an older, authority figure.

✓ Different cultures also have specific rules about what is permissible touching and what is not. These rules depend on various factors such as gender, social hierarchy, and the relationship between individuals.

✓ A sensitive teacher will employ appropriate cross-cultural skills that signal respect toward their students of different cultural backgrounds. Once students feel respected and comfortable in their classrooms, they will be able to learn.

Chapter 12

Discourse

Key Issues

- ○ The meaning of discourse
- ○ Organization patterns of conversations and written texts
- ○ Cross-cultural conversational and rhetorical patterns
- ○ ESL learners' communicative ability depends on understanding the discourse rules of the target language

...conversation takes place between a teacher (T) and her ESL student (S):

...l me about the picture you drew?

...Sam.

T: *What kind of a dog is he?*

S: *She a poodle. She got beautiful hair.*

T: *What do you like to do with your dog?*

S: *I like to play ball with her. I kick the ball, she run and catch it.*

T: *It sounds like fun. Does your dog also sleep with you?*

S: *Yeah, she sleep on my bed, near my feets. She like to make . . . (scratches his head in search for the right word, and hesitates for a moment, then makes the sound of a dog snoring.) She make noise.*

T: *Oh, you mean she snores?*

S: *Yes, she like to do that.*

Do you think there is conversational flow in this dialogue? Why or why not? How does the teacher help the student to stay within the topic and keep the conversation going?

WHAT IS DISCOURSE?

Much of what we have studied so far has focused on how we process language at the sentence level, not on how humans process larger units of discourse. In this section, we will focus mainly on conversational and rhetorical patterns and compare how these styles may vary across languages.

Discourse: Cross-Cultural Conversational Patterns

Maintaining a conversation in any language requires a set of skills. Some skills are generally employed in many languages, but the way in which each is carried out in real time communication may vary from language to language. Research suggests that the ability to maintain a conversation in a second language requires the following:

a) **Turn-taking:** To have successful oral interaction, participants must understand the implicit rules governing when and how long a person speaks, when and how long a person should remain silent, who can nominate topic shifts, and so forth. These rules may be different from one language to another, and may cause misunderstandings that can affect student's ability to succeed in school. For example, native speakers of English accept the notion that only one person speaks at a time, whereas in Hawaiian and other languages that have a longstanding tradition of didactic storytelling, overlapping talk is permis-

2 The following conversation is between two teachers (T1 and T2) who have been observing a group of ESL children learning to write in English.

T1: *Did you notice Maria's* (a Spanish speaking girl) *story had a beginning, a middle, and an end?*

T2: *Yes, I think she's making a lot of progress in writing. What did you think of Hoang's story?*

T1: *Well, I didn't like it as much as Maria's. Hoang tends to move away from his topic quite often; instead of talking about his hobby, he sometimes includes information about what other family members like to do that has nothing to do with him or the topic. I don't know . . . it's too distracting, I suppose.*

What assumptions do these English-speaking teachers make about what makes good writing? What inferences can you draw about how writing is organized in different languages?

sible. This is particularly problematic when learners encounter classroom discussions that require students to respond individually.

b) **Topic selection and relevance:** One of Grice's conversational maxims is that participants generally try to cooperate by exploring and maintaining topics of interests to all participants. Other factors in determining topic selection are based on the context of the interaction, social relationships between the participants, and the purpose of the communication. For example, cultures may have different views about the meanings of words such as freedom, sexuality, leadership, democracy, or security and have different levels of comfort in speaking openly about these topics in the public arena. While AIDS and homosexuality may largely be accepted for public discussion in America, traditional cultures may frown upon their members who speak about these issues publicly because they run counter to the cultural, religious, or moral principles of the group. Hence, members may shy away from certain topics to protect the face of the collective group.

c) **Conversational repair:** When communication breakdown occurs, participants use various techniques of self-correction and clarification to eliminate misunderstandings. For example, speakers repeat or paraphrase their message (*Uh . . . what I mean to say is . . ., As I've said earlier . . ., Can you say that again?, What do you mean?,* etc.). These strategies enable learners to overcome some of the difficulties they experience in sending and receiving messages.

d) **Appropriateness:** The varieties or styles of speech that native speakers adopt depend on various factors such as age, gender, and cultural backgrounds. Native speakers learn to employ speech register, a term used to describe the varieties of speech styles that are appropriate for individual contexts. Casual conversations between two close friends may feature slang and spontaneous speech that may not be used in a formal speech register, such as when a student makes an oral presentation on an academic topic to his/her teacher and peers. It should also be noted that what is an appropriate topic in one cultural context may be considered taboo in another. For example, in American culture, it is generally not appropriate to ask personal questions related to age, salary, and weight; the freedom to ask these questions depends on how close the relationship is between participants, the context, and the cultural norm in which these questions may be asked. Some topics that are innocuous in the American culture are offensive in other cultures. For example, in the Arab culture a person would never ask a man about his wife, or a woman about her husband. This question exceeds the boundaries of benign conversation.

WRITING ACROSS CULTURES

Just as there are rules of language use in oral discourse, there are similar rules in written discourse. In the middle 1960s, research in contrastive rhetoric suggested that culture affects second language writers' preference of rhetorical and organizational patterns. In Kaplan's (1988) investigation of expository paragraphs written in English by ESL learners from various linguistic backgrounds, he found four different discourse structures that contrasted with English linearity, as shown in the figure below (Figure 12.1):

First, let us examine a sample passage written by an English-speaking student:

> ### PASSAGE 1
>
> (1) Underage drinking is becoming a problem in our community. (2) Every Monday and Tuesday I hear kids telling each other about last weekend and how they went out and got "plastered" or "wasted," and how stupid their parents are for not noticing. (3) For the rest of the week they go around planning what they are going to do next weekend. (4) When I hear them talking I just think to myself, "If they only knew." (5) I know.
>
> (6) I am a teenage alcoholic. (7) All through my junior high and high school years I thought I was cool because I drank. (8) Little did I know that the situation was getting out of hand. (9) By the time I was a freshman in high school it was getting so I needed a shot of whiskey just to get me out of bed. (10) It got worse. (11) Next I started taking drinks to school and drinking them at lunch. (12) I had to have a drink just to feel "normal." (13) My grades went down and my athletic ability, which had always been excellent, also went down (Connor, 1987:70).

How would you describe the organization of ideas in Passage 1? Looking at Passage 1 carefully, notice that the initial sentence introduces the topic of discourse and the subsequent sentences develop the topic by supporting examples. Although not all English texts are linear, native speakers of English generally expect written texts to have minimal digressions or repetitions, unlike the patterns classi-

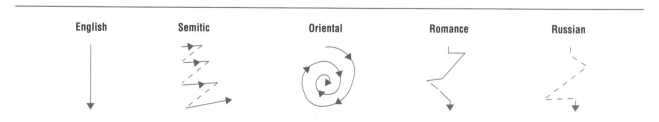

FIGURE 12.1

fied as Semitic, Oriental, Romance, and Russian. During the last fifteen years, contrastive rhetoric has expanded its focus by investigating specific differences in overall organizational structures and other rhetorical devices in writings across languages.

As studies on contrastive rhetoric have noted, cultures vary in the rhetorical devices they use to present words, sentences, and paragraphs to their readers. These studies argue that these rhetorical differences do not illustrate that one language is better than the other; rather, they simply reflect how languages adhere to their own particular patterns of thought. These rhetorical devices have significant effect when writers transfer the rhetorical form of their first language that does not conform fully with the rhetorical form of the target language. The result may raise problems for the target language reader.

To illustrate how cultures vary in the rhetorical devices they use to present words, sentences, and paragraphs to their readers, let us turn to Passage 2. Passage 2 has been translated from Korean.

PASSAGE 2

(1) Foreigners who reside in Korea, as well as those who study the Korean language in foreign countries are, despite their deep interest, ignorant of the basis on which the Korean alphabet, Hangul, was formulated. (2) The Korean alphabet, composed of combinations of lines and curves, at first seems more difficult than Japanese Kana for those who use the Roman alphabet, and as the combination of vowels and consonants multiplies, it appears more difficult to memorize all the combinations.
(3) This seemingly complicated combination of vowels and consonants can, on the contrary, be mastered with no more effort than is needed to learn the Roman alphabet or Japanese Kana, for one must merely memorize two dozen vowels and consonants, the principal letters of the Korean alphabet.

(4) The sounds of these five words are of the same kind as k, t, p, s, ch, however they are named hard sounds because the sounds are harder than k, t, p, s, ch. (5) Some people think these sounds are the same as g, d, b, z, j, because st, sp, ps, sch which are used with g, d, b, as sounds today are combina-

tion words. (6) And some people say, "The words which mark hard sounds are sk, st, sp." (7) They say, "g, d, b are not Korean. (8) These were made to mark Chinese." (9) So they wanted to take g, d, b out of Korean (Eggington, 1987:154).

How would you describe the organization of ideas in Passage 2? Unlike Passage 1, the writer in Passage 2 introduces the topic in the initial sentence, then moves away from the topic in sentences (2)–(3), then back to the subject in sentence (4). Later, the subject is further developed by what it is not, rather than what it is, as demonstrated in sentences (5)–(9). It appears that Korean discourse approaches the subject indirectly and has a looser style of development than English rhetoric, where a main idea is introduced and subsequent ideas must be directly connected to the main theme. A similar rhetorical pattern has been noted for Japanese and Chinese. Texts in Korean follow a four-part structure—*Ki-Sung-Chon-Kyul*—which is similar to the Japanese *Ki-Shoo-Ten-Ketsu* framework which has origins in classical Chinese poetry. This framework follows the pattern shown below:

introduction and loose development
↓
statement of the main idea
↓
concepts indirectly related to the argument
↓
conclusion of the main idea

From an English perspective, the Korean text may appear poorly focused, when in fact, it is the preferred rhetorical pattern in Korean academic discourse.

Differences in rhetorical patterns between Arabic and English have also highlighted that patterns of thinking vary across languages. One rhetorical difference between Arabic and English is found in the use of paragraphing in writing. Paragraphs are segments in a text that have distinct units of meanings and serve to help readers follow writer's divisions of thought with relative ease. A paragraph has to contain a series of sentences that convey a specific theme or unit of meaning. In other words, paragraphs must have unity and coherence. Hence, paragraphing is a type of visual signal to help readers move from one point to another. Passage 3 is a translation of an Arabic newspaper article. (Shiyab, http//www.translationdirectory.com/article619.htm) that reflects Arabic paragraphing style.

PASSAGE 3

It must be understood that the national administration of this country must go in line with the armed forces because both of them aim at protecting the country and maintaining its security and stability.

Along this kind of understanding, His Highness, Jabir Al-Ahmad, clearly spelt out the importance of strengthening the armed forces, and re-examining the capabilities of these forces in such a way that they become the protecting armour of Kuwait.

And at the same time, affirming Kuwait's commitment toward its (sister) Arab countries.

However, these matters are only a small part of Kuwait's worries, which include third-world countries, the non-aligned states, the Islamic and Arab countries, and Palestine at the center of all this.

How many paragraphs are found in Passage 3? Does each paragraph express a specific theme or unit of meaning? After examining the passage closely, you will find that the passage contains four paragraphs with three themes—one in paragraph 1, another in paragraphs 2 and 3, and the third in paragraph 4. To the English writer, Passage 3 may appear somewhat confusing because there is no specific theme or idea expressed in each paragraph, which forces readers to supply their own visual. Plus, the illogical division of paragraphs 2 and 3 may add more confusion to an English reader. This lack of visual signal may pose genuine problems for English readers who expect writers to make everything as clear as possible to the reader. Shiyab concludes that Passage 3 reflects a pattern of Arabic paragraphing used for aesthetic purposes typically found in Arabic journalistic texts. Other rhetorical devices have also been noted in the English texts translated from Arabic and other languages. Additional discourse patterns found in Arabic and other languages are as follows:

Arabic: English texts written by Arab students are characterized by repetition, over-emphasis, and parallelism, where the first idea is completed in the second part, as well as the use of more oral features heavily influenced by classical Arabic which reflects oral traditions (Kaplan, 1966; Ostler, 1987). Sa'Adeddin (1989) stresses that these differences reflect a preference for the "aural style," a mode that reflects solidarity and shared cultural beliefs. He argues that Arabic writers may also write in a "visual" style just as English writers do; but this style is generally not preferred by Arabic writers because the writing appears distant and non-interactive to them. Similar patterns have been found in comparisons of Hebrew and English (Zellermeyer, 1988).

Spanish: Spanish ESL writers tend to write longer sentences (Reid, 1988; Lux, 1991; Lux and Grabe, 1991) and use many coordinating and subordinating clauses (Reppen and Grabe, 1993).

Thai: Studies have found that Thai writers tend to use more repetition (Bickner and Peyasantiwong, 1988), and prefer narrative structures that employ a high frequency of figurative language, e.g., metaphors, similes (Indrasutra, 1988), and personification. These preferences may reflect the fact that narrative plays a greater role in Thai culture and instruction than it does in English.

These differences in rhetorical styles affect the ability of non-native speakers to communicate in the English-speaking discourse community. However, these differences do not in any way indicate that there is something deficient or inferior about a language or the cognitive abilities of non-native speakers. Rather, these differences must be considered differences in cognitive styles (Reid, 1993).

Beginning ESL writers must learn the rhetorical conventions in English discourse to write well in their second language. Classroom activities and tasks must provide ample opportunities for children to experiment with language in written communication. Free writing activities, and shared or independent reading activities are ways in which ESL writers can learn the conventions in written communication. These must be included in any training program for ESL learners and should not be delayed until ESL writers have developed good oral and listening skills in English.

Points to Remember

✓ The study of discourse examines how humans process units of conversational and written discourse beyond the sentence level.

✓ Studies have shown that conversational and rhetorical patterns vary across languages.

✓ Maintaining a conversation in any language requires a set of skills, including turn-taking ability, topic selection and relevance, conversational repair ability, and determining the appropriateness of topic and speech style within a specific context.

✓ While these conversational skills are required in all languages, the way each subset is carried out may vary from culture to culture. Cultures have various sets of social norms governing when and how long a person speaks or remains silent, who can nominate topics, how males and females address each other, and so forth.

✓ Just as there are rules for language use in oral discourse, similar principles apply in written discourse. Research in contrastive rhetoric suggests that culture affects second language writers' preferences for rhetorical and organizational patterns.

✓ These cross-cultural preferences in rhetorical and organizational patterns should not be interpreted as deficiencies in a language or in a student's cognitive abilities.

✓ Teachers should not prematurely judge students' social and written skills as deficient, as students may already be competent in their first language. Instead, teachers must be prepared to help ESL learners understand discourse patterns in English by providing modeling and samples of English discourse, and by reading and writing activities, even if the learner is not yet proficient in English.

Chapter 13

Dialectal Variations

Key Issues

- Differences in regional dialects
- Differences between standard and nonstandard
- Features of different varieties of World Englishes
- The process of English language acculturation
- Attitudes toward World Englishes

SCENARIO

Ms. White's first grade classroom consists of 18 students. Although most of her students are originally from Florida, several of the students come from the Northeast and the Midwest. In one of her vocabulary lessons, Ms. White showed students pictures of a tap, a water-fountain, a boy carrying a bag, a bottle of Sprite, and a pail. She asked her students to name these items.

Ms. White: *Johnny, what's this?* (pointing to the picture of a tap)

Johnny: *It is a faucet.*

Anna: *No, it is a spigot.*

Mary-Lou: *No, it is a tap.*

Ms. White: *All of your answers are correct. People in different parts of America use different words for the same item.*

Can you guess which regions of the United States Johnny, Anna and Mary-Lou are from? Can you guess the term people from Wisconsin use for water-fountain? What do people from Iowa call a bottle of Sprite and a bucket? How about the New Yorkers; what word would they use to describe someone carrying something?

REGIONAL DIALECTS

In Pennsylvania one often hears the words *youse* and *youns*. This may sound funny to the ears of those who are familiar with only the standard dialect of the English language; nevertheless, such differences do not hinder communication. Dialects are variations within a language that may be intelligible to the speakers of that language; for instance, a Bostonian English speaker may not have difficulty understanding a Texan English speaker. On the other hand, languages that are mutually unintelligible are languages that have separate systems, such as Chinese and Swahili.

A dialect atlas contains maps that exhibit regional variations in a language. Isoglosses are lines on the map that represent the boundaries between dialects, demarcating regions that use particular features (usually phonological or lexical). For instance, people in the northern and eastern parts of Pennsylvania use *pail* and *curtains* instead of *bucket* and *blinds*. There are several major regional dialects in the United States. The main dialect areas in the eastern United States are the Northern, Midland, and Southern regions. Refer to the following table for lexical features of United States regional dialects.

Lexical Variation

TABLE 13.1

American Regional Dialects

Northeast	South	Midwestern	West
brook	branch	creek	creek
faucet	spigot/spicket	tap	hydrant
johnnycake	corn pone	corn bread	corn bread
pail	bucket	pail	bucket/pail
tonic	coke/cold drink	soda/pop	pop
string beans		snap beans	
quarter of five			quarter till five
bag			sack
sick to my stomach			sick at my stomach
(cherry) pit			(cherry) seed

The following tables show lexical differences between American, Canadian, and British English.

TABLE 13.2

Canadian English and American English

Canadian English	American-English
chesterfield	sofa
serviette	napkin
eh?	huh?
faucet	tap

TABLE 13.3

British and American English

Food		Clothing		Motor Vehicles	
British English	American English	British English	American English	British English	American English
bangers	sausages	grip	hairpin	bonnet	hood
chips	French fries	jumper	sweater	boot	trunk
cooker	stove, range	knickers	underpants	drop top	convertible
prawn	shrimp		(women's)	dynamo	generator
fizzy drink	soda	nappy	diaper	lorry	truck
		trousers	pants		

Phonological Variation

Examples of phonological variation in regional dialect are: in eastern New England, postvocalic /r/ is not heard in words such as *barn*, *four*, *daughter*, and /a/ is used for /ae/ in words such as *aunt, bath,* and *half* (O'Grady, 1989). Also in this region the linking /r/ is a phonological variation. For instance, in the sentence *The boys who play the tuba are in the school band*, note that for speakers who have linking /r/ in their phonological rule, *tuba* will be pronounced with /r/ at the end. The phonological rule for this is to insert an /r/ between a word ending in a vowel and another word beginning with a vowel. In Midland, the postvocalic /r/ is retained, as in car, as opposed to eastern New England and Southern English. In Southern English, the /s/ assimilates the voicing of the adjacent vowels to yield /z/ in words such as *greasy*.

Morphological Features

Tables 13.4 and 13.5 list some morphological differences between Appalachian, African-American, and standard American English.

TABLE 13.4

Appalachian English (AE) vs. Standard English (SE)

AE	SE
clumb	climbed
het	heated
ruck	raked
drug	dragged

TABLE 13.5

African-American English (AAE) vs. Standard English (SE)

AAE	SE
He need to get a book from the shelf.	He needs . . .
She want us to pass the papers to the front.	She wants . . .

Syntactic Variation

Tables 13.6 and 13.7 list some syntactic differences between Appalachian (AE), African-American (AAE), and standard American English (SE).

TABLE 13.6

Appalachian English (AE) vs. Standard English (SE)

AE	SE
He might could make one up.	He could make one up.
I useta couldn't count.	I used to not be able to count.
He ain't never done no work to speak of.	He has never done anything to speak of.

TABLE 13.7

African-American English (AAE) vs. Standard English (SE)

AAE	SE
I didn't have no lunch.	I did not have any lunch.
The tea always be cold.	The tea is always cold.

What do you notice about the differences between these dialects and standard English?

STANDARD VERSUS NON-STANDARD

Read the following statements:

1. He come a-running.
2. He must didn't hear me.
3. I didn't have no lunch.
4. She be late every day.
5. He does not have anything.
6. She don't know nothing.
7. I think /th´k/ Jill is a nice person.
8. His cigar smells bad.

Which of the above statements do you consider standard speech? What makes a dialect standard or nonstandard? Is standard dialect more correct than non-standard? Does it have more grammatical rules than non-standard? A dialect is considered standard or nonstandard on the basis of these three factors:

1. prestige—prestige corresponds to the social status of the speakers of the dialect. (The language spoken by the wealthy and the educated is usually more standard than that spoken by the working class.)
2. ethnicity—the speakers' race (the Spanish spoken in Spain is considered more standard than Guatemalan Spanish.)
3. region—the parts of the country in which the dialect is spoken. (In the United States, the Midwestern dialect is considered more standard than the Southern.)

Within a speech community, there may exist a standard speech variety perceived by speakers as higher in status. Some teachers reprimand their students when they do not speak "proper" English— "proper" meaning standard English. What is "proper" or standard English? It is a dialect perceived by the members of the speech community as being prestigious because it has been defined as such by the community. Standard English has formal and informal levels. The formal standard appears mainly in writing, public speeches, and television news scripts. It is taught in schools and is characterized by restrained vocabulary and strict adherence to grammatical elements, such as subject-verb agreement and tenses. The informal standard takes into account the context in which it is used and is flexible and subjective. Examples are conversations at parties and talk around an office break area.

Most teachers are obligated to enforce the use of standard English in their classrooms. Diaz and Weed (1995) suggest that they often choose one of the three following philosophical positions on the teaching of standard English:

○ Replacive or eradicationism: Standard English supplants the dialect of vernacular-speaking students. Teachers see their roles as correcting students' "errors."

○ Additive or bidialectism: Maintains both the standard and the vernacular variety for use in different social situations. Teachers may encourage students to use colloquialisms to lend flavor to creative writing or dialogue, while reserving standard English for formal classroom contexts.

○ Dialect rights: Rejects the necessity to learn and practice standard spoken English. Teachers do not teach standard English (Wolfram, 1991).

Teachers who subscribe to any one of the above positions need to understand the consequences of their actions. Teachers who subscribe to the first position may be sending a message to students who speak other dialects of English that their dialect is inferior. In some cases, in which students who speak a vernacular language have been enrolled in ESL classes without their parents requesting the classes, parents have shown anger and disapproval. Parents may find such placement insulting and inappropriate because their children already speak English as their native language. Teachers who take the replacive eradicationism stance should understand and address the social functions that dialects serve.

Teachers who choose the second position (additive or bidialectism) realize that they are preserving their students' civil rights; they are helping to combat the myth that anything other than standard English is deficient. Teachers who have studied dialect variation are more likely to respect their students' respective dialects of English and convey information about English variation within the United States.

Teachers who choose the third position (dialect rights) are preventing students from developing a second dialect of English that may benefit them in a society that harbors language prejudice against substandard dialects of English. Teachers who show students how standard English currently plays a role in their lives, and how their own dialect is different from other systems, give students a knowledge base for developing a second dialect. Moreover, language awareness instruction is crucial in examining dialect prejudice. Such instruction is beneficial not only to vernacular speakers, but to all students.

Scenarios

1 Joe: *Hey, Hamid! What are you up to? Do you have any plans next week?*

Hamid: *Well, Joe, my sister is getting married next week. So I've got to go back to my kampung.*

2 Sally: *The movie is boring, eh?*

Nancy: *Well, I like it actually.*

World Englishes

Are there any words in the preceding scenarios that you do not recognize as belonging to standard American English? Can you tell from what language backgrounds the speakers might be? In the first scenario, the second speaker used the Malay word *kampung* to mean hometown or village. In the second scenario, the first speaker used a Canadian question tag *eh* as a confirmation check. There are a number of studies that have documented a growing number of Englishes used internationally (Platt & Weber, 1980; Kachru, 1985; Pakir, 1991). Many developing and developed nations in the world not only use English extensively at the social level, but also adopt English as an official language—meaning that official government business is conducted in English. Kachru (1985), a leading sociolinguist in this area, found that these varieties fall into two major groups: native and non-native. As shown in Figure 13.1 below, native varieties of English are spoken by native speakers of English from countries such as Britain, the United States, Canada, and Australia (the inner circle). On the other hand, the non-native varieties are models of English spoken in countries such as Malaysia, Singapore, Jamaica, Africa nations, and India (the outer circle). Although the countries in the inner circle set the standards for English that countries in the outer circle must model, oftentimes contact between two cultures and languages may make language acculturation difficult to resist. Examine the following

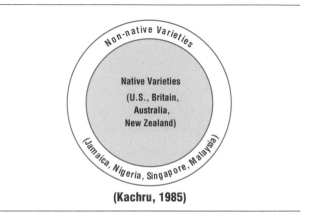

(Kachru, 1985)

FIGURE 13.1 Native and non-native varieties of English.

samples of English which are divided into two groups: native and non-native. The italicized words are typical linguistic features of different varieties of English.

Other Native Varieties

Canada

○ "The *bill* please." (bill = check)
○ I drove 50 *clicks* last week. (clicks = kilometers)
○ My *hoase* (house) is *oat* (out) in the country.
○ It's really cold out, *eh?*
○ *Washing powder* = laundry soap
○ *Washing up liquid* = dishwashing liquid

(For more examples see www.//canadian.demon.co.uk/lang.htm.)

Australian English

- *arvo* = afternoon
- *dinkie die* = the whole truth
- *egg nishner* = air conditioner
- *Whyne chevva cold share* = Why don't you have a cold shower?
- *billabong* = river pool
- *kookabura* (a native bird)

(For more examples see www.uta.fi/FAST/US1/ REF/aust-eng.html.)

New Zealand English

- *big sitter* = sleeper sofa
- *eketahuna* = a small town devoid of basic amenities and remote from the outside world, similar to the American usage of timbuktu.
- *home and hosed* = safe, completed successfully
- *hottie* = hot water bottle
- *anklebiter* = toddler, kids

(For more examples see http://nz.com/NZ/Culture/ NZDic.html.)

Non-Native Varieties

Singapore/Malaysia

- Ginger tea is good for your sore throat—it is very *heaty.*
- I got *presen* from *dem.*
- They *chop* your ticket when you go in (to the fair). (Singapore)
- She doesn't like any fruit, *la.*
- You want a *rubber, isn't it*? or You speak English, *is it*?
- Alamak, he is a *lawyer buruk*! (My gosh, he has the sharp-tongued wit of a lawyer. Typically used in a negative sense.)

(Platt & Weber, 1970)

Caribbean English

- *Gimme wat me wan lemme gwan* (Give me what I want, let me go home). (Jamaican Patois)

- "Urmilla: *Girl, I in big trouble. Big, big trouble. If you know what tiger go and do! He go and invite two Americans he does work with to come for Indian food tonight.*

  Rita: Is wat happen to him at all? He crack? He is a damn fool in truth. He bringing wite people to eat in dat hut? Tiger must be really going out of he head, yes. . . ." (excerpt from Samuel Selvon's novel, *A Brighter Sun,* Trinidad 1971).

(Comrie et al., 153 & 156)

Nigerian English

- I like her. *She's a nice fellow.*
- *One pig big pass all we pigs came into our yard* (A pig bigger than all our pigs come into our yard).

(Comrie et al., 153)

Indian English

- There will be *kirtan* and *ardasa* for the peace of the departed soul.
- His *soyem* Fateha will be solemnised on . . . and all the friends and relatives are requested to attend the Fateha prayers.
- *police wala* = policeman
- *lathicharge* = to attack with a baton

(Kachru, 1991)

What linguistic features contribute to such different varieties of English? And what purpose do they serve for the speakers who use them? English has spread to linguistically and culturally pluralistic societies and the brand of English that emerges in a particular area reflects the locality and needs of the speakers within that community. Studies of World Englishes (Platt and Weber, 1980; Kachru, 1985; Quirk, 1985) have documented features of the many varieties of English and have raised questions about how these features meet the needs of speakers' sociocultural contexts.

Also notice that the English language as spoken around the world has gone through phonological, morphological, and lexical innovations. These innovations involve the borrowing of local words and the redefinition of English words in new contexts, in simplifying of sounds to fit the phonology of the local language, and the simplifying of grammar. Differences among these varieties of English may be reflected at one or more linguistic level, as described below.

A. Lexical

1. **Contextual redefinition of English lexical items:**

   For example, the word *heaty* as shown in the earlier example refers to foods that make the body hot, whereas the opposite concept—*cooling*—refers to the reverse effect. These concepts are based on long-established Chinese beliefs (Tongue, 1974). The word *chop* in Singaporean/Malaysian English means to stamp something. *Fellow* in Nigerian English refers to both males and females. The word *crack* in Trinidad English means "crazy."

2. **Local word borrowings:**

   These lexical items give flavor to different varieties of English. They may carry cultural content and punch not found in another English language variety. For example, Indian English samples reflect lexical items that are culturally specific to death announcements; these words reveal the religious and cultural backgrounds of the deceased. The Singaporean/Malaysian expression *lawyer buruk* literally translates into "razor-sharp and manipulative wit," which can be good or bad depending on the context of its utterance. Just as many Native American words have entered the American English lexicon, Australian and New Zealand English have words that come from the Aboriginal languages. Words like *eketahuna*, *kookaburra*, and *billabong* have been borrowed for plants, animals, or landscapes that were unknown in Europe or anywhere outside of Australia and New Zealand.

   New words are also created by combining words from two different languages, such as *lathicharge* and *police wala*, which mean "an attack with a baton" and "a policeman" respectively in Indian English.

B. Phonological

The following are phonological innovations of different varieties of English:

1. Deletion of final consonants, such as /s/ in *presents* in Singaporean and Malaysian English.
2. Sound substitution, such as consonants /d/ for /th/ as in *them* or *that* in Singaporean/Malaysian and Caribbean English, vowels /o/ for /aw/ as in *house* and /oa/ for *out* in Canadian English.
3. Sentence intonation that employs a rhythmic pattern not found in many native varieties; for example, in the sentence *I wanted a bicycle,* there will be more frequent breaks between syllables in Singaporean English, producing an overall staccato effect.
4. Combination of syllable reduction and sound substitution such as the /ay/ for /ey/ in *g'dye, myte* for good day, mate and /ah/ for /r/ as in *egg nisher* for air conditioner in Australian English.

C. Grammar

Some of the differences in grammatical features that make one variety of English distinct from another are as follows:

1. Omission of auxiliary verbs such as the *be* verbs in Caribbean and Singaporean/Malaysian English: *I in big trouble.*
2. Use of different tag questions such as *is it* or *isn't it* in Malaysian or Singapore English to signal confirmation of a previously mentioned or implied fact or a question that requires a yes or no answer. A similar phenomenon is evident in Canadian English, where *eh* is used at the end of a question to signal don't you think?
3. The use of extra particles at the end of a word to show solidarity, rapport, or informality such as *la* in Singapore and Malaysian English.

4. The use of different words to denote grammatical function, i.e., *pass* in Caribbean English expresses comparison.

Now you may consider some of these varieties of English to be "broken English"; however, studies have shown that these non-English features are typical and systematic within a particular variety and thus should be viewed as different from the linguistic norm of the native speaker's variety. Similar phenomena can also be observed in the speech of native English speakers. Take for example Appalachian English constructions: *I was a-washing one day* and *I can't hardly read it* (Language Files, pg. 378). Although many native speakers may label the use of prefix *a-* in verbs and double negation as ungrammatical, these constructions are systematic and regular in Appalachian English.

Like any regional dialect of native speakers' English, different varieties of World English also fall within a continuum of standard versus nonstandard, depending on notions associated with the social prestige of the speakers who use a particular variety. Thus, dialect is accorded power because the speakers are in a position of political, economic, and educational power, not because the dialect itself is superior. In addition, some varieties of English such as those spoken in Singapore, Malaysia, Nigeria, India, and the Caribbean, have been nativized, a phenomenon found when a speech variety is acquired in a non-English culture or context, resulting in the birth of a new variety of English.

Teachers who will be dealing with ESL learners must be aware that some of their students may be using a different variety of English from their own. In some cases, English may be the students' primary language, and hence make them native speakers of English in their own countries of origin. However, upon arrival in the American classroom, these students will immediately realize that their brand of English may not be readily understood by teachers who speak another standard model of English. This experience can frustrate learners who have seen themselves as competent English speakers. Teachers must handle this delicate situation in a sensitive manner to avoid increasing students' anxiety levels and thus impeding learning. Although it is important that students communicate intelligible messages, teachers must not cast judgments based on a student's dialect or the accent the student employs. Teachers should also refrain from disparaging students' English because a student's home language or dialect is, on the social level, an important identity marker. By not respecting a student's dialect, teachers are indirectly disparaging the student's family, friends, and values, a practice which can be detrimental to the student's development and positive self-concept. Teachers should not try to replace the learner's home dialect or variety with the language of the school; instead, they should empower students by allowing them to maintain their home dialect while learning a new language and showing how these speech registers are appropriate for various contexts. Students must be encouraged to speak and write in their home language or dialect and, at the same time, learn to master the language of the normative culture in their society if they are to succeed in school.

✓ Dialects are variations within a language that may be intelligible to other speakers of that language.

✓ A dialect atlas contains maps that exhibit regional variation in a language.

✓ Isoglosses are lines drawn on the map representing boundaries between dialects. These lines also demarcate the region that uses a particular feature (usually phonological or lexical).

✓ The main dialect areas in the eastern United States are the Northern, Midland, and Southern regions.

✓ A dialect is considered standard or nonstandard on the basis of prestige, ethnicity, and region.

✓ Within a speech community there exists a standard speech variety perceived by speakers as higher in status than other speech varieties.

✓ Teachers who are obligated to enforce the use of standard English in their classrooms should be aware of three possible philosophical positions: replacive or eradicationism, additive or bidialectism, and dialect rights.

✓ As English language use has become internationally widespread, new varieties of native and non-native English have emerged.

✓ The differences between native and non-native varieties of English are reflected on one or more linguistical level: phonology, grammar, and lexical.

✓ The linguistic features of varieties of English also convey social, emotional, and cultural meanings that make them distinct from one another.

✓ Native and non-native varieties of English fall on a continuum of standard versus nonstandard, involving the perceived social class of the speakers; the language itself is not inferior.

✓ Teachers can empower students by validating the fact that the learner's home dialect or variety of English is important and allowing them to use their home language whenever appropriate; however, teachers must also help learners master the language or dialect of the dominant culture to help them excel in school and in the culture at large.

Chapter 14

Development of the English Language

Key Issues

- A language tree traces the relationship between languages
- The Indo-European language family contains English and other languages
- Historical events influenced the evolution of the English language
- Examples of lexical borrowings found in English
- The language origins of borrowings in English
- Word meanings are not fixed
- Words shift in meaning over time

SCENARIO

Ms. Duncan noticed that her Spanish- and French-speaking students did much better in comprehending the passage read in class than did her Thai students. She found that her Spanish and French speakers recognized some English words such as *vigilante*, *incommunicado*, and *assault* in their reading passage because these words are similar in form and meaning to the words in their native language. Because these words are central to the overall meaning of the text, they were able to use their word knowledge to make good predictions about the main ideas of the text. On the contrary, her Thai students struggled because there were too many unfamiliar words.

What knowledge did Ms. Duncan's Spanish and French-speaking students rely on for comprehending the reading passage in English? What generalizations can you make about Spanish, French, and English? What generalizations can you make about English and Thai?

LANGUAGE FAMILIES

Just as we have a family tree to trace the genealogy of our ancestors, we have a language tree that traces the relationship among languages that have contributed to the makeup of the English language. The following diagram displays a partial family tree of the Indo-European languages, showing how some words in English are similar to those in German, French, and Italian. For instance, English *mother*, German *mutter*, French *mere*, and Italian *madre*. English and German are "sister" languages, with a common parent, while English and French are "cousins," sharing a common ancestor (Indo-European), but with distinct parent languages. Refer to Figure 14.1 of the Indo-European language family.

HISTORY OF THE ENGLISH LANGUAGE

The evolution of the English language has been influenced by many historical events, such as the con-quest of English speakers by speakers of other languages like those from Scandinavia and France. In addition, through trade and colonialism, English speakers have come into contact with other language groups, such as Chinese, Japanese, Swahili, and Spanish. Dramatic changes in the English language also reflect intellectual attitudes toward languages, as well as social, political, and religious influences in history. For example, Latin was the language of the Church in the early era of Christianity, as well as the language of the upper social class and of intellectuals. As such, many religious words with Latin roots have been incorporated into English. Similarly, at the height of Greek civilization, the Greek language was perceived as a language associated with intellectuals and the upper social class, thereby eventually bringing about spurts of Greek borrowings in the English language.

Table 14.1 gives a chronological account of the historical events that have been major influences in shaping the development of the English language.

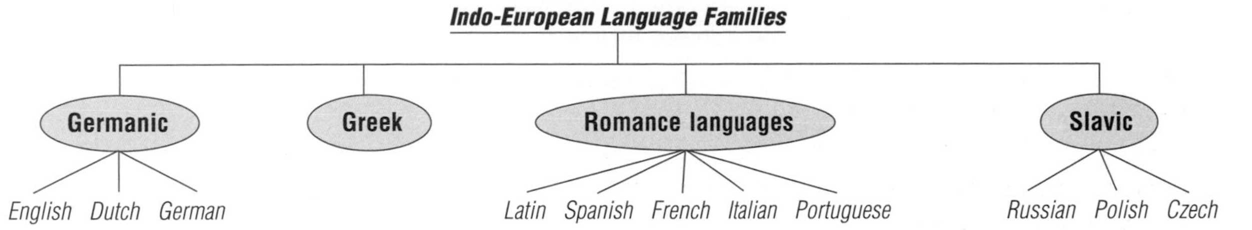

Indo-European Language Families

```
                        Indo-European Language Families
        ┌──────────────┬────────────────────┬─────────────────────┐
    ( Germanic )    ( Greek )      ( Romance languages )        ( Slavic )

  English Dutch German        Latin Spanish French Italian Portuguese   Russian Polish Czech
```

Word Families

English					
English	*mother*	German	*mutter*	French *mère*	Italian *madre*
English	*mosquito*	Spanish	*mosca (fly)*		*mesea (fly)*
English	*alligator*	Spanish	*lagarto (lizard)*		
English	*delicatessen*	German	*delikatesse*	French *delicatessen*	Italian *delicatessen*
English	*housewife*	German	*hausfrau*		
English	*stove*	Latin	*extufa*		Italian *stufa*
English	*hospital*	Latin	*hospes*		Italian *ospedale*
English	*massage*	French	*masser*	Portuguese *amassar (to knead)*	Italian *massaggio*
English	*savvy*	Spanish	*saber (to know)*		Italian *sapere*
English	*two*	Italian	*due*	Russian *dva*	Italian *(to know)*
English	*three*	Italian	*tre*	Russian *tri*	
English	*sister*	Italian	*sorella*	Russian *sestra*	

FIGURE 14.1

TABLE 14.1

A Chronological Table of the History of English—External History

Dates	Events	Language Influence	Stages
700–900? B.C.	Settlement of British Isles by Celts	Celtic—in London, Dover, Avon, Cornwall	Pre-English
55 B.C.	Beginning of Roman raids	Latin—preserved in a few forms: -chester < *castra 'camp'*	
43 A.D.	Roman occupation of "Brittania"		
Early 5th c.	Romans leave British Isles		
449 A.D.	Germanic tribes defeat the Celts	Germanic—Anglo-Saxon	Old English (450–1100)
ca. 600 A.D.	England converted to Christianity (Borrowings: *abbot, altar, cap, chalice, hymn, relic, sock, beet, pear, cook, rue, school, verse*)	Latin, via the Christian Church	
ca. 750 A.D.	*Beowulf* writings are composed (only extant manuscript written ca. 1000 A.D.)		
9–11th c.	Invasions by Scandinavians (Borrowings: *birth, sky, trust, take, skirt, disk, dike;* simplified pronoun system)	Scandinavian	
1066 A.D.	Battle of Hastings—Norman Conquest (Borrowings: *court, enemy, battle, nation, crime, justice, beef, pork, veal, mutton, charity, miracle*)	Norman French, Latin via Norman French for learned vocabulary	
ca. 1200 A.D.	Normandy and England are separated		Middle English (1100–1450)
13th–14th c.	Growing sense of Englishness		
1337–1450	Hundred Years' War		
1340–1450	Chaucer		
1476	First English book is published; spelling standardized		Early Modern English (1450–1700)
1564–1616	Shakespeare (Greek & Latin borrowings: *anachronism, allusion, atmosphere, capsule, dexterity, halo, agile, external, insane, adapt, erupt, exist, extinguish*)	Latin and Greek, via the influence of printing and the Renaissance in Europe	
16th–19th c.	Imperialism (Borrowings: *mogul, rajah, safari, loot, bandana, pajama*)	Swahili, Hindi, Tamil, Chinese, etc., via the various colonies	Modern English (1700–present)
19th–20th c.	Development of North American, Australian, African, Caribbean, and South Asian varieties of English; Scientific and Industrial Revolution	Technical and regional vocabularies	

(Language Files, 335)

ENGLISH BORROWINGS

Read the following list of words now considered to be mainstream English. Have you noticed any words in another language that are similar to these? What are they? In what languages do you think these words originated? (Hint: check a dictionary.)

| chaperone | Florida | cuisine | zero |
| mustang | succotash | cinnamon | papaya |

Like all languages, English has been influenced by other languages throughout its development and has borrowed a huge number of vocabulary items from many languages. The following Tables 14.2 and 14.3 include samples of borrowed items. Some of these words may still appear foreign, while others have been partially naturalized to sound like English. Teachers may use this knowledge to their advantage by drawing on word cognates to help ESL learners make the connection between their first and second language. It may also make ESL learners beam with pride when they see how their culture or native language has influenced the English language they hear today, and may thereby increase their motivation to learn the new language.

TABLE 14.2

Samples of English Borrowings

	Food-related	Health and Fitness	Fighting/ Crime Words	Arts/Pop Culture
Spanish	Empanadas Tostadas Nachos Potato Chili Cafeteria Barbecue		Federal (officer) (detective) Vigilante (jail) Incommunicado Guerrilla	Tango Cha cha Conga
Greek	Oleo margarine (Latin and Greek) Gyros	Biopsy Carcinogen Leukemia Oncology Panacea Euthanasia Gymnasium Sarcoma Isotonic (exercises)	Helicopter Periscope Genocide	Drama Theater Tragedy Dialogue Episode Comedy
Dutch	Crullers Waffles		Bazooka	
Chinese	Bok choy Mandarin Tea Chow time Ketchup	T'ai chi	Gung ho Snorkel	

(continued)

TABLE 14.2 (continued)

Samples of English Borrowings

	Food-related	Health and Fitness	Fighting/Crime Words	Arts/Pop Culture
French	Hash Dessert Hors d'oeuvres Baguette Pralines Frappes Filet Bisque Stew Boil	Hospice Polyp Massage Masseur Masseuse	Sabotage Assault Barricade Commandant Lieutenant Soldier Enemy Troops Parachute	Vaudeville Shows Disco
Arabic & Yiddish	Sherbet Candy Kebab Bagels Challah Nosh Couscous Knish Matzoh ball			
German	Bratwurst Delicatessen Frankfurter Noodle Pretzel Pumpernickel Schnitzel Hamburger		Flame throwers	
Latin		Penicillin Surgeon Diet Tumor	Torpedo	

TABLE 14.3

Samples of English Borrowings

	Food-related	Animals	Dwellings	Arts/Pop Culture
Native American	Shawnee cake (Johnny cake) Journey Succotash	Caribou Moose Opossum	Igloo Wigwam	
African/African American vernacular	Yams Okra Gumbo		Crib (house)	Wannabe (wanna be) Bust out, chat, cut, break (synonyms for rap)

SCENARIO

A young boy wants to praise his mom.

Son: *Mom, you're a beast.*

Mother: *I'm a what? You want to be grounded, young man?*

Son: *No, you don't understand, Mom. I'm saying you're cool.*

LEXICAL AND SEMANTIC CHANGE

What do you think is happening in this situation? You probably noticed that both mother and son have different expectations of what the word *beast* connotes. This example illustrates how words, like grammar and other aspects of language, change over time and how meanings are determined by the speakers' needs—linguistic or social. Evidently, the word *beast* is now being used in a positive sense, unlike its original meaning. Such semantic changes occur in several forms: (1) by extending new meaning to the original word meaning, (2) by reducing the referent of the original word, (3) by expressing opposite connotations from its original, and (4) by creating a new hybrid. Table 14.4 illustrates several types of lexical and semantic changes in the English language over time (Comrie and et al., 1996). The arrows indicate the lexical and semantic changes that each word has undergone.

As teachers, it is important to realize that language is not a set of formulaic rules for learners to master. Although teachers must help learners in developing standard English, they cannot be overly prescriptive in their approach to how speakers use language. As you have probably noticed, many of the words in Table 14.4 have become obsolete and may not be a part of the mainstream English we hear today. On the other hand, there are also some words that were introduced in specific domains that have now entered mainstream English. Because language use is socially and contexually bound, it is not surprising to find young learners picking up terms and using them for expressive functions. The rule of thumb is to keep an open mind and allow students to use these words to express themselves. At the same time, instruction should also teach students the appropriate speech registers for a variety of contexts. As we have noted, some words may require cultural information not readily available in the ESL learners' schemata, and thus may require explanations from the teacher.

TABLE 14.4

Examples of Lexical and Semantic Change in the English Language

Domains	Sample Words	Time
Holidays	Carol (Ring Dance) → Christmas Carols (Choral Singing)	Before 18th century
	Pudding In The Belly → Stuffing	
	St. Nicolas → Santa → Santa Claus (clipping from Dutch Sinterklaas)	18th–19th century
	All Saints Day (All Hallows day) → Halloween	
	Rockets → Firecrackers	
	Armistice Day → Veterans Day	20th century
Sports	Kicking the Bladder (A.D. 43) → Fut Balle (12th century) → Football (which includes soccer, rugby, and American football)	Before 18th century
	Rounders (South England) → Baseball	18th–19th century
	The Number of Cats → The Number of Bases in Baseball	
	Game Plan (specific to sports) → A General Term for Advance Strategy → Plan	
	Scramble (mixing foods as in eggs) → War Terms (in WWII to connote speed and disorganization) ↻ In Football (to refer to quarterback's efforts to stop onrushing offense)	
	Slapping Five → High Five → Gimme Five → Gimme Some Skin	20th century
Health	Stress (4th century—Emotional and physical exhaustion) → Burnout (cessation of jet engine operation)	Before 18th century
	Quacks (1600s; Persons Who Sell Medicine Door to Door) → Snake-Oil Salesman (1920s) Spawns Words like Alternative Medicine (1990s)	20th century–present
	ARC (AIDS-related complex) AIDS Virus → HIV (human immunodeficiency virus)	
Pop Culture/Rap	Blue Devils (meaning depression) → Blues (music)	18th–19th century
	Hillbilly Music → Country Music	
	Cowboy Movie → Gun Opera → Horse Opera → Western Movie	
	Picture Show → Motion Picture → Flick (slang term)	20th century–present
	10 (a 1979 movie title) → She's a 10 (a beautiful woman)	
	Gump (popularized by the movie Forrest Gump) → Gump Our Way to Bosnia (to refer to military strategy)	
	Beat → Kick (the beat in RAP music) ↻ Scratch extends to mean "to move a record back and forth for percussion effect in rap music"	20th century–present
Cyberspace	Information + Superhighway = Computer Communication Systems	20th century–present
	Hacker (an expert programmer) → An Expert Programmer Who Performs Illegal Activities	
	Surf + Net = Surf the Net (navigating the Internet)	
	Bogus (1960s; silly or stupid) → Bogotify ("make bogus") and Bogue Out ("act bogus")	

Points to Remember

✓ A language family tree traces the relationship between languages.

✓ English and German are sister languages, sharing the same parent language (Germanic), while English and French are "cousins," sharing a common ancestor, the Indo-European Language.

✓ Many historical events, such as the conquest of English-speaking countries by speakers of other languages, have influenced the evolution of the English language.

✓ Attitudes toward languages, as well as social, political, and religious influences, reflect the dramatic change in the English language.

✓ 700–900 B.C. to 449 A.D. marks the Pre-English era; 450 A.D. to 1100 A.D. marks the Old English era; 1100 A.D. to 1450 A.D. marks the Middle English era; 1450 to 1700 A.D. marks the Early Modern English era; and 1700 to the present marks the Modern English era.

✓ English has been influenced by many languages over time and has borrowed many vocabulary items.

✓ Some of these words have been adapted to fit the phonology of the English language, while others may still appear foreign in sound and spelling.

✓ Teachers can help ESL students by drawing their attention to word cognates.

✓ ESL students may be further motivated to learn English if they are aware of the way the language reflects the diversity of its speakers.

✓ Word meanings are not static.

✓ New words are created based on speakers' linguistic and social needs.

✓ Changes in word meanings occur in different forms. A word may extend meanings of the original word or narrow the referent of the original word.

✓ Words may have the opposite connotation from their original meaning.

✓ A hybrid or new word may be created from original expressions.

✓ Teachers should not be overly prescriptive in their approach to how speakers use language.

Part Three

A KNOWLEDGE BASE
FOR LANGUAGE THEORIES
AND APPLICATIONS

Chapter 15

First and Second Language Acquisition

Key Issues

○ The stages of first and second language acquisition

○ The student's internal system of grammar

○ Developmental errors in language acquisition

SCENARIOS

1

Child: *Nobody don't like me.*

Mother: *No, say "Nobody likes me."*

Child: *Nobody don't like me.* (repeated eight times)

Mother: *Now listen carefully, say "Nobody likes me."*

Child: *Oh, nobody don't likes me.*

2

Adult: *Whose toy is that?*

Child: *That dog toy.*

Adult: *Oh . . . That's the dog's toy.*

Child: *Aha . . . That dog toy.*

3

Child: *Mommy, Daddy goed to work.*

Mother: *Yes, your daddy went to work.*

FIRST LANGUAGE ACQUISITION

In the first scenario the child does not simply imitate or repeat an adult's utterances, even though the adult has given the child the correct form. In the second scenario the child may try to imitate an adult, but may not yet be able to do so accurately. In the third scenario the child develops a personal system of grammar and produces novel utterances he or she has never heard from an adult. If language learning is simply a process of imitation and memorizing rules and words, how do children learn these rules when most are not explicitly given to them? The scenarios above demonstrate that children often learn to figure out these rules on their own. The study of language acquisition attempts to determine how children acquire the grammar which provides a foundation for their ability to speak and interpret verbal messages.

OTHER EXAMPLES

1. A child says, [næna] for banana, [dedo] for potato, [wio] for wheels

2. A child may say "take" first, then "took," and then "taked," and finally say "took" consistently.

3. A child may acquire the -ing verb forms as in "she going" before the past or third person present, as in "she went" or "she goes."

As shown in example one, children will simplify a word by deleting the first syllable. (A syllable is a structure consisting of one consonant or a consonant cluster followed by a vowel.) The deletion of initial consonant or consonant clusters in these words may be attributed to the fact that the first syllable is an unstressed syllable and is thus not a perceptually salient or prominent sound. The ability of children to dissect the syllable structure of a word depends on whether the stressed syllable is generally longer and louder than the unstressed syllable. In examples two and three, we see that certain inflectional morphemes are acquired in stages before they become more adult-like. The question, then, is how do children learn all the rules of the language they are exposed to? The following section will discuss the developmental stages of first language acquisition regardless of what the first language may be.

DEVELOPMENTAL MILESTONES IN LANGUAGE LEARNING

Crying, Cooing, and Babbling Stage

During the first year of life, an infant's cooing, crying, and babbling reveal early signs of language-like behaviors. Although the child's strings of consonant- and vowel-like sounds do not have any intelligible meaning to an adult, some psychologists and linguists have argued that these behaviors carry specific functions. One function is to provide practice for later speech. Another is to provide a means for socialization between the child and others in his or her environment. When adults talk to infants, they often encourage them to babble by nodding and rewarding them with a big smile. This experience is socially rewarding for children and provides incentives for continuing their efforts to develop speech. However, there are also those who have suggested that babbling is related to biological maturation, an early sign of when a child's brain reaches a critical level of development that predisposes the child to language. Whatever the reasons, it is apparent that children are able to process complex linguistic input early on in life and continue to proceed at a relatively fast pace.

In the following sections the different linguistic stages for language acquisition will be discussed. However, these stages are simply averages, and do not, in any way, suggest that all learners in a specific age group are similar. Despite variability within an age range, all learners go through similar stages, no matter what their first language may be. In the following section, the linguistic stages in the acquisition of phonology, morphology, syntax, and semantics will be discussed. Although the examples are drawn from children learning English as a first language, the general principles are relevant to other first languages. It is important to note that since the study of first language acquisition deals with very young informants, interpretations of children's language samples are often based on an adult's perspective, not on the child's own system of grammar.

LINGUISTIC STAGES

Acquisition of Phonology

At a very early age, children must learn to distinguish and master the phonemes in their language. Since there are infinite numbers of words to learn, it would be impossible for children to simply memorize individual words. Instead, they learn to break words into smaller units of sounds and sound combinations that they can manage and use to create new words. Table 15.1 summarizes the consonants, vowels, and syllable structures that are acquired in stages.

As children are learning new words, they begin to understand that words have sounds and meaning. In their attempt to learn their first words, they will show many variations in pronunciation. Some may be able to approximate adults' productions, while others may produce a very distorted production that is not very comprehensible to anyone. As can be seen in Table 15.1, children, in the early stages, tend to treat entire words as if they were single sounds and are unaware of the changes in meaning induced by variations in sounds. In other words, they treat the entire word as a single unit, paying less attention to the parts of the word. However, in order to learn more words, they must learn to break down words and use different sound combinations to produce new words. Several sound patterns are developed earlier.

TABLE 15.1

Early Stages of Children's L1 Phonological Productions

	Stages	Examples
1. **Consonants**	**Early stage:** /p, b, m, w/ acquired first. Labial before alveolars, palatals, and velars Stops and nasals	/ba/ for *bottle* *telebision* (with a /b/ instead of /v/) /da/ for *daddy* /ma/ for *mommy* /du/ for *juice*
	Later: Liquids /l/ Fricatives /f, v, θ, ð, s, z, š, ž, h/	/wɪo/ for *wheel* /wʊv/ for *love*
2. **Vowels**	**Early stage:** Vowels /a, i, u/ These are universal vowels, i.e., they occur in many languages and tend to be acquired before rare ones. Also, they are very distinct from each other along the front-to-back and vertical dimensions.	/dada/ for *daddy* /si/ for *see* /pun/ for *spoon*
3. **Syllable structure**	**Early stage:** (C) V (initial C may be dropped) CV structure preferred first *(Reduplication of syllable structure is common.)*	/tu/ for *Matthew* /su/ for *shoe* /gagi/ for *doggie* /gud/ for *good* /top/ for *stop* /mama/ for *mommy* /baba/ for *bottle*
	Later: CVC CCVC (initial cluster) CVCC (final cluster)	/buh/ for *bird* /boken/ for *broken* /kwɪk/ for *quick* /dæns/ for *Janet's*

Initially, children tend to acquire sounds that are maximally different from one another. It is no surprise that children acquire /pa/, /ba/, /ma/ first because these labial sounds /p, b, m/ are distinct from the vowel /a/ and thus the CV-syllable structure seems to be the preferred structure in many young children's productions. Earlier in Chapter 6, you learned that bilabials are produced by a complete ob-struction of the airstream, whereas the vowel /a/ is produced by a wide opening in the vocal tract. Later, they will produce consonant clusters such as /tr/ in *tree* and /kw/ as in *quick*. Consonants that share similar properties like /l/ and /r/ are mastered last.

In addition, children may sometimes delete consonant or vowel sequences in multi-syllabic words. Consider this: the first syllable of words such as *ba-*

nana or *potato* may sometimes be deleted because they are not as loud and prominent as the other syllables in a word. Hence, linguistically novice children may not pay attention to parts of words that are unstressed. Once children learn to distinguish between stressed and unstressed syllables, they will learn to dissect continuous strings of speech more easily.

In summary, children acquire the phonological system of their native language in developmental stages. They must learn to master fine motor coordination and receive a lot of input, good models of language, as well as encouragement from people around them to support their language development.

Acquisition of Morphology

Children also exhibit predictable stages in acquiring morphemes in their first language. (See Table 15.2.) Words that are acquired first typically have concrete referents and relate directly to the immediate environment.

In addition, morphemes and words that carry important semantic information tend to be produced before functional morphemes. For example, children acquire the *-ing* morpheme as in *walking* before the third person present marker *-s* as in *walks*, because *-ing* indicates "action in progress," whereas the *-s* present tense morpheme seems redundant to the child because it does not affect meaning, except to show subject agreement. Children tend to acquire plurals quite early, but they may not have complete

mastery of this form until a later stage of development. For example, children may not produce any plurals at first. Later, when children discover the plural *-s*, they may apply *-s* to irregular nouns like *feet* and *men*, producing *feets* and *mens* respectively. This misapplication of rules is known as overgeneralization. Children will outgrow these deviant forms with time and practice.

Only eight inflectional morphemes exist in English, while derivational morphemes are much more extensive. Because of this, little is known about the acquisition of derivational morphemes as opposed to inflectional morphemes. Nevertheless, evidence suggests that the acquisition is somewhat systematic and predictable. The more productive the morphemes are (i.e., they can be attached to many free morphemes), the greater the chances are that the morphemes will be acquired first. This explains why the *un-* or *-ly* is acquired before *-hood*, and *-ize*.

Acquisition of Syntax

Children's first signs of syntactic knowledge do not begin until the age of one. From Table 15.3, you will learn that children begin by producing single-word utterances that consist of words like nouns and verbs. Although children are limited to one-word production in the early stages, they can understand and possibly intend to convey more meaning in their production. This is evident from how children are able to understand other's speech consisting of more than one word. As their vocabularies expand, they

TABLE 15.2

Early Stages of Children's L1 Morphological Productions

	Stages	Examples
1. Inflectional/grammatical morphemes	Early stage: (Ages 2–5) -ing acquired first, followed by: past *-ed*, plural *-s* and *-es*, possessive *'s*, third person present *-s*	*She playing* *She wented/goed* *Feets* for *feet, ducks, dogs, horses,* /dæns su/ for *Janet's shoe*
2. Derivational morphemes	Productive morphemes like *-er, -ly, un-* tend to be acquired first before morphemes such as *-hood, -ize*	*Un-* + *happy* *Farm* + *-er* *Careful* + *-ly*

will produce two-word utterances that reflect a consistent set of word orders or semantic relation. For example, the phrase *Mommy go* shows agent-action relationship whereas *baby there* shows object-location relationship. Later, children will learn to combine and expand their two-word utterances to form utterances consisting of three or more words.

Children also go through various stages in their development of negatives. At first, they will simply put *no* at the beginning of a sentence to show negation, such as the phrase *no toy*. Then, the *no* or *not* is inserted in between the subject and the verb, producing sentences such as *baby no sleep* or *I not thirsty*. They will tend to use somebody and something in negated sentences such as *I don't see something*. As children are continuously exposed to adult grammar, their speech will become more adult-like by using *anybody* or *anything* in negated sentences.

Children also show creativity in learning the rules of question formation. Initially, children produce questions by using a rising intonation such as *Mommy cup?* Later, they will place auxiliary verbs in the front of a question. At this time, they do not know how to use *wh-* words to form questions. Once they can produce *wh-* words, they will insert *wh-* words in declarative sentences, producing an utterance such as *Why I can't go?* It takes a while before they finally figure out the subject and verb inversion in questions. It is clear that children do not simply imitate speech that they hear around them, nor do they make random errors all the time. In fact, for the most part, children's productions reveal their active construction of rule learning and application that evolves over time, resulting in finely tuned adult grammar. Table 15.3 summarizes salient syntactic structures that children acquire over time:

TABLE 15.3

Early Stages of Children's L1 Acquisition of Syntax

	Stages	Examples
1. Length of utterance	Holophrastic stage (one word)	/gek/ for *bug* /bet/ for *bed* /dak/ for *sock* /ge/ for *crayon*
	Two-word stage (Telegraphic speech; i.e., function words are omitted as focus is given to semantic content.)	/weo go/ for *wheel go* *Mommy book* (possesser + possession) *this shoe* (demonstrative + entity) *Katie eat.* (agent + action) *Baby there.* (object + location) *Kick ball.* (action + object)
	Multi-word stage (Some telegraphic speech still evident.)	*Janet eat cookie.* *Throw red ball.* *Mummy no go.*
2. Plurals	Initially, no plural marker is used	*Man, toy*
	Then plural *-s* acquired first, followed by irregular plurals	*Mans, feets, dogs, toys* *Mens, footses* *Men, feet*

(continued)

TABLE 15.3 (CONTINUED)

Early Stages of Children's L1 Acquisition of Syntax

	Stages	Example
3. Negatives	Put *no* in front of sentence	*No milk, no go.*
	Then insert a negative word *(no, can't, don't, not)* in between the subject and the verb or adjective. (*Be* verb is often omitted.)	*Baby no sleep.* *I not break doll.* *I not thirsty.*
	Use negation with *somebody* or *something*	*I don't see something* instead of *I don't see anything.*
	Then replaced with *nobody* or *nothing* and later with *anybody* or *anything*	*I don't see nothing.* *I don't see anything.*
4. Questions	Use rising intonation followed by:	*Mommy cup? More juice?* *Daddy going?*
	(Around age three) Use *can, will* and other auxiliary verbs in yes/no questions; auxiliary verbs precede subject	*Are you sad?* *Is he going?*
	Do not invert subject and verb in *wh-* questions	*Why I can't go?* *Why you are sad?* *Where he is going?*
	Invert subject and verb in *wh-* questions	*Where's Daddy going?*

Acquisition of Semantics

Although semantics is the least understood field of all linguistics areas, there are some generalizations that can be made about how children learn vocabulary in their own languages. The acquisition of vocabulary words does not occur in set stages, but there is evidence that children develop vocabulary in two systematic ways. Table 15.4 below summarizes the process:

TABLE 15.4

Early Stages of Children's L1 Acquisition of Semantics

	Examples
Lexical Semantics: 1. *overgeneralization:* Unlike adults, children use a word to label items that typically do not belong to the same class.	A child may use *ticktock* to refer to clocks, parking meters, the dial on a set of scales.
	A child may use *doggie* to refer to furry things, slippers, other animals that move, such as ducks, toads, and so forth.
2. *narrowing:* applying a word to a smaller set of referents than is done in adults' lexicon.	A child may not consider an *olive* a fruit or *whales* mammals as these are quite far removed from the other members of the same class.

(continued)

TABLE 15.4 (CONTINUED)

Early Stages of Children's L1 Acquisition of Semantics

	Examples
Sentence Semantics:	
3. interpreting passive sentences as if they were active (age 4–5)	*She pushed him.* (active) and *She was pushed by him* (passive) may be interpreted as *She pushed him.*
4. difficulty interpreting bare infinitives: subordinate clause comprising an infinitive verb without a subject	*I told you where to sit* is correctly interpreted as *I told you where you should sit.* But *I ask you where to sit* is incorrectly interpreted as *I ask you where you should sit* instead of *where I should sit.*
5. principle of order of mention	A child may correctly interpret the sentence *He came home before he ate lunch* as *First he came home, then he ate lunch.* But a child may incorrectly interpret *Before he ate lunch, he came home* as *First he ate lunch and then he came home.*

(Parker & Riley, 2000)

Earlier, in Chapter 9, we stated that one way of determining word meanings is by analyzing their semantic features that single out classes of words with shared properties. For example, the word *table* can be used with *dining table, bistro table, study table,* and *end table* because all of these things are objects to put things on. However, this semantic concept has to be learned by children. This process is not always easy because many words may shift meaning from one occasion to the next. Thus, it is natural that in the early stages, children will learn to link words they hear to their own experiences and their primitive conception of word meaning, resulting in productions such as *ticktock* to mean "anything that ticks," and *doggie* to refer to "any animal that moves." Likewise, children may narrow a class of noun, based on the same process; and thereby conclude that a tomato is a vegetable and not a fruit. Linguists have claimed that children's overgeneralizations and narrowing of words reflect their incomplete definitions of word meanings that are different from what adults possess.

A child's acquisition of semantics is inextricably bound to syntax. For example, linguists have learned that some children may not fully acquire passive structure until much later (around six to ten years). Thus it is not unusual to hear children interpreting passive sentences, such as *She pushed him* and *She was pushed by him* as if they were active sentences. It appears, in this case, that meaning is determined by the order of constituents; this phenomenon is also observed in children's interpretations of sentences with main and subordinate clauses. For example, the sentence *Before he ate lunch, he came home* may be interpreted as "he ate lunch first, followed by the act of coming home." Like the passives, the bare infinitives in English are acquired relatively late. Bare infinitives are structures that do not have an overt subject, for example *I told you where to sit.* Children may interpret the sentence *I told you where to sit* as "I told you where you should sit" because native speakers interpret the subject of where to sit by determining the closest noun phrase to the left. However, there are exceptions. Many native speakers will interpret *I ask you where to sit* to mean "I ask you where I should sit" and not "where you should sit," even though you is the closest noun phrase to the left.

You will notice that the first language acquisition process is rule governed and develops in predictable stages. Children do not simply parrot adults' speech. In fact, children produce errors in their speech that reflect an active process of rule testing through trial and error. As they acquire more knowledge and confidence in using a language, these errors will disappear and their language becomes more target-like over time. Words that are acquired first are usually words related to the immediate linguistic environment; they are grounded in the "here and now" principle.

SCENARIO

The following is a retelling of Little Red Riding Hood by Chen, a five-year-old Chinese girl.

Teacher: *Have you read this book, Chen? Do you know the story?*

Chen: *Yes. I know.*

T: *Will you tell me?*

C: *Yep. There was a girl and she was—she wented to her grandma house and then she see animal.*

T: *Wolf.*

C: *Yep. Wolf. The wolf want to eat her and . . . (hesitates) eh . . . I don't know.*

T: *Yes? And so what did she do?*

C: *(Chen thinks for a moment.) She ranned home and she see a man with gun.*

SECOND LANGUAGE ACQUISITION

In this scenario, Chen, a second language learner of English, does not just reproduce words and sentences that she has heard uttered by native speakers, but experiments with English language rules and produces novel words such as *ranned*, *wented*, and *grandma house* as well as omitting the article before a noun.

Some of the patterns of errors made by second language learners are similar to those of children acquiring English as their first language (refer to the section on first language acquisition). Although second language learners vary greatly in their acquisition of a second language, they progress through similar second language developmental stages. The following sections discuss the patterns in second language acquisition.

DEVELOPMENTAL MILESTONES IN SECOND LANGUAGE LEARNING

Silent Period

In the comprehension stage, also known as the silent period or preproduction stage, the learner simply listens and absorbs the sounds and rhythms of the new language. As listeners become familiar with the flow of the speech sounds of the new language, they also start to pick up on isolated specific words in the perceived strings of new and unfamiliar sounds. They are also internalizing knowledge of what makes an acceptable sentence in a new language. During this stage, learners may appear anxious when asked to produce speech. Therefore, teachers with second language learners at this stage of their second language learning process should not force them to speak. They should not feel frustrated when students do not respond to them; this is a normal, initial stage that second language learners go through in learning a new language. During this stage, teachers can provide a lot of comprehensible input by using visuals, manipulatives, gestures, and context clues, and modeling expected behavior and encouraging students to join in group chants and songs. Teachers are advised not to overtly correct errors, as this may heighten learners' anxiety levels and does not guarantee they will internalize the rules; instead, teachers should provide learners with a rich language environment in which they can use the input to the best of their abilities.

After the silent period, learners will go through early production (one- or two-word stage), speech emergence (phrases and short sentences), and intermediate fluency (begin to engage in discourse). All of these stages involve linguistic elements such as phonology, morphology, syntax, semantics, and pragmatics.

LINGUISTIC STAGES

Acquisition of Phonology

There are several reasons why second language learners may not initially produce the sounds of the target language correctly. This failure may be attributed to the following factors:

A. Speakers may transfer the segmental structure of L1 to L2. An example is the L2 phonemic distinction that L1 lacks. Japanese has one phoneme /r/ with allophones l and r; thus they do not make a distinction between /l/ and /r/, whereas in English there is a phonemic distinction between the two. Therefore, Japanese or Chinese speakers may experience difficulty in producing /r/.

B. Speakers may also transfer phonological rules from L1 to L2. German speakers devoice the word-final obstruents when learning English, yielding both *back* and *bag* as /baek/ because in German the word-final obstruents must be voiceless.

C. Speakers may also transfer phonotactic constraints (i.e., conditions for a permissible sequence of segments) from L1 to L2. For example, in English it is permissible to string three consonants in the syllable-initial cluster such as *straight* and *splendid*. Speakers whose native languages do not permit this will put in a vowel to break up the cluster. For instance, Spanish speakers will say /estop/ for *stop*, /especial/ for *special*, and Arab Egyptian speakers will say /firɛd/ for *Fred* and /čildirən/ for *children*.

Acquisition of Morphology

Second language learners go through predictable stages in acquiring morphemes in their second language. These stages are similar to the stages children go through in acquiring English as their native language. The plural morphemes PLU (*boy/boys*) are acquired before the present PRES (*He eat/eats pizza*) and possessive POSS (*girl bag/girl's bag*) morphemes. Morphemes are also acquired according to their morphological function rather than their phonological form.

The examples in Table 15.5 show the order of grammatical morphemes acquired by children learning English as a second language. Dulay and Burt (1983) reported that children from different first language backgrounds seem to have a similar order of acquiring the English morphemes. For instance, the (PLU) morpheme as in *boy/boys* and (progressive) as in *cry/crying* are acquired earlier than (third person singular) as in *like/likes* and (POSS) as in *Mom cup/Mom's cup*. Studies have found that nonnative English speakers in their acquisition of the (PLU) forms seem to have misanalyzed the irregular plural form as a root form and thus inflect it again with the regular plural suffix, as in *sheep/sheeps*.

As for the derivational morphemes, *-er*, *-ly*, *un-* in words such as *longer*, *lovely*, *untidy* are acquired sooner than morphemes such as *-hood*, *-ize* in words such as *brotherhood* and *familiarize*.

TABLE 15.5

Early Stages of Children's L2 Acquistion of Morphemes

	Stages	Examples
1. Inflectional/ grammatical morphemes	Early stage: (3–5 years old) s, es- -ing followed by third person singular pres -s past -ed and possessive -'s,	*boys and girls, sheeps, feets,* *noses, cause them hungry* and *crying* Many like pizza. *She boughted it at the store.* *Mom kuh* cup
2. Derivational morphemes	Productive morphemes such as -er, -ly, un- tend to be acquired before morphemes like -hood, -ize.	*longer, lovely, untidy* *neighborhood,* *familiarize*

Acquisition of Syntax

Second language children produce these syntactic structures during their second language acquisition process, as shown in Table 15.6.

TABLE 15.6

Early Stages of Children's L2 Acquisition of Syntax

	Stages	Examples
1. Length of utterance	Holophrastic stage	*kuh (cup)*
	Two-word stage (telegraphic speech; i.e., function words are omitted as focus is on meaning)	*He cry; Hims back*
	Multi-word stage (Some telegraphic speech still exists.)	*I not cry; Tran nots here.* *She boughted it at the store.* *Mary didn't wanted it.*
2. Negatives	Put *no* in front of sentences by: inserting a negative word *no* or *not* between the subject and the verb or adjective (*Be* verb is often omitted)	*I not cry.* *Tran nots here*
	Use negation with the incorrect auxiliary	*Lucy doesn't gots the glue.*
3. Questions	Use rising intonation followed by:	*Tan is reading?*
	The production of *wh-* questions begins	*What you study?* *What the time?*
	Auxiliaries such as *is, are, was* appear, but are not yet inverted systematically with the subject	*Why I can't color?* *What she is singing?* *Why you don't draw?*

Table 15.6 shows three components of the acquisition process of syntactic structures by English learners: length of utterance, negation, and questions.

Length of utterance: English language learners go through the holophrastic stage (*cup*) to the telegraphic stage (*He cry*) and the multi-word stage (*I not cry*).

Negation: O'Grady (1989) reported that regardless of native language background, English language learners' most common first attempt at negating in English is to place the negative particle *no* (or occasionally *not*) before the phrase to be negated as in *I not cry* and *no eat*.

Questions: In the initial stage of forming questions, English language learners tend to add rising intonation to their sentence structures, such as *Tan is reading?* Then the attempt at *wh-* questions begins, however, the auxiliary is usually omitted such as *What you study?* Another stage in forming questions is when the auxiliaries are not yet inverted systematically, as in *What she is singing?*

Acquisition of Semantics

In acquiring semantics, second language learners go through stages similar to the stages first language children go through in learning words. Studies have documented several generalizations about these stages. Table 15.7 displays the stages in which English language learners acquire meanings. The common developmental strategy that children learning English as a second language employ is the overgeneralization of the superordinates due to their limited vocabulary (*animal* instead of *dog*). Other developmental strategies are the inappropriate use of synonyms (*long* instead of *tall*) and the use of circumlocutions which involve substituting a descriptive phrase for a word that the learner has not yet acquired (*a lady who is carrying a baby* instead of *a pregnant lady*). Perhaps the most common difficulty that English language learners face in the semantic domain is the acquisition of idioms (*break a leg*) and with words that have one form but many meanings (*diamond, bank*).

TABLE 15.7

Early Stages of Children's L2 Acquisition of Semantics

	Examples
Lexical Semantics	
1. Overgeneralization: Using superordinates due to limited vocabulary	*animal* instead of *dog; small* instead of *little (I have small money)*; *boys and girls* instead of *children*
2. Inappropriate use of synonyms	*My brother is long and thin* instead of *tall.* *I will borrow you the book* instead of *lend.*
3. Use of circumlocutions in place of an exact word	*A lady who is carrying a baby* instead of *a pregnant lady*
4. Acquisition of idiomatic expressions, *polysemes* (one form with related meaning) and *homonyms* (one form with unrelated meaning) takes longer	*Break a leg, run up, run down, run out; mouth* used for eating, opening of river; diamond (baseball, stone)

First Language Acquisition

✓ Cooing, babbling, and crying are precursors to true language development. They not only enable infants to experiment and practice different sounds for later speech; they also provide a means for infants to communicate their needs to others. All of which motivates infants to continue developing their language-learning potential.

✓ Children's first language acquisition occurs in developmental stages. At the phonological level, sounds that are easy to produce will be acquired first, i.e., labial consonants are acquired before alveolars, palatals, and velars. Universal vowels and vowels that are distinctive from one another will be acquired first. Syllable structures consisting of consonants and vowels are acquired first, followed by two- or three-consonant clusters in the initial or final positions of a word.

✓ Grammatical morphemes are acquired in a predictable order. Inflectional morphemes such as *-ing,* past *-ed,* plural *-s* are acquired before possessives *-'s* and third person *-s.*

✓ Syntactic structures are acquired in a predictable order from one- to two-word stage to multiple-word stage. Sentence types such as negatives and questions are also acquired in stages.

✓ Children's development of semantics is systematic. They may overgeneralize by extending or narrowing the meaning of a word to include referents that are not included in the adult's lexicon.

✓ Initially, children may treat passive sentences as if they were active. They may also have difficulty interpreting bare infinitives and interpret sentences based on the order of the words in a sentence.

✓ Children do not simply imitate adults' speech or memorize the rules and words of a language.

✓ Children develop their own internal system of grammar by testing the rules themselves, applying the rules, and later modifying their grammar to match that of adults. During this process, children may make overgeneralization errors that are produced by misapplying rules to instances where they do not apply.

✓ Children may not correct their overgeneralized productions even if they are corrected by adults because their own system of grammar may not be developed enough to accommodate such changes.

✓ Children's early vocabulary is centered in the "here and now"; they relate to their immediate experiences.

(continued)

Second Language Acquisition

✓ Some patterns of errors made by second language learners are similar to those made by children acquiring their first language.

✓ Some second language learners will go through a silent period at the initial stage of their second language acquisition process.

✓ The stages that learners go through in learning their second language are:

  ○ Silent period/pre-production stage

  ○ Early production (one- or two-word stage)

  ○ Speech emergence (phrases and short sentences)

  ○ Intermediate fluency (begin to engage in discourse)

✓ Second language learners go through a predictable order of acquiring grammatical morphemes and syntactic structures in English, just like children learning their first language.

✓ Errors made by second language learners may be attributed to transfer of L1 rules to L2.

✓ Second language learners also demonstrate some similarities to first language learners in their acquisition of word meanings. They may overgeneralize the meaning of a word. Second language learners, due to their limited vocabulary, may also substitute words or phrases.

✓ Errors produced by second language learners are also considered developmental, just as in first language acquisition.

Chapter 16

Non-Linguistic Factors That Influence Second Language Acquisition

Key Issues

- ○ Relationship between age and length of exposure to second language acquisition
- ○ Differences in cognitive styles and their influence on second language acquisition
- ○ Differences in personality traits and their influence on second language acquisition
- ○ Types of motivation and success in language acquisition
- ○ Relationship between social distance and language acquisition

Examine the following comments about second language learners:

I don't understand why Rosa is not showing that much progress in her English. She has been in the U.S. for seven years and she gets to hear English all the time. Her parents want her to do well in school and believe that her future will be better here than in Mexico. On top of that, she gets a lot of English everywhere. So what's preventing her from learning English well?

I notice that many ESL children are very fluent in English, but their parents may not be as fluent, even though they have been in America for the same length of time. Children are like sponges, always absorbing information.

The only way to learn is to speak and use the language constantly. But how will these ESL children learn if they refuse to speak in class or answer our questions? They must learn to participate in class if they want to do well here.

Look at Hoang. He has been here for only two years but his English is improving every minute. He likes to talk in class, participates in every class discussion, and is not afraid to ask questions when he doesn't understand. I think he will pick up the language very quickly.

Do you think the views expressed are justified? Why or why not? Can you offer alternative explanations for why individuals have different levels of success in learning a second language?

In earlier chapters, the role of linguistic variables in second language acquisition was discussed. The following factors may also have some influence on second language acquisition.

AGE

There is a prevailing assumption that children learn a second language more readily than adults. This view is largely influenced by Lennenberg's (1964) "critical period hypothesis," which states that the age span during which children must have exposure to language to build critical left brain structures which enable them to gain native-like competence is between birth and just before puberty. While researchers may have differing views about the implications of the critical period hypothesis in second language learning, it is generally accepted that children who are exposed to another language at a very early age have a greater chance of producing native-like fluency and accent. Length of exposure to the language has also been shown to correlate positively with proficiency. It is not unusual to expect that those who begin learning a second language at an early age may simply have longer exposure to the language and ultimately achieve greater proficiency. Moreover, young children are typically less self-conscious about learning a second language; they are not expected to perform at a cognitively higher level than adults, and thus experience less anxiety. All of these factors may promote acquisition.

On the other hand, adults may be more efficient at learning a new language because they bring with them extensive knowledge, mature cognitive skills, and strategies for problem-solving that may facilitate second language acquisition. Adults, however, may not be able to produce accent-free speech if they acquire the second language after puberty. Moreover, non-native adults may also choose to speak English with an accent to maintain or project their personal or cultural identity through their speech, or modify the degree of accent in their speech, depending on the context.

COGNITIVE STYLES

Cognitive styles refer to the way learners approach problem-solving tasks, conceptualize, and organize information. Cognitive styles may mediate between emotion and cognition; for example, one's emotional state may elicit tendencies toward reflectivity or toward impulsivity. In other words, if a student is in an impulsive mood, the student may demonstrate an impulsive style of learning. And if the student is in a reflective mood, he or she may be more likely to exhibit a reflective learning style. These distinctions may have several implications for language acquisition. Researchers have found that children who are more reflective tend to make fewer mistakes in reading than impulsive children (Kagan, 1965). Conversely, children who are more impulsive tend to be faster readers; they adopt a strategy of reading for understanding by guessing from context and they are not overly concerned with errors. Such a style could have positive effects on language learning.

What important considerations for second language learning can we then draw from these differences in cognitive styles? Knowing that learners exhibit these differences, teachers must be mindful not to judge errors made by impulsive learners who may be taking more risks with language. But then again, the reflective learner must be given time to react and respond to instructional material and other activities done in the classroom.

Additional cognitive styles are field independence and field dependence. Field independence is

an analytical ability that enables learners to distinguish and analyze the parts from the whole. Field dependence, however, means a person analyzes information in a holistic way and does not easily distinguish the parts from the whole.

How does this information relate to second language learning? It appears that classrooms that focus on structure drills and other activities involving analysis and attention to specific details and explicit rules may work well for field-independent learners. Field-dependent learners may do better when instruction does not focus explicitly on rule learning, but introduces language structures through contextually embedded activities such as story reading, oral discussions, group work, and so on.

It is important that teachers view these cognitive styles as general tendencies which may be exercised in varying degrees by learners, depending on the context, and thus refrain from labeling students as either type. More importantly, teachers must be cognizant that each individual is unique and help learners develop flexibility in the way that they learn.

... Livin' my life like it's golden ...

PERSONALITY TRAITS

There are certain personality traits that are believed to correlate with good second language acquisition, although supporting empirical studies are somewhat inconclusive. Impulsivity and risk-taking behaviors appear to be important to successful learning of a second language. Good language learners who have fewer inhibitions will be more willing to take a calculated risk and will try to figure out the language as much as they possibly can. Beebe (1980) found that Puerto Rican children learning ESL displayed significantly greater risk-taking behaviors with an English-speaking interviewer than with an English-speaking bilingual. He reasons that ESL learners will unconsciously adjust their speech for the interlocutor—in this case making more elaborations and explanations for the English-speaking interviewer and thereby demonstrating more risk-taking behaviors. Such a learner may be well-suited for the less formal learning environment.

It is often accepted that extroverted learners will acquire language at a faster rate than introverted learners. This is because extroverts, by nature, are more assertive, adventurous, responsive, talkative, and, consequently, more inclined to continue learning the language. However, Suter (1976) and Busch (1982) found no correlation between extroversion and pronunciation skills in English. Busch (1982) also found that extroversion correlates with length of exposure to English and that introversion affects performance on language tasks involving grammar and reading. These disparate findings suggest two things: (1) the effect of personality on language acquisition may be inversely related. It is possible that learners who have long exposure to the second language may become more extroverted and (2) extroversion may enhance communicative language ability more than knowledge of linguistic rules or academic language learning.

Stephen Krashen (1981), a leading figure in the field of ESL, also stresses the negative effect that anxiety plays in language learning. Learners who generally have a high global self-esteem (overall self-assessment), or specific self-esteem (self-evaluation on specific tasks such as writing a paper, driving a car, and so on), and low inhibitions may have a better chance at achieving successful language learning than those with a lower sense of self and many anxieties. Thus it is important that teachers help learners become comfortable by providing instruction that is clear, meaningful, and appealing, while offering support in the form of encouragement so that students remain interested in their own learning.

SOCIAL PSYCHOLOGICAL FACTORS

ESL learners' motivation and attitude may also influence the degree of success in second language acquisition. Gardner and Wallace's (1972) significant study on motivational factors affecting second language acquisition identified two basic types of motivation: instrumental and integrative. Instrumental motivation refers to motivation for learning a language based on instrumental reasons, such as getting promoted to a higher grade, gaining admission to a good program of study, competing for scholarships, doing well in classroom tasks and tests, and so forth. Integrative motivation refers to the learner's desire to identify with the members of the target culture and to understand and appreciate the values and knowledge of the target culture and its speakers. Graham (1984) asserts that a learner who is integratively motivated may not have to "lose oneself" in that process. It is also important to note that the degree of success achieved by learners may be motivated by attitudes that are both instrumental and integrative. For example, ESL children in the United States may wish to learn English to do well in school and to "fit in" with the mainstream student population; however, because young learners may not have the fully developed attitudes of their adult counterparts, their attitudes toward a culture may have little or no effect on their second language acquisition.

In addition, Maslow's (1970) hierarchy of needs points to equally important forms of motivation: intrinsic and extrinsic. Intrinsic motivation refers to the learner's internal desire and self-determination to learn. For example, ESL learners in the United States may recognize that English is an important tool of communication in their classrooms, and thus may work hard to acquire fluency. If the learners are studying a second language to fulfill a parent's wish, then the motivation is extrinsic.

In what way do these forms of motivation affect language learning? Learners who are instrumentally and intrinsically motivated may do equally well in acquiring another language. But the former may lack the persistence for learning the target language once a specific task is accomplished, or when the external reward or punishment related to the behavior is removed. Learners who learn to appreciate and value target language speakers and to achieve a sense of self-satisfaction may do well in the long run, as they are more likely to persist in learning and increasing their abilities in the language.

Another socio-psychological factor focuses on attitudes of second language learners. Because second language learning involves the integration of the cultural skills, values, and ideas of the new culture, second language learners' attitudes toward the target language culture and its members may either contribute to or hamper language acquisition. In Schumann's (1978) acculturation model, he asserts that success in second language acquisition requires learners to adapt to the target culture. How well the learners adapt to the new culture depends on the social distance between the learner and the target language group. Social distance is determined by the differences in size between groups, the ethnicity, and the political and social status of the second language group. The more learners perceive themselves to be politically or socially inferior to the target language group, or perceive their cultural values or ideas to be in conflict with those of the target language and culture, the greater the social distance.

Equally important is how teacher and peer attitudes can influence learning ability. Teachers and mainstream peers must display respect for second language learners, their cultures and language groups, and be willing to accept them for who they are and not judge them through the lens of their own culture. Only then will students be empowered.

Points to Remember

✓ Age correlates with second language acquisition. Younger children are more likely than adults to acquire native-like pronunciation. However, adults are cognitively more advanced in acquiring grammar and vocabulary in a second language.

✓ Cognitive style is a significant factor in language acquisition, because learners will respond to the form of instruction that matches their learning styles. Since each learner is unique, teachers must diversify language instruction as much as possible. Exposing students to different learning styles will help them become more versatile in their learning approach.

✓ Learners who exhibit fewer risk-taking behaviors and high inhibitions may create high affective barriers which impede language acquisition.

✓ The relationship between extroversion and language acquisition is not conclusive. Extroversion may not always be a factor in acquisition; rather, it may be a consequence of language acquisition. In fact, both extroverts and introverts may become successful at language acquisition. Extroversion may be a factor in promoting natural communicative ability.

✓ ESL learners' attitudes and motivations may also affect language acquisition. Learners with integrative motivation, a desire to identify with and appreciate the values and the members of the target culture, may be more likely to continue learning and persevere through obstacles they encounter in their learning. The motivation to succeed is increased if the learners are internally—as opposed to externally—driven to learn a language.

✓ ESL learners with instrumental motivation, a desire to learn a language for utilitarian purposes, may also do well in acquiring a language; but this motivation may be reduced once learners have met their target goal. Similarly, learners whose desire to learn is instrumental and intrinsic may also do as well as learners who are extrinsically and instrumentally motivated.

✓ Learner attitudes toward the target language culture and its members may also influence how well they adapt to the new culture. The greater the social distance, the more difficulties learners will have with learning the second language.

✓ Teachers must demonstrate respect for and acceptance of the values of second language learners, their families, and their cultures.

Chapter 17

First and Second Language Acquisition Theories and Models

Key Issues

- ⭘ Theoretical perspectives of language acquisition
- ⭘ A child develops his or her own system of grammar
- ⭘ Krashen's Monitor Model
- ⭘ Cummins' BICS and CALP
- ⭘ McLaughlin's model of language processing: controlled and automatic
- ⭘ Bialystok's model of language processing: implicit versus explicit knowledge
- ⭘ Application of Bialystok's and McLaughlin's models: focal versus peripheral levels
- ⭘ Stages of interlanguage within Selinker's Interlanguage Theory

SCENARIO

Kayla: *I can't believe your sweet little Ginger is already talking! How old is she? What were her first words?*

Consuela: *She's eighteen months. Her first words took me by surprise. She said "Mo," the nickname we gave to the lost and hungry little puppy we found under the bridge nearby our house. Ten months later, she was saying "Mo, go cookie."*

Having read the previous scenario, can you explain how children, who have no knowledge of language at birth, acquire language?

FIRST LANGUAGE ACQUISITION THEORIES

We have already established that language involves a complex and rule-governed system. How then, do children, who at birth have no knowledge of language, suddenly develop the ability to use sounds, morphology, and syntactic and lexical rules to produce sentences they may never have heard before by the time they turn five? Do children simply imitate what they hear from adults and other children around them? Or do they actually seek out patterns, hypothesize, and test rules of the language they hear around them? Do children pick up their first language through intensive teaching? These are the fundamental questions that a theory of first language acquisition attempts to answer. The following section will discuss several theoretical perspectives on language acquisition.

Behaviorism

A major influence on the behaviorist perspective came from B.F. Skinner (1957) who argued that language learning is a culturally determined and learned behavior. Behaviorist proponents claimed that learners learn by undergoing training and practice through a series of stimulus and response chains and operant conditioning, all reinforcers that moti-

vate the formation of a language habit. In other words, a person's utterance becomes a stimulus which, in turn, will initiate a response. This response will then act as a stimulus and the cycle continues. Language learning, like learning how to walk, requires effort and training. Behaviorists also claimed that learning how to write is not universal across cultures because some cultures do not have a history of written language. Learning how to write, then, involves a conscious effort and specific training, as well as culturally based knowledge and a willingness to learn by trial and error. Thus, this perspective emphasized the importance of environmental factors which shape what the learner will eventually know and learn.

However, this perspective fails to account for how children can produce novel utterances they have never heard before. It also fails to explain instances of regression evident when children are developing their own system of grammar. The fact that children may initially be able to orally produce the word [stop] for *stop*, later regress to [tʰap], and eventually sound more adult-like, is evidence of language regression, a natural phenomenon in the acquisition process. In addition, children are sometimes impervious to adult error correction at various levels, indicating that they do more than simply imitate and repeat adults' utterances.

Nativist/Mentalist Perspective

Unlike the behaviorist view, the nativist believes that language learning is biologically determined. In other words, each person is endowed with an innate ability to learn language. Noam Chomsky, a major influence on this paradigm, refers to our basic innate language learning capacities as the Language Acquisition Device (LAD). This LAD contains general knowledge about the basic properties common to all languages, including phonology and phonological rules, distinctive features, and so forth. Since human beings are already born with this "grammar" in place, little emphasis is given to how environment affects the acquisition process. This view asserts that environment only serves to trigger the LAD which determines what children will acquire.

The nativists also contend that children actively construct grammar for themselves by actively listening to the language around them and trying to determine the patterns in the utterances. For example, a child's initial hypothesis on how to form past tense verbs is to add /-ed/ to all verbs, thus producing forms such as *wented*, *holded*, and *eated*. When they discover that the rule no longer matches the adult form, they will modify or add another rule which will eventually match the adult form. It is for this reason that the nativist perspective is sometimes referred to as the mentalist view.

Another compelling reason for the innate theory is the effect that error correction has on children. As we saw in the first scenario in Chapter 15, a child progresses through language in predictable stages. The child will not respond to error correction if the child is not developmentally ready. Similarly, the child acquires much of his or her language ability before coming to school, thereby supporting the innate structures argument.

Even though nativists and behaviorists differ fundamentally on how much language is innate, they agree that some innate structures are necessary at the initial stages of learning. While the nativist perspective credits children as active learners and recognizes the complexities of the acquisition process, it fails to account for the fact that adults and caregivers do provide children with negative feedback or correction on their production. Several stud-ies have documented that adults correct their children's utterances covertly (Hirsch-Pashek, Treiman and Schneiderman, 1984), as the following example suggests:

Teacher: *What did you see, Maria?*

Maria: *I see baby ducks.*

Teacher: *At the park? You saw baby ducks at the park? How wonderful!*

Therefore, the theory that children simply figure out the rules on their own may lack sufficient support. In addition, recent neurological findings have revealed the importance of mental stimulation through social interaction in stimulating proper brain development, which strengthens other pathways for learning in young children. Children who are not given adequate mental stimulation and opportunities for interaction with adults and peers before puberty may "wire their brains" differently than their counterparts who have rich socialization experiences.

Social Interactionist

Social interactionists believe that human language emerged from the social role that language plays in human interaction. Like the behaviorists, they believe that environment plays a key role and that adults in the child's linguistic environment are instrumental in language acquisition. However, there is a fundamental difference in how the behaviorists and social interactionists view that process. While the behaviorists view learners as empty vessels into which information must be poured, the social interactionists view learners as participants who are actively negotiating meaning with those with whom they interact. Speech between a mother and child or between a native and non-native speaker reveals conversational strategies that focus on the meaningful and intentional use of language, all of which foster language acquisition in young children. One influential advocate of this perspective was the Soviet psychologist Lev Vygotsky (1978). He believed that learners bring two levels of development to their learning: an actual developmental level and a potential developmental level. These two levels are referred to as the Zone of Proximal Development.

Through social interaction, adults and peers can assist learners to move from their zone of actual development to the zone of potential development, by using simplified language, choosing topics that are concrete in the learner's immediate environment, and providing elaboration and clarification so that learners can understand input provided to them.

Figure 17.1 summarizes the basic similarities and differences between the behaviorist, nativist, and social interactionist perspectives.

Brain-Based Principles

Studies have revealed that the human brain is made up of thousands of nerve cells or neurons that form a communication network in the brain. These connections in the brain enable us to process and interpret different kinds of information from many different stimuli, including visual, tactile, oral, auditory, and olfactory (smell). The human brain also has areas that specialize in different cognitive functions. The left brain hemisphere is responsible for analytical reasoning, temporal ordering, and arithmetic and language processing; whereas the right brain hemisphere is in charge of processing non-linguistic sounds, including music and information requiring visual and spatial skills. Scientists have also found that the specialization of cognitive functions in the brain can be reversed at an early age if there is injury to one part of the brain. For example, if a young child suffers an injury to the part of the brain responsible for language processing, the right brain hemisphere can develop that function to compensate for the loss in the left hemisphere. However, individuals who have completed the "hard wiring," or specialization of functions, in the brain cannot re-

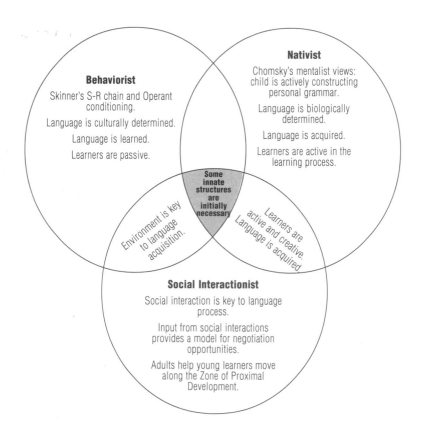

FIGURE 17.1 Venn Diagram which summarizes the salient characteristics of the three language theories.

verse the functions, regardless of the severity of the brain damage.

However, recent discoveries about the brain reveal a profound insight about new windows of opportunity. While important discoveries are being made about the brain as we write, there are sufficient insights about the brain available today to benefit teachers in their efforts to enhance classroom instruction. A study conducted by neuroscientists Joy Hirsch and Karl Kim at the Memorial Sloan-Kettering Cancer Center in New York shed light on how children and adults use different parts of their brains when learning a second language. Using an MRI scanner, brain scans of individuals learning a second language during their adult life and their childhood years, respectively, were taken as they thought aloud about what they had done the day before—first in their first language and then in the second language. Results showed that those who were learning a second language as adults used a distinct region in the Broca's area as their first language, the language processing center for managing speech productions. Those who were learning a second language as children made use of the same area of the Broca to produce speech. Both groups, however, showed similarities in their use of the Wernicke area, the language processing area for understanding and interpreting information. Hirsch explains that the difference between adults and children can be attributed to the way the brain is hard wired. Those who learn another language when they are young may "intertwine sounds and structures from all languages into the same area."("The Bilingual Brain" in *Discover*). Once this hard wiring is complete, new sounds and structures must be processed by a different area of the brain. Researchers also agree that these differences might be caused by the differences in the way young children learn another language as compared to adults.

Findings from brain studies also provide useful information for how teachers can enhance learning by improving their delivery of instruction, by improving student's levels of motivation and active participation, and by eliminating potential barriers to learning. Above all, they underscore the fact that all students have the ability to learn. Caine and Caine (1997; 1991) list several major principles of brain-based knowledge and their applications for language teaching which are summarized in Table 17.1.

PARALLEL DISTRIBUTED PROCESSING

In the past two decades cognitive scientists have compared the human brain's information processing capabilities to those of a computer. Earlier computer metaphors of the brain presuppose that information is taken in, processed in a single central processor in the working memory, and then stored in the long-term memory for future retrieval. This model of a computer-like human brain also assumes that the brain processes information in a sequential or serial manner. However, a group of cognitivists (McClelland, Rumelhart and Hinton, 1986) has proposed that the human brain is capable of processing many kinds of "messy" cognitive tasks on a daily basis and hence developed a model called parallel distributed processing (PDP), a processing system which is similar to the workings of the brain.

In the PDP model, the processing units are compared to the connections between neurons in the brain. When stimulated by the environment, the connections between neurons will be activated, forming a web of association. The PDP proponents reason that humans are far better than computers when considering many pieces of information simultaneously. They contend that processing occurs in parallel forms and proceeds simultaneously along many different dimensions. For example, the reading process does not move from simple decoding to holistic processing for comprehension. Instead, the processes move at many different levels. As we read, we also simultaneously attend to the lines, curves, and angles in letters, the meaning of words, the syntactic structures, our knowledge of the content, our reading purpose, and our attempt to integrate the meanings of new words with the constructed meaning in our memory. In other words, top-down (holistic), bottom-up (decoding), and a combination of top-down and bottom-up processing can occur simultaneously in a single act of reading. While little is known about whether the PDP model will be the "wave of the future" in the cognitive sci-

TABLE 17.1

Brain-based Principles and Their Pedagogical Implications

Principle	Pedagogical Implications
1. The brain is a complex adaptive system. It can simultaneously process many pieces of information.	Instruction that provides a variety of experiences and uses different methods and approaches can activate many different aspects of the brain, thereby increasing learning potential.
2. The brain is a social brain. Learning is influenced by the levels of social interaction with others.	Instruction should include cooperative techniques that encourage student-student interaction and provide opportunities for learners to take more control, work more democratically and cooperatively, and become independent thinkers and explorers.
3. The search for meaning is innate.	Activities and materials presented in a meaningful, relevant, and interesting manner allow students to make the emotional connection which enhances long-term memory. Learning is also enhanced by familiarity with routines and schemes already present in the learners.
4. The brain searches for and generates patterns on any incoming messages.	Instruction that is fun and contains an emotional "hook" will allow the brain to search and create meaning more so than activities that require learners to react passively.
5. Emotions are crucial to memory.	Instruction should not make learners feel physically or emotionally threatened. It should support and validate the abilities, talents, and backgrounds of learners.
6. The brain processes parts and wholes simultaneously.	Language structures and vocabulary are best learned when they are embedded in meaningful contexts of problem solving and activities using natural language.
7. Learning involves both peripheral and focused attention.	Music, art, and other kinds of rich environmental stimuli can support natural language acquisition. Teachers' enthusiasm, acceptance, and sensitivity to learner needs can also send subtle signals that support learner growth.
8. Learning involves both conscious and subconscious processes.	Instruction must allow learners to experience and do something with language, as well as to review what they have learned so that they can reflect, take charge, and negotiate personal meanings.
9. There are at least two types of memory: spatial and rote learning systems. The spatial system is analogous to episodic memory, which stores personal, autobiographical experiences in long-term memory. The rote learning system is akin to memorization of discrete, unrelated bits of information which is motivated by rewards.	Instruction must involve novel experiences that tap into the spatial system and not focus on memorizing language structures. Structures must be contextually introduced through demonstrations, drama, pantomimes, story reading, retelling activities, and so forth.
10. Learning is enhanced by challenging and stimulating instruction. High levels of stress and anxiety may inhibit learning.	Teachers must create a low anxiety classroom by praising learners for their accomplishments, and by utilizing learners' values, knowledge, and background experiences to further learning. They must also maintain reasonably high expectations of their students. Introducing sensory activities can help students tap into their physical abilities as well as their intellectual strengths, and can raise the comfort levels of students.
11. Each brain is unique. Different environments and experiences give individuals their own unique characteristics.	Instruction must include all learners' learning styles and encourage expression of understanding through all senses.

ences, its strong resemblance to certain aspects of human cognition may offer insights into human learning.

SECOND LANGUAGE ACQUISITION THEORIES AND MODELS

So far you have read about the factors and conditions that influence first language acquisition. Do you think that these theories can adequately explain the second language acquisition process? Consider these questions: Why do children acquire second language oral fluency better than adults? Do children learning their first language and children learning their second language go through the same acquisition process? Are the circumstances surrounding children and adults learning a second language the same? Even though the first language acquisition theories may also apply to the second language acquisition process, they may not be able to fully capture the complexity of a second language acquisition process. First language acquisition theories are not sufficiently equipped to explain the degrees of levels of success that second language learners achieve. The following section offers other models and theories that examine factors and circumstances which can influence second language acquisition.

Krashen's Monitor Model

Some scholars refer to Stephen Krashen as an armchair theorist, although his second language acquisition model appeals to many. In his Monitor Model, Krashen outlines five hypotheses: (1) Acquisition vs. Learning Hypothesis, (2) The Natural Order Hypothesis, (3) The Monitor Hypothesis, (4) The Input Hypothesis, and (5) The Affective Filter Hypothesis. There are many implications for the classroom that can be drawn from Krashen's Monitor Model. For instance, Krashen uses the metaphor of a filter that facilitates or hinders learning. When students are placed in a safe, secure, and caring environment that challenges them to learn, the affective filter will be lowered and, according to Krashen, learning will take place. But when the learning environment is threatening, full of anxiety, and is not challenging enough, the affective filter will be raised and learning will be blocked. Refer to Figure 17.2 for explanation and application of Krashen's Monitor Model.

Cummins' Second Language Framework

Jim Cummins (1981) makes a distinction between social language and academic language. Social language refers to everyday conversational language which is context embedded—supported by the use of illustrations, realia, demonstrations, and so forth. Studies have shown that second language learners acquire social language in approximately two years and academic language in five to seven years. Since social language deals with the here-and-now language, second language speakers tend to acquire it faster than they acquire academic language, the language of school tasks which is more abstract and decontextualized. Communication involving academic language is harder because it is context-reduced (little or no context clues).

Teachers may find it puzzling that ELLs who maintain fluent spoken English have difficulties in reading and writing. This can be explained by Cummins' second language framework that differentiated students' social language and academic language. Refer to Cummins' four quadrants for appropriate tasks and strategies to help ELLs at varying proficiency levels move from social language (quadrant 1) to academic language (quadrant 4) (Refer to table). In Table 17.2 several examples of specific strategies at different stages of language proficiency are listed. In quadrant 1, strategies such as developing survival vocabulary and following demonstrated directions are cognitively undemanding (easy) and contain high contextual clues. These activities are best employed when teaching second language learners who are at the pre-production or early production stage of language acquisition. As these learners become more proficient in the target language, teachers can gradually increase the degree of task difficulty, activities from Cummins' quadrants 2 and 3 can be used. Activities in quadrant 4, such as understanding academic presentations without visuals or demonstrations, lectures, and making

HYPOTHESES	APPLICATIONS
The Affective Filter Emotional variables such as anxiety, motivation, and self-confidence play a part in language acquisition.	A safe and secure environment Cooperative learning, mutual respect, and high expectations
The Input Hypothesis Language is acquired when learners understand messages (comprehensible input). They must be exposed to messages a bit beyond their level of proficiency, i.e., i +1.	Teachers should provide comprehensible input in many forms, e.g., use of visuals, less complex structures, paraphrases, slower and more enunciated speech. E.g., students understand messages with "unacquired" grammar with the help of context.
The Monitor An error-detecting mechanism that is responsible for accuracy. It is an editor that confirms or repairs student utterances. There are three types: optimal, overusers, and underusers. Overusers refer to conscious grammar all the time. Underusers do not refer to their conscious grammar at all, and optimal users monitor when to focus on form.	Students may not internalize teachers' explicit corrections because of their developing grammatical system. Therefore a teacher's modeling of correct sentences provides a rich input for students to use later in developing and monitoring accuracy in speech and writing. In addition, students should be given time to detect and self-correct their errors. Hence, teachers should focus more on correcting students' errors in writing by giving ample time for students to review their written productions and maximize their use of the monitor for error correction.
The Natural Order Hypothesis Certain rules within a language are acquired before others. Correct usage of grammatical structures is acquired gradually by children acquiring their first and/or second language.	Grammatical structures need not be the center of curriculum organization. Problem-solving structures will promote acquiring of rules.
Acquisition vs. Learning Learning = formal knowledge of a language (rules). Acquisition = language acquired at the subconscious level (child's acquiring his first language).	Communicating meaning is more important than drill and practice. Learners are given time to internalize language before they respond. Partial and incomplete utterances are acceptable.

FIGURE 17.2 Krashen's Monitor Model

formal oral presentations, are examples of cognitively demanding tasks that are context-reduced; i.e., offer few or no clues. These types of tasks are meant for high intermediate and advanced second language learners.

Cummins also argues for the significance of common underlying proficiency (CUP) in second language learning as opposed to separate underlying proficiency (SUP) which assumes that content and skills learned in the primary language will not transfer to the target language. Cummins' theory of CUP implies that knowledge and literacy skills in a student's native language will transfer to his or her learning of a target language. In other words, children learning to read and write Mandarin Chinese develop concepts about print and the role of literacy that make learning to read and write English easier, even though Mandarin Chinese and English do not share a similar writing system. Cummins strongly asserts that once children build a strong foundation in the native language, learning a second language, as well as learning in general, readily builds upon this foundation. Bilingual education is based on the above assumptions about learning.

McLaughlin's Attention-Processing Model

McLaughlin and Bialystok, proponents of cognitivist theory in the second language acquisition field, have criticized Krashen for his "simplistic account" of conscious versus subconscious processes in the acquisition versus learning hypothesis. McLaughlin and Bialystok argued that for knowledge to be stored in the long-term memory, learners have to be aware of this knowledge; this conflicts with Krashen's notion that acquisition takes place in the subconscious mode and learning takes place in the conscious mode. Following McLaughlin's argument, learners who "acquire" as opposed to "learn" a second language must have a certain level of

TABLE 17.2

Language and Content Activities within Cummins' Quadrants

Cognitively Undemanding (Easy)

	A		**C**
	◯ Developing survival vocabulary		◯ Engaging in telephone conversations
	◯ Following demonstrated directions		◯ Reading and writing for personal purposes: notes, lists, sketches, etc.
	◯ Playing simple games		
	◯ Engaging in face-to-face interactions		
	◯ Participating in art, music, and physical education		

Context-Embedded (Clues) ←→ *Context-Reduced (No Clues)*

	B		**D**
	◯ Participating in hands-on science and mathematics activities		◯ Understanding academic presentations without visuals or demonstrations: lectures
	◯ Making maps, models, charts, and graphs		◯ Making formal oral presentations
	◯ Solving math computational problems		◯ Solving math word problems without illustrations
	◯ Making brief oral presentations		◯ Writing compositions, essays, and research reports in content areas
	◯ Understanding academic presentations through the use of visuals, demonstrations, active participation, realia, etc.		◯ Reading for information in content areas
	◯ Understanding written texts through discussion, illustrations, and visuals		◯ Taking standardized achievement texts
	◯ Writing academic reports with the aid of outlines, structures, etc.		

Cognitively Demanding (Hard)

(Adapted from Chamot and O'Malley, 1987; Cummins, 1981)

awareness, i.e., operate at a conscious level; it cannot all be subconscious.

In their model of the second language learning process, McLaughlin and his colleagues prefer the terms controlled and automatic processing mechanisms to Krashen's acquisition versus learning distinction. McLaughlin defines the controlled processing mechanism as a limited and temporary capacity, while the automatic processing mechanism is referred to as "relatively permanent" processes (McLaughlin et al. 1983:142). An example of controlled processing is the learning of a new skill, such as soccer. When one first learns to play soccer, one can deal only with the basic elements of kicking the ball, passing the ball to another player, or defending the ball from being taken away by the opponent. Everything else about the game is far too complicated for the beginner's limited capacity.

Meanwhile, automatic processing, according to McLaughlin, is similar to what expert learners do. The expert learner can manage many types of information simultaneously because certain sub-skills have become automatic. However, learners with limited linguistic capacity may not be able to juggle as much linguistic information simultaneously. Learners who have developed expert skills are able to manage processing of a more "accomplished" skill where the hard drive of their brain can manage hundreds and thousands of bits of information simultaneously. For example, language proficient learners may do several things at once while understanding and sending verbal messages in a conversation. They pay attention to selective words and try to find a match between the sounds they hear and the words in their mental lexicon; they pick up intonation cues to interpret messages, and assess a speaker's purpose, body language, and setting to fill in gaps in understanding; finally they apply appropriate discourse rules based on their knowledge of the setting in giving their responses. Because proficient language users have a more developed grammar and vocabulary system, they are able to attend to other aspects of the communication system that less proficient language learners are not. McLaughlin and others also maintain that these two types of processing skills may utilize peripheral attention (similar to inductive learning) and focal attention (similar to deductive learning).

Their view of controlled and automatic processing has several implications for the second language classroom. One implication can be demonstrated by how a child acquires language. Children generally do not pay attention to the learning of forms or grammatical rules; instead, their focus is on communication of meaning. For instance, in kindergarten and lower grade classrooms, children are exposed to a rich print environment and contextually embedded language that encourage children to internalize language naturally.

Another implication of McLaughlin's model can be seen in how adults learn a second language. Unlike young children, older second language learners may be able to articulate rules and analyze language, but may not be able to transfer this knowledge to communicative situations that require the use of such knowledge. Language instruction for older children and adults tends to emphasize learning of rules and vocabulary pertinent to their program of study. This is normally expected, because older learners are cognitively more mature and have the learning experience to analyze and understand rules. As such, they may be more receptive than children to classrooms that focus on rule learning, an unnatural context for language learning. Newer proponents in the second language field maintain that language can be acquired without explicit focus on forms. They stress that language can be internalized if learners are exposed to meaningful and authentic language through engaging learner-oriented activities appropriate to the students' language developmental process. In other words, communication should be the goal of any language instruction.

Bialystok's Analysis/Automaticity Model

Bialystok's model of second language learning is similar in many ways to McLaughlin's in that they both emphasize the importance of introducing authentic and contextually embedded language through meaningful activities. But Bialystok's model goes further in accounting for how automatic processing is accomplished by second language learners.

Bialystok maintains that language processing involves the use of both explicit and implicit knowledge. Explicit knowledge refers to a person's knowledge about a language and their ability to articulate that knowledge. Implicit knowledge refers to information that is automatically and spontaneously used in language tasks. According to Bialystok, the distinction between automatic and spontaneous processing refers to the relative access the learner has to both of these forms of knowledge. This access hinges on the learner's control, defined as "the ability to intentionally focus attention on relevant parts of a problem to arrive at a solution" (Bialystok and Mitterer 1987:148). An example of how control affects language processing is demonstrated by the performance of native and highly proficient non-native speakers. Whether native speakers can or cannot provide an analysis of their explicit knowledge of their L1 grammar, all native speakers can automatically and spontaneously process and produce utterances in their L1. On the other hand, non-native speakers may be able to analyze and explain L2 grammar, but may go through a time delay in the production of L2 because they are less experienced with their second language than L1 speakers are with their first language.

In other words, second language learners need more time to process linguistic input because they have to move back and forth between explicit and implicit knowledge of the language in interpreting linguistic messages. This insight underscores the need for teachers to be patient with second language learners, giving them ample time to process verbal messages—especially those communicated orally. Teachers also need to include a variety of elicitation techniques appropriate for learners at different stages of linguistic proficiency. These include dialogue journals or reading response logs, in addition to asking students to respond orally in class.

What practical applications for the second language classroom can be drawn from McLaughlin's and Bialystok's models? Both McLaughlin and Bialystok suggest that the ultimate goal of using language is to communicate, and therefore, second language learning should focus more on meaning and not on form. While second language learners should be introduced to graded complexity of language structures, explicit teaching of forms should be done at a peripheral level. Once learners become engaged in activities that encourage them to use language in a purposeful and meaningful way, they will eventually learn the forms of the language. (See Table 17.3.)

It appears that McLaughlin and Bialystok see parallels between controlled/focal attention and Krashen's conscious learning of a language in addi-

TABLE 17.3

Practical Applications of McLaughlin's and Bialystok's Models

	Controlled	Automatic
	new knowledge; limited capacity	well trained, capacity is practically unlimited
Focal intentional attention	grammatical explanation word definition copy a written model "memorizing" a dialogue prefabricated patterns	scanning editing, peer-editing advanced L2 learner focuses on models, clause formation, etc.
Peripheral incidental attention	simple greetings TPR/Natural approach new L2 learner fully completes a brief conversation	open-ended group work rapid reading, skimming free writes normal conversational exchanges of some length

Source: Brown, 1994: 285.

tion to similarities between peripheral/automatic cell processing and Krashen's acquisition route, a subconscious process of language acquisition.

SELINKER'S INTERLANGUAGE THEORY

Selinker's 1972 Interlanguage theory maintains the separateness of a second language learner's system and gives the system a structurally intermediate status between the native and target languages. According to Selinker, second language learners are producing their own self-contained linguistic system. The system is not a native language system, nor the target language system, rather it falls between the two. It is the best system that the second language learner possesses to provide order and structure to linguistic stimuli (see Figure 17.3).

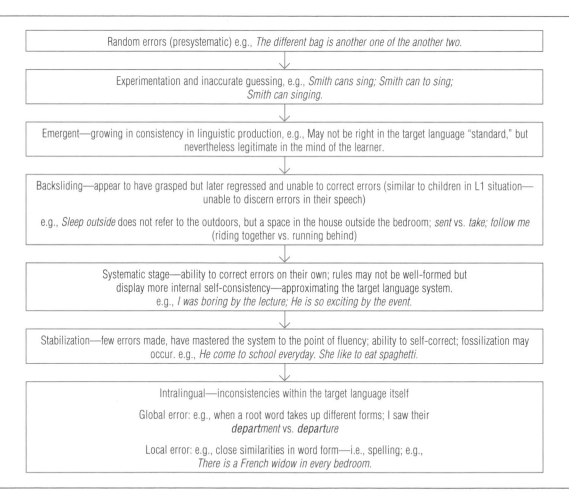

Random errors (presystematic) e.g., *The different bag is another one of the another two.*

↓

Experimentation and inaccurate guessing, e.g., *Smith cans sing; Smith can to sing; Smith can singing.*

↓

Emergent—growing in consistency in linguistic production, e.g., May not be right in the target language "standard," but nevertheless legitimate in the mind of the learner.

↓

Backsliding—appear to have grasped but later regressed and unable to correct errors (similar to children in L1 situation—unable to discern errors in their speech)

e.g., *Sleep outside* does not refer to the outdoors, but a space in the house outside the bedroom; *sent* vs. *take; follow me* (riding together vs. running behind)

↓

Systematic stage—ability to correct errors on their own; rules may not be well-formed but display more internal self-consistency—approximating the target language system.
e.g., *I was boring by the lecture; He is so exciting by the event.*

↓

Stabilization—few errors made, have mastered the system to the point of fluency; ability to self-correct; fossilization may occur. e.g., *He come to school everyday. She like to eat spaghetti.*

↓

Intralingual—inconsistencies within the target language itself

Global error: e.g., when a root word takes up different forms; I saw their
*depart*ment vs. *departure*

Local error: e.g., close similarities in word form—i.e., spelling; e.g.,
There is a French widow in every bedroom.

FIGURE 17.3 Stages of Interlanguage Development

✓ Children's first language acquisition occurs in developmental stages. At the phonological level, sounds that are easier to produce will be acquired first. Grammatical morphemes and syntactic structures are acquired in a predictable order.

✓ Children do not simply imitate adults' speech or memorize rules or vocabulary. They develop their own internal system of grammar by testing the rules out themselves, applying them, and later modifying their grammar to match that of adults.

✓ The behaviorist theory maintains that language must be taught and learned through frequent practice, training, and reinforcement. It places heavy emphasis on the role of the learner's linguistic environment as a primary source for influencing language acquisition.

✓ The nativist maintains that all humans have an innate capacity to learn a language. The child's linguistic environment triggers the innate language capacity, or the LAD, and plays a minor role in language acquisition. Children are actively constructing their own grammar, as evidenced by their unresponsiveness to adults' error correction and their novel productions.

✓ The social interactionist emphasizes the role of social interaction in language acquisition. Adults provide scaffolds by modifying their speech, using more concrete references, correcting errors through modeling and examples, negotiating meanings, and expanding on children's productions. These factors promote language acquisition.

✓ Brain-based theories stress that language learning is more than just a cognitive function. These highlight how factors such as affective filters, comprehensible input embedded in meaningful contexts, background experience, and learning approaches influence language acquisition.

✓ Krashen's Monitor Model consists of five hypotheses: the Acquisition versus Learning hypothesis, the Natural Order hypothesis, the Input hypothesis, the Monitor hypothesis, and the Affective Filter hypothesis.

✓ The term "social language" refers to everyday conversational language. It is supported by contextual clues. Second language learners acquire this skill level within two years.

✓ Academic language is the language of school tasks that are usually abstract and decontextualized. Second language learners take five to seven years to acquire CALP.

✓ It is important for teachers to understand that second language learners who have good conversational skills (BICS) may still have difficulties in performing their school-related tasks (CALP).

✓ Teachers should design and use activities within Cummins' four quadrants to advance students from the level of language proficiency they are in (e.g., for pre-production and early production, use activities such as developing survival vocabulary, playing simple games, and engaging in face-to-face interactions before asking students to write or orally present on topics containing complex concepts and language).

✓ McLaughlin, in his second language learning model, makes a distinction between controlled and automatic processing. Controlled processing is limited and temporary, while automatic processing tends to be permanent and is more adept at processing more information.

(continued)

✓ Bialystok's model focuses on the distinction between explicit and implicit knowledge. Explicit knowledge refers to a person's knowledge about a language and the ability to articulate it, while implicit knowledge refers to knowledge that is automatically and spontaneously used in language tasks. This model focuses on the element of control.

✓ Both McLaughlin's and Bialystok's models suggest that because the ultimate goal in using language is to communicate, learning or acquiring a language should emphasize meaning instead of form.

✓ Selinker's Interlanguage Theory proposes that second language learners produce their own self-contained system that falls somewhere between the L1 and the L2 systems.

Chapter 18

Meeting the Needs of English Language Learners

Key Issues

- ○ Challenges twenty-first century teachers face in meeting the needs of English language learners

- ○ Approaches to attaining and organizing background information to help meet the needs of ELLs

- ○ Stages in second language acquisition

- ○ ESL strategies to employ in the classroom

SCENARIO

On a bright sunny morning, the school secretary walked into Ms. Clark's first grade class with a new student. She said: "This is Ika, Ms. Clark. She's been assigned to your class. She doesn't speak any English. Her parents just arrived from Russia this week." "Welcome, Ika!" said Ms. Clark, taking Ika by the hand and making a place for her on the floor next to herself. Ika became the eighth English language learner in Ms. Clark's class of 32. Unfortunately, none of the other ELLs speak Russian, though Ms. Clark has four other languages represented in her class, and she speaks only English!

Meeting the needs of a multilingual population is not an easy task for any teacher. Because diversity seems to be the norm rather than the exception in today's society, teachers are continuously challenged to find ways to be effective in their everyday teaching.

BEST PRACTICES FOR ELL INSTRUCTION

In a review of the research on characteristics and optimal conditions in schools and classrooms for ELLs, the following best practices were listed:

○ a supportive school-wide climate
○ a customized learning environment
○ articulation and coordination within and between schools
○ the use of native language and culture in instruction
○ a balanced curriculum that includes both basic and higher-order skills
○ explicit skill instruction
○ opportunities for student-directed instruction
○ use of instructional strategies that enhance understanding
○ opportunities for ELLs to employ language in meaningful contexts
○ systematic valid and reliable student assessment
○ staff development in effective ESL instruction
○ home and parent involvement

(August and Hakuta, 1997a)

In addition to the above, teachers must provide a meaningfully based context-rich and cognitively demanding curriculum. In the American Educational Research Association (2004) published piece on boosting academic achievement of ELLs in terms of literacy, the following critical components are provided: (1) explicit instruction in word recognition through phonological awareness, practice reading, phonics, and frequent in-class assessment; and (2) explicit instruction in skills that are needed to comprehend the text, such as vocabulary building in context, strategies to aid comprehension, and academic oral language development.

One of the major understandings that practitioners and scholars have reached is that ELLs cannot be provided special assistance only in the English language. Other assistance such as bilingual education, richer and more sustained collaboration between content area teachers and English language specialists, specifically designed academic instruction in English (SDAIE), and/or sheltered English instruction must also be considered (Varghese, 2005). Other best practices found in the literature include:

○ integrating language and content instruction
○ lessons and units that foster concept development, practice, and application
○ building background knowledge by providing concrete experiences
○ ensuring that textbooks and trade books are at the students' instructional level

- balanced literacy instruction
- cooperative/interactive learning
- providing a caring and trusting environment
- addressing learning styles and multiple intelligences

(Violand-Sanchez, 2005)

In her article, "Success for Second Language Learners" (1991), Lisa Johnson, a teacher, discusses basic approaches to organizing information and background material that can serve as a foundation for understanding ELLs' needs and for helping them to grow and develop. She discusses two broad categories: "Getting Set" and "In the Classroom" as detailed below.

Getting Set

- Finding out how much school experience the English language learner has had.
- Determining the student's English language proficiency level.
- Keeping a record of the information attained to have a baseline measurement when later assessing the student's academic and language growth.
- Employing the "buddy system" to pair a newcomer with a student from the same language background who has already developed some English language competency.
- When a buddy is not available in the same classroom, looking in other classrooms or among adults in the school to provide at least some emotional support for the newcomer.
- Learning as much as possible about the student's cultural background, traditions, and behavior patterns. This information may be obtained with the aid of the school's media specialist, the school district's office of multicultural affairs, county ESL or bilingual teachers, the public library, as well as from parents, siblings, and community members who share the same linguistic background.
- Respecting the silent period of newcomers. This is a time when students are observing and internalizing new language meanings and patterns.

During this time, involve them in activities where they respond non-verbally, such as total physical response (TPR). They will begin to speak when they are ready.

In the Classroom

- Employing the thematic approach to teaching lessons/units. These provide ample opportunity for English language learners to be immersed in the related language for a longer period of time, thus allowing students to be involved with the same concepts, vocabulary, and language structures in different contexts. This reinforcement gives the repetition these students need without becoming simply "rote" memorization of facts.
- Engaging students in many activity-oriented and hands-on experiences provides concrete experiences that makes input much more comprehensible for English language learners.
- Emphasizing small group work and teamwork allows all students to contribute at their own levels. Small group activities also encourage ELLs to share in a less threatening environment. Teams/small groups must be balanced, taking into consideration ELL's English language development.
- Providing a "print rich" environment, yet ensuring that it is comprehensible to the students. Labeling everything in the classrooms is an excellent way to provide this "comprehensible input." Word lists (with pictures) of vocabulary/concepts are also helpful in providing a print rich environment.
- Setting time aside to read to the students, making sure numerous pictures and objects are used to introduce and clarify new vocabulary/concepts. Big books, predictable books, and pattern books are particularly effective for ELLs.
- Welcoming the richness of cultural diversity in the classroom. Using ELLs' places of origin as part of social studies units gives geography, for example, a new meaning. It is a golden opportunity for native speakers to learn about different parts of the world in a more meaningful way.

○ Studying art, music, cuisine, and the language(s) of the cultures represented in the classroom. Examining many cultures is a way to help students recognize and value similarities and differences among cultural groups.

○ Reading multicultural versions of the same fairy tale is a great way to learn about these cultures, as it helps students to realize the common elements as well as the differences.

○ Using charts and graphs helps English language learners understand new concepts while acquiring the English language. Charts and graphs help make the input comprehensible because they are less dependent on language.

Diversity in the classroom poses significant challenges to teachers nationwide. The traditional teacher role of imparting knowledge to a homogeneous group of students is a thing of the past. All teachers today are language teachers. The teaching of all subjects, i.e., social studies, science, or mathematics, is attached to the need to develop language before the students can acquire historical, scientific, and mathematical knowledge and concepts.

As mentioned in Chapter 17, English language learners progress through similar second language developmental stages, although they vary greatly in their acquisition of the new language. This places tremendous demands on teachers who teach ELLs. To meet these demands, teachers must develop a greater understanding of the complexity of second language acquisition and be cognizant of specific strategies needed to effectively meet the needs of English language learners.

SECOND LANGUAGE ACQUISITION

There are four stages in oral language development:

1. **Silent, pre-production, or comprehension stage**
   a. This stage is similar to the period of time that infants (from birth to approximately nine or ten months) are listening and interacting with those around them in a non-verbal fashion.
   b. Pre-production is used to describe the phase similar to that of the period when infants do not yet produce language.
   c. Comprehension equates with the fact that infants and toddlers initially comprehend much more language than they are able to produce; comprehension precedes production.

2. **Early speech emergence**
   Language begins to emerge slowly; one-word sentences, then two-word sentences, and then simple grammatical structures are employed.

3. **Speech emergence**
   Language continues to evolve; phrases and short sentences are employed.

4. **Intermediate fluency**
   More complex language is employed; the learner engages in discourse. The use of more complex sentences is evident.

There is a sequential order in which language develops: (1) listening, (2) speaking, (3) reading, and (4) writing. What implications does this theoretical knowledge have for classroom teachers in the twenty-first century?

Stages of Language Development and Teaching Strategies

1. Teachers will have students in their classrooms who are in the "silent period." Though these students are not speaking English yet, they are being exposed to the language constantly while at school. However, this language needs to be made "comprehensible" for them to begin to understand what is being said. There are a series of language modifications teachers can employ to make their input "comprehensible." The ESOL literature refers to these as "motherese" or "parentese" because they are associated with

what mothers or caregivers do when communicating with babies. These are:

○ Use of simple language
○ Use of gestures, facial expressions
○ Slowing down
○ Enunciating clearly
○ Repeating
○ Rephrasing

In addition to the use of motherese/parentese, teachers must use visuals such as pictures, objects, realia, charts, and graphs to ensure that the input they are providing non-English speakers is comprehensible.

2. During the silent period, English language learners can be involved in lessons. Although they are not yet speaking, they can respond non-verbally to commands given by the teacher. The use of pictures, objects, and realia are excellent ways to get students involved in this fashion. The teacher may ask students to sort pictures, arrange objects, or select specific pictures/objects to ascertain their comprehension of the lesson presented. For example, the teacher may ask students to select pictures of the famous monuments in Washington, D.C. described in the lesson, or to select pictures that show the House of Representatives and the Senate after studying U.S. government. In this way students can participate in lessons before they speak any English. This helps develop a positive self-concept because students feel successful when they are able to be involved in the lessons, though their oral language development is still very limited.

3. Using pictures, objects, and realia is also necessary when introducing new vocabulary in context, since there is much vocabulary students will need to acquire knowledge and concepts. Visuals help students attach meaning to what is being said. They make "input comprehensible" (Krashen, 1981). Another way of encouraging comprehensible input is by simplifying the language and language structures employed in instruction. Repeating key points in different contexts is very effective, as is rephrasing what has been said. Some teachers have a tendency to speak fast; slowing down is essential. These "sheltering" techniques are essential when teaching second language learners.

The following are effective strategies for involving students who are in the "early speech emergence stage":

○ asking questions that require only a yes/no answer:
 Is this the Washington Monument?
 Is this the House of Representatives?

○ asking either/or type questions:
 Is this the Washington Monument or the Lincoln Monument?
 Is this the House or the Senate?

○ asking short answer questions that can be answered with one or two words.

As ELLs develop more language, teachers can continue to involve them in activities that require more complex language and language structures.

Meeting the needs of the students in today's classrooms requires teachers to modify their teaching strategies by incorporating second language acquisition techniques. Modifying the language employed to conduct lessons, using visuals, and involving students in lessons by allowing them to respond non-verbally while in the silent stage are effective strategies. By employing these strategies in their classrooms, teachers will begin to make a positive impact in meeting the needs of their diverse student population.

✓ Background information teachers acquire about their students is necessary and helpful in providing for their needs.

✓ English language learners progress through similar second language developmental stages.

✓ There are four stages in oral language development: pre-production, early speech emergence, speech emergence, and intermediate fluency.

✓ Using visuals, modifying the language employed to teach lessons, and involving students by having them respond non-verbally in the initial stages of second language development are all excellent ways of meeting the needs of second language learners.

✓ Motherese/parentese strategies include: use of simple language, use of gestures and facial expression to convey meaning, slowing down, enunciating clearly, repeating, and rephrasing.

✓ There are numerous modifications teachers must make to provide the optimum learning environment for ELLs.

Chapter 19

Strategies and Styles

Key Issues

- ○ Differences between learning strategies and styles
- ○ Role of strategies and styles in language acquisition
- ○ Communication strategies
- ○ The Cognitive Academic Language Learning Approach (CALLA)
- ○ Gardner's Multiple Intelligences
- ○ Classroom application of styles and strategies

SCENARIO

A teacher is doing a shared/modeled writing activity with a group of second graders in a mainstream classroom. There are some ESL learners in the class. Today, the teacher, Mrs. Abrams (T), will demonstrate to the students (S1, S2, and so on) how she composes by thinking aloud about the steps she takes and the decisions she makes as she writes.

T: *Children, last week we read a story about a little boy's favorite person, who happens to be his hero. We also discussed what makes a person a hero and why. Well, today we are going to write about our own personal hero. Let's write this together.*

Now where do I begin?

Maybe we should name one person whom we admire most. Then we will list some reasons why we like the person. OK, whom do you admire most?

(Students shout several answers: Michael Jordan, Pokémon Pikachu, grandfather, etc. Since there are many suggestions, the students are asked to vote on someone they all agree to be a hero. Finally everyone agrees on Michael Jordan as their hero.)

T: *What makes Michael Jordan a hero?*

S1: *He plays good basketball. He can jump very high.*

T: *OK. I will draw a circle and write "Plays basketball well," and "He can jump," in each circle. Does anyone know if "basketball" is one word or two words?*

S2: *Two words.*

S1: *No, it is one word.*

T: *Maybe, we will write it as two words now. Later, we will check to see if we are correct. Now, what else do we like about Michael Jordan?*

S3: *He is very funny. I like his movie* Space Jam.

S4: *I laughed so hard when I watch this movie.*

T: *OK, we will draw another circle, and inside it we will write, "funny."*

What observations did you make while reading this scenario?

What are some general approaches the class is learning to use to process information before they begin to write? The teacher is highlighting several different strategies for organizing and generating ideas before writing. She also will demonstrate the use of "wordweb," a graphic organizer to help students focus, generate, and organize ideas, instead of concentrating on grammar and mechanics. In other words, the teacher is modeling brainstorming strategies in the pre-writing stage. Does this influence how learners process and understand information? What type of learners would benefit most from the teacher's use of a wordweb and verbal explanations?

Now reflect on the strategies you have used or still use when learning to read and write in your first language and in another language. Do you apply the same strategies in all learning situations? What type of a learner are you? What kind of instruction inhibits or promotes your ability to learn effectively?

STRATEGIES

What Are Learning Strategies?

Second and foreign language educators have been seeking ways to help learners in their efforts to be successful in learning and communicating in their target language. These efforts have brought about much discussion regarding how learning strategies can provide positive support to students in their attempts to learn a new language. First of all, there are several definitions of learning strategies. According to McDonough (1995:3), "language learning strategies are used with the explicit goal of helping learners improve their knowledge and understanding of a target language. They are the conscious thoughts and behaviors used by students to facilitate language learning tasks and to personalize the language learning process." Operationally defined, learning strategies are "the strategic techniques used by language learners to comprehend and process new information more deeply, to help to recall old information, and to apply knowledge and skills to facilitate problem-solving" (Nyikos, 1991). They are the tools we use to

make learning more effective, engaging, and rapid. According to Stern (1992:261), "the concept of learning strategy is dependent on the assumption that learners consciously engage in activities to achieve certain goals and learning strategies can be regarded as broadly conceived intentional directions and learning techniques."

Schmidt (1994) and Cohen (1996a) further explained that all language learners use language learning strategies either consciously or unconsciously when processing new information and performing tasks in the language classroom. However, if learners are unable to identify any strategies associated with the task at hand, then the behavior would simply be referred to as a process, not a strategy. For example, a learner may use the behavior of skimming the title, headings, and subheadings of a text or previewing pictures to get an overall idea before doing a close reading of a text. If the learner is at all conscious (even if peripherally) as to why the previewing is taking place, then it would be a strategy. Since language classroom is like a problem-solving environment in which language learners are likely to face new input and difficult tasks given by their instructors, learners' attempts to find the quickest or easiest way to do what is required, that is, using language learning strategies, is inescapable. Many research studies in the field of learning strategies for foreign language and second language learning (Brown 1989; Cohen, 1990; O'Malley and Chamot, 1990; Oxford, 1990; Nyikos, 1991) have underscored the fact that language learning is a very complex cognitive skill and have linked the use of appropriate strategies to successful language performance (Rubin, 1975; Wenden, 1985). In order for students to become competent in a new language, they must be given the tools needed for effective learning.

What Are Communication Strategies?

While learning strategies are typically strategies we use for processing input, communication strategies are verbal and non-verbal strategies for producing clear messages in the second language. As we know, language processing may involve both comprehension and production simultaneously (Tarone, 1981), thus making it difficult to separate the two.

However, these distinctions illuminate the nature of communication. Figures 19.1, 19.2, 19.3, and 19.4 provide taxonomies for the two types of strategies: learning and communication strategies.

Few studies have looked at the explicit relationship between strategy instruction and second learners' performance in the target language. In his study of the effects of strategy instruction on high school students in Hungary who were learning English as a foreign language, Dörnyei (1995:80) found that explicit instruction on three communication strategies (topic avoidance and replacement, circumlocution, and fillers and hesitation devices) "provides these learners with a sense of security in the L2 by allowing them room to maneuver in times of difficulty. Rather than giving up their message, learners may decide to try and remain in the conversation and achieve their communicative goal." Cohen (1996b) went beyond the limited number of specific communication strategies used in Dörnyei's study (1995) and found that instruction in communication strategy was beneficial when learners are engaged in discussions of speaking strategies, given the opportunity to review checklists of possible strategies, and practice those strategies in class. He added that learners should work on developing their own list of strategies that they will use in different language learning and using situations.

How can understanding learning and communication strategies be helpful in second language classroom learning? One of our most important goals is to train learners to become autonomous by showing them the "how to" of learning a language in the most efficient and productive way. Because ESL learners have varied experiences, training, and linguistic proficiencies, teachers are in a better position to help them if they understand a myriad of effective strategies and apply them in their teaching techniques and materials. Of course teachers should not force learners to adopt specific strategies and cannot expect all learners to immediately embrace all strategies; some students may bring preconceived ideas about what instruction should be like,

based on their previous training (Bialystok, 1985). In addition, learners may forget the effective strategies they use consciously or unconsciously or be unsure of strategies they used when learning their L1 which can be transferred to L2. Consequently, they may not be able to make the transfer. It is vital, then, that these strategies be revived through instruction and guided practice. Ultimately, strategic instruction will offer students opportunities to practice an array of effective strategies from which to choose when they encounter different classroom tasks and life situations. The instructional strategy CALLA was developed for the sole purpose of providing learners with tools to learn.

CALLA LEARNING STRATEGIES

While the Natural Approach and TPR (Total Physical Response) promote the acquisition of social language, CALLA (Cognitive Academic Language Learning Approach) is a strategy that promotes the acquisition of academic language. Chamot and O'Malley (1994), the creators of CALLA, intended it to help second language learners become autonomous learners by empowering them to achieve academically. CALLA integrates content (the core curriculum's key concepts and ideas), language (the language needed to access the content), and strategies (students' own use of special techniques to help them learn).

CALLA learning strategies are divided into three strategic categories: metacognitive, cognitive, and social affective.

A. Metacognitive Strategies

There are five sub-categories of metacognitive strategies: advanced organization, advanced preparation, organizational planning, selective attention, and self-evaluation. Figure 19.1 outlines each metacognitive strategy.

Advanced Organization
(Preview main ideas and concepts of the material to be learned by skimming the text for organization)

Advanced Preparation
(Rehearse the language needed for oral and written tasks)

Organizational Planning
(Plan the parts, sequence, and main ideas to be expressed orally or in writing)

Selective Attention
(Attend to or scan key words, phrases, linguistic markers, sentences, or types of information)

Self-Evaluation
(Judge how well one has accomplished a learning activity after it has been completed)

FIGURE 19.1 Metacognitive Strategies

SCENARIO

1 Application of Metacognitive Strategies

Ms. Lott's second grade class has been reading a series of stories on a related theme—geographical locations. The students have read "Buffy's Orange Leash" which takes place in the United States, "Soccer Sam," which takes place in Mexico, and "Nessa's Fish," which takes place in the Arctic. Today they will be reading a story, "Slippery Ice," which takes place in Antarctica. Before the students read the story, Ms. Lott previews main ideas and concepts by reviewing the locations of past stories on a world map, using an overhead transparency. Student volunteers locate Antarctica on the world map. Then Ms. Lott rehearses the language needed for oral and written tasks by displaying a pocket chart consisting of words that describe penguin actions (taken from the story). Students will act out the actions as they read the story. Next, they will create a song to the "Twinkle, Twinkle Little Star" tune, using all the words they have learned about penguins. Ms. Lott helps students select key words and phrases by displaying a penguin poster and distributing cards in the shape of a fish to help students concretize concepts related to penguins. On this card, each student writes a word that retells the story he or she has read. Students will then organize the word cards on the poster around the penguin creating a wordweb. After students have read the story and related activities have been completed, Ms. Lott asks students what they have learned from the story. She also asks what learning activities they liked best and why.

The teacher in the previous scenario used all five sub-categories of metacognitive strategies. Can you locate them?

B. Cognitive Strategies

There are nine sub-categories of cognitive strategies: contextualization, elaboration, grouping, imagery, inferencing, note-taking, resourcing, summarizing, and transfer.

Figure 19.2 illustrates the sub-categories of cognitive strategies.

Contextualization
(Place a word or phrase in a meaningful sentence or category)

Elaboration
(Relate new information to what is already known)

Grouping
(Classify words, terminology, or concepts according to their attributes)

Imagery
(Use visual images—mental or actual—to understand and remember new information)

Inferencing
(Guess meanings of new items from text, predict outcomes, or complete missing parts)

Note-taking
(Write down key words and concepts during reading or listening activities)

Resourcing
(Use reference materials such as dictionaries, encyclopedias, or textbooks)

Summarizing
(Make a mental or written summary of information gained through listening or reading)

Transfer
(Use what is already known to facilitate a learning task)

FIGURE 19.2 Cognitive Strategies

2 Application of Cognitive Strategies

Ms. Lott's class is reading another book, *Tacky the Penguin* by Helen Lester. She asks students to examine the cover, then has them discuss why the penguin on the cover might be considered tacky. Students are encouraged to respond freely, using their word knowledge and the picture. She also asks students to tell her in what part of the world they think the story might take place. After students do choral reading, Ms. Lott shows them a wordweb with the word *tacky* in the center. They are asked to brainstorm for other words that are similar in meaning. As the students provide the words, Ms. Lott puts them in the smaller circles which extend from the big circle containing the word *tacky*. Once students have finished with the reading activity, Ms. Lott tells them to act out scenes from the story as she reads the story again. She specifically asks them to act out the words describing the actions of the penguin. She selects several lines in the story and assigns students specific roles in the story to act out. Students wear teacher-made costumes when performing the skit. After the skit, the students answer comprehension questions, filling out blanks and writing short answers. They are told they will conduct further research on penguins and Antarctica. At the end of the lesson, Ms. Lott asks students what three things they have learned from the story. Then the students are asked to write their own imaginary story about penguins in Antarctica.

Can you identify specific cognitive strategies in the previous scenario?

C. Social Affective Strategies

There are three sub-categories of social affective strategies: cooperation, questioning for clarification, and self-talk.

Cooperation
(Work together with peers to solve a problem, gather information, check a learning task, or get feedback on oral and written performance)

Questioning for Clarification
(Ask a teacher or peer to clarify or explain, rephrase, or give examples)

Self-Talk
(Use mental techniques to boost one's own confidence and reduce anxiety when completing a task)

FIGURE 12.3 Social Affective Strategies

Can you identify the social affective strategies in the following scenario?

SCENARIO

3 Social Affective Strategies

Ms. Lott's lesson objectives are for students to identify the adjectives and verbs used in the two stories ("Tacky the Penguin" and "Slippery Ice"), and for them to describe the events in proper sequence when retelling the stories. For this lesson, she uses the cooperative learning structure—jigsaw reading. First, she groups students in fours. These groups are the home groups.

Each member of a home group is assigned a number, 1, 2, 3, or 4. Students must learn about the others on their team and look out for one another. Then, Ms. Lott assembles an "expert" team, consisting of students who have the same number; for instance, all number ones form a group, number twos get together and form another group, and so on. Each "expert" group is given a task to do. The tasks for this lesson are:

Group #1: Locate, color, and label the geographical areas in which each story is set.

Group #2: Identify three verbs and three adjectives in the stories and draw or act them out.

Group #3: Using a Venn diagram, compare and contrast the characters in the two stories.

Group #4: Retell the stories using the excitement map—an extension of a simple retelling.

Ms. Lott gives each "expert" group fifteen minutes to complete its task. Then, she reassembles the home groups and asks each member to teach his or her assignment to the others in their group. Every member in the "home" group must have the information that covers all of the given tasks. Then, Ms. Lott tells the students they are going to play a game called "Jeopardy." She writes comprehension questions about the two stories and puts them in a hat. She will draw one question at a time and pick a number (1–4) to answer the question. Because students do not know whom she will pick to answer the question, everyone must know the answer, so they have to work together and teach one another to answer the question correctly. In this game, students not only help one another, but they must boost each other's confidence and cheer each other on. Each member must convince other members that they can provide the correct answer. After a series of questions, the winning team receives a prize. The game is competitive, yet fun.

COMMUNICATION STRATEGIES

It is not enough for second language learners to be able to read, write, and understand basic knowledge in their L2; they must also be able to communicate and get things done. Del Hymes (1974) developed a term called *communicative competence* which he defines as one's ability to use the language appropriately in a variety of contexts. This means knowledge of grammar alone is not enough to guarantee second language learners the ability to use the language appropriately in social contexts. Canale (1983) identifies four elements of communicative competence: grammatical, sociolinguistic, discourse, and strategic competence.

Grammatical competence focuses on the accuracy of the language "code," i.e., vocabulary, grammar, pronunciation, and spelling.

Sociolinguistic competence involves the appropriate use of language in varied social settings, i.e., requesting information, refusing assistance, and other social etiquette.

Discourse competence is the learners' ability to appropriately engage in conversation. Learners need to know the skills of combining and connecting phrases and sentences. They also need to know conversational rules, such as giving and taking of the floor while talking, and written discourse rules, such as using appropriate address for different audiences.

Strategic competence pertains to the way language is used, both verbally and non-verbally, to achieve communication goals. Strategic competence is used for two main reasons: (a) to make meaning clear in communication; and (b) to embellish communication. The sub-categories of strategic competence are illustrated by the following scenario.

SCENARIO

4 Strategic Competence—A Yellow Ribbon

It is sharing time in the classroom. Miguel has brought in an Easter basket. Although he is relatively inexperienced in communicating in English, he is anxious to share his basket with the class. Miguel communicates in English with Spanish intrusion, relying on his Spanish to fill in for words not yet part of his limited English vocabulary. Miguel tells the class about his basket with smiles and gestures; then the teacher encourages the class to raise their hands and question him about his basket.

Miguel: *This basket. I'm got little candy for . . . for . . . dia de Pascua (Easter). I'm got huevos de colores* (colored eggs) *blue, green, yellow. I'm got little pollitos* (chicks). *Me sit and eat chocolate con mi hermana* (with my sister).

Teacher: *Girls and boys, now you may ask Miguel questions about his basket. Remember to raise your hands!*

Adeleine: (Raising hand.) *What color is the ribbon?*

(continued)

Miguel:	*Ribbon?* (taken aback by the unfamiliar word "ribbon," looks around the classroom as if searching for a cue to the meaning. Finally, his gaze rests on Maria. Maria points to the ribbon in Adeleine's hair; Miguel has found his cue.)
Miguel:	*A yellow ribbon!* (Look to Adeleine for confirmation. Adeleine nods yes. Miguel is elated.)
Carlos:	*Can I have a green egg you have in your Easter basket?*
Miguel:	*What?* (Looks puzzled.)
Carlos:	*Can I have the green egg? Look—Look—Look* (Forms an egg shape with his hands).
Miguel:	(Stares in basket.)
Carlos:	*Green egg.* (Gets up and points to the green egg in basket.)
Miguel:	(Smiling) *O.K. Here green egg!*

(Source: Ventriglia, L. 1979. *Conversations of Miguel and Maria: How Children Learn a Second Language.* Addison Wesley Publishing Company. Pp. 69–70.)

This scenario illustrates how a brief conversational exchange between native speakers and beginning non-native speakers can be a complex and laborious task. Here, we will focus on what Canale calls second language learners' strategic competence. In strategic competence, communication goals are achieved by the manipulation of language, both verbal and nonverbal. Elaine Tarone (1981) provides a taxonomy of strategic or communication strategies as shown in Figure 19.4.

Now that we know the different strategies second language learners use in their target language communication, let us analyze the strategies that Miguel used in the yellow ribbon scenario. Notice that Miguel uses the language switch strategy in reverting to chunks of Spanish. He appeals for assistance by repeating or imitating the word ribbon to show signs of uncertainty about what the word means. Here, he did not ask a question, but used non-verbal gestures (looking at Maria and staring in

the basket). Carlos also uses mime to explain his question to Miguel (forms an egg shape with his hands).

As teachers of second language learners, we need to understand the communication strategies our students use. It is important that teachers complement students' communication and learning strategies with instructional strategies appropriate to their level of linguistic proficiency. For example, when second language learners use the circumlocution strategy, teachers should understand that they have not acquired the appropriate term and will try to explain the concept using related terms available to them. At this point, the teacher may supply the word in context and ask learners to repeat the word, or restate the word for the learner. A teacher who understands the basic elements of communication strategy will focus on key words and use various communication strategies to facilitate their students' understanding and delivery of a message.

Approximation
(a substitute word that the second language learner knows is incorrect, but has semantic features similar to the desired item, e.g., *points/dots*; *rounds/circle*; *pipe/waterpipe*)

Word Coinage
(make up a new word to communicate a desired concept, e.g. *water bird* for *duck*)

Circumlocution
(the second language learner describes characteristics or elements of the object or action instead of using the appropriate term in the target language, e.g., *the lady who is carrying a baby in her tummy* for a *pregnant woman*)

Literal Translation
(word-for-word translation from the native language, e.g., *Go sleep outside* referring to sleeping not in the bedroom, but in the living room)

Language Switch
(use of L1 without bothering to translate, e.g., *pollitos* (chicks))

Appeal for Assistance
(learner asks for the correct term, e.g., "What is this? What do you call this?" Or uses non-verbal gestures)

Mime
(non-verbal strategies are used instead of the term for lexical item, e.g., forms egg shape with hands)

FIGURE 19.4 Classification of Communication Strategies (Tarone, 1981)

LEARNING STYLES

While learning and communication strategies deal with specific techniques for problem-solving, learning styles refer to the general approaches to learning that may persist even though the content and nature of problem-solving changes. Learning style is thus defined as the "habitual strategies determining a person's typical modes of perceiving, thinking, and problem solving" (Messick, 1976:5). Howard Gardner's (1983) seminal work on multiple intelligences describes several distinct intelligences, all of which can be nurtured in many different ways over time. These intelligences influence the way one learns and processes new information. Gardner further states that individuals may draw upon more than one intelligence in any problem-solving task and that these intelligences may work in harmony. The following Table 19.1 gives an overview of several types of intelligences and applications for teaching and assessing students with regard to these forms of intelligences.

TABLE 19.1

Applications of Multiple Intelligences in Instruction and Assessment

Intelligence	Characteristics	Teaching	Assessing
Linguistic	Loves to read, write, tell stories, enjoys verbal interactions	Do storytelling activities, creative writing, reports and essays, oral and silent reading, memory games	Oral/written reports Dialogue journals Reading response Thinking/learning logs Memorization
Bodily-Kinesthetic	Loves to move, touch, gesture, use body language	Do sports, dance, acting, experiments, craft projects, field trips	Physical demonstrations Role playing Mime/Charade games Read aloud with finger puppets Interpret story through dance
Spatial/Visual	Loves to visualize/create a mental picture, to draw and design, or to play with things in order to understand new information	Use visuals, charts, maps, and other graphic organizers to sort information Use video and computer-assisted instruction	Posters, charts, diagrams, illustrations, model constructions
Musical	Loves listening to melodies and is sensitive to pitch and rhythm	Do singing activities and poetry readings, reader's theatre, jazz chants	Write a rap/song/ballad to display understanding Create sound effects for reader's theatre or skit
Logical-Mathematical	Loves to work with numbers, figure out and explore patterns and relationships, do experiments, solve puzzles	Do math games, simulation, and thinking games	Solving mathematical and logic problems Student inventions Classify ideas Show relationship and pattern between ideas
Interpersonal	Loves to interact with people and show leadership skills Good at communicating, negotiating, organizing	Whole and small group discussions of topics Class debates, oral interviews, reader response to peer writing, think-pair-share reading activity, jigsaw activity, structured controversies, board games	Group summary/report of video, reading, or problem-solving activities Group negotiates on a solution to controversial problems or dilemma
Intrapersonal	Prefers independent work and is self-directed and motivated	Independent tasks on special interest topics Reflective journals, self-assessment journals	Student portfolios where learners make personal choices of work to be included in the portfolio Reading or writing rubrics of individual students Self-made multimedia projects/reports

What is the practical application of the multiple intelligence theory/learning styles theory for second language classrooms? First and foremost, because teachers will work with diverse groups of learners, it is essential that they understand the concept of learning styles and learners' language-learning capabilities so that they can develop language-learning materials to address these differences. With this knowledge, teachers will position themselves to better help students identify their strengths and shortcomings, and to facilitate the transfer of their strong skills to new learning.

Second, ESL students must learn to adapt their learning styles to the educational culture of their new environments in order to be better prepared for American classrooms. Some studies of learning styles have demonstrated differences between mainstream and minority students in American classrooms. Research in the area of learning styles of children who are native English speakers suggests that learners have four learning style preferences: visual, kinesthetic, tactile, and auditory learning (Dunn, 1983, 1984; Reinert, 1976).

However, Backes (1993) found that Native American high school students preferred sharing and community learning environments, and indirect, reflective, and experiential learning, while mainstream students preferred concrete-sequential learning, a mode of thinking that typifies logical-mathematical intelligence. Reid (1987) also found differences in learning styles between ESL students in intensive English classes in the United States and their native English speaking American counterparts. Most ESL students preferred tactile and kinesthetic learning; however, those who had been in American classrooms longer had adapted their learning styles and become more auditory and less tactile. These findings suggest that students' learning style preferences or predispositions may be nurtured by their respective cultures or learning environment.

Third, ESL students in elementary classrooms who had little experience in American classrooms may benefit from training that allows them to expand on their existing styles. Fourth, since learners may exhibit differences in learning styles, it is important that teachers also include methods of assessment that are balanced and reflective of different intelligence (suggestions for alternative assessment methods will be discussed further in the section on assessment). This does not mean all forms of intelligence must be covered in assessing student performance. What is important is that teachers provide several methods of assessment from which students can choose. For example, they might ask a student to answer guided questions about a reading passage by drawing a diagram or picture that describes the text, or by analyzing the text and drawing comparisons and contrasts to other texts, or by performing a drama that highlights the important ideas.

Lazear (1991) suggests four steps in planning lessons for teaching multiple intelligences: triggering particular types of intelligence through a variety of materials and exercises using multiple sensory systems; amplifying and teaching a particular intelligence; integrating different intelligences into daily activities; and encouraging student reflection about their own intelligences, how they work, and how they relate their intelligences to their daily lives. Joy Reid (1998) offers specific ways for teachers to modify their lesson plans to match different styles. First of all, teachers should include activities that allow students to do both group work (collaborative learners) and some individual work (independent learners). Second, assignments should be written (visual learners) and spoken (auditory learners); this can be achieved by including activities such as note-taking, reading-writing, and discussions. Third, include hands-on activities such as role-play and demonstrations for concrete learners and individual problem-solving tasks for abstract learners. Finally, teachers should allow reflective learners to do activities which require time for examining options, and present active learners opportunities for spontaneous learning experiences.

- ✓ The Cognitive Academic Language Learning Approach (CALLA) integrates content, language, and strategies.

- ✓ CALLA consists of three main categories of strategies: metacognitive, cognitive, and social affective.

✓ Metacognitive strategies attend to organizational skills and self-evaluation; cognitive strategies include, among others, contextualization, imagery, summary, and note-taking. Social affective strategies include cooperation, questioning, clarification, and boosting one's self-confidence.

✓ Communicative competence is defined as one's ability to use language appropriately in a variety of contexts. There are four main communicative competencies: grammatical, sociolinguistic, discourse, and strategic.

✓ Strategic competence involves paraphrasing, borrowing, appealing for assistance, mime, and avoidance.

✓ Teachers should have informed knowledge of the communication strategies second language learners employ, so that they can match instructional strategies to learning strategies.

✓ Learning styles, or multiple intelligences, refers to the general ways in which we process and respond to information in our environment.

✓ Learning styles account for differences in how students learn. Gardner identifies multiple forms of human intelligence. Because teachers will most likely encounter culturally and linguistically diverse classrooms in the future, it is important that they understand how students learn, and diversify their teaching styles to accommodate their students' learning style preferences.

✓ ESL students may have already developed culturally distinct learning style preferences, and must learn to adapt their learning styles to their target language classroom, to function well in their new learning environment. Teachers can ease ESL learners' transitions into their new classroom cultures by including students' dominant learning styles in their instruction, as well as exposing them to other ways of learning. In this way, learners will expand their learning styles and have more options to choose from and apply to different kinds of problem-solving tasks.

Chapter 20

Language Learning Errors and Strategies for Error Correction

Key Issues

- ○ Major types of learner errors
- ○ The role of error correction in language acquisition
- ○ Some techniques for error correction

SCENARIO

Examine students' and teachers' comments below regarding learning errors and error correction:

Students' Comments:

"My teacher tells me this is very good work. But when I get my work back, my paper is full of errors. I think my teacher didn't like my work."

"I just can't say anything without making mistakes. That is why I keep quiet."

"I know I don't say it right. I want to learn. I want my teacher to correct all my mistakes."

Teachers' Comments:

"I don't understand what my students are saying, so how can I correct them?"

"My students are making the same mistakes over and over again, although I've corrected their errors many times."

"I've got to correct all their errors; otherwise, I'm not doing my job!"

What do you notice about the way students and teachers view error correction in language learning? Although there is no doubt that both recognize that making errors is a natural part of the learning process, they have different opinions about error corrections. Because language learning involves emotional, psychological, and cognitive states, teachers should not ignore the effect that error correction has on language acquisition.

At the same time, teachers face a dilemma: if errors are left uncorrected, they will remain permanent or fossilized in a student's linguistic system. The question is, then, what errors should be corrected and how should they be treated? The answer to this question will largely depend on the student's linguistic proficiency, educational background, and risk-taking behavior (Diaz-Rico and Weed, 1995).

LEARNER ERRORS

The following factors are useful in guiding teachers in providing appropriate error correction:

a) Teachers should not correct every error that learners make in speech and writing. If a learner is still at the early stages of language acquisition, teachers should encourage the student to experiment with language and not worry too much about accuracy. If the student says, *"I wear blouse blue"* or *"I no go in there,"* the teacher should respond *"Oh, you wear a blue blouse?"* or *"You did not go in there. What did you do then?"* The important thing is to remember that learners are still getting the correct structures they need; focusing too much on their errors will cause unnecessary anxieties that can hamper learning.

b) As learners get more confident with their new language, teachers can focus on specific errors that interfere with communication. Research (Burt and Kiparsky, 1972; Burt, 1975) suggests that there are certain types of errors that may hinder communication. These are considered global errors. These errors are usually characterized by incorrect word order pattern, omission or incorrect use of transitional expressions, and omission or incorrect use of lexical items that carry significant information, and incorrect use of words caused by poor pronunciation. Examples of global errors are listed below:

Incorrect Sentence Structure:

- *The bus use many people. (Many people use the bus.)*
- *Not do homework principal will call to office. (The principal will call students to the office if they do not do their homework.)*
- *If we practice sports, we will enjoy together. (If we practice sport together, we will enjoy ourselves.)*
- *This way, can gain plenty of experience. (missing subject: This way, we can gain plenty of experience.)*
- *Hungry and poor drove Timoen to despair. (missing gerund: Being hungry and poor drove Timoen to despair.)*

On the other hand, learners may also commit errors that do not hinder communication. These are considered local errors but meaning can still be inferred from context. These errors are usually characterized by misuse of verb tense, incorrect use of verbs to describe conditions/state of being, or incorrect use of inflectional morphemes, omission of articles such as *a*, *an*, or *the*, and so on. Examples of the different types of local errors are as follows:

Misuse of verb tenses:

- *People will feel sick every time they saw these.*

- *Our interviews were conducted face to face, and the time taken on each person is 15 minutes.*
- *I knew Marcella since 1970.*
- *I wish you are staying here with me.*

Omission of plural *-s* and misuse of singular and plural nouns:

- *He has many problem.*
- *These knifes need to be sharpened.*
- *The Chineses celebrate their New Year in February.*

Misuse of count and uncountable nouns:

- *He gave me useful advices.*
- *He collects antique furnitures.*
- *She traveled with a lot of luggages.*

Misuse of plurals of compound nouns:

- *She bought two photos albums.*
- *He has two son-in-laws.*

Errors in comparative constructions:

- *I have more big toys at home.*
- *I prefer reading than watching films.*
- *Day after day, I felt weak than before.*

Errors in reported speech:

- *I don't know why did this happen.*
- *Marisol's friends advised her don't be so proud.*

Errors in subject-verb and pronoun agreement:

- *I can't work anymore; my body feel weak.*
- *Everybody were waiting to see what would happen next.*
- *Advertising are essential for modern businesses.*
- *Though my grandmother is old, she is very strong.*

Missing *be* verb:

- *It never easy for me to forget a good friend. (It is never . . .)*
- *This subject not very popular among middle school students. (This subject is . . .)*

Miscelleanous:

- ○ *Maria, my best friend likes Barbie dolls (missing comma: my best friend,)*
- ○ *I have eight years old (misuse verbs that describe state or conditions: I am eight years old.)*
- ○ *I ate big apple. (Article omission: I ate a . . .)*

Some of these errors may sound odd to a native speaker, but they do not interfere with communication. Teachers should also bear in mind that they should not overcorrect errors rarely committed by students. Correction should consistently focus on the most frequent errors, rather than on isolated errors.

In summary, the criteria for selecting errors to correct depends on several factors: (a) the students' needs and their personal reactions to error correction, (b) the comprehensibility of the message, and (c) the frequency of particular types of errors. Depending on the cultural and training backgrounds of English language learners, some students expect grammar instruction and expect their teacher to correct their errors. Unless their grammar needs are met, they may not be receptive to try other indirect techniques of error correction that require learners to self-correct with some teacher assistance.

c) Teachers should not judge grammatical and lexical forms used in non-standard or non-native varieties as errors. While these varieties may have their unique syntax, semantic system, grammar, pronunciation, and rhythm, they are not linguistically inferior. Like every other language, it is fully systematic, grammatical, symbolic, and poses no barrier to abstract thought. However, as discussed in Chapter 13, teachers are responsible for making sure that their English language learners develop the standard form used in school. Hence, teachers must stress the importance of keeping both language systems so that their students can navigate through a variety of situations in which they are expected to use language.

STRATEGIES FOR ERROR CORRECTION

The following are some strategies for ESL student error correction, that, with a teacher's help, will promote self-correction.

- ○ Pinpoint the error.
- ○ Rephrase the question or explanation.
- ○ Explain a key word or grammatical rule.
- ○ Repeat student answers with correction.
- ○ Provide cues for students to self-correct; for example, using fingers to represent each word produced by the learner. Then tell students that the finger that is down denotes that the word is grammatically incorrect. Ask learners to correct their errors, giving further hints as necessary.
- ○ Compile some samples of high frequency errors made by the whole class, keeping the students' identities anonymous. Circle the errors and ask students to correct them.
- ○ Ask students to listen to their taped oral reading, and another tape produced by a more proficient peer. Then ask them to compare differences in pronunciation between the two tapes.
- ○ Purposely make errors committed by students, and ask them if they can spot anything wrong.

Because error correction may influence learners' attitude towards learning the target language, here are some "don'ts" of error correction:

- ○ Do not overly correct learners' errors, especially speech errors. This can increase their reluctance to participate in discussions and experiment with language in both oral and writing activities.
- ○ Do not try to correct too many errors at a time as this may put undue burden on their processing ability. The rule of thumb is to correct global errors first before local errors or correct errors that students frequently produce first before other less frequent errors.
- ○ Do not correct student's errors in front of the whole class as this may make them embarrassed.

○ Do not judge grammatical forms and word choice used in non-standard varieties or non-native varieties as incorrect. When teachers do this, they are undermining the role and function of the learners' native language experience and knowledge as an important bridge to acquiring the target language.

Points to Remember

✓ Although errors are natural in language learning, teachers must correct errors so that they do not remain permanent or fossilized in students' linguistic systems.

✓ Teachers should first focus on global errors (those that hinder communication), rather than local errors (those that do not interfere with communication).

✓ Teachers should not overcorrect isolated errors which are not committed frequently. Too much emphasis on accuracy can heighten learner anxiety, which, in turn, will impede learning.

✓ Teachers must take into consideration the learners' needs, level of linguistic proficiency, and personal reaction to error correction.

Chapter 21

Language Methodologies

Key Issues

- ○ Chronological development of language methodologies
- ○ Principles and techniques of various language teaching methodologies

SCENARIO

Students sit in a semicircle, attentively listening to the dialogue, presented on tape, of a conversation between two friends talking after class.

Susan: *Hi Carlos! How are you today?*

Carlos: *Fine, thanks. And you?*

Susan: *Fine. Are you going to the cafeteria?*

Carlos: *No, I'm going to the library.*

Susan: *I am going to the library too. Can I walk with you?*

Carlos: *Sure, let's go.*

The teacher asks the whole class to repeat the taped dialogue, line by line. He models the pronunciation of some of the words. Then, he asks students to work in pairs; one student assumes the role of Susan and the other Carlos. After five minutes of practicing the dialogue, the teacher asks students comprehension and vocabulary questions.

The previous vignette depicts one of the methodologies presented in Table 21.1. The table presents the chronological development of foreign language teaching over a period of more than a century.

Although these methodologies were first used in foreign language teaching, over the years they have been adopted into the teaching of English as a second language (TESOL) and are frequently used in the mainstream classroom today.

The methodologies in TESOL have not always subscribed to student-centered approaches. In fact, the Grammar Translation Method was one of the earliest methods in foreign language teaching at the start of the twentieth century, and was first used in the teaching of classical languages. It focuses on learning the grammar of the target language. Using this method, students will not only be able to appreciate literary works written in the target language, but they will also be familiar with the grammar of their native language. Since students learn the target language for the purpose of reading literary works,

reading and writing skills are greatly emphasized, while speaking skills are considered less important.

The Direct Method (DM) became popular as a reaction to the Grammar Translation Method (GTM). Since GTM failed to teach students to communicate, the DM focuses on teaching students to communicate in the target language. In this method, students are required to communicate in the target language without reverting to their native language; therefore, translation is not allowed.

During World War II, there was an urgent need in the United States to teach foreign languages to the military. Although DM teaches learners to communicate in the target language, learners were not learning the target language fast enough. At the time, works in descriptive linguistics and behavioral psychology were prevalent, and exciting ideas in both fields contributed to the birth of yet another method in language teaching—the Audio-Lingual Method (ALM). Like the DM, the goal of the Audio-Lingual Method is for students to communicate in the target language. There are many similarities and differences between the principles of both methods.

More and more language methods surfaced in the early 1980s, as a lot of work was done in second language acquisition. Scholars such as Krashen and Tracy Terrell outlined another language learning method called the Natural Approach. The pendulum has shifted in language teaching, and now focuses on the way children learn their first language. Since children acquire their first language without the imposition of grammatical rules, the Natural Approach integrates techniques drawn from other methods which emphasize the promotion of comprehensible and meaningful activities over the teaching of grammatical rules.

Total Physical Response (TPR), an offshoot of the Natural Approach, was developed by James Asher. He asserted that speech comprehension is displayed through physical action in an informal and low anxiety learning environment.

The methods in language teaching have come a long way. From GTM to current methods, such as the Whole Language and Cognitive Academic Language Learning Approach (CALLA), the emphases and foci in language teaching have again shifted. Now, the most significant goal in language teaching is for learners to achieve communicative competence in the target language. The Whole Language approach and CALLA advocate teaching language through the use of meaningful content areas and the integration of language acquisition skills.

A summary of the principles and techniques of the above-mentioned methods are presented in Table 21.1.

TABLE 21.1

Time Period	Method	Explanation	Techniques	Error Treatment Classroom	Teacher's Role	Student's Role	Current Application
Until the late 19th century	Grammar Translation	Based on the way Latin and Greek are taught. The purpose of this method is to teach the reading of literary works in the target language. There are no linguistic or learning theories to support this method.	Memorization of grammatical rules and vocabularies. Direct translations to and from another language are intellectual exercises that enhance students' comprehension of how their own language functions. Little or no emphasis on oral skills, as the focus is on reading and writing. The rules are reinforced in drills and translation exercises. Classes are taught in students' native language. Bilingual dictionary is used.	Accuracy in bilingual translation is the focus in correction and feedback. Peers or teachers correct mistakes.	Following a traditional way of teaching, the teacher is the authority figure in the class, helping students read literature in the target language. They provide translation and corrections when necessary. Input is in the form of the unidirectional lecture format.	Students follow teacher's instruction closely. They have very limited opportunity to work with their peers.	Use of dictionary. Provide translation when necessary. Label words and items in L1.
Late 19th–early 20th century	Direct	Purpose is to promote communication in target language without translating. The premise is that the second language should be learned as naturally as possible, just as children learn their native language.	The use of native language is forbidden. Grammar is taught inductively through fill-in-the-blank exercises. Contextualization of language within a situation or topic is employed.	It is very important that students produce correct pronunciation and grammar. The teacher can use a variety of means to elicit self-correction.	Teachers must have native or near-native fluency in target language, as they will be modeling and controlling the flow of "natural" input in the target language. Teachers foster environments in which students' participation is elicited.	Students are active participants, communicating their thoughts and ideas frequently. They absorb as much input as possible so that they can begin to think in the target language.	Small group work. Grammar can be provided peripherally. Use social language to teach academic language. Use topics of real interest, such as hobbies, movies, etc.

TABLE 21.1 (continued)

Time Period	Method	Explanation	Techniques	Error Treatment Classroom	Teacher's Role	Student's Role	Current Application
1940–1950	Audio-Lingual (Charles Fries)	Language is viewed as a habit-formation process, reflecting the theory of behavioral psychology. L2 should be learned without reference to L1. Speaking and listening precede reading and writing as language is equated to speech.	Stimulus-response drills; memorization of dialogues; exclusive use of L2; grammar rules are taught indirectly; the order of skills learned: listening, speaking, reading, writing.	Students' responses are positively and immediately reinforced. Errors are immediately corrected to avoid the forming of bad habits. First, students are asked individually to repeat the corrected word or sentence. Later the rest of the class will do the same.	Teacher is in control of all activities in class. Provides students with a model for imitation, directs all activities, making corrections and providing reinforcement where necessary.	Students mimic and memorize dialogs and patterns. They work in language lab with tapes to practice listening and speaking.	Initial memorization of relevant canon utterances in target language. Skits using dialogues.
Late 1970's, early 1980's	Natural Approach (Krashen and Terrell)	A second language is learned using the same process that children use to learn to speak. The method integrates Krashen's hypothesis of L2 language acquisition and observations on acquisition of L1 and L2 languages. Students need to acquire a huge inventory of vocabulary to understand and use speech. Meaning is emphasized over grammatical accuracy. The method proposes to develop students' BICS and CALP.	The content of lessons reflects students' needs and language proficiency levels. Class activities are meaningful, and repetition of grammatically perfect sentences is avoided. Games and problem-solving tasks are used in class. Students' silent period is acknowledged.	Students are free to make errors. Corrections are made through restatement or modeling of correct utterances.	Teachers provide instruction that is comprehensible, by using a variety of interesting activities that meet students' needs, proficiency skills, and class objectives. Teachers create a conducive and relaxed learning environment that does not pressure students to speak when they are not ready.	Students are encouraged to participate in communicative activities that promote language acquisition. They focus on context and key words to arrive at the general meaning. Inference skills are highly promoted.	Low anxiety class atmosphere where learning and acquisition of language will take place. Use communicative activities such as role play, drama, and skits. Use realia and authentic materials, such as magazines and newspapers.

TABLE 21.1 (continued)

Time Period	Method	Explanation	Techniques	Error Treatment Classroom	Teacher's Role	Student's Role	Current Application
1974	Total Physical Response (TPR) (Asher) Whole Language (Kenneth and Yetta Goodman)	Action and speech are combined in an informal and stress-free learning environment. Comprehension speech precedes speech, as speech will emerge naturally. TPR syllabus is sentence-based; focusing on grammar and vocabularies through meaning is the primary emphasis.	Physical action is used to teach language. Students indicate comprehension through movement and actions. Students listen and respond physically to oral commands for first ten hours of instruction. Use target language only.	Errors are tolerated by teachers as meaning and comprehension is the major focus. Errors are expected, and only major ones are corrected at first. Correction of errors should always be made in context and in a non-threatening manner.	The teacher plans and directs activities. Language input is provided in the form of commands. As students become more in control of their learning, teachers guide their interaction individually, as well as on a whole-group basis.	First, students observe the behavior modeled by teachers and volunteers. Students should show comprehension through action, although they are not required to produce language until they are ready. Students should understand different combinations and sequences of commands and adapt to new situations.	Use TPR to act out difficult words. Observe students' silent period. Correct errors that hinder communication.
1970's & early 1980's		Learning proceeds from whole to part. Learning should take place in the L1 language to build concepts and facilitate the acquisition of the L2 language.	Lessons are purposeful and student-centered. Cooperative learning.	Making errors is a normal process in learning. Errors are corrected meaningfully and in a contextualized manner.	Teacher makes informed decisions about teaching, learning, reading, and writing. Focuses on literacy and the process of learning, rather than the products.	Students experiment and take risks when learning the new language. They should see themselves as producers of knowledge and not be afraid to make mistakes.	Student-centered classroom. Use literature in class. Content-driven language curriculum.
1987	CALLA (Chamot and O'Malley)	See Chapter 17					

✓ The Grammar Translation Method, which originated in the late nineteenth century, uses techniques such as memorization of grammatical rules and vocabularies, direct translations, and drill exercises to teach the target language. The purpose of the method is to teach the reading of literary works in the target language.

✓ The Direct Method, which began in the early twentieth century, forbids the use of native language in the class. Grammar is taught inductively through fill-in-the-blank exercises. Language is taught in context.

✓ The Audio-Lingual Method was first used in the 1940s. It is based on the behaviorist view of language learning. The order of skills learned are listening, speaking, reading, and writing. L2 should be learned without reference to L1.

✓ The Natural Approach emerged in the late 1970s and early 1980s. It is based on how children acquire their first language and integrates Krashen's hypotheses: affective filter, the "input hypothesis," natural order, and acquisition versus learning. Teachers should provide a comfortable, low anxiety classroom that is conducive to learning. Learners' silent period is acknowledged, and communicating meaning is emphasized over grammatical accuracy.

✓ Total Physical Response, commonly known as TPR, is a method that uses physical actions to teach language. Students show comprehension through movement and actions. The learning environment is stress free. Since comprehension precedes production, learners can use non-verbal responses, such as nodding and pointing, or acting out the answers.

✓ Whole language was developed in the early 1980s. It centers on the idea that learning proceeds from wholes to parts. Lessons in this approach are student-centered and purposeful. Curriculum is literature-based and cooperative learning is used.

Part Four

A KNOWLEDGE BASE IN ASSESSMENT AND EVALUATION

Chapter 22

Assessment and Evaluation for the English Language Learner (ELL)

Key Issues

○ Assessment: What is it?

○ Why we need to assess

○ What the teacher must know about the English language learner

○ Assessment: Formal and informal

○ Standardized testing: Unfair evaluation for English language learners

○ The No Child Left Behind Act of 2001

SCENARIO

Ahmed is a student from Saudi Arabia entering Gibbons Elementary for the first time. The teacher is using a proficiency test to place him in the correct level. The test shows a picture of a young woman in a classroom pointing to a blackboard. As the teacher asks Ahmed who the woman is, he stares at the picture and does not appear to know how to answer. Why not?

Mrs. Freeman, the guidance counselor from Lauderway Elementary School, is testing Yoshi to see at what language level he should begin school. Mrs. Freeman shows him a colorful picture with foods such as rice, eggs, bread, bananas, pumpkins, lemons, cherries, and apples. She says, "Name three things in the picture that you might find in pies." Yoshi stares at the picture and does not answer. Why not?

Nong, who speaks halting English, is being tested for English level placement and is asked to draw a picture of breakfast. She draws rice, a fish head, and soup. Her teacher believes Nong did not understand the question. What happened here?

Carlos is sitting with his new teacher, who is trying to assess his English knowledge. In her conversation with him, she asks him to complete the following sentence: *My brother and I like to play football. His favorite position is quarterback and my favorite position is* _____. Carlos looks questioningly at his teacher, not understanding what he is being asked. Why not?

What problems can you surmise about the previous scenarios? If you were the teacher of these students, what assumptions would you make about their respective language levels? Would you be assessing their language or their cultural knowledge?

Would you think Ahmed was English deficient, or even developmentally delayed, because he did not know to label the woman in the picture as a teacher? Would it have occurred to you that boys have only male teachers where he is from, and the concept of having a female teacher is alien to him?

When Yoshi was asked about pies, he could not answer the question because pies are a manifestation of American culture and do not exist as a component of the typical Japanese diet.

People in the United States eat a variety of foods for breakfast, but it is probably safe to say fish heads, rice, and soup are not among them. Bacon, eggs, toast, and coffee are more likely to conjure up images of American breakfast foods. However, for Nong, this is a common meal and she prefers the head of the fish to the body.

When Carlos was asked about football, his favorite sport, he was thrilled. He and his brother love the game, but to them, football is *futbol*, the word for "soccer" in Spanish.

WHAT IS ASSESSMENT?

Classroom teachers need to be accountable for the effectiveness of their teaching. To evaluate students, they need to collect information about their students' progress so that they can modify and improve instruction, evaluate the curriculum, and measure the language gains the students make. Assessment of language proficiency of English learners serves the same purpose as assessment of other areas of student learning. The primary goals of assessment are: to gain information about the nature and extent of students' learning and to determine the appropriate educational plan for students. Assessment also allows us to conduct both formative (ongoing evaluation of student performance to guide teaching and assess learning by collecting and analyzing student work) and summative (the end results) program evaluations. What has to be kept in mind is what is being measured—language or content. Are students being tested on how much content they know, or how much English language they have acquired?

Unfortunately, often too much reliance is placed on a single standardized assessment instrument, when assessment should be an ongoing collection of information gathered during and after instruction to judge the student's overall progress. Additionally, the misuse or misinterpretation of assessment data or cultural bias within the instruments (as exemplified in the scenarios at the beginning of the chapter) result in incorrect diagnoses, student misplacements, inappropriate or inadequate programs, and student under-achievement.

WHY ASSESS?

Testing and assessment are very different. Mitchell (1992) states that a test is a "single-occasion, unidimensional, timed exercise, usually in multiple choice or short-answer form." Conditions for every test taker are the same, which is why they are called *standardized tests*, and the norms for comparison are the same for every participant. Assessment is completed on a broader scale; it is a collection or a varied sample of work done by students to ascertain what they know or can do. Testing can only be one part of assessment. We need to assess because testing alone cannot accurately evaluate the English learner.

English learners are often misclassified as having learning disabilities when the problem is really limited English language proficiency (Baker, 2000).

Erickson (1981) writes:

> *"The consequences of misclassifications due to inadequate or inappropriate tests may include improper placement, insufficient instruction, and, as a result, lower academic achievement than would have been reached if appropriate instruments and proper placement had occurred. The ultimate consequence of such testing may include increased dropout rates and perpetuation of unequal educational opportunity for language minority students."*

Schools must comply with federal and state laws (*Lau* v. *Nichols*, 1974; Title VII of the Elementary and Secondary Act, 1968, etc.) which mandate appropriate instruction for non-native speakers of English. This is not possible without assessing how much a student knows upon entry to the school, as well as how the student is progressing throughout the program. Administrators must know where to budget monies, what programs to initiate and fund, and what trained personnel need to be hired to teach these students. Without accurate and reliable assessment, a grave injustice is done to the future of our English-learning population, as they cannot progress toward the future without knowing where they are in the present.

More and more educators of ELLs subscribe to the idea that English language proficiency and academic content should be assessed from a holistic viewpoint. Data can be gathered from a great variety of sources such as the following:

1. School records (including previous test records), portfolios (samples of students' work), guidance reports, attendance and health records, and referral forms.
2. Interviews—formal and informal—with parents, teachers, and other appropriate school personnel.
3. Anecdotal records or direct observations of students in the classroom, the playground, at "specials" (art, music, P.E., etc.), in the cafeteria, and in daily interactions with native-English speakers.
4. Informal instruments such as checklists, rating scales, cloze testing (a reading and appropriate language use assessment technique in which

words have been deleted from a passage and the student must identify them correctly by filling in the blanks), writing samples, and curriculum-based tests constructed by classroom teachers.

5. Standardized tests designed by specialists, and administered, scored, and interpreted under standard conditions.

SCENARIO

Mrs. Cooper teaches third grade at Spring Street School in a small town in Massachusetts. The town's population is mostly Anglo, mainstream, and native English-speaking. All her students speak English fluently with no accents and are functioning at grade level. There is nothing to indicate that anyone is of an ethnic group other than the English-speaking Anglo majority. One little boy, Roman, is having tremendous difficulty spelling. Although the teacher keeps telling him to sound out the words, his spelling test looks like this:

Apul (apple)

Thot (thought)

Eskool (school)

Pipul (people)

Nedd (needed)

Poot (put)

Mrs. Cooper decides to speak to Roman's parents because, in her assessment of the situation, he obviously is not studying for his spelling tests; however, the student teacher, bilingual in English and Spanish, took one look at his test, went over to Roman's desk, and said to him, *"Roman, hablas español?"* Roman's eyes brightened in surprise and answered, *"Si, Señora. Hablamos español en casa."* The student teacher went to her cooperating teacher and said, "Mrs. Cooper, Roman is sounding out his spelling words. Phonetically, these are perfectly sounded out in Spanish!" Mrs. Cooper had no idea that Roman was from a Spanish-speaking family, because he had no accent, no Hispanic surname, spoke fluent English, and did not "look" Hispanic. Assumptions can be misleading and lead to grossly inaccurate judgments.

WHAT DOES THE TEACHER HAVE TO KNOW ABOUT THE LANGUAGE LEARNER?

Teachers need to know as much as possible about their students for many reasons. First, they need to know what languages are spoken at home. Upon entry to many schools, parents and guardians must complete a Home Language Survey, which asks:

1. Is a language other than English used in the home? If yes, language used_____.
2. Did the student have a first language other than English?
3. Does the student most frequently speak a language other than English?
   (See samples of Home Language Surveys in the Appendix.)

If any question is answered in the affirmative, it is a signal that language services might be needed. The Home Language Survey should alert administrators and teachers to further evaluate proper placement for the student. Often incorrect assumptions are made on the basis of appearances. For example, an individual with a foreign surname such as Chin might not speak a word of Chinese, or a child named Samuel Brown might have been raised in Mexico and not know any English. José Bautista was born in the Dominican Republic, moved to Haiti when he was a baby, and attended a bilingual school where the language of instruction was English. His father was a doctor of Dominican descent, but spoke only English to José. José learned Haitian Creole from his playmates, but he is English dominant. If administrators did not know his background, where would he be placed based on his name, his country of origin, or his accent?

How much previous education has the student had? Is he or she literate in the native language? Is the native language a written or oral language? (Some native languages are only oral and do not have a written form.) What kind of a student was the child academically in the native language? Was the student's education interrupted by political upheaval, war, economic strife, migration, familial problems, or other forms of unrest? How much edu-

cation do the parents possess? Do they speak English? Why did the family come to the United States? Was it a happy move? Did it shatter or reunite the family? Did the child know he or she was coming to the United States, or was there no time for the closure of saying goodbye to friends and family? These social and psychological factors carry a powerful influence when it comes to learning another language or living contentedly in another country.

Once in school, the student must be evaluated to see how much language is being learned, how well he or she is doing in class, and when enough language has been learned to reclassify and progress to a higher level. Finally, accurate records of assessment must be kept to know when enough advancement has been made to warrant exiting the ESOL program and being mainstreamed. After exiting the ESOL program, assessment must continue in order to ascertain the child's progress, for assurance that he or she is functioning at grade level. If the student is having difficulty, other services and counseling should be provided, including support through alternative programs and learning strategies. With accurate, precise, and ongoing assessment, teachers and administrators can differentiate among, and offer proper treatment for, language, academic, psychological, physical, and emotional problems.

TYPES OF ASSESSMENT: FORMAL AND INFORMAL

The Florida Department of Education Office of Multicultural Student Language Education (OMSLE) has produced an Instructional Language Assessment CD. Originally developed by Sandra H. Fradd, Ph.D., it offers the comparison of formal and informal measures of language assessment found in Table 22.1.

Testing, both formal and informal, plays a key role in ESL teaching and planning, by identifying (1) linguistic skills (phonology, morphology, syntax, and vocabulary), and (2) integrated language skills (reading, writing, listening, and speaking) (Carrasquillo, 1994). Both linguistic skills and integrated language assessment instruments are similar

TABLE 22.1

Types of Assessment: Formal and Informal

Formal Measures	Informal Measures
—are based on statistical norms for representative populations	—can be based on classroom activities and materials
—are designed to compare individuals and groups with norms representative of the general population	—can be designed to determine students' strengths and needs
—are administered according to specific guidelines in terms of seating, test format, response time, and responses made	—can be used whenever appropriate
	—are time consuming and not easily scored
—are administered by trained and credentialed personnel	—can be used by teachers, assistants, and peer tutors
—are usually English language based	—can incorporate both English and other languages
—are usually composed of questions requiring short answers, or often multiple choice responses	—can use a variety of response modes and contexts
—can be interpreted across settings	—are not easily interpreted across settings

in that they are designed to measure outcomes based on the academic content being taught; however, there are some major differences.

VALIDITY

Validity refers to the adequacy and appropriateness of the interpretations made from assessments in regard to the specific use of assessment results. Does the assessment accurately measure what it is intended to gauge? Because language learning involves mastery of skills in different areas, it is important to test the learner's skills from a global perspective across domains and tasks, considering the total product, rather than individual sub-skills (vocabulary, grammar, pronunciation, inferring meaning, etc.) of language. Informal testing instruments better serve this purpose than standardized tests, which are often designed to measure outcomes and content common to students who belong to the ethnic majority of the United States. For example, if we ask a child who was raised in the United States mainstream culture to finish this sentence: *Jack fell down and broke his* _____, it would be an easy task. However, if we ask a child who has no familiarity with this common nursery rhyme, the child would be unable to answer. The flexibility of informal testing allows adaptation of the content to avoid cultural biases and to measure

a greater variety of sub-skills. At some time within their educational experience, all students will be expected to perform on standardized tests; therefore, it is a good idea to prepare them by systematically teaching test-taking skills.

RELIABILITY

Reliability refers to the consistency of assessment results obtained over a given period of time, when scored by different raters, or over different measurements of samples of the same behavior. Does the assessment consistently measure what it is intended to gauge, no matter who administers the test? Reliability is expressed statistically as a correlation coefficient indicating the degree of relationship between two sets of scores, with 1.0 being the greatest degree of correlation, and zero being the lowest. Simply speaking, if we give an achievement test today, will the test scores be consistent if we give the test tomorrow or next week? Consistency makes validity possible, and justifies generalizations about assessments (Linn and Granlund, 2000).

It is important to remember that although reliability (consistency) of measurement results is necessary to obtain valid results, it is not sufficient in isolation. In other words, it is possible to have consistent results that provide the wrong information, or measurement results that are consistently interpreted incorrectly.

While standardized tests are generally quite reliable (between .80 and .95) compared to more accurate informal assessment instruments, the results obviously will not be useful if they are not valid.

PRACTICALITY

Practicality refers to the economical aspects of the assessment instrument with regard to time, labor, and money. The ideal assessment instrument would include ease of administration and scoring, while producing results that are correctly interpreted by school personnel. For instance, while interview testing may provide a good measure of oral communication proficiency, this type of instrument requires the luxury of time and energy—commodities the typical classroom teacher lacks. Conversely, while standardized tests provide ease of administration and scoring, the results rarely yield true data that are useful for ESOL educators.

Although there are some standardized tests designed specifically to assess English language proficiency, most are inadequate for target language evaluation. These tests are usually administered once or twice a year, do not monitor students' ongoing progress in language acquisition, and usually cannot measure all the components involved in language learning (reading, writing, listening, speaking, communicative competence, etc.).

Probably the most salient disadvantage in standardized testing is the inability to assess linguistic or communicative competence, skills critical to language acquisition. Linguistic competence is the ability to control pronunciation, morphology, and syntax. Communicative competence refers to the ability to use language to achieve a particular purpose (Krashen and Terrell, 1983).

WHY DO STANDARDIZED TESTS RESULT IN UNFAIR EVALUATIONS FOR ENGLISH LANGUAGE LEARNERS?

The problem of cultural bias in standardized testing has already been mentioned. Other problems that result from cultural differences stem from the ways in which tests are taken in other countries. The idea of multiple choice questions is unheard of in many other countries. For example, in Haiti the traditional type of test given is the essay test. Among other typical testing procedures in the United States, "bubbling in" answers to a test on a Scantron sheet is a foreign concept to students from many other cultures; without guidance and training, new students in the United States will not know what they are expected to do in this new testing situation.

In some other countries it is not considered cheating to work together, ask another student for the answer, or to work in groups. Individual work is prized as a valued commodity in the United States, and if another's work is not cited in the references, it is considered plagiarism. Korean students, for example, believe it is an honor to quote another author's work without citation, and honestly cannot understand the commotion resulting from submitting a "plagiarized" assignment.

Law and Eckes (1995) believe that standardized tests tend to fragment skills, and do not really measure reading ability. Students may demonstrate their knowledge in vocabulary or grammar, but the tests may not measure reading or writing ability as a whole. Additional problems with standardized testing include:

- ❍ the inability to show whether the student knows the material or not (because of multiple choice answers);
- ❍ only lower-order thinking skills are tested;
- ❍ they measure correctness based on a single occasion, instead of measuring random competence;
- ❍ the tests cannot tell where or why the student failed;
- ❍ all language and thinking skills are tested through the confines of reading and writing; and
- ❍ standard tests have no context from which to draw meaning and inference.

For English learners, the primary goal of NCLB is to help English learners meet academic standards and become proficient in English as quickly as possible. Schools are held accountable for adequate yearly progress (AYP) that is measured according to state benchmarks. All students must make progress over a term of three years, or remedial action will be made to improve programs. English learners must meet annual English language development objectives [Title I, Section 1111(b)(1), and Title III, Section 3122(a)(1)]. However, test scores are disaggregated from the general population to show progress of English learners.

The NCLB Act is a prime example of inequitable challenges facing the English learner. By testing students in a new language, it is likely that language proficiency is being measured instead of academic knowledge. Standardized tests from the United States are normed for the native English speaker, and English learners cannot compete with students who have received years of education in their native language (Coltrane, 2002; Menken, 2000). Although it may be inequitable, state educational agencies (SEAs), LEAs, and schools are required to maintain the same academic content and achievement standards established for all children.

THE NO CHILD LEFT BEHIND ACT (NCLB) OF 2001

The No Child Left Behind Act that was passed in 2001 has made an impact on standards-based high-stakes testing for all states. In an effort to increase academic achievement in reading and mathematics, this act advocates annual testing for all students in grades 3–8, including English learners who may not be proficient in the language. English language development must be assessed yearly, as long as students are labeled "ESOL" and are in programs that receive Title III funds from the government. (Title III is the English Language Acquisition, Language Enhancement, and Academic Achievement Act.) Local education agencies (LEAs) are offered Title III funds to develop and implement English language instruction in educational programs.

Points to Remember

- ✓ Assessment of content learning must not be confused with how much language the student knows.
- ✓ Assessment is used:
    - ○ for appropriate student placement;
    - ○ to gain information about the student's learning;
    - ○ to conduct formative and summative evaluations.

- ✓ In evaluating students, we need to collect information about their progress to modify and improve instruction, evaluate the curriculum, and measure language gains they make.

- ✓ Testing and assessment are different. Testing is a single-occasion exercise under specific conditions that are the same for everyone. Assessment is a broader collection of work samples indicating the caliber of work the student is doing.

- ✓ Inappropriate assessment can lead to inappropriate placement, instruction, and achievement, resulting in minority students dropping out of school.

- ✓ ESOL students should be assessed holistically, using alternative procedures from a variety of sources.

- ✓ Teachers must know what languages the student speaks, how much academic background the student possesses, and as much personal information as possible to correctly place, evaluate, and instruct the ELL student.

- ✓ Standardized tests are unfair to the new language learner because they can be culturally and linguistically biased; they cannot accurately measure how much the student truly knows. What they indicate instead is how the ELL student measures up to the native English-speaking student.

Chapter 23

Responding to a Court-Imposed Consent Decree:
A Look at Initial Placement and Assessment

Key Issues

- A Court Imposed Consent Decree and Settlement
- Home Language Survey
- Language placement and classification

SCENARIO

Lina, a German girl who has moved to the United States to live with her American-born aunt, went to her neighborhood high school with her aunt to register. They were handed a Home Language Survey, on which they indicated that German was Lina's first language. But upon hearing Lina speak English with her aunt, the guidance counselor placed Lina in a regular classroom. The aunt pointed out that Lina had been in the country for only four months and still needed ESOL instruction; but, the aunt had to make a special request for language services. The guidance counselor incorrectly assumed that because Lina could speak "survival" English (enough to be understood clearly), she could function academically in a class of native-English students.

COURT-IMPOSED CONSENT DECREES

A Look at Initial Placement and Assessment

As a result of noncompliance with federal laws ensuring equal educational opportunities for all students regardless of national origin, ethnicity, or language, many states or school districts are often mandated by court order to develop and implement strategic plans to deliver comprehensible instruction for language minority students.

A good example of a consent decree would be the August 1990 ruling passed in the state of Florida. As in a number of other states, Florida was obligated to adhere to the 1990 META Consent Decree, a court-enforced agreement between the Florida Board of Education and a coalition of eight groups represented by Multicultural Education, Training, and Advocacy, Inc. (META) and Florida legal service attorneys. The META Consent Decree guaranteed the identification and provision of services for Florida students whose native language is one other than English. The consent decree settlement terms consist of six principal issues:

1. Identification and assessment
2. Equal access to appropriate programming
3. Equal access to appropriate categorical and other programming for Language Enriched Pupils (LEP)
4. Personnel
5. Monitoring
6. Outcome measures

Notice how many of these items refer to, or are related to, assessment and evaluation. Let us look at each section of the decree separately and ascertain how much of the consent decree can be complied with simply by using some form of assessment.

Section one of the META Consent Decree requires: application of the Home Language Survey; establishment of ESOL committees to decide language learning eligibility factors and formulate a plan for English learners; English language assessment, classification, and reclassification; and post-reclassification monitoring. This entire process of identification and assessment cannot be undertaken without trying to evaluate the English learner before, during, and after he or she enters school.

Section two of the decree contains five requirements:

1. submission of a district English language learning plan (which cannot be done without assessment of students' needs);
2. provision of basic ESOL instruction (which cannot be done accurately without having assessed the student);

3. provision of ESOL instruction and/or home language instructional strategies in basic subject areas (again, assessment comes first);
4. identification of interim staffing and in-service measures (which can only be done after assessing students and needs); and
5. procedures for parental involvement.

Section three of the consent decree requires equal access to appropriate programs for English learners, all of which require assessment before placement in any program.

Section four addresses personnel, certification and inservice, exemptions, the supply of personnel, in-service evaluation, and implementation of a schedule for these plans. Clearly, English learners must be assessed prior to knowing what personnel to hire for each school and how to plan subsequent programs.

Sections five and six of the consent decree refer to monitoring issues and outcome measures. Assessment is the only way to measure and monitor progress and determine the extent to which a school district is in compliance with consent decree stipulations. As a result of application of the aforementioned state-mandated guidelines, ongoing assessment is required to monitor the degree to which student achievement is improved. As a direct consequence of examining the consent decree section by section, we begin to see the tremendous importance, value, and consequences of assessment and evaluation.

SCHOOL REGISTRATION

When a new student registers for school, the administration must determine language proficiency for proper placement. Among other documents, a Home Language Survey is completed by the parent or guardian. If the parent answers yes to any of the three questions below, it is determined that the student might need language services and a language proficiency placement test is given.

1. Is a language other than English used in the home?

2. Did the student have a first language other than English?
3. Does the student most frequently speak a language other than English?

Many language placement tests exist, but some popular proficiency tests used to identify, assign, and reclassify English learners are:

The Language Assessment Scales (LAS);

The IDEA Proficiency Test (IPT);

The Maculaitis Assessment Program (MAC);

The Bilingual Syntax Measure (BSM);

The Peabody Picture Vocabulary Test (PPVT); and

The Language Assessment Battery (LAB).

A language proficiency test may test oral or written skills in a language but is primarily given to determine into what language level the student will be placed. Testing is an inexact science, but it provides an approximate indication from which the English learner can progress.

One popular oral test that is administered to beginning level students is the Idea Proficiency Test (IPT), published by Ballard & Tighe. By using visuals and a question and answer format, the level of vocabulary, syntax, comprehension, and verbal expression can be measured. The test is featured at: thttp://www.ballard-tighe.com/IPTOnline InserviceTraining/IPTOral/IPTIOralEnglish_Com ponentsAndAreas.htm. A written exam is also available to accompany the oral exam. The written test determines vocabulary, vocabulary in context, reading for understanding, reading for life skills, and language usage (see http://r3cc.ceee.gwu.edu/standards_assessments/EAC/eac0118.htm).

Nationwide, standardized tests are often used, but later, individual states and districts might create their own proficiency tests according to their individual needs. A list of language proficiency tests from a variety of states can be found at the end of this chapter

Although assessment of English learners varies from state to state and district to district, for purposes of this book we will use the procedures of a

Florida school as an example of the procedures followed when a newcomer begins school.

The first step is to identify potential English learners, based on the Home Language Survey portion of the school registration form (a sample form is included in the Appendix). If the student meets the definition of an English learner, then he or she progresses to step two.

Step two involves checking previous records for language learning status or prior language testing to determine if the student has been assessed for oral language proficiency in English. If no records exist or the student has just arrived from another country, the student is assessed for language proficiency using an oral evaluation such as the IDEA Proficiency Test I or II, depending upon grade level. If the student speaks some English, he or she is assessed starting at the appropriate age level on the IPT. If no English is spoken at all, the student is assessed starting at the lowest level on the IPT. This test determines the student's proficiency level.

Step three is to complete the Initial Aural/Oral Language Classification Assessment Form (see Appendix for sample). The student's level is recorded as one of the following:

A1—No English, Non-English Speaker (NES)

A2—Limited English Speaker (LES), limited understanding

B1—Intermediate English Speaker (LES), communicates with simple phrases

B2—Intermediate English Speaker (LES), communicates in English about everyday situations, but lacks academic language terminology

C1—Advanced English Speaker (LES), understands and speaks fairly well

C2—Full English Speaker (FES), reads and writes English comparable to native English-speaking counterparts

D—Full English Speaker (FES)

E—Monolingual English Speaker

(For further descriptions of these classifications, see Appendix.)

Students designated A1 through C1 are entitled to receive ESOL services, and those labeled C2 are placed in a basic program, pending reading and writing assessment to determine exiting criteria. If the student does not require ESOL services, the form is placed in the cumulative folder and the process ends there. If the student is given an active ESOL status designation (A1–C1), the official ESOL folder is initiated and the student's information is entered into the AS400 data collection system for the county.

Step four includes sending all information gathered to the county ESOL department and sending the Initial Aural/Oral Language Classification Assessment Form to the parent or guardian. A meeting is arranged to explain ESOL program procedures and to have the parent or guardian sign the yellow LEPSEP folder. This initial meeting is called the LEPSEP (Limited English Proficient Student Education Plan) meeting.

Step five is to inform the classroom teacher of the student's ESOL classification level and report any other pertinent information. The teacher is now responsible for executing the LEPSEP in the classroom. From this point on, the assessment is no longer one of proper English language placement, but one of assessing academic progress and learning.

Finally, the No Child Left Behind Act of 2001 has influenced English learner assessment. According to statute, ELLs in every state are assessed annually to determine if they are progressing adequately in acquiring English proficiency in the five domains of speaking, listening, reading, writing, and comprehension. Each state's academic standards will determine whether benchmarks are being met.

A SAMPLE OF PROFICIENCY TESTS BY STATES:

Arizona: The Standard English Language Proficiency Assessment
http://www.ade.az.gov/asd/lep/testaccommodations2005-06.pdf

California: California English Language Development Test (CELDT)
http://www.cde.ca.gov/ta/tg/el/

Georgia: Language Assessment Battery in English (Mandatory)
http://www.glc.k12.ga.us/pandp/esol/tguide/tg-12b.htm

Hawaii: English Proficiency Test (EPT) and native language proficiency (NLP)
http://doe.k12.hi.us/specialeducation/esllsped.htm

Iowa: English Language Development Assessment (ELDA), Iowa Test of English Language Learning
(ITELL) http://www.state.ia.us/educate/ecese/is/ell/doc/gdelps.html

Kansas: Kansas English Language Proficiency Assessment "Kelpa"
www.ksde.org/sfp/esol/kselprofasses.ppt

Massachusetts: Massachusetts Comprehensive Assessment System (MCAS) with accommodations for
English learners who have been in the United States up to three years
http://www.aps1.net/District/MCAS/mcas2.htm

Nebraska: Consortium created English Language Development Assessment (ELDA)
http://www.serve.org/_downloads/publications/ell.pdf

Nevada: (PreLAS) Pre Language Assessment Scale for grades K-1 and the (LAS) Language Assessment
Scale, the LAS Oral, and the LAS Reading/Writing for 2nd grade and above
http://www.doe.nv.gov/statetesting/langprofassess.html

New York: Language Assessment Battery (LAB-R)
http://www.nycenet.edu/daa/test-info

New York: New York State English as a Second Language Achievement Test (NYSESLAT)
http://www.nycenet.edu/daa/test_info/

Oregon: (Oregon ELPA) Oregon English Language Proficiency Assessment
http://www.ode.state.or.us

South Dakota: The Dakota ELP assessment
http://doe.sd.gov/oess/title/IIIela/faq.asp

Texas: Reading Proficiency Tests in English (RPTE)
http://www.tea.state.tx.us/assessment.html

Virginia: Any of the following tests can be used
Council of Chief State Schools (CCSSO) State Collaborative on Student Standards and Assessments
(SCASS), the Idea Proficiency Test (IPT), Language Assessment Scale (LAS), and Woodcock-Munoz
Language Scale (WMLS). http://www.pen.k12.va.us/VDOE/Instruction/ESL/AssessmentInstruments.pdf

✓ The Home Language Survey must be completed for each English learner; however, further information, such as literacy level in the home language, literacy background experience, or language preference is needed to aptly meet the needs of all students.

✓ To comply with a consent decree mandate, the entire process of identification and assessment must be coupled with an evaluation of the English learner before, during, and after entering school.

✓ The student is tested for initial placement and classification and documentation is kept in a folder as an official record.

Chapter 24

How Does a Classroom Teacher Assess and Evaluate an English Learner?

Key Issues

- ○ Assessing and evaluating the English learner
- ○ Maintaining student assessment documentation

SCENARIO

Roody arrived from Haiti as a non-English speaker when he was ten years old and was placed, age appropriately, in the fourth grade. Although Roody was not a mean-spirited child, his behavior soon became a problem, as he was annoying other children, ignoring the teacher, and making classroom life miserable. The teacher decided to meet with his parents for an academic conference, but was advised by the bilingual counselor not to call Roody's house. In the Haitian culture, parents revere the teacher and are not called to the school, except when the child is a serious behavior problem; this means the child will most likely be punished corporally at home. The teacher did not want the boy to be punished—he only wanted to discover what was bothering Roody so he could help him to learn. Finally, a Haitian-Creole speaking liaison contacted the parents on behalf of the teacher and a conference was arranged. Through a discussion with the parents, the teacher discovered that Roody was bored and frustrated in class; although he could not understand English well enough to grasp the language arts content, he had learned the math content two grades earlier in Haiti. As a result, an individual educational plan was created for Roody; he would go to the fifth grade teacher's highest math group while a tutor was found to help him with his academic English. Roody's behavior improved dramatically once his keen mind was challenged and the world in English began to make sense.

HOW DOES A CLASSROOM TEACHER ASSESS AND EVALUATE AN ELL?

English learners must receive instruction in basic subject areas that is understandable, given the student's level of English proficiency. Assessment of student learning, especially in the content areas, can pose problems because separation of language proficiency and knowledge of content is difficult. Teachers need to distinguish if content has been mastered or if language has interfered with student learning. Many tests that seek to measure academic knowledge actually measure only language proficiency (Chamot and O'Malley, 1986; DeGeorge, 1988; Holmes, D., Hedlund, P., & Nickerson, B. 2000; Menken, 2000).

Just as a second grade mainstream teacher might read a mathematical problem to a poor reader for assessment of the child's understanding of mathematical concepts, we must adapt our assessment instruments for ESOL students to appraise actual content knowledge. If we ask a child, "What is the sum of four and four?," the student might not respond because he or she does not know the meaning of the word "sum." How many times do these errors occur for both native and non-native English-speaking children without our knowledge? In fact, these misunderstandings occur between native English-speakers all the time. You hear words and interpret them through the meaning you know, but the meaning is not always what the speaker was trying to imply. Take this example: a tourist from Massachusetts visits a friend in Tennessee and the following dialogue ensues:

Northerner: *Hi Janie. Could you give me a ride to the mall? My car won't start.*

Janie (Southerner): *I don't care a bit to do that.*

Northerner: *OK. Do you know where I can catch a bus to the mall then?*

Janie: *Why do you want to take a bus? I said I don't care to take you.*

Northerner: *Right. That's why I want to take the bus.*

Janie: *No, get in the car and I will take you.*

Northerner: *Well, I don't want to put you out.*

Janie: *I don't know what you mean.*

Can you see what is happening? To the Northerner, when you say *I don't care to do it*, it means *I don't want to do it*. To the Southerner, *I don't care to do it* means she is happy to do it. Both participants are native English speakers, with their own background knowledge, but the language interferes with meaning. Imagine the misunderstandings that occur when a person is learning a language. An English learner calls the teacher "*Teacher*," not knowing the correct way to address a teacher in the United States, yet is politely translating the appropriate form of address from the native language to the target language (English). Again, right information, wrong word. The same phenomenon applies to assessment; the language used may interfere with the meaning the student receives. It is impossible to accurately assess a student's content knowledge with standardized testing if the student does not understand the intended meaning of the words.

For the most accurate placement of the new student, the teacher needs to know as much as possible about the student. After the initial placement test is administered to determine the level of English proficiency, assessment of the student's home language proficiency, previous schooling, academic level, family history, background, and any other pertinent information must be considered. This is important because these factors can determine future success or failure in the classroom.

Because the most common way to assess English learners is through an oral language proficiency test and Home Language Survey, a wide range of skills and abilities are not being identified. How will you know if the new young boy can read or write in his native language, or if he ever attended school at all? If he comes from a wealthy Haitian family, it can be assumed the student has attended school, has studied in French, has learned

Haitian Creole from speaking with his peers, and maybe has had English training as well. He might even be ahead of his grade-level counterparts in the United States. But for a student coming from a less-advantaged family, formal schooling may never have been an option in the home country. What considerations would you have to make for these students?

Another scenario: look at a ten-year-old student who has escaped from a war-torn country, has had one year of formal training before escaping her village, speaks little English, and is now staying in the United States until the war in her country is over. How and where will you place her? She has the academic skills of a first-grader, yet is age ten. Will you place her with the other first-graders where she will not struggle academically, or will you assign her to a fourth or fifth grade class so she can develop socially with her peer group?

Other important factors to consider are the reasons for immigration. The Haitian student who was wealthy in his country has come to the United States because his father is going to practice medicine. The poorer Haitian student has come to the United States to seek economic freedom and a better life. The student escaping her homeland until the war is over probably has expectations of returning home soon. Which student would be encouraged to learn English quickly, aspire to high academic achievement (seen as the key to success in life), and embrace the United States culture? Obviously, the student who expects to return to her country will have less motivation to learn the language.

What about previous literacy levels? Some cultures do not have a written language, but have very strong oral storytelling traditions. Undoubtedly, the literate student has an easier time than the student with no previous literacy skills, because prior knowledge can be transferred to the new language (Smith, 1993). The student with no prior literacy skills must learn to read and write through a foreign language, a monumental task for some learners.

Overall, programmatic assessment of the ESOL student is accomplished by seeking information about the student's prior school experiences, using school records or home country transcripts; interviews with parents, guardians, and interpreters; and any other evidence of the student's previous educational history. Ideally, the student is tested in the home language for content knowledge so that language capability is not confused with content knowledge. If no tests are available for measuring the student's previous academic background, the teacher must devise ways to test prior knowledge. (See Betty Lacaya's narrative in "Notes from the Field.")

Many teachers who are inexperienced in teaching non-native English-speakers are unaware of the complex set of issues and implications these students bring with them. Often the teacher unknowingly refers the student to special services when the difficulty is purely from linguistic interferences. This is why students learning another language are overrepresented in special education programs (Crago, 1990). They are referred for testing when the teacher mistakenly believes the child's English language "dis"ability indicates academic or mental ability. However, sometimes the reverse is true—the teacher, after years of experience, knows the student has serious developmental concerns beyond academic English tasks, and refers the student to special services only to be denied. The reasons for denial could be the particular school's retention policy, inability to test the student in the native language, lack of official documentation of problems, or any number of reasons.

Maintaining Student Documentation

Any school district that is subject to a consent decree must comply with the stipulations to protect the rights of the English learner. Parents or guardians of all incoming students must complete the Home Language Survey to determine the native language. Appropriate steps are taken to determine if language proficiency assessment is needed, and if so, a proficiency exam is administered. Depending on the results, the student is assigned to the assumed correct level and some type of program is assigned to meet the needs of the student.

Let us examine the process a new student from Colombia undergoes as she tries to register at her neighborhood school. Rosa Castillo and her parents approach the secretary in the front office of Crocker School and receive a packet of documents to complete. One document, the Home Language Survey, includes these questions, and the Castillos answer like this:

1. Is a language other than English used in the home?   Yes
2. Did the student have a first language other than English?   Yes
3. Does the student most frequently speak a language other than English?   Yes

Because this Home Language Survey is so superficial, we can learn that Rosa speaks a language other than English, but cannot tell which languages she uses to communicate with her friends; how many other languages she speaks and with whom; which language she is literate in, if any: and any number of other pertinent points that are conspicuously absent. However, if the form is expanded to ask crucial questions, such as questions about other languages the student speaks, it could be helpful. For example, a student from Paraguay may speak Guarani as a first language, yet speak Spanish as a second language. Even if no one in the school system speaks this student's native language, if the second language is known, someone can certainly help to communicate with the student in Spanish.

According to the Home Language Survey, the student meets the state definition of Limited English Proficient (LEP), and the school must provide oral/aural assessment within twenty days of completion of the survey. If, for some reason the period needs to be extended, an additional twenty days are allowed if the parents are notified in writing.

In this particular county, the instruments for assessing language proficiency are:

○ the Pre-IDEA Oral Language Proficiency Test (Pre-IPT)—Pre-K and Headstart (ages 3–5),
○ the IDEA Oral Language Proficiency Test I (IPT-I)—Grades K–6,
○ the IDEA Oral Language Proficiency Test II (IPT-II)—Grades 7–12.

Many schools in the county have a trained oral language assessor—perhaps the assistant principal, the guidance counselor, an ESOL teacher, or even you, the classroom teacher. Staff from the Multicultural/Foreign Language or ESOL Department may also go to the schools to assess oral/aural proficiency if requested.

After a proficiency test is scored, a corresponding level of English knowledge is determined, using an acceptable language level classification chart. In this text, we will use the Broward County Language Level Classification from A1 to E (see Appendix). In this county, a LEPSEP (Limited English Proficient Student Education Plan) folder is initiated for the student, and the classification level (according to the county's determination) is noted on the placement test, as well as the assessment form (Initial Aural/Oral Language Classification Assessment Form, 2590E, see Appendix). Students who score in the A1–C1 category are entitled to ESOL services. Parents are notified of the child's eligibility in their native language (if they speak one of the four major languages in Broward: Spanish, Portuguese, French, and Haitian Creole).

If a student transfers into Broward County from another school district, language levels are reclassified into Broward's terms. For example, a student moves from Dade County (Miami) into Broward County. The counties' classifications are correlated this way:

Dade County	Broward County
Level I	A1/A2
Level II	B1
Level III	B2
Level IV	C1
Level V	C2

The exit date is noted and the student is monitored for the next two years by teachers, principals, and designated ESOL contact persons, according to Florida state guidelines.

Students who are in grades 4 to 12 are assessed in the same manner, but their standardized achievement test scores are also factored into the equation. Students from other counties do not have to be reassessed for entry into the ESOL program. Although parents cannot waive the child's right to ESOL services, they may choose the method of delivery. Students can stay in their neighborhood school setting and receive instruction in the mainstream classroom with ESOL strategies, or they can choose to attend an ESOL cluster school.

After the LEPSEP folder (Form 4399—see Appendix) is generated for the new ESOL student, it must be updated and reviewed annually, as well as whenever necessary. This folder contains ESOL program exit and monitoring information, as well as recommendations made by the ELL's Committee (consisting of parents, teachers, school administrators, and designated ESOL personnel). These documents provide legal proof that the student is receiving services, the school is following the prescribed laws for language minority students, and language skills are progressing through the years, as well as the documentation necessary to receive state ESOL funding.

Points to Remember

✓ A consent decree that protects the rights of language learners mandates that English learners must receive instruction that is comprehensible to them, and they must be provided instruction in basic subject areas, given the student's level of English proficiency.

✓ Teachers need to distinguish if content has been mastered, or if language is interfering with student learning.

✓ Many tests measure language proficiency instead of academic knowledge.

✓ When students are judged by oral language proficiency, a wide range of skills and abilities are not being identified.

✓ Reasons for immigration can influence second language acquisition.

✓ Knowledge about the student's background and previous literacy skills can help the teacher assess the student more accurately.

✓ States must comply with the stipulations of their consent decree requirements. A Home Language Survey is completed by the parents, and documentation is kept for each English learner.

✓ Students transferring from county to county keep the same fluency classification; only the language is adapted to reflect the code of the new county.

Chapter 25

ESOL Students and Standardized Tests

Key Issues

- ○ ESOL students and standardized tests: The issues
- ○ Modifications allowed for writing assessments
- ○ How student assessment documentation is maintained
- ○ District and state policies
- ○ Timeframe for testing ESOL students

SCENARIO

When giving tests in another language we need to remember what it is like when the mind goes through a series of thinking processes. Let us assume you are a native English speaker and the teacher asks you a question in Spanish. We will walk through an example of the process your mind would go through in this situation. The Spanish alphabet is similar to English, so if you see the question in written form you will be able to make educated guesses through clues. Now imagine the difficulty you would experience if you were asked the question orally, with no literacy clues, in a classroom with all eyes on you, waiting for the answer. *¿De qué color es el carro del hombre?* First you have to translate in your mind what is being asked. You can see (or hear) the word *color*, which is the same in English; then you notice "*carro*," which you probably assume means "car." You then make an educated guess and conclude that the question has something to do with the color of a car. Great! Now you have translated the question in your mind. You decide the answer will be red, but now you have to think of how to say "red" in Spanish. Your mind frantically searches for the translation as the teacher (if he has not moved on to another student yet) and the entire class await your answer.

Finally, you remember that red is *rojo*, but now you have to try to recall what the correct pronunciation is, because you vaguely remember that the *j* has an odd pronunciation like an *h*. As you practice the answer in your mind, you get ready to blurt it out. Just as you are ready, the teacher announces, "Susie doesn't seem to know. Can anybody help her out?" as other classmates clamor to answer the simple question.

ESOL STUDENTS AND STANDARDIZED TESTS

Can you see from the above example why an ESOL student needs more time to process information? Succinctly, this is the formula a beginning second language student goes through:

1. The question is asked in English.
2. The mind translates to the native language.
3. The question is pondered.
4. The answer is formulated within native-language understanding.
5. The answer is translated back into English.
6. The student must pronounce the answer in English.

Whew! Exhausting, is it not? That is one reason English language learners might appear fatigued, or frequently suffer from minor ailments such as headaches or stomachaches (Ariza, 1991).

In complying with state mandates, modifications must be provided for ESOL students which correspond to their immediate level of English expertise, in accordance with an approved district ELL plan. However, students' needs should be determined individually when considering precise modifications. Individuals who administer any statewide assessment test must be adequately trained by the school district; the district must provide qualified personnel (such as the ESOL district coordinator) to ensure appropriate testing conditions prevail.

Modifications should be made for the English learner when faced with the ubiquitous standardized test. The following suggested testing modifications for ESOL come from a memorandum sent to all Florida school district superintendents. These regulations have been applied to the High School Competency Test (HSCT) since 1996, and have been in effect for the Florida Comprehensive Assessment Test (FCAT) and the Florida Writing Assessment since 1997. We will begin with the HSCT and FCAT.

1. Additional time may be allowed for testing, as long as the entire test is taken on the same day.
2. The ELL may use a dictionary that they are accustomed to using in instructional settings, e.g., Spanish to English—English to Spanish. A native language dictionary is not provided.
3. The ELL may be tested in a separate room with the ESOL person administering the test. Minors must adhere to the wishes of their parents or guardians regarding this option.
4. The ESOL or bilingual teacher administering the test may answer questions the student has about test directions or instructions.

(See Appendix for types of accommodations made by other states.)

For the mathematics section of the test, the ESOL or bilingual teacher may explain a word or phrase that will help the student understand the question, but may not help solve the problem. Teachers must be careful not to answer questions in a way that allows the student to infer the correct answer. When the test is administered to a group of students, a question may be explained to the entire group if it will benefit all participants. If clarification is needed by only one student, it must be given individually without disturbing other examinees.

The same caveat applies to the reading section. The teacher must be careful not to answer questions in a manner that would provide an answer and is prohibited from answering questions about reading passages or any of the possible answers. Again, the student can use a dictionary, but he or she must be able to read and answer in English.

Writing Assessment Modifications

1. Testing time may be extended beyond the time specified in the administration manual and the test may be given in brief segments throughout the day. However, testing must be completed the day it starts.
2. Home-language-to-English—English-to-home-language dictionaries may be used during testing, as they are familiar tools in daily instructional settings. Dictionaries in English only or the native language only are not permitted.
3. At the discretion of parents, ELLs may choose to take the test in a separate room with an ESOL or bilingual teacher.
4. The teacher may not read the prompt, nor answer any questions about the prompt that the students may ask. Only general test directions may be translated into the native language.

Some examples of writing prompts are:

1. Write about the best day in your life. Tell what you did.
2. Your friends come to visit you from another country. What would you do to show them the United States?
3. Write about how your life would be if you had gone out west in a covered wagon.

The first two prompts could be responded to by any student, because the concepts are universal. But look at the third prompt. What does it mean to go out west? What is a covered wagon? How much background knowledge would you need to write this scenario? The third question was actually taken from a standardized test given several years ago. Would this question be fair to an English language learner not from the United States?

DISTRICT AND STATE POLICIES ON ASSESSMENT: WHEN DO ENGLISH LEARNERS TEST?

All states follow their own guidelines to ensure that English learners are not denied access to educational programs and that English learners receive adequate and appropriate instruction. To achieve these objectives, districts and schools must identify and provide accurate academic assessment data. If the standard tests are impossible to administer, adjustments and alternative measures must be provided. Because of the significant influx of non-English speaking migrants to the state, Florida has addressed the issues of fair academic assessment by the following policy:

1. If English learners have been receiving ESOL services for a period of less than two years (two years from date of entry into the ESOL program), they may be exempted from taking the norm-referenced test, but must be assessed by alternative means as determined by districts and schools.
2. Students who have exited the ESOL program, or students who have been classified as ELL but do not receive services, must take all norm-referenced tests by virtue of their classification.
3. ELL classified students in the ESOL program for a period of less than two years (two calendar years from the date of entry into the ESOL

program), with the approval of the majority of the ELL Committee, may be exempted from taking the Grade Ten Assessment Test and the Florida Writes performance assessment. However, assessment must be made by other means.
4. ELL students receiving services for less than two years may be exempted from taking the HSCT (High School Competency Test) temporarily. However, no high school diploma is awarded until the test is taken and passed. ELLs who are not receiving services, or who have exited the program, are not temporarily exempted from this test

It is of utmost importance that parents are informed of the school's decisions about inclusion or exclusion of their children in testing procedures. They need to understand the ramifications of exemption, especially with regard to taking the HSCT. Finally, although school districts are not required to offer translated versions of norm-referenced tests, alternative assessments that reflect student accomplishments must be provided for those students who are exempted from district and statewide tests.

Points to Remember

✓ According to law, modifications must be made for ESOL students based on their current level of language knowledge. We cannot wait until they "know enough English" to instruct them in academic content.

✓ Extra wait time is crucial when questioning second language learners. Their minds are processing what is being asked and are translating data from one language to another.

✓ In many states, ESOL students who have been receiving services for less than two years from the date of entry into the ESOL program may be exempted from taking a norm-referenced test, but they must be assessed by alternative means, as determined by districts and schools.

✓ Suggested guidelines for testing modifications for English learners need to be determined, and followed, with the approval of the ESOL Committee, districts, and schools.

Chapter 26

Why Alternative Assessment for English Language Learners?

Key Issues

○ English fluency versus content knowledge

○ Types of alternative assessment

○ Authentic assessment

○ Grading the ESOL student fairly

SCENARIO

Mrs. Matsuno, a teacher with little experience in alternative testing for ESOL students, was at the end of her patience with Akemi. Nothing had changed in Akemi's academic behavior—she still was not responding as the teacher expected, even after being in the United States for more than eight months. The other students were busy answering the questions on the Civil War unit test while Akemi had barely made an attempt to read the test questions. In frustration, Mrs. Matsuno grabbed a piece of paper and tossed it on Akemi's desk. "Here, draw a picture." At least she had given the child a way to keep busy. To the teacher's surprise, Akemi started drawing a clear, epic-style depiction of the Civil War, with President Lincoln, soldiers with vivid uniforms representing Northern and Southern armies, and illustrations that clearly showed she had understood the content of the unit. Mrs. Matsuno was overwhelmed! She had unwittingly discovered a successful way to alternatively assess her student.

WHY ALTERNATIVE ASSESSMENTS FOR ENGLISH LANGUAGE LEARNERS?

When assessing ELLs, always keep in mind that lack of English fluency does not signify lack of intelligence. It should not be assumed that students are below grade level because they cannot do grade level work in English. In fact, English-learning students are often bored or frustrated when forced to sit through lessons addressing academic content they have already mastered in their native language. Such students may respond by acting out or tuning out.

Chamot and O'Malley (1994) describe six basic reasons why alternative assessment is valuable and more accurate in assessing instruction for ESOL students.

1. Authenticity—Assessment reflects actual classroom tasks in local curriculum content and provides true information about language acquisition.
2. Variety—Student performance is assessed from a variety of perspectives, instead of relying on a limited number of measurements; this provides a global perspective from which to draw conclusions about progress.
3. Process Orientation—Progress is monitored with respect to learning processes and strategies, as well as product output.
4. Continuity—Student performance is ongoing and monitored throughout the school year.
5. Instructional Assessment—Instruction can be adapted to individual student needs, and feedback on instructional effectiveness is readily provided.
6. Collaborative—Teachers can interact holistically to share their views of students performance throughout a variety of scenarios.

Alternative assessment is the practice of judging student progress by methods, instruments, and documentation other than standardized tests. These methods can include portfolios, journals, interviews, etc., that demonstrate the student's ability to complete grade-level work. Authentic assessment, performance assessment, and naturalistic assessment are also valuable indicators because they demonstrate the child's true abilities.

Authentic assessment incorporates real-life functions. The English learner can demonstrate achievement by producing information, such as being able to make a telephone call to the bus company to inquire about a route. Performance assessment requires the student to make a correct response, indicating knowledge of a skill, concept, or method of completing a task (O'Neill, 1992). Naturalistic assessment entails observing performance and behavior informally within a natural setting (Chittendon, 1994).

Assessment and instruction should go hand in hand, as they are interdependent. Carefully designed assessment should be authentic and conducted in conjunction with developmentally appropriate activities that reflect the ELLs true environment, both in and out of school (Cummins, 1982; DeGeorge, 1988; O'Malley & Valdez Pierce, 1996). Throughout the entire process of teaching and learning, authentic assessment should be ongoing, methodical, and linked to all subjects taught. In this way the instructor can judge the English learner's progress holistically, as well as objectively, and accurately analyze reading, writing, listening, speaking, cultural knowledge, and communicative competence.

Although the choices for alternative assessments are comprehensive, we will discuss the most common types in use today.

Portfolios

Probably the most popular example of an alternate assessment is the portfolio. Students, teachers, professors, private and public employees, artists, job seekers, and any number of individuals are expected to showcase their work in the form of portfolios to indicate their progress and competence. Portfolios for ESOL students are collections of information about the student that indicate progress in learning which enable teachers, parents, and administrators to evaluate the student's achievement, growth, and thinking processes. Portfolios can also include communications with students, other teachers, parents, and administrators about the student's progress, with specific representation of his or her work (Chamot and O'Malley, 1994; O'Malley & Valdez Pierce,1996).

According to Paulson et al. (1992), in addition to being simply a collection of student work, a portfolio is "a purposeful collection of student work that exhibits the student's efforts, progress, and achievement in one or more areas . . . the collection must include student participation in selecting contents, the criteria for selection, the criteria for judging merit, and evidence of student reflection." Thus, a collection of student work can only become a portfolio if the student contributes input, allowing the student to play a role in his or her own academic growth.

The advantages of assessment by portfolios are many, according to Valencia et al. (1990).

○ This type of assessment capitalizes on the student's best work instead of focusing on errors.
○ Assures that assessment is ongoing during instruction. No time is lost in testing.
○ Drives instruction, as teachers learn directly from the ongoing process of teaching what to teach, how to teach, and when to teach (Teale, 1987). Portfolio assessment is multifaceted, because it embodies cognitive, affective, and social processes.
○ Both teacher and student are involved in an active, reflective partnership. The student selects the work to be shown and must justify his or her choice.
○ It is authentic. Assessment occurs as students are actively learning.

WHAT SHOULD BE INCLUDED IN PORTFOLIOS?

There is no right or wrong way to put together a student portfolio, unless a school or district mandates a specific procedure. Typical contents of a portfolio include:

○ Drawings;
○ Writing samples;
○ Language Experience Approach stories dictated to the teacher;
○ Poetry, haiku, creative writings, or other assignments;
○ Letters;
○ Invitations;
○ Greeting cards;

- ○ Visual representations created by the student, such as charts, maps, semantic maps, webs, graphic organizers, pictures of bulletin boards, and science or other projects;
- ○ Evidence of solo or group activities in which the student has participated;
- ○ Audio tapes of verbal progress;
- ○ Videotapes of student participation in dramatic representations, choral readings, role playing, skits, or of the student leading the class in some activity, teaching/sharing something about his or her culture, telling or reading a story, interviewing someone, giving a puppet show, dramatizing a commercial, etc.;
- ○ Learning log;
- ○ Checklist of achievements, such as a vocabulary list, rubrics of criteria mastered, SOLOM matrix (see references), etc.;
- ○ Reading inventories;
- ○ Selected work samples;
- ○ Parent/teacher conference report;
- ○ Self-evaluation;
- ○ Copies of pertinent data such as report cards and test scores;
- ○ Book reports;
- ○ A list of books read;
- ○ Lab reports submitted;
- ○ Research papers;
- ○ Evidence of collective group work in which the student took part;
- ○ Work dated at the beginning, middle, and the end of the year, to measure self-progress.

As we can see, the list of contents for a student's portfolio can be endless. However, it is important that teachers keep portfolios as well, containing student work accumulated throughout the year; these should include cumulative portfolios of the student's long-term records and another portfolio with grades, records, notes, and observations. This is not merely efficient record keeping, it is also a way to maintain legal documentation for future reference, crises, or substantiation.

Teacher-Made Tests

For students temporarily exempted from standardized tests, teacher-made tests can be substituted for standardized computation/calculation and reading/language exams. However, all substitute testing must be approved by the ELL committee, follow the district ELL plan, and be tied to the test subject content from which the ELL was originally exempted to ensure congruence with the standard test.

Abbreviated Standard Tests

Many school districts have developed alternative tests to assess the skills and benchmarks that are used to measure achievement of goals and standards. These are often called test prototypes. In addition, many private textbook and computer software publishers have marketed test prototypes that correspond to state standardized tests that can be adopted as alternative assessments for individuals exempted from formal testing.

Protocols

When a teacher needs to assess a particular skill or wants to assess a certain content area, students can be assigned a specific academic activity to perform. For example, if a teacher needs to assess skills in oral reading, the student is asked to read aloud. The results are obvious indicators of achievement.

Rating Scales/Inventories

Teachers can use these methods to record behaviors and student progress. Daily or weekly behavior, academic progress, or emotional episodes can be recorded. For example, when trying to eliminate a linguistic or grammatical interference, a teacher could write: *Yesterday Wang, who is working on his pronunciation of "th," corrected himself twice, and today he corrected himself five times.* Such documentation should not be judgmental, rather it should merely report progress.

Anecdotal Records

Anecdotal records are notes jotted in a narrative form at the end of the day or during a free moment. The teacher, paraprofessional, or staff member working with the student can also record what happened in the classroom, on the playground, in "specials," at lunch, with other students, while the student is alone, etc. The teacher can clarify student behavior or performance, and major changes can be revealed over time. However, this manner of assessment does have drawbacks, as the teacher must have ample time to collect the data and the perception to make sense of the information collected. Therefore, it might be best to save this method for selected individuals who need more one-on-one attention.

Miscue Analysis

Teachers use miscue analysis as an assessment tool to ascertain how a reader processes the printed word (Goodman & Goodman, 1972; Goodman, 1973). An analysis of reading weaknesses and strengths can be made by the kinds of errors made. In the case of an English language learner, the teacher must be sure the "mistakes" are not caused by pronunciation problems, but truly represent difficulty in reading. In miscue analysis the student reads aloud a meaningful passage of about 500 words, while the teacher records the performance. The teacher can hold a copy of the same text to make notes. After the reader finishes, the teacher asks probing questions to see what the child has remembered. Some miscues can be:

Insertion—the reader says a word that is not in the text

Omission—a word is omitted

Substitution—one word is replaced with another while reading

Teacher supplies word—if the reader struggles with a word, the teacher supplies one

Immediate correction—the reader says a wrong word and then self-corrects

The teacher, who knows the students, will be the best judge of their reading comprehension. However, sometimes a student will read aloud beautifully and not understand what he or she has just read; conversely, the student will not read well aloud, but will understand the passage after reading silently. In such cases, the teacher might not realize what is happening. In the first case, the student demonstrates excellent pronunciation, and in the second example, the student cannot pronounce the words correctly, yet comprehends the text. A younger student might have acquired a native-like accent, but not possess CALP (Cognitive Academic Language Proficiency, Cummins, 1981), whereas the older student might have excellent prior knowledge and be able to understand, but not be able to speak well. Identifying such reading patterns enables teachers to plan an appropriate reading program for their students.

IRI

An IRI (Informal Reading Inventory) is an assessment tool that involves teachers taping students as they read passages with varying degrees of difficulty (grade levels). After reading, students are asked comprehension questions. The tape is replayed and the teacher can then do a miscue analysis to see if the student's comprehension is reflected in his or her patterns of miscues. The results indicate the reading grade level.

Running Records

A running record is one way to evaluate a student's daily progress in reading. Usually they can begin after about two hours of training (Clay, 1989). This method is similar to a miscue analysis, as the student reads while being recorded, and the teacher stands behind the reader checking off errors. Some teachers prefer not to record the reader, but the recording allows teachers to avoid classroom interruptions and they can play back the performance at a later date. Unlike IRI's, there is no text to mark, and so the teacher has to write quickly—another reason why recording is useful. Running records are a successful way to evaluate text difficulty, to group students, to monitor progress, and observe difficulties, while allowing readers to move at their own speeds (Clay, 1979, 1989; Zorillo, 2002).

Journals

Journals are an excellent venue for learners to begin practicing their writing. Students usually either love keeping journals or hate it. Journals can be formal notebooks or they can be made of folded and stapled paper. A teacher can make journal writing valuable to English language learners, and at the same time have an excellent vehicle for assessing their writing skills. If given a writing task, even students who appear to have an excellent grasp of English will almost always make errors, and the teacher will find areas that need substantial practice. Ironically, many students (especially from Asian countries) write native-like English, yet cannot speak or understand English well, because their past language education focused on literacy, not communicative competence.

Personal Journals

A personal journal may be the first encounter a student has in writing about personal thoughts. Where, when, and how often journal writing is assigned depends on the teacher's preferences and objectives. The teacher may respond if the journal writer wishes, but should not correct. Often students are delighted when the teacher writes back a personal response. This technique works wonders for those who are too shy or timid to talk to the teacher. By responding in writing, the teacher can begin to build a very strong, personal bond with the writer. The journal writer must feel that his or her writing is personal and that trust must be fostered by the teacher.

Dialogue Journals

A dialogue journal (Kreeft, 1984; Peyton & Staton, 1993) is just that—the student writes and the teacher responds. Students can keep writing about the same topic, or a new topic can be announced at each writing time. This is a great opportunity to encourage new writers to participate in a meaningful activity. Students usually savor reading what their teacher has to say. Be aware, however, that certain topics or language may present problems and the teacher may need to explain why the writing is inappropriate. Also, teachers may learn distressing details about a student's life, such as an abusive relationship, a par-

ent going to jail, or the fact that his or her friend is contemplating suicide, and may need to decide how he or she should intervene because the student's writing might be a legitimate call for help.

Buddy Journal

Buddy journals are ongoing conversations between two individuals in written form (Bronley, 1989, 1995). The partners can be in the same grade, class, or reading group, or they can be older students in different classes, schools, grades, and with the advent of electronic mail, even in different countries. The students can brainstorm topics, or topics can be assigned by the teacher. This is an ideal way to create a meaningful activity, as the writers are motivated to write because they will receive an answer. Again, the teacher may have to monitor the journals for appropriateness.

Learning Journal

A learning journal is an ideal way to teach metalinguistic awareness, as English language learners are encouraged to write about their learning process. This may be a little difficult because students must be taught what to look for and what to write about. For example: *Today I made a mistake and everyone laughed when I said soup instead of soap. I hate it when they laugh at me.* Guiding questions can be posed so that language learners can understand how they are learning and the processes they are going through. Typical questions could be: *What did you learn today?; How did you know you learned it?; How did you feel when you took that reading test today?; What is the hardest part about English?* By reading the journals, teachers are able to cull salient points to focus and build on, while helping students to understand the language learning process.

SOLOM (See Appendix)

The California State Department of Education has created an oral language observation instrument called the SOLOM (Student Oral Language Observation Matrix). Throughout the year, the teacher has the opportunity to see students in a variety of meaningful and complex communication situations. Because teacher observations are cumulative and free from the stresses of artificial testing situations, the assessment of students yields greater reliability than the one-shot standardized test (Goodman, Goodman, & Hood, 1989). The SOLOM test focuses on oral language traits such as comprehension, fluency, vocabulary, grammar, and pronunciation. Each student is assessed for these traits, and the appropriate box checked off. After tallying the scores (each trait receives a certain number of points), teachers can rate students as "non-English proficient," "limited English proficient," or "fully English proficient." With this assessment tool, the teacher must be linguistically sensitive, as the test can be subjective.

Checklists

Checklists are wonderful, fast, and convenient alternative assessment tools for ESOL students, because they are adaptable for any lesson and can be completed quickly. Checklists include the behaviors or skills that are to be assessed; the teacher simply checks off the appropriate skill. When creating a checklist, the teacher must think about all the behaviors, tasks, skills, and so on, that he wants to see the student master. At the bottom of the checklist, space should be left for additional categories which are certain to present themselves during the process of learning. Checklists can be made for one lesson, or for many throughout the year. The date, the behavior, the task, activity, etc. should be recorded for later reference. Because this is a holistic assessment, it is a natural way to document achievement, mastery, or failure. Be cautioned, however, that checklists can be limiting; when teachers focus exclu-

sively on certain things, they may miss other significant occurrences.

Rubrics

A rubric is a predetermined list of criteria to determine the grade for or quality of an assignment, a product, project, or task. For example, the teacher can grade a student on the following basis:

For a grade of A the student must:

Attend every class;
Receive no less than 90 percent on the test;
Turn in superior written work on time;
Prepare for and participate in each class.

For a grade of B the student must:

Miss no more than one class;
Receive no less than an 80 percent on the test;
Turn in very good written work;
Prepare for and participate in most classes.

For a grade of C the student must:

Miss no more than two classes;
Receive no less than 70 percent on the test;
Turn in good written work;
Prepare for and participate in some classes.

Academic Rubric

You can create your own rubric by using the tool found at this website: *Create rubrics for your project-based-learning activities.* (2005). Retrieved from the Rubistar website on November 16, 2005, from http://rubistar.4teachers.org/index.php. Teachers can prepare rubrics for ESOL students according to the objectives they want to achieve.

SCORING RUBRIC FOR ORAL PRESENTATION

4 Communicates a purpose or idea in a clear, specific manner. Superior effort, 2–3 mistakes.	**3** Uses good techniques to communicate ideas; purpose is clear. Makes 4–6 mistakes.	**2** Demonstrates an attempt to communicate with adequate success. Makes significant errors or omissions; more than 7–9 mistakes	**1** Demonstrates little or no clarity; reason for assignment is unclear; more than 10 mistakes; unacceptable assignment.

Electronic Documentation

Audio and video documentation are ideal methods of capturing the student's abilities from beginning (placement) to end (exiting the ESOL program). Initial interviews can determine proper placement, based on oral proficiency and receptive language understanding, and can be played back at any time to measure progress, evaluate learning, and to plan further instruction. As an additional bonus, students can see and hear their own progress. The teacher can videotape students as they participate in skits, role playing, theatrical works, solo and choral recitations, interviewing, presentations, debates, and any number of opportunities that personify the English language learners as they engage in language interaction.

Interviews and Conferences

One simple way to judge how much students know is to sit down and talk to them. Teachers can phrase questions to elicit responses that indicate mastery of a grammatical concept. For instance, if a teacher wants to know if the student can use *do* and *did* appropriately, the teacher can ask a specific question requiring that form to answer correctly. Teachers who tell a student, *Tell me what you did during the spring vacation*, will soon learn if the student knows the past tense. If a student is told, *Ask me what I did on my birthday last year*, and the student responds, *What you did on your birthday last year?*, we know there is a problem with the *do* structure in English. In this way, teachers can clearly see where comprehension breaks down and where strengths lie.

Interviews and conferences may be formal or informal, but they involve more than just talking to the student. The aim is to get the student to talk, so teachers must listen and let the student speak. This will be difficult if there are thirty other students clamoring for attention. If teachers want to use this method, they need to plan for its success by choosing a time when they will be able to concentrate on the individual at hand, and ask questions that require more than a yes or no answer.

Self-Assessment

Some students come from countries where the teacher (as master) talks and the learner memorizes, and creativity is not encouraged. English learners in American classes must be trained to become reflective and to evaluate their own work. Provocative questions such as: *What is my best work this week? What do I need to practice more to improve my spelling? What do I need to become a better writer?* will help learners to assess themselves and see where they have improved, as well as where they need to improve. This procedure will take much practice and guidance, because many students raised in other cultures are not expected to focus on themselves, and they feel uncomfortable doing this.

GRADING THE ENGLISH LEARNER

One of the greatest dilemmas facing the classroom teacher is the issue of fair and accurate grading of English learners, when the categories on their report cards do not truly reflect the ESOL student's quality of work or academic progress. Sadly, a report card often only reflects the student's work in comparison to the rest of the class. In addition, a poor grade can carry such a social stigma that the children often unfairly judge their own worth by the grades they receive. When grades include absences or behavioral issues, the final tally is skewed, and academic ability is neglected. Compounding the grading issue is the uncertainty and disparity concerning the literacy level in the native language. It is unfair and quite impossible to compare a competent literate with an emerging literate, as there is no common standard to measure standard performance.

Rhodes and Shanklin (1992) have suggested a number of guidelines that can be used in obtaining more accurate grades. Teachers should grade only:

1. The student's best work;
2. Material relevant to the student's learning; and
3. Progress and end product.

Students should:

1. Know what skills and topics will be graded (to ensure their best effort is directed at the right objectives); and
2. Be taught to know how to critique their own work and what to learn to improve their grades.

And, finally, teachers should strive to improve their own grading practices.

As previously recommended, extra time can be allowed to provide for delayed language processing; interpreters can be available, and the testing format can be revised to make testing more comprehensible for the second language learner. As grading procedures become more defined and precise, the process of determining accurate grades will become more smooth.

Finally, conventional report cards can be replaced by a quarterly summary report that evaluates student performance across the curriculum in narrative form, with corresponding rating scales (Meisels, 1996/1997), and written comments about the significance of the grade.

Points to Remember

✓ Lack of English fluency does not indicate lack of intelligence. The student might possess the content knowledge in his or her native language.

✓ Alternative assessments judge student progress through methods, instruments, and documentation other than those used in standardized tests.

✓ Authentic assessment incorporates real-life functions; the English learner can demonstrate achievement by producing information to demonstrate competency. The student can call the bus company and inquire about the correct route to take, order a meal from a menu, pay a bill, etc.

✓ Assessment and instruction should go hand-in-hand, as they are interdependent; both should be authentic and designed to be done in conjunction with developmentally appropriate activities that reflect the English learner's true environment (Cummins, 1982; DeGeorge, 1988; Kauchak, Eggen, & Carter, 2002).

✓ Portfolios, teacher-made tests, writing samples, etc. are some examples of alternative assessments.

✓ When assessing an English-language learner using the IRI (Informal Recording Inventory), be careful not to judge comprehension by pronunciation. The fact that a child can pronounce words while reading does not indicate reading comprehension. Likewise, a child may not be able to pronounce words correctly, but may possess total understanding of the passage.

✓ Report cards do not truly reflect the ELL's quality of work or academic progress. They do, however, compare the student to the rest of the (native-English-speaking) class—an unfair evaluation.

✓ Rubrics can be created to measure your own language and content objectives.

Part Five

TEACHER REFLECTIONS: NOTES FROM THE FIELD

To help present and future teachers deal with the issues surrounding alternative assessment of ELLs, we thought it would be most helpful to hear from teachers already in the field, dealing with testing and assessment issues on a day-to-day basis.

Marci Maher, who received her ESOL endorsement through her undergraduate teaching program at Florida Atlantic University, is a new fourth grade teacher in Broward County, Florida. She talks about what it is like for her to comply with state mandates, meet the needs of all the students in her charge, and juggle the mind-boggling array of administrative tasks demanded of her as a classroom teacher.

MARCI MAHER:

ESOL students come to the classroom not knowing what to expect. You don't know anything about their academic or personal history. You need to teach them, and they need to learn. Communication is limited. They feel hopeful, you feel hopeful. Then reality sets in. How in the world do you teach a child who cannot speak or understand English? Where do you begin? How do you make them feel a part of the classroom?

From my own experience as a brand new teacher, I can assure you that it is with great apprehension and a little bit of fear that one takes on the challenge of teaching the ESOL child. When you look into the eyes of foreign children, you want to convey so much to them. You want so much for them to benefit from what you have to offer in the classroom, knowing that as hard as you try, without the proper resources, these children will lose precious time in their academic development, leaving gaps where seeds of knowledge need to be planted and nurtured. These children need uninterrupted learning, as do all children. Yet these children's lives were interrupted when they were transported to a new country through no choice of their own. What can teachers do? This situation is here to stay, as more and more people from other countries enter the United States from all over the world.

In all fairness to the teacher and to the ESOL student, the school should provide the teacher with materials such as computer programs, bilingual books, tests to measure the child's academic level in the native language, and bilingual translators who are immediately accessible. This way, not so much time is lost during the adjustment period for the ESOL child. However, the reality is that this might not happen, so a well-prepared teacher will gather his or her resources and prepare material long before the inevitable ESOL child arrives.

I would like to share some of the steps I have taken to aid an ESOL child in my class who is classified "A2." To set the scene, "Pedro" had just arrived from Brazil in January. I had been teaching fourth grade for six weeks.

Pedro did not speak, read, or comprehend any English. Where does a teacher begin with a child such as Pedro? I decided to take the following steps:

○ First, I tested him on a computer reading program called "The Rosetta Stone." He did fairly well.

○ I got some phonics books on a second-grade level to increase his decoding and encoding skills to our fourth-grade level.

○ Next, I arranged for him to be in a third-grade reading group. Exposure to reading in a less intimidating level was recommended to me by experienced teachers. He also sits in on my reading groups.

○ I scheduled him to have a daily half-hour reading skills session in the computer lab.

○ I found a Brazilian peer buddy from the fifth grade who would partner with him, show him around, and explain things to him in his native language.

○ Whenever possible, but at least three times a week, I sat with Pedro and read one-on-one with him. Afterwards, we worked with word lists and phonics skills.

○ Pedro received a spelling list once a week, as did the other children—but he received words modified to fit his circumstances.

○ Pedro had a peer buddy in my class who spoke Spanish. He understood most of what he heard, but not all. I spoke some Spanish and I think he understood some of what I said as well. Pedro participated in all other subjects such as math, science, social studies, art and physical education. His classmates readily accepted him and socially, the transition has been smooth.

As you can see, teaching the ESOL student requires quite a bit of coordinating and organizing in addition to

(continued)

all the regular classroom duties. It is no easy feat. I am a teacher who is receptive and open to teaching ESOL students and I am ready to go the "extra mile." Individuals who are not open to foreign cultures and believe students should learn English before being placed in the regular classroom may have difficulty teaching ESOL students and might feel resentment. However, the law is clear and we must make modifications for ELL students.

What happens to the ESOL child in a negative type of environment? Obviously, there is not one answer, but I suggest that all new teachers prepare for their future ESOL students by knowing the legal issues, knowing what is expected of them as teachers, and preparing themselves to be able to respond to the needs of these lovely children.

Betty Lacayo is a veteran fourth grade teacher in St. Lucie County, Florida, with many years of experience teaching ELL students. She has learned to meet their needs, adapt and modify content areas, and create alternative instruments to assess learning and instruction.

In the following pages, she shares her thoughts, based on her years of experience. She explains what transpires in her school when a new ESOL student registers and how she copes with the day-to-day instructing and assessing of ESOL students.

BETTY LACAYO:

After identifying a new ESOL student through the Home Language Survey, the guidance counselor (the designated ESOL tester) administers the routine test given to ESOL students (the IDEA Oral Language Proficiency Test), which will determine for me whether or not the student is a non-English speaker (NES) or a limited English speaker (LES). If a child is LES, a norm-referenced test is administered. My school uses the MAT (Metropolitan Achievement Test). If students score below the 32nd percentile they are placed in an ESOL program. An NES student is immediately placed in an ESOL classroom (that is, mainstreamed in a regular class with a teacher who either is in the process of attaining, or has attained, the ESOL endorsement).

Monitoring during the program includes an annual ELL committee review of the student's current English language proficiency test data, academic achievement record, and current classroom performance to determine if there is a continued need for ESOL services. Students may not exit the program if they score an NES or LES on the IDEA test. In our county we use a classification system of A1, A2, B1, B2, C1, C2 and then exit the ESOL Program. We also conduct an annual ELL committee review before moving up a classification or exiting the program.

St. Lucie County School Board (like other counties) offers an ESOL Quick Reference Guide. These booklets contain key information pertaining to the practical application of ESOL program requirements. They also

include a step-by-step outline of school-based procedures, including identification procedures, assessment, placement, parent notification, the ELL plan, exit procedures, and the monitoring of a student's performance after exiting the program.

After the guidance counselor gathers the classification information, she passes along the results to me as the classroom teacher, and then I have to pretty much fend for myself. Once receiving the ESOL child in my class, I sit and have a very informal interview (in a conversational manner) to determine the child's English ability. If the student is Spanish or Haitian-Creole speaking, I have the ESOL teacher assistant speak to them to determine whether or not they have attended school in the past and have learned to read and write in their native language. If I have a student from a country other than a Spanish or Haitian-Creole speaking country, I am at a great disadvantage and can only hope that the county has someone to come help me interpret. Otherwise, I have to start at the "bare bones" basics. When students come into my class as non-English speaking, I start by having them help me label things around the classroom using index cards. This helps to acclimate them to the classroom layout. As they work on the cards, I also observe their writing skills and hand coordination with a pencil and paper. Consequently, the language they speak determines the activities I plan for them. When children speak Spanish, I am able to modify activities and am confident with the tasks I have created for them. I adapt activities to our current theme

(continued)

of study in the classroom so students feel a part of our classroom community. Haitian students are a bit more difficult, because the majority of the Haitian children we see at our school have never attended school anywhere. With other nationalities, it is extremely difficult to place them at their current level of academic ability, but in my opinion, observation is the most powerful tool. I watch to see if the students know how to hold a book and turn the pages correctly. I look to see how well the student is able to copy the alphabet for some sign of previous writing practice. If students have basic reading and writing skills in their native language, I immediately research the linguistic and grammatical interferences that occur between their native language and English so that I have a good basis for ascertaining where I need to start.

There are numerous ESL books and other books that make you aware of the cultural differences you can expect to encounter with your students from afar. The best plan of action I take is to try to get to know my student's culture so I can understand how the student thinks and why he or she may behave in ways that reflect the values of that culture.

Every teacher with ESOL students has been tormented over the question of what to do about assessing these students. Wanting to be fair and grade according to ESOL students' abilities, teachers are forever in search of new methods to adapt their assessment procedures to fit the needs of these students.

Knowing traditional assessments have not been effective in my assessment of ESOL students, I have searched for alternative methods. I have adapted several methods of assessment of reading and language arts. Because I integrate subject areas across curriculum, most science and social studies grades are pulled from reading and language arts lessons and assignments. Math, being the great equalizer, is graded separately and is only modified when word problems are involved.

Because every ESOL student comes into my classroom with different needs, I tailor my curriculum and methods of assessment accordingly. Fortunately, my experience has been that the "typical" ESOL student coming into my fourth/fifth grade classroom has some (limited) English and is able to read and write in his or her native language. The following ESOL assessment adaptations are for this type of ESOL student.

An example of a reading assessment I use is what I refer to as a "backward S." I use this assessment method when I want to determine if a student has comprehended the main events and sequence of a story plot. After reading a story in a whole-group setting, I will have the students brainstorm the events that have taken place. Once these events are charted, I have the students place story events along the "backward S" in the order in which they have occurred.

The ESOL adaptation of this lesson begins after the ESOL students have participated in the brainstorming session. I meet with them as a group and have them recall story events orally to me (typically ESOL students will not participate in whole-class brainstorming sessions; they listen intently but do not like to volunteer answers until they are comfortable with speaking English). The ESOL students are usually eager to participate at this point, because they have had the process and format modeled for them by their fellow students. After listing the events, they illustrate the recalled events and construct a simple sentence or two placed under the illustration describing the story event. Next, they paste these illustrations along the "backward S" in proper sequence. This lesson enables me to assess their ability to sequence a story, recall events, and construct a simple sentence.

Using adaptations of books is another way I assess an ESOL student's comprehension of a story. After reading a short story, we discuss events in the book and any connections they have made with the story line. Next, we discuss how to change the text of the book to make an entirely new story. Once we have discussed the new plot, I help the students write the story using a Language Experience Approach. After the dictation is written on chart paper, the ESOL students work to construct a new book, making illustrations and composing text.

When working with non-fiction material, I teach research reporting. Using a matrix, I outline the research in matrix form and students use the format to construct a research paper. When adapting the report for ESOL students, I use a basic matrix. I pluck basic facts from the non-fiction book they are reading and have them fill out this matrix. After completing the basic matrix, ESOL students will construct sentences from researched material and compile the report.

When using alternative methods of assessment, I am sensitive to the efforts of my ESOL students and celebrate any work they produce. Every year I partner with a primary (K–2) teacher and establish "little buddy readers" for my ESOL students. The choice of buddies is generally determined by the grade levels at which my ESOL student, and the buddy are reading. (Typically, the

(continued)

buddy's reading level is just below the current level of my ESOL student.) Work produced by my ESOL students is always shared with their buddy, along with the primary grade classes.

Another great benefit of the "buddy system" is that it allows my ESOL students to go into the primary classroom as a "teacher assistant." The time spent in the primary classroom allows the ESOL student to be exposed to guided reading lessons that are filled with helpful reading strategies.

Adaptations of vocabulary lists have proven to be effective when integrating an ESOL student's native language with English. Although the method I use is limiting, my ESOL students enjoy vocabulary time. When constructing a weekly vocabulary list, I use words that relate to our current theme of study. Because the vocabulary words are used in content, it is crucial that their meanings become real to my students. I adapt vocabulary lists for my ESOL students by choosing between five and eight vocabulary words having root meanings that come from their native language.

When I assign vocabulary words, the class finds the definitions for homework, and the next day we collectively compose the list of words with their meanings. During this process, I ask my ESOL students to point out and underline root meanings they may recognize in their native language. For example, my Hispanic students recognize the word *dentures* from the Spanish word *dentadura*. I illustrate that *diente* means *teeth* in English. This example not only gives Spanish-speaking students a chance to feel a part of the lesson, it also helps the English-speaking students to learn the root meaning of dente, which will expand their vocabulary as they search for new words with that root meaning, e.g., *dentist, dental, orthodontist,* etc.

"Cloze" assignments prove to be quite helpful for practice in correcting grammatical points and assessing an ESOL student's grammar acquisition. After practice in correcting common syntactical errors (by having the students fill in the blanks with the correct grammar), I can determine their awareness of the proper syntax in English. But I make sure to always have them practice before I actually give a cloze activity as an assessment.

Over the years, I have observed ESOL students participate with more success in smaller cooperative groups than in a large, whole-group setting; but many critics erroneously believe cooperative grouping does not allow opportunities to assess students. When I have cooperative groups in my classroom, I discuss the grading criteria with my students before we break into groups.

Whether I am grouping my students homogeneously or heterogeneously, the ELL student typically does well in the group. I believe students learn from their peers and cooperative groups help to alleviate anxiety the English learning students may feel in a group setting. It also helps to keep the learning environment diverse and interesting. Literature circles (a cooperative grouping method) are a prime example of getting students to discuss the books they have read. In literature circles, students choose the books they want to read, and through a series of questions, they discuss different elements of the story. My ESOL students typically tend to gravitate toward books that are on their current level and are quite proud to be able to discuss the book, rather than being asked to "write a book report." As literature circles are taking place, I circulate to make sure everyone has a role in the group. The students do well as facilitators in this academic setting.

As you probably can surmise, my classroom practices are very functional. I use manila folders to record anecdotal records. It is a simple and extremely manageable process. I try to have a conference with my students once a week and alternate reviewing independent reading and writing projects. I divide the class into four groups: Monday Group, Tuesday Group, Wednesday Group, and Thursday Group. Fridays are reserved for any students who were absent on their conference day. During a writing conference, the students bring what they would like to discuss or share with me. Sometimes it is a daily journal entry or a writing project they are working on (such as a research report, etc.). We talk for about five minutes and discuss any problems they may be having with their writing. I only edit things they are to publish (we consider published work as work written for others to read). I never edit their daily journals. After their conference, I pull their manila folder and write a quick comment on what I observed during the conference. For example, if I observed the student having difficulty with verb tense, I will note that on the anecdotal record (e.g., *Susie has changed tense in her narrative story about the party she had over the weekend).* The following week we review the comments on the anecdotal record and I look for improvement in the area.

For a reading conference, students bring selections they want to share with me. I have them read to me aloud, and then we discuss what they are reading. It can be a chapter book we are reading together as a class, a book they are reading independently, or any other reading material. It is at this time that I observe if they are using decoding strategies when coming to an unfamiliar word and if they are employing comprehension strategies. I

(continued)

make brief notes of what I observe (e.g., Johnny used good word attack strategies when reading the word *accomplish*).

As an educator who knows traditional assessments do not work for this diverse population, creating alternative methods of assessment has proven to be a challenging experience. I have learned that I must respect the native culture of my ESOL students as I familiarize them with their new culture. I must also be considerate of their sense of pride in their accomplishments, as I continue to search for new methods of assessment that will uplift their learning spirits and reflect their true academic abilities. If I am able to inspire my English-learning students to be excited about the work they produce in my class, I believe they will feel like they are an integral part of our classroom communnity.

Appendix of Documents and Forms

○ Menu of Alternative Assessment Recommended for English Language Learners (Broward County Schools)

○ S.T.A.R. Diagnostic Report of Skills Assessment of Reading (Printout of Diagnostic Report from Miramar's Elementary School software program)

○ Collaboration Rubric (contribution by Bianca Swanson, a graduating student of Florida Atlantic University's Teacher Education ESOL integrated program)

○ Developmental Stages of Writing

○ Portfolio Cover Sheet

○ Exited Students Form

○ Sample Exit Criteria Grades 4–12

○ ESOL Program Exit Information

○ Language Reclassification Form

○ Reclassification of ESOL Students

○ LEPSEP Folder (three sheets)

○ Recommendations Based on Annual Review (one sheet)

○ IPTI (Idea Proficiency Test)—English Forms C and D

○ Home Language Survey: Samples from Various School Districts

○ School Board of Broward County ESOL Instructional Strategies Matrix

○ Language Level Classifications

○ Elementary School Language Reclassification Chart

○ Secondary School Language Reclassification Chart

○ Sample ESOL Program Delivery Options

○ Initial Aural/Oral Language Classification Assessment Form

○ Identification of Students Whose Primary or Home Language is Other than English

○ The IDEA Oral Proficiency Test (IPT)

○ Aural/Oral Language Proficiency Tests for Assessment and Placement of ELLs

- ○ TESOL ESL Standards for Pre-K through Grade 12 Students
- ○ ESOL Program Initial Language Classification Assessment Form
- ○ Easing the Paper Load: Ten Techniques of Responding to Writing
- ○ Developmental Reading Rubric
- ○ ESL Reading Rubric
- ○ Summary Evaluation Guidelines
- ○ Holistic Oral Language Scoring Rubric
- ○ Analytic Oral Language Scoring Rubric
- ○ Analytic Scoring Rubric for Writing
- ○ Sample Parent Letter for Student's Portfolio
- ○ Elementary School Reading/Writing Portfolio Cover Sheet
- ○ Middle School Reading/Writing Portfolio Cover Sheet
- ○ High School Reading/Writing Portfolio Cover Sheet
- ○ Portfolio Evaluation Summary
- ○ Self-Assessment of Oral Language
- ○ Self-Assessment of Academic Language Functions
- ○ Self-Assessment of Communication Strategies in Oral Language
- ○ Self-Assessment of Speaking Ability
- ○ Self-Assessment of Reading Strategies
- ○ High-Stakes Assessment for English Language Learners
- ○ Types of Accommodations Provided, by State

MENU OF ALTERNATIVE ASSESSMENT RECOMMENDED FOR ELLS

Interview

Content Retelling

Content Dictation

Cloze Procedure

Graphic Representation

Student Self-Rating and Evaluation

Checklist

Venn Diagram/Semantic Map

Writing Sample

Journal

Group Testing

Technology

Audio and Video

Debate

Role Play

Games

Observation/Anecdotal

Portfolio

01/05/00

S.T.A.R.
- Diagnostic Report -
Miramar Elementary School
Miramar, FL US

Page 1

Student Name:
    Teacher: Administrator, S.T.A.R.
     Grade: 2

Student ID:
    Section: 2C-ESL
    Test Date: 01/06/00

Diagnostic Code: 2B

The diagnostic information presented below is a generalized skills assessment based on the student's performance on the test.

IRL: Pre-Primer
 GE: 1.2
 PR: 9
NCE: 21.8

At this stage, students begin to read conventionally. They apply emergent reading skills (print and book concepts) to unfamiliar text and learn to read primers and other early reader texts. Students build their understanding of print through repeated readings of familiar text and through exposure to a variety of literature.

At this level, students are concentrating on word recognition. They learn to segment words systematically, and to identify initial and final consonant sounds, consonant clusters, and long and short vowel sounds. They also learn how to identify simple phonograms such as -at, -en, and -op, to help them decode. They use their growing knowledge of phonics and word structure to gain meaning from printed text.

At this stage of reading development,   is expected to
    - develop the ability to read aloud more independently;
    - develop listening comprehension with increasingly difficult materials;
    - continue to build sight word vocabulary;
    - develop effective word-recognition skills;
    - use context clues and illustrations to decode unfamiliar words.

For optimal reading growth,   needs to
    - work on mastering basic word attack skills;
    - listen to books read aloud at school and at home daily;
    - have opportunities to read aloud to and with fluent readers;
    - have time set aside daily for independent silent reading at school.

       reading level is below the 25th percentile for this grade placement.
Therefore, corrective measures such as the following should be taken:
    - Increase the amount of time spent reading aloud to the student.
    - Actively involve parents, paraprofessionals, and volunteers to act as tutors.
    - Use paired reading tutoring to increase word recognition in context.
    - Further assess the nature of the reading difficulty.

If   is using the Accelerated Reader(TM) reading management system, the

Student Name:

student's estimated Zone of Proximal Development (ZPD) for independent fiction
reading is 1.2 - 2.2. This range is approximate. Success at any level also
depends on the student's interest, prior knowledge, and other factors. The
following techniques will help assure continued optimal growth:
- For nonfiction reading, reduce the ZPD range by one-half to a full
  grade level.
- For read-aloud activities and paired reading, increase by one to three
  grade levels.
- Adjust the reading level and ZPD so that the student maintains an
  average percent correct of 85 percent or higher on the AR tests.
- Use the Accelerated Reader tests to enhance motivation for and
  increase amount of independent reading.
- Use Accelerated Reader tests as closure to develop listening
  comprehension skills and to provide closure to read-aloud experiences.
- Use the At-Risk Report and Student Record Report for a more in-depth
  analysis.

Your Name: _____ Group Topic: _____

Group Members: _____

Collaboration Rubric

	Beginning 1	**Developing 2**	**Accomplished 3**	**Exemplary 4**	**Score**
Contribute					
Research & Gather Information	Does not collect any info that relates to the topic.	Collects very little info—some relates to the topic.	Collects some basic info—most relates to the topic.	Collects a great deal of info—all relates to the topic.	
Share Information	Does not relay any info to teammates.	Relays very little info—some relates to the topic.	Relays some basic info—most relates to the topic.	Relays a great deal of info—all relates to the topic.	
Be Punctual	Does not hand in any assignments.	Hands in most assignments late.	Hands in most assignments on time.	Hands in all assignments on time.	
Take Responsibility					
Fulfill Team Role's Duties	Does not perform any duties of assigned team role.	Performs very few duties.	Performs nearly all duties.	Performs all duties of assigned team role.	
Share Equally	Always relies on others to do the work.	Rarely does the assigned work—often needs reminding.	Usually does the assigned work—rarely needs reminding.	Always does the assigned work without having to be reminded.	
Value Others' Viewpoints					
Listen to Other Teammates	Is always talking—never allows anyone else to speak.	Usually doing most of the talking—rarely allows others to speak.	Listens, but sometimes talks too much.	Listens and speaks a fair amount.	
Cooperate with Teammates	Usually argues with teammates.	Sometimes argues.	Rarely argues.	Never argues with teammates.	
Make Fair Decisions	Usually wants to have things their way.	Often sides with friends instead of considering all views.	Usually considers all views.	Always helps team to reach a fair decision.	
Behavior	Interrupts class while teacher is speaking.	Talks while teacher is talking or reading.	Listens quietly but talks a little.	Listens quietly and raises hand if they have a question.	
Posture	Not sitting properly in their seat or space.	Sits in spot but is touching or annoying others around them.	Sitting in spot slouching or leaning to the side.	Sitting up straight in their spot.	
Contributions	Always calls out questions and answers posed.	Sometimes calls out questions and answers posed.	Answers and asks questions but calls out rarely.	Raises hand to ask and answer questions.	

Contributed by Bianca Swanson, Student in TESOL 4081, Florida Atlantic University.

DEVELOPMENTAL STAGES OF WRITING

Many students will illustrate—then write—illustrate—then write—which is a process of revision. This enhances the writing process and is necessary for writing.

Stage 1: Random Illustration

○ Scattered and no sense of story.
○ Kindergarten students spend a lot of time in this phase.
○ A Readiness Stage—to get to the product you are looking for.

Stage 2: Picture Grounded in One Topic

○ One story goes with the picture.
○ Sense of story is evident: Beginning, middle, and end.
○ Many students stay in this stage a while.

Stage 3: Illustration with Letters Randomly Written on the Bottom

○ Usually consonants and very few vowels.
○ Starting to realize that the letters are used to communicate a story.
○ When they read back to you—can match story to letters and can end at end of letters.

Stage 4: Copying Words from Around the Room

○ Do have a sense that a word means something—but need to move them along so that the words come from the student.

Stage 5: Write on the Same Topic Day After Day

○ Help student with another topic.
○ It is important to break this pattern and help student move onto something else.
○ Talk through the story first—then encourage the student to write.
○ If student has a fear of writing and spelling words—encourage invented or transitional spelling.

Stage 6: Saying Something about the Picture (Not a Story Yet)

○ Writes lists to go with the picture or labels the picture.

Stage 7: Invented Spelling with Sound/Letter Correspondence and Is a Sentence

○ Spacing between words is still not apparent.

Stage 8: Sentence with a List of Pictures and/or Words

○ Example: One day I went to the aquarium. I saw fish, dolphins, and whales . . . (Things in the picture)

Stage 9: A Story: Beginning, Middle, and End

○ Share student's work by putting it on the overhead and demonstrating what a sense of story is to the class.

Adapted from The Writing Project: Teacher's College, Columbia University.

PORTFOLIO COVER SHEET

Student Name: _____ Date: _____

Class: _____

Type of assignment _____

I have chosen to place this item in my portfolio because _____

_____

_____

_____

From this assignment I learned _____

_____

_____

_____

One thing I want to tell you about this assignment is _____

_____

_____

_____

When I look at this assignment

    I like _____

    _____

    I would improve _____

    _____

If I were to give myself a grade on this assignment, it would be a grade of _____ because

_____

_____

Teacher signature _____

Comment:

The School Board of Broward County, Florida
MULTICULTURAL/FOREIGN LANGUAGE/ESOL EDUCATION DEPARTMENT

EXITED STUDENTS FORM
CLASS RECORD

Date: _____   **School Year:** _____

School/Cluster: _____

Name and Title of Person Completing this Form: _____

List all students who have met the exit criteria for the school year. All students must be classified "C2" on the LEPSEP Folder to be eligible to exit the ESOL Program. If the student's social security number is not available, please give the FSI number.

NOTE: Exited students are coded LF during the monitoring period of 2 years.

Last Name	First Name	Grade*	Date of Birth	SSN # or FSI #	Basis of Exit**	Tests	Exit Date
						Reading _____ Name of Test _____ Date _____ % scored / Writing _____ Name of Test _____ Date _____ % scored	
						Reading _____ Name of Test _____ Date _____ % scored / Writing _____ Name of Test _____ Date _____ % scored	
						Reading _____ Name of Test _____ Date _____ % scored / Writing _____ Name of Test _____ Date _____ % scored	
						Reading _____ Name of Test _____ Date _____ % scored / Writing _____ Name of Test _____ Date _____ % scored	
						Reading _____ Name of Test _____ Date _____ % scored / Writing _____ Name of Test _____ Date _____ % scored	

*Current Grade Placement
**Choose one: A = Aural/Oral
                 R = Reading and Writing (Language)
                 L = LEP Committee

White Copy: Multicultural/Foreign Language/ESOL Education Department
Yellow Copy: ESOL Curriculum/Contact Person
Pink Copy: Principal/Data Processing

Form 2590L/Revised 04/00:jb

SAMPLE EXIT CRITERIA GRADES 4–12

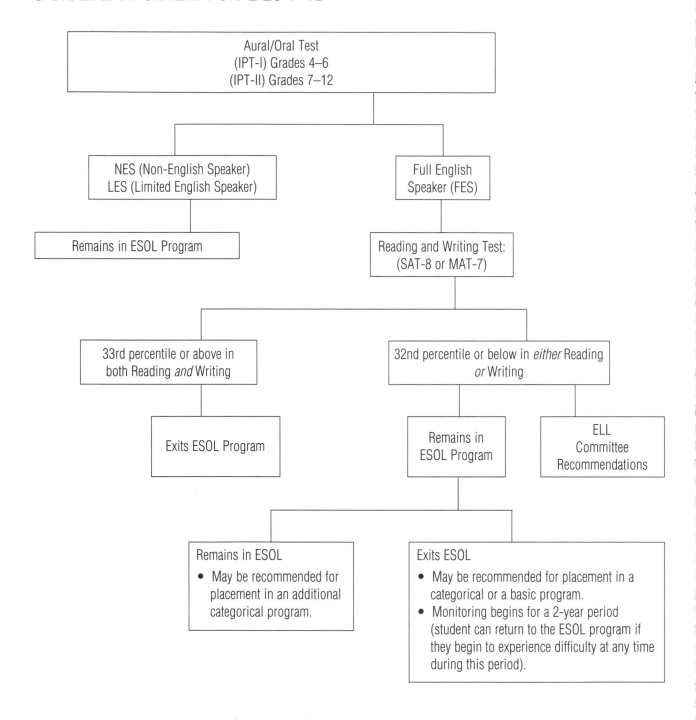

ESOL Program Exit Information

- Aural/Oral Language Assessment _____ Assessment Date _____ Language Classification _____
  - IPT I/II
- Reading/Writing (Grades 4–12)
  - **FCAT-NRT**
    - Reading Comprehension Subtest _____ %ile
      Assessment Date _____
  - ELL Committee Recommendation Date _____
    ESOL Program Exit Date *(EXIT) _____
    Reassigned School _____ Next School Year _____

    (If applicable)

Metropolitan Achievement Test
  Reading Comprehension Subtest _____ %ile
  Language (Writing) Subtest _____ %ile
  Assessment Date _____

  _____ Grade _____

  (If applicable) *(Next School Year)*

POST RECLASSIFICATION INFORMATION (Monitoring Information)

	First Report Card After Exiting	End of First Semester After Exiting	End of First Year After Exiting	End of Second Year After Exiting
DATE				
SIGNATURE				
COMMENTS				

POST-RECLASSIFICATION INFORMATION (Initial date a **former** limited English proficient student is **reclassified** as limited English proficient.)
LEP Committee Review Date *(RECLASS) _____ Home School or ESOL Cluster Assignment _____

Basis for Post-Reclassification _____ ELL Committee Exit Review Date *(EXIT) _____

Grade: _____ Date: _____   Grade: _____ Date: _____
Members: *Members:*
Principal or Designee _____   Principal or Designee _____
ESOL Teacher _____   ESOL Teacher _____
Parent(s) _____   Parent(s) _____
Other Signature(s)/Title(s): _____   **Other Signature(s)/Title(s):** _____
ELL Committee Recommendations: _____   *ELL Committee Recommendations:* _____

Grade: _____ Date: _____   Grade: _____ Date: _____
Members: *Members:*
Principal or Designee _____   Principal or Designee _____
ESOL Teacher _____   ESOL Teacher _____
Parent(s) _____   Parent(s) _____
Other Signature(s)/Title(s): _____   **Other Signature(s)/Title(s):** _____
ELL Committee Recommendations: _____   *ELL Committee Recommendations:* _____

*Descriptors used in TERMS data base

The School Board of Broward County, Florida
Multicultural/Foreign Language/ESOL Education Department

LANGUAGE RECLASSIFICATION FORM
CLASS RECORD

School: _____

Teacher: _____

Date: _____

List all students who are being reclassified and check (✓) the appropriate column.

Last Name, First Name	SSN # or FSI #	Country of Birth	Grade	A^1–A^2	A^2–B^1	B^1–B^2	B^2–C^1	C^1–C^2
								U
								S
								E
								E
								X
								I
								T
								F
								O
								R
								M
								U
								S
								E
								E
								X
								I
								T
								F
								O
								R
								M

Form 2590K Revised 04/00:jb

White Copy:	*Multicultural/Foreign Language/ ESOL Education Department*
Yellow Copy:	*ESOL Teacher*
Pink Copy:	*Principal/Data Processing Clerk*

RECLASSIFICATION OF ESOL STUDENTS

Teachers of English learners are responsible for changing students' language classifications in accordance with elementary and secondary district guidelines (Appendices I & J).

How to use the charts:

1. Find the student's current language classification on the chart.
2. Look at the descriptors at the next highest level. Decide if the descriptors typify the student's present language functioning.

   ○ If descriptors are appropriate, assign a new language classification at the next highest level.
   ○ If descriptors are inappropriate, the language classification remains the same.

3. The new language classification must be documented on the LEPSEP folder (Appendix E) and on the *Language Reclassification Form-Class Record)* (Form 2590K, Revised 1/97, Appendix K).

Note: ELLs may be reclassified at any time during the school year. Teacher judgment is recommended when reclassifying students. It is important to know the ELLs are not given only the aural/oral language assessment instrument for reclassification.

GRADING

Grading English learners is a difficult task because teachers must separate the students' content area knowledge from their knowledge of English. Therefore, teachers should assess what students know and can do, rather than their ability to express this in English. When grading English learners, the following factors should be considered:

   ○ Student's level of English proficiency.
   ○ Student's previous schooling.
   ○ Teacher's delivery of comprehensible instruction through the use of ESOL Strategies.

In summary, it is important to remember that grading of English learners should include a variety of alternative assessments (Appendix L).

INSTRUCTIONAL PROGRAM RECOMMENDATIONS

Option 1: LEP students receive instruction in a **self-contained** setting in English/language arts and content areas. **ESOL strategies must be used in the instructional delivery.**

Option 2: LEP students receive instruction in a **self-contained** setting in English/language arts. Content areas can be delivered through a combination of **self-contained and/or basic program classes. ESOL strategies must be used in the instructional delivery.**

Option 3: LEP students receive instruction in English/language arts and content areas through the **basic program. ESOL strategies must be used in the instructional delivery.**

Write date if program option changes.

GRADE _____	GRADE _____	GRADE _____	GRADE _____	GRADE _____
Option 1_____ Date	Option 1_____ Date	Option 1_____ Date	Option 1_____ Date	Option 1_____ Date
Option 2_____ Date	Option 2_____ Date	Option 2_____ Date	Option 2_____ Date	Option 2_____ Date
Option 3_____ Date	Option 3_____ Date	Option 3_____ Date	Option 3_____ Date	Option 3_____ Date
GRADE _____	GRADE _____	GRADE _____	GRADE _____	GRADE _____
Option 1_____ Date	Option 1_____ Date	Option 1_____ Date	Option 1_____ Date	Option 1_____ Date
Option 2_____ Date	Option 2_____ Date	Option 2_____ Date	Option 2_____ Date	Option 2_____ Date
Option 3_____ Date	Option 3_____ Date	Option 3_____ Date	Option 3_____ Date	Option 3_____ Date

CURRENT STUDENT SCHEDULE MUST BE ATTACHED (MIDDLE AND HIGH SCHOOL).

CATEGORICAL PROGRAMS

Check if the student is attending any of the following: School Year (s)

_____Title I Math   _____

_____Title I Reading   _____

_____Dropout Prevention   _____

(See Consent for Placement in CUM Folder)   _____

_____Exceptional Student Education (See IEP)   _____

_____Other _____   _____

          Name of Program

ADDITIONAL COMMENTS: Use this section to make the Student Education Plan more specific for the student as needed. Also include any recommendations for referrals to special programs and any specific performance statements.

_____

_____

_____

_____

Student is in need of Reading/Writing/Math Academic Improvement Plan.

❑ Yes   (Develop Academic Improvement Plan and insert in LEPSEP Folder)   Date:_____

❑ No   Date:_____

Student is in need of:

❑ Summer School/Extended School Year (ESY)   Date:_____

THE SCHOOL BOARD OF BROWARD COUNTY, FLORIDA
MULTICULTURAL/FOREIGN LANGUAGE/ESOL EDUCATION DEPARTMENT
LIMITED ENGLISH PROFICIENT STUDENT EDUCATION PLAN (LEPSEP)

Name _____

(Last)   (First)   (Middle)

Date of Birth _____ **Place of Birth** _____

Date of Entry into U.S.A. _____

Student Language _____ **Parent/Guardian Language** _____

Home Language Survey Date *(REFDTE) _____

School	Year	Grade
_____	20 ___ –20 ___	_____
	20 ___ –20 ___	
	20 ___ –20 ___	
	20 ___ –20 ___	
	20 ___ –20 ___	
	20 ___ –20 ___	
	20 ___ –20 ___	

This is an initial LEPSEF _____ Date _____ Signature _____ Date _____ Signature _____

(ESOL Designee)   (Parent Signature)

Initial Placement Information: **ESOL Program Entry Date *(ENTRY)** _____

■ **Aural/Oral Language Assessment**   Assessment Instrument _____ Initial Language Classification _____ Assessment Date *(CLASS) _____

STUDENTS C2-LP (LEP Committee Recommendation)

Students (4th–12th grades) classified as fully English proficient **(C2-LP)** on an Aural/Oral Test with Reading/Language (Writing) Assessment pending must be referred to the LEP Committee. The LEP Committee must determine whether to place the student in the ESOL program within 20 school days from the completion of the Aural/Oral Test.

The LEP Committee's determination is:

☐ ESOL Program (C1–Y)   ☐ Basic Program (C2-LP: Valid for up to one year) _____ Date _____

    FCAT-NRT

        Reading Comprehension Subtest _____ %ile

        Assessment Date _____

■ **Reading/Writing (Grades 4–12)**

    Metropolitan Achievement Test

        Reading Comprehension Subtest _____ %ile

        Language (Writing) Subtest _____ %ile

        Assessment Date _____

LANGUAGE RECLASSIFICATIONS

From A1 to A2	Date _____	Grade _____	Assessor _____	Home/Cluster School _____
From A2 to B1	Date _____	Grade _____	Assessor _____	Home/Cluster School _____
From B1 to B2	Date _____	Grade _____	Assessor _____	Home/Cluster School _____
From B2 to C1	Date _____	Grade _____	Assessor _____	Home/Cluster School _____
Status Unchanged	Date _____	Assessor/School _____	Date _____	Assessor/School _____
	Date _____	Assessor/School _____	Date _____	Assessor/School _____

*Descriptors used in TERMS data base

Recommendations based on Annual Review:

_____ 2nd yr. ESOL Program Placement   Date _____   Current Classification _____

Assessment Data _____ Signature _____

                                                                           (ESOL Designee)

_____ 3rd yr. ESOL Program Placement   Date _____   Current Classification _____

Assessment Data _____ Signature _____

                                                                           (ESOL Designee)

This is a **recommendation** for a: ***(REEVAL)**

_____ 4th yr. ESOL Program Placement   Date _____   Current Classification _____

Assessment Data _____ Signature _____

                                                                           (ESOL Designee)

_____ 5th yr. ESOL Program Placement   Date _____   Current Classification _____

Assessment Data _____ Signature _____

                                                                           (ESOL Designee)

_____ 6th yr. ESOL Program Placement   Date _____   Current Classification _____

Assessment Data _____ Signature _____

                                                                           (ESOL Designee)

LEP COMMITTEE MEETINGS

Grade: _____ Date: _____	Grade: _____ Date: _____	Grade: _____ Date: _____
Members:	*Members:*	*Members:*
Principal or Designee _____	Principal or Designee _____	Principal or Designee _____
ESOL Teacher _____	ESOL Teacher _____	ESOL Teacher _____
Parent(s) _____	Parent(s) _____	Parent(s) _____
Other Signature(s)/Title(s):	Other Signature(s)/Title(s):	Other Signature(s)/Title(s):
_____	_____	_____
_____	_____	_____
Recommendations:	Recommendations:	Recommendations:
_____	_____	_____
_____	_____	_____
_____	_____	_____
_____	_____	_____
_____	_____	_____
_____	_____	_____
_____	_____	_____

Descriptors used in TERMS data base

IPT I – ENGLISH, FORMS C AND D
IDEA PROFICIENCY TEST LEVEL SUMMARY

At LEVEL A, a student can do less than half the skills listed in LEVEL B.

At LEVEL B, a student can:
1. tell his/her name and age.
2. identify family and common school personnel, classroom objects, basic body parts, common pets, and fruits.
3. use present tense verb "to be."
4. use regular plurals.
5. answer simple "yes/no" questions appropriately.
6. follow simple directions involving basic positions in space.

At LEVEL C, a student can:
1. identify common occupations, clothing, farm animals, and foods.
2. express himself/herself using the present progressive tense (s/he is working) of common verbs.
3. use negatives and subject pronouns correctly.
4. use mass nouns appropriately.
5. follow the teacher's directions related to identifying positions on a page.
6. repeat simple sentences correctly.
7. comprehend and remember major facts of a simple story.

At LEVEL D, a student can:
1. identify modes of transportation and household items.
2. name the days of the week.
3. describe common weather conditions.
4. use possessive pronouns correctly.
5. ask simple future tense questions.
6. understand and express comparative and quantitative concepts.
7. follow directions of teacher involving movement in space.
8. repeat complex sentences correctly.
9. understand and identify moods in a simple story.
10. express himself/herself using the present and future tenses.
11. express creative thoughts in complete sentences.

At LEVEL E, a student can:
1. identify content area vocabulary.
2. use superlatives and past tense correctly.
3. understand and name opposites of key words.
4. ask past tense questions.
5. discriminate differences in closely paired words.
6. describe and organize the main properties of common objects.
7. identify main idea and descriptive details of a story or TV show.

At LEVEL F, a student can:
1. identify the seasons and unusual occupations.
2. use conditional tense of verbs.
3. discriminate fine differences in closely paired words.
4. express himself/herself using past tense correctly.
5. comprehend and predict the outcome of a story.
6. recall and retell the main facts of a story.
7. explain positive and negative attributes of friendship.
8. share meaningful personal experiences.

Note: Skills noted above are sampled in test levels. Level Summary is only an indicator of oral language skills student possesses.

HOME LANGUAGE SURVEY

Samples from Various School Districts

The Broward County, Florida, Home Language Survey

Colorado Home Language Survey

Maine State Department of Education, Home Language Survey

Pennsylvania Department of Education, Home Language Survey

Sequoia Choice School, Arizona, Home Language Survey

St. Lucie County, Florida, Home Language Survey

Ysleta Independent School District, Texas, Home Language Survey

THE SCHOOL BOARD OF BROWARD COUNTY, FLORIDA
Multicultural/Foreign Language/ESOL Education Department
Home Language Survey

1. Is a language other than English used in the home? ☐ Yes ☐ No
   If yes, language used _____
2. Did the student have a first language other than English? ☐ Yes ☐ No
3. Does the student most frequently speak a language other than English? ☐ Yes ☐ No

Relationship of person completing the survey to student?   Mother   Father   Guardian   Self

_____
Signature of person completing survey   Date

(Haitian-Creole)

1. Eske ou pale yon lòt lang ki pa angle lakay-ou? ☐ Wi ☐ Non
   Si wi ki lang? _____
2. Eske elèv-la pale yon lòt lang ki pa angle? ☐ Wi ☐ Non
3. Eske elèv-la pale yon lòt lang ki pa angle tour tan? ☐ Wi ☐ Non

Relasyon ant moun ki ranpli fòm-sa ak elèv-la?   Manman   Papa   Gadyen   Elèv-la menm

_____
Siyati moun ki ranpli fòm sa-a   Dat

(French)

1. Est-ce qu'il y a une langue autre que l'anglais parlée a la ☐ Oui ☐ Non
   maison? Si oui, quelle langue? _____
2. Est-ce que la langue maternelle de l'étudiant est autre que l'anglais? ☐ Oui ☐ Non
3. Est-ce que l'étudiant parle souvent une langue autre que l'anglais? ☐ Oui ☐ Non

Ille de parenté de la personne remplissant ce questionnaire
avec l'enfant?   Maman   Papa   Guardien   Soi-même

_____
Signature de la personne remplissant ce questionnaire   Date

(Portuguese)

1. Outro idioma que não seja inglês é falado em casa? ☐ Sim ☐ Não
   Caso Sim, idioma falado _____
2. O estudante tem como primeiro idioma outro além do inglês? ☐ Sim ☐ Não
3. O estudante fala mais frequentemente um idioma que não seja inglês? ☐ Sim ☐ Não

Qual é o parentesco da pessoa, em relação ao estudante,
completando este levantamento?   Mãe   Pai   Tutor(a)   O Próprio

_____
Assinatura da pessoa completando este levantamento   Data

(Spanish)

1. ¿Se habla en la casa otro idioma que no sea el inglés? ☐ Sí ☐ No
   Si es así, ¿Cuál idioma es hablado? _____
2. ¿Es el primer idioma del estudiante otra lengua que no sea el inglés? ☐ Sí ☐ No
3. ¿Habla el estudiante con más frecuencia otro idioma que no sea el inglés? ☐ Sí ☐ No

¿Cuál es el parentesco de la persona que completa esta
encuesta con el estudiante?   Madre   Padre   Tutor   Yo mismo

_____
Firma de la persona que completó esta encuesta   Fecha

Comments: _____

Form 4402/cd Rev. 9/96

COLORADO

Dear Parents:

The English Language Proficiency Act in the State of Colorado requires all school districts to identify all students whose dominant language is not English. The purpose of this form is to provide the schools with essential information to help us promptly identify those students who might be in need of tutorial assistance in English, when English is not the primary language spoken in the home.

It is required by law that the information on the reverse side of this letter be kept on file for every student in the public school system. Please help us keep our files up-to-date and/or identify students in need of our services, by completing this form and leaving it in your child's school. If it is not possible to fill out the form immediately, please return it to the school as soon as possible. Thank you for your help.

Sincerely,

Gene Cosby, District Superintendent

Student's Name _____ Grade Level _____ Birth _____

Date _____

School _____ Country of Birth _____

Phone Number _____

Parent(s)' Names _____

Address _____

Is your child's primary home language other than English?
yes ☐ **no** ☐

If "No," stop at this point and sign.

Parent/Guardian Signature _____ Date _____

IF ANY PART OF THIS FORM IS UNCLEAR, PLEASE ASK FOR ASSISTANCE. <u>THIS FORM IS ALSO AVAILABLE IN SPANISH.</u>

1. What language(s) is used to communicate at home?

_____

2. Can your child read and write in that language(s)?

   Yes _____ No _____

3. How often do the members of your family speak that language(s) at home?

		Always	Usually	Seldom	Never

   a. This child
   b. Mother/Guardian
   c. Father/Guardian
   d. Brothers/Sisters
   e. Others living in the home

4. This student SPEAKS:
   a. Only the other language and no English
   b. Other language more often than English
   c. Equally or difficult to determine
   d. English more often than other language(s)
   e. Only English

5. This student BEST UNDERSTANDS:
   a. Only the other language and no English
   b. Other language more often than English
   c. Equally or difficult to determine
   d. English more often than other language(s)
   e. Only English

6. Which language(s) did your child first learn when s/he began to speak?

7. Which grades has your child completed? (circle those which apply)

   in an English only program

   in a language(s) other than English

   in a Bilingual Ed. program

   in an ESL program

Parent Signature _____

Date _____

MAINE STATE DEPARTMENT OF EDUCATION
Augusta, Maine 04333-0023
HOME LANGUAGE SURVEY

STUDENT'S

NAME_____SCHOOL_____

GRADE_____SCHOOL   UNIT   OR

TOWN_____DATE_____

Directions: Answer each question by putting the appropriate number in the box at the end of each question. If you answer "9. Other," specify the language.

1. What language do you **MOST OFTEN** use when speaking to your child?
    1) English   4) Vietnamese   7) Spanish
    2) French   5) German   8) American Sign
    3) Passamaquoddy   6) Khmer   9) Other (specify)_____ [

2. What language did your child **FIRST** learn to speak? 1   2   3   4   5   6   7   8   9   [

3. What language does your child **MOST OFTEN** use when speaking to brothers, sisters, and other children at home?   1   2   3   4   5   6   7   8   9   [

4. What language does your child **MOST OFTEN** use when speaking to you and other adults in the home? (grandparents, aunts, uncles, guests)   1   2   3   4   5   6   7   8   9   [

5. What language does your child **MOST OFTEN** use when speaking with friends or neighbors, **OUTSIDE** the home?   1   2   3   4   5   6   7   8   9   [

*This survey, approved by the U.S. Office for Civil Rights, is available in these languages from our office:

Somali	French	Khmer	Passamaquoddy	Chinese	Dari
Polish					
Greek	Spanish	Lao	Vietnamese	German	Russian
Amharic					

TO THE TEACHER: (1) If you have observed this student use a language other than English, please indicate other language here:_____

(2) Was the child's first language development interrupted at some point in time, due to adoption, relocation of family, etc?

_____

http://www.state.me.us/education/esl/hls.htm   9/1/2001

LE DÉPARTEMENT D'ÉDUCATION
Augusta (Maine) 04333-0023
SONDAGE LINGUISTIQUE

Nom   de   l'   étudiant_____

École_____

Classe_____

Ville_____Date_____

Directions: Répondez à chaque question en mettant le numéro approprié dans la boîte a la fin de chaque question. Si vous répondez "9. Autre," spécifiez langue.

1. Quelle langue utilisez-vous le **plus souvent** quand vous parlez à votre infant?
    1) Anglais   4) Vietnamien   7) Espagnol
    2) Français   5) Allemand   8) Langue par signe
    3) Passamaquoddy   6) Khmer   9) Autre (spécifiez) _____
2. Quelle fût la **première** langue que votre enfant a parlé?   1   2   3   4   5   6   7   8   9
3. Quelle langue parle-t-il/elle le **plus souvent** avec les autres enfants à la maison?
    (fréres, soeurs, etc.)   1   2   3   4   5   6   7   8   9
4. Quelle langue parle-t-il/elle le **plus souvent** avec vous et les autres adultes à la maison
    (grandparents, tantes, oncles, visiteurs)?   1   2   3   4   5   6   7   8   9
5. Quelle langue parle-t-il/elle le **plus souvent** avec ses amis et voisins, hors de la maison?
                                                        1   2   3   4   5   6   7   8   9

*Ce sondage, sanctionné par L'Office des Droits Civils des E.-U. est disponible dans les langues suivantes par notre bureau:

Somali	Français	Khmer	Passamaquoddy	Dari	Allemand
Polonais					
Grecque	Espagnol	Laotien	Vietnamien	Chinois	Russe	Amharique

PENNSYLVANIA DEPARTMENT OF EDUCATION

HOME LANGUAGE SURVEY

ANNOTATED SAMPLE
HOME LANGUAGE SURVEY
Used to determine a primary or home language other than English (PHLOTE).

The information provided in italics provides an explanation as to why the question is being asked and is intended to help guide you as you prepare your own version of a home language survey. The survey you construct will be dictated by your needs. Some of the questions listed below, if not included in your survey, may be included in a student profile or background sheet, depending on various factors and your school district's needs. Your version of a home language survey may be as long or as short as you like. Just remember to include the questions required by the Office for Civil Rights. They are marked by an asterisk.

Instructions: At registration, please ask all parents or guardians the following questions about the language use of the child. Print responses. If **one** of the answers is a language other than English or the country of origin is other than the United States, contact _____(the person in the district responsible for language proficiency assessment or instructional placement). Otherwise, the student is considered English language proficient and no further action is needed. A copy of this survey shall be placed in the student's permanent folder.

These instructions assume that the survey will be administered when the parent or guardian is enrolling the student. Generally, the district will have an interpreter available at that time. Districts may choose to send the survey home to the parents. While this is useful for some purposes, there is always the chance that the survey will not get to the parent/guardian or that they will not be able to answer it because it is in English. It is the district's responsibility to provide a version in the preferred language or mode of communication of the parent/guardian. Should you decide to send the survey home, the instructions will need to reflect what you want parents to do and should be written in clear, concise terms.

Name_____ Date_____

Date of Birth_____Age_____Grade_____

Parent/Guardian Name_____

Telephone (_____)_____Country of Origin_____
        Area code

Other countries of residence (please list)_____

The country of origin is especially important in cases where English is the language of the country, but the students do not speak a standard American dialect. They will require some instruction, especially in listening and speaking, to be able to participate in mainstream classrooms successfully. Parents do not have to respond to this question.

The questions listed below are in some logical order. Please note that only the ones marked with an asterisk are required for Office for Civil Rights purposes. The others are designed to assist you to more accurately determine the role of language in the student's personal and educational life.

What was the first language your child learned to speak?* *May be the language of a caretaker/relative, rather than that of the parents.*

What language(s) does your child speak most often at home?* *May indicate preference and/or dominance.*

What language(s) does your child read?

What language(s) does your child write?

What language(s) has your child studied in school?

What language(s) do you use when speaking to your child? *As students become proficient in English, parents may speak to their children in the native language, although the student will sometimes respond in English.*

What language(s) is spoken most often in your home?*

Does your child understand, but not speak a language(s) other than English? *This would indicate receptive knowledge of a language(s).*

What language(s) does your child speak with grandparents, aunts, uncles, cousins, babysitters? *Helps to determine the amount of another language(s) a child is exposed to and its influence on the acquisition of English.*

What language(s) does your child use with brothers and sisters? *This will help to determine student's language preference.*

What language(s) does your child speak with friends and neighbors? *The neighborhood language may be different from that of home and school.*

Other than the languages studied in school, does your child speak any languages other than English? Which ones? *Knowing which others will provide insight into possible language interference.*

What language(s) do you (parents/guardians) read? *This is important for determining the language of documents you send home.*

Do you (parents/guardians) read English? *Some parents/guardians may have a good command of written English, but are not able to speak it fluently. They may want documents sent home in English.*

What language(s) do you (parents/guardians) write?

Survey conducted/completed by:_____
This may require the signature of the parent/guardian if it is a version that has been sent home.

Contact Person:

Bureau/Division: Bureau of Curriculum and Academic Services,

Telephone: (717) 783-6649
FAX: (717) 783- 3946
TTY: (717) 783- 8445
Code: ESL
Last Modified Date: August 29, 2000
Expiration Date August 2001

SEQUOIA CHOICE SCHOOL
1460 S. HORNE, MESA, AZ 85204
PH(480)649-7737 FX(480)649-0747

Home Language Survey

Arizona law requires that we ask all parents/guardians to answer questions about languages used in the home environment. Please answer each question carefully. We appreciate your cooperation in providing this information. PLEASE PRINT(If you are not sending through the internet).

STUDENT'S LEGAL NAME(LAST, FIRST, MIDDLE)

DATE

ADDRESS

CITY

STATE   ZIP

PARENT-LEGAL GUARDIAN (LAST, FIRST, MIDDLE)

FATHER / MOTHER / OTHER(SPECIFY)   HOME PHONE NO.

BIRTH DATE   BIRTH PLACE

ETHNIC ORIGIN

TRIBE (IF NATIVE AMERICAN)

PREVIOUS SCHOOL ATTENDED

NUMBER OF YEARS IN SCHOOL IN THE U.S.A.

ADDRESS OF PREVIOUS SCHOOL

CITY

STATE   ZIP CODE

In what language would you prefer school communication?

ENGLISH   OTHER (SPECIFY)

1. When your child first began to talk, what language did he, she learn first?

2. What language does your child speak most frequently at home?

3. What language(s) do the parents/guardians speak most often at home, regardless of the language spoken by the child?

Has your child been enrolled in any program for Language Acquisition such as English as a Second Language (ESL) or Bilingual?
__ NO __ YES (PLEASE SPECIFY)

SIGNATURE OF PARENT OR GUARDIAN

DATE

Submit form thru the web

or print the form out and mail it to the address at the top of this form.

EXCELLENCE IN EDUCATION

THE SCHOOL BOARD OF ST. LUCIE COUNTY

Means Court Center
532 North 13th Street
Fort Pierce, Florida 34950-8219   (561) 468-5000

ST. LUCIE COUNTY SCHOOL DISTRICT
*** HOME LANGUAGE SURVEY ***

STUDENT:_____ DATE:_____

SCHOOL:_____ GRADE:_____ BIRTHDATE:_____

BIRTHPLACE:_____ PARENT/GUARDIAN:_____

Check (✓) Yes or No for each of the following questions.

A. Is a language other than English used in the home?

    _____ Yes _____ No   If yes, what language_____

B. Did the student have a first language other than English?

    _____ Yes _____ No   If yes, what language_____

C. Does the student most frequently speak a language other than English?

    _____ Yes _____ No   If yes, what language_____

NOTE: If the answer to at least one of the above questions is yes, your child will be assessed to determine if he/she is limited English proficient.

Date student first enrolled in any school in the USA or its territories: (month/day/year)_____

USA city and state/territory where first enrolled:_____

_____   _____
Signature of person completing survey   Date

Relationship to student?   _____ Mother _____ Father _____ Guardian _____ Self
                                _____ Other (Identify) _____

Your cooperation is requested in accurately completing the form and returning it to the school as soon as possible.
* *
OFFICE USE:(To the Terminal Operator)
If the answer to question B and/or C is "yes," create an I02 screen with the LEP code of "LP" and the Basis of Entry code of "T".

Distribution: Cumulative Folder: (White)   Terminal: (Yellow)   Resource Teacher: (Pink)   Parent: (Goldenrod)
Revised 6/97   Form #FED0023A

ACCREDITED SYSTEM-WIDE BY THE SOUTHERN ASSOCIATION OF COLLEGES AND SCHOOLS

The School Board of St. Lucie County is an Equal Opportunity Agency

Ysleta Independent School District
Home Language Survey

The State of Texas requires that the following information be completed for each student that enrolls in a Texas public school. This survey shall be kept in each student's permanent record folder.

NAME OF STUDENT:

Last   First   Middle   Grade   Age

(1.) What language is spoken in your home most of the time?

What language do you speak most of the time?

Signature of Parent or Guardian   Date

DISTRITO ESCOLAR INDEPENDIENTE DE YSLETA
ENCUESTA DEL LENGUAJE DEL HOGAR

El estado de Texas requiere que la siguiente informacion se complete para cada estudiante que se matdcula en una escuela poblica de Texas. Esta encuesta se archivar en el expedients del estudiante.

NOMBRE DEL
ESTUDIANTE: _____
                Apellido   Primer nombre   Segundo nombre   Grado   Edad

(1.) ¿cual idioma se habla en su casa la mayoria del tiempo?

(2.) ¿Qué idioma habla su hijo la mayoria del tiempo?

Firma del Padre o Tutor   Fecha

A. Methodologies/ Approaches		
	A1	Total Physical Response (TPR)
	A2	Natural Approach
	A3	Cognitive Academic Language Learning (CALLA)
	A4	Whole Language Approach
	A5	Language Experience Approach (LEA)
	A6	Retelling a Story
	A7	Activating Prior Knowledge

B. Visuals		
○ Graphic Organizers	B1	Flow Charts
	B2	Maps
	B3	Charts
	B4	Graphs
	B5	Pictures
	B6	Semantic Webbing/Mapping
	B7	T-Charts
	B8	Venn Diagrams
	B9	Story Maps
	B10	Timelines
	B11	Computer/Software
○ Other Audio/ Visuals	B12	Realia
	B13	Videos/Films/CD ROM
	B14	Demonstrations
	B15	Captioning
	B16	Labeling
	B17	Music/Songs
	B18	Jazz Chants/Raps
	B19	Cassettes—Music/Books
	B20	Language Master

C. Interactive Strategies		
○ Cooperative Learning Activities	C1	Peer Buddy
	C2	Small Group Activities
	C3	Pairs and Threes
	C4	Jigsaw
	C5	"Corners"
	C6	Think/Pair/Share
	C7	Group Reports, Projects
	C8	Panel Discussions/Debate
	C9	Choral Reading/Read Around Groups

D. Other Interactive Strategies		
	D1	Field Trips
	D2	K-W-L (Know/Wants to Know/Learned)
	D3	Role Play
	D4	Games
	D5	Dialogue Journals

E. Modified Class Work (Based on Level of English Proficiency)		
	E1	Vary Complexity of Assignment
	E2	One-on-One Instruction with Teacher or Aide
	E3	Modify Nature of Assignment
	E4	Substitute Diagram for Paragraph
	E5	Use of Home Language for Instruction
	E6	Explain Key Concepts
	E7	Repeat/Paraphrase/Slow Down
	E8	Vocabulary with Context Clues
	E9	Reading with a Specific Purpose
	E10	Use Simple, Direct Language (Limit Idioms)
	E11	Use all Modalities/Learning Styles
	E12	Provide Meaningful Language Practice
	E13	Drills (Substitution, Expansion, Paraphrase, Repetition)
	E14	Matching with Visuals
	E15	Unscramble Sentences, Words, Visuals
	E16	Categorize Vocabulary
	E17	Context Clues
	E18	Outline Notes
	E19	Directed Reading/Thinking Activity (DRTA)
	E20	Semantic Feature Analysis
	E21	SQ3R (Survey, Question, Read, Recite, Review)
	E22	Summarizing
	E23	Notetaking
	E24	Wordbanks
	E25	Repetition
	E26	Question-Answer Relationship (QAR)

F. Multicultural Resources		
	F1	Guest Speakers
	F2	Use of Community Resources
	F3	Cultural Sharing
	F4	Varied Holiday Activities

G. Alternative Assessment Instruments		
	G1	Interview
	G2	Content Retelling
	G3	Content Dictation
	G4	Cloze Procedure
	G5	Graphic Representation
	G6	Student Self-rating and Evaluation
	G7	Teacher Rating Checklist
	G8	Writing Sample
	G9	Group Testing
	G10	Observation/Anecdotal
	G11	Portfolio

LANGUAGE LEVEL CLASSIFICATIONS AND DESCRIPTIONS

In order to assist schools in determining what the language classifications mean when students are at different points through their second language development, the following descriptions have been developed:

A¹   Non-English Speaker or minimal knowledge of English
Demonstrates very little understanding.
Cannot communicate meaning orally.
Unable to participate in regular classroom instruction.

A²   Limited English Speaker
Demonstrates limited understanding.
Communicates orally in English, with one- or two-word responses.

B¹   Intermediate English Speaker
Communicates orally in English, mostly with simple phrases and/or one sentence responses.
Makes significant grammatical errors which interfere with understanding.

B²   Intermediate English Speaker
Communicates in English about everyday situations with little difficulty but lacks the academic language terminology.
Experiences some difficulty in following grade level subject matter assignments.

C¹   Advanced English Speaker
Understands and speaks English fairly well.
Makes occasional grammatical errors.
May read and write English with varying degrees of proficiency.

C²   Full English Speaker
Understands and speaks English with near fluency.
Reads and writes English at a comparable level with native English-speaking counterparts; may read and write the native language with varying degrees of proficiency.

D   Full English Speaker
Speaks English fluently.
Reads and writes English at a comparable level with English-speaking counterparts.

E   Monolingual English Speaker

Note:
In the Broward County Public Schools, when an ELL is classified as C^2, the student exits the program. His/her academic performance is monitored for two years, as required by state guidelines, by the principals, teachers, and designated school ESOL curriculum contact person(s).

Language Arts/ESOL Performance-Based Curriculum

Elementary School Language Reclassification Chart

	A¹*	A²	B¹	B²	C¹	C²
Listening Comprehension	Demonstrates understanding of only a few words or learned phrases. Unable to communicate in English.	Demonstrates limited understanding of familiar vocabulary when spoken slowly. Able to comprehend language only with high levels of contextual support with numerous repetitions.	Demonstrates understanding of familiar vocabulary at slower than normal speed. Able to comprehend language with some degree of contextual support with repetitions.	Demonstrates extensive understanding of familiar vocabulary and classroom discussion at slower than normal speed. Able to comprehend language with little contextual support. Some repetition may be needed.	Demonstrates understanding of social and academic language comparable to native speaker of same age and grade level.	Demonstrates thorough understanding comparable to that of native speakers of same age and grade level. Able to comprehend language without contextual support.
Verbal Expression	Unable to produce understandable speech, making conversation almost impossible.	Very difficult to understand. Generally reluctant to speak. Language difficulties often cause resticence. Can communicate with learned phrases.	Able to handle basic social conversation. Conversation/discussion is invariably interrupted due to the constant need to search for the "right words."	Mispronounces words sporadically but can be understood clearly. Conversation/discussion is generally fluent, with occasional lapses while searching for the "right words."	Participates effectively in social conversation and classroom discussions.	Conversation/discussion is as proficient and unconstrained as that of native speakers of same age and grade level.
Voabbulary/Grammar	Uses extremely limited vocabulary and incorrect grammar. Deficiencies in vocabulary/grammar make conversation almost unintelligible.	Uses limited vocabulary and incorrect grammar which make comprehension very difficult. Can respond to simple questions using one- or two-word responses.	Uses limited conversation due to insufficient vocabulary/grammar. Produces repeated errors in vocabulary and structure which occasionally conceal meaning. Frequently rephrases to be understood.	Produces a few significant errors caused by language interference, but can be understood. Occasionally uses awkward terms and tries to rephrase to make meaning clear.	Demonstrates good control of more difficult grammar and uses advanced vocabulary.	Uses vocabulary, grammar, and idioms comparable to that of native speakers of same age and grade level.
Reading	May recognize some familiar letters/words/numbers, if applicable to age and grade level.	Recognizes a few short, simple words/phrases, if applicable to age and grade level.	Reads and comprehends short, simple sentences, if applicable to age and grade level.	Reads and comprehends short paragraphs, with assistance, if applicable to age and grade level.	Reads and comprehends near grade level, if applicable.	Reads and comprehends selections on grade level, if applicable.
Writing	May point or write some familiar letters/words and/or basic information, if applicable to age and grade level.	Able to print or write short basic words/phrases with frequent mistakes, if applicable to age and grade level.	Able to print or write short, simple sentences, if applicable to age and grade level. Frequent errors occasionally conceal meaning.	Makes a few crucial mistakes with more complex academic tasks, but meaning is understood, if applicable to age and grade level.	Makes a few noticeable mistakes but is approaching native speaker's writing competence, if applicable to age and grade level.	Writing competence is comparable to that of a native speaker, if applicable to age and grade level.

*The A¹ classification includes those students with varying degrees of literacy skills in their own language and/or English.
NOTE: Individual variations will occur depending on student ability and background.

Secondary School Language Reclassification Chart

	A¹	A²	B¹	B²	C¹	C²
Listening Comprehension	Minimal comprehension, may understand only a few words and learned phrases (e.g., "What's your name?").	Understands simple phrases and conversation within context when spoken slowly and with several repetitions.	Increased comprehension of conversation containing familiar vocabulary when spoken at a slow pace; limited ability to understand without face-to-face contact.	Comprehension of most social conversation and classroom discussions at slower than normal speed. Rewording and repetition may be necessary. Increased ability to understand without face-to-face contact.	Understands social conversation and classroom discussions at normal speed.	Understands social conversation and classroom discussions; understands without face-to-face contact; understands conversation between native speakers.
Verbal Expression	Communicates with actions and gestures. Limited verbal production.	Speaks with hesitation and with frequent lapses into silence; can communicate limited number of survival needs using simple learned phrases.	Speaks with some hesitation and uses mostly learned phrases and simple sentences; some errors in speech. Can express survival needs and has increasing ability to handle basic social conversation.	Speaks with general fluency in everyday situations, but hesitates in classroom discussions while searching for the correct manner of expression.	Participates effectively in social conversation and classroom discussions; can express complex ideas; can handle familiar and unfamiliar situations.	Speaks fluently in everyday conversation and expresses abstract concepts in the classroom as expected of native speakers.
Vocabulary/ Grammar	Vocabulary may consist of a few isolated words; Limited recognition and usage of basic grammatical structures.	Limited vocabulary; can ask and respond to simple questions with one- or two-word learned responses; usage/recognition of basic grammar.	Frequently uses incorrect terms and tries to reword to clarify meaning; increasing control of basic grammar, but still makes frequent errors.	Sometimes uses incorrect terms and must reword ideas to compensate for lack of vocabulary; has control of basic grammar but makes errors in word order and more difficult grammar.	Can use vocabulary to express exact meanings and has good control of basic and more difficult grammar.	Use of vocabulary and idioms is similar to that of a native speaker; better control of grammar.
Reading	Recognition of letters of the alphabet, numbers, and a few simple sight words (name, address, stop, etc.). May be minimal.	Reads and understands sight words, short phrases, and learned sentences; limited comprehension of simplified academic textbooks.	Reads short, simplified academic textbooks and materials; cannot comprehend basic (non-simplified) academic textbooks and other materials on grade level.	Reads and comprehends simplified academic textbooks and materials; tries to read basic (non-simplified) materials but needs assistance.	Reads some basic academic materials and textbooks on grade level with partial understanding, but still needs assistance; reads and comprehends non-simplified everyday material on familiar subjects.	Reads and comprehends basic textbooks and academic materials at grade level.
Writing	May be able to write letters of the alphabet, numbers, and very basic personal information (name, address, etc.).*	Writes common sight words and short, learned phrases; can complete simple worksheets with one- or two-word responses.	Writes phrases and short simple sentences; makes frequent errors and needs assistance.	Writes short paragraphs on familiar subjects, but makes errors and needs assistance; has difficulty with more complex academic writing tasks.	Completes routine writing tasks for social and survival purposes with accuracy; makes errors and needs assistance with writing for academic purposes (essays, written reports, etc.).	Writing ability for social, survival, and academic purposes is similar to that of native speaker at same grade level.

*The A¹ classification includes those students with varying degrees of literacy skills in their own language and/or English.
NOTE: Individual variations will occur depending on student ability and background.

SAMPLE ESOL PROGRAM DELIVERY OPTIONS

1. **ESOL Cluster School**

   A cluster school serves its own ELL students and also ELL students from other schools that do not offer self-contained ESOL classes. A school designated as an ESOL Cluster provides self-contained classes in ESOL/language arts and the content areas.

2. **Home School (Self-Contained Classes)**

   A home school that has a sufficient number of its own ELL students provides them with self-contained classes in ESOL/language arts and the content areas.

3. **Home School (Basic Program with ESOL Strategies)**

   A home school that does not provide self-contained ESOL classes due to an insufficient enrollment of ELL students. ELL students receive instruction in the basic program using ESOL strategies.

4. **The Nova Center**

   New ELL students entering the Broward County Public Schools have a choice of receiving ESOL services at the Nova Center for Applied Research and Professional Development. The enrollment at the Nova Schools is limited and ELL students are registered on a first-come, first-served basis.

Definition of terms used:

1) ELL

   English Language Learner

2) Self-contained

   a class in which all students are ELLs. Bilingual assistance is provided by the teacher and/or paraprofessional

3) ESOL

   English for Speakers of Other Languages

4) Basic Program

   a class with students who are non-ELL and ELL combined. The teacher instructs in English and uses ESOL strategies.

5) ESOL Strategies

   a variety of methods and techniques used for teaching ELLs.

The School Board of Broward County, Florida
Multicultural/Foreign Language/ESOL Education Department
INITIAL AURAL/ORAL LANGUAGE CLASSIFICATION ASSESSMENT FORM

Student's Name: : _____ Date:_____
                    (Last)   (First)   (Middle)

Home Address: _____
           Street Number   City   State   Zip

Phone (Home): _____ Phone (Work):_____ Name:_____
                                                      (Parent/Guardian)

Date of Birth:_____ Sex M ☐ F ☐ Social Security #_____or FSI #_____Grade:_____
                                    (optional)

Country of Birth:_____ Home Language:_____

Date of Entry into the U.S.A._____ Home School:_____

Comments/Observations:_____

INTERVIEW ON FREQUENCY OF LANGUAGE USAGE	English	Home Language	Both
What language do people usually speak at the student's home?			
What language does the student speak at his/her home?			
What language does the student usually speak with his/her best friend when he/she is not at school?			

Test Administered:_____ Test Score Level:_____

Assessor's Signature:_____Language Classification:_____

Cluster School Placement (If Applicable):_____

LANGUAGE LEVEL CLASSIFICATIONS

A¹ Non-English Speaker or minimal knowledge of English
Demonstrates very little understanding; Cannot communicate meaning orally. Unable to participate in regular classroom instruction.

A² Limited English Speakers
Demonstrates limited understanding; Communicates orally in English with one- or two-word responses.

B¹ Intermediate English Speaker
Communicates orally in English, mostly with simple phrases and/or sentence responses; Makes significant grammatical errors which interfere with understanding.

B² Intermediate English Speaker
Communicates in English about everyday situations with little difficulty, but lacks the academic language terminology. Experiences some difficulty in following grade level subject matter assignments.

C¹ Advanced English Speaker
Understands and speaks English fairly well; Makes occasional grammatical errors; May read and write English with variant degrees of proficiency.

C² Full English Speaker
Understands and speaks English with near fluency. Reads and writes English at a comparable level with native English-speaking counterparts; may read and write the native language with variant degrees of proficiency.

D Full English Speaker
Speaks English fluently. Reads and writes English at a comparable level with English-speaking counterparts.

E Monolingual English Speaker

LEP CODE: ☐ LY   ☐ ZZ
(Check one)   ☐ LP

Please fill in percentile scores for C2-LP students in grades 4-12.
Reading Score:_____
Writing (Language) Score:_____
Date:_____

CODE	DEFINITION
LY	Limited English Proficient (LEP) student.
LP	C2-Student placed in Basic Program pending Reading and Writing assessment.
ZZ	Does not need ESOL services.

Form #2590E (Revised 04/98) jb

White Copy: Multicultural/Foreign Language/ESOL Education Dept.
Yellow Copy: LEPSEP Folder
Pink Copy: Data Processing Clerk

THE SCHOOL BOARD OF BROWARD COUNTY, FLORIDA
MULTICULTURAL/FOREIGN LANGUAGE/ESOL EDUCATION DEPARTMENT

IDENTIFICATION OF STUDENTS WHOSE PRIMARY OR HOME LANGUAGE IS OTHER THAN ENGLISH

SCHOOL _____ DATE _____

CONTACT PERSON _____ POSITION _____

NAME (Last, First, Middle)	DATE OF BIRTH	GRADE	TEACHER'S NAME	PRIMARY/HOME LANGUAGE	FOR ESOL PROGRAM USE ONLY		
					FSI NUMBER	LANGUAGE CLASSIFICATION	DATE	ASSESSOR'S INITIALS

PLEASE USE THIS FORM TO REPORT ALL STUDENTS WHO INDICATE A PRIMARY/HOME LANGUAGE OTHER THAN ENGLISH. Upon receipt of this form by Multicultural/Foreign Language ESOL/Education Department , an appointment will be set up with your school to assess these students for an INITIAL LANGUAGE CLASSIFICATION.

DO NOT WRITE BELOW THIS LINE - OFFICE USE ONLY

_____
Principal/Designee

Comments: _____

White Copy: Multicultural/Foreign Language/ESOL Education Department   Yellow Copy: Language Assessor   Pink Copy: Home School
Form 2590A (Revised 4/98:jb)

266   Appendix of Documents and Forms

The IDEA Oral Proficiency Test (IPT)
How Scoring Correlates to Language Level at Two Florida Schools

Pre IPT   <u>Pre-Kindergarten (3 and 4 years old)</u>

Level A	A^1/A^2	1–3 Errors = A^1	4–6 Errors = A^2
Level B	B^1		
Level C	B^2		
Level D	C^2*		
Level E	C^2		

*   May be classified C^1 if their performance indicates a lack of English proficiency in readiness skills appropriate for age.

IPT 1   <u>Kindergarten</u>

Level A	NES A^1/A^2	10–12 Errors = A^1
		7–9 errors = A^2
Level B	LES B^1/B^2	5–6 Errors = B^1
		3–4 Errors = B^2
Level C	FES C^2*	
Level D	FES C^2*	
Level E	FES C^2	
Level F	FES C^2	

IPT I	1st Grade	2nd–3rd Grades	4th–6th Grades
Level A	NES A^1	NES A^1	NES A^1
Level B	NES A^2	NES A^2	NES A^2
Level C	NES B^1	NES B^1	NES B^1
Level D	LES B^2	LES B^2	LES B^2
Level E	FES C^2*	LES B^2	LES B^2
Level F	FES C^2*	FES C^2*	FES C^1/C^2

- Students in kindergarten through third grade may be classified as C^1 if their performance indicates a lack of English proficiency in academic and readiness skills.

IPT II	Level A	NES A^1
7–12 Grades	Level B	LES A^2
	Level C	LES B^1
	Level D	LES B^2
	Level E	LES B^2
	Level F	FES C^1/C^2
	Mastery	FES C^1/C^2

Note: Classifications D and E should always be considered if applicable.

DADE COUNTY CORRELATIONS

Dade County	**Broward County**
Level I	A^1/A^2
Level II	B^1
Level III	B^2
Level IV	C^1
Level V	C^2 (Monitor for two years, as of exit date)

Aural/Oral Language Proficiency Tests for Assessment and Placement of ELLs

Name of Testing Instrument	Description	Grade Level(s)	Languages	Administration Method/Time	Publisher/ Distributor
Balado Listening Comprehension Test	Language dominance; determine language functional level & strengths & weaknesses in both languages.	K–12	English & Spanish	Individual or group; 30—40 min. hand scored; listen to verbal cue and place an "X" on drawing	SCHOOL BOARD OF BREVARD COUNTY DIVISION OF INSTRUCTIONAL SERVICES 1274 S.Florida Ave Rockledge, FL 32955 (407)531-1911 Dr. Carl R. Balado University of Central Florida (407)275-2054
Basic Inventory of Natural Language	Proficiency; dominance; screening; placement; diagnosis	K—adult	English, Spanish, Vietnamese, Armenian, Japanese, Korean, & Cantonese	individual/group 10—15 minutes oral; hand/machine scoring	CHECpoint Systems, Inc. 1520 N. Waterman Ave. San Bernardino, CA 92404 (800) 635-1235 FAX (909) 384-0519
Crane Oral Dominance Test	Tests language dominance	K–12	English & Spanish	Individual 20 minutes	Bilingual Education Services Inc. 2514 S. Grand Ave. Los Angeles, CA 90007-9979 (800) 448-6032 or (213) 749-6213 Crane Publishing Co. 1301 Hamilton Ave. P.O. Box 3713 Trenton, NJ 08629 (609) 393-1111
Dade County Oral Language Proficiency Scale	Listening and speaking skills based on student's responses to oral and visual stimuli	PreK —12	English	Individual	Dade County Public Schools Purchasing Depart. 1450 N.E. 2nd Ave Miami, FL 33132
Dade County Secondary Level Placement Test	Listening & speaking skills based on student's responses to oral and visual stimuli	6 –12	English with instructions in Haitian Creole	Individual Group Approximately 75 minutes	Dade County Public Schools 1450 N.E. 2nd Ave Purchasing Depart. Miami, FL 33132

Name of Testing Instrument	Description	Grade Level(s)	Languages	Administration Method/Time	Publisher/Distributor
			and Spanish		
Idea Oral Language Proficiency Tests (IPT I and IPT II)	Proficiency; lang. dominance; placement; diagnostic; exit Spanish version developed specifically for Spanish speakers	IPT I/ K-6 IPT II 7-12	English & Spanish	Individual; 8-14 min. Oral, pointing performance Hand scored	Ballard & Tighe Publishers 480 Atlas St. Brea, CA 92621 (800) 321-4332 FAX (714) 255-9828
Language Assessment Battery (LAB)	Proficiency; Dominance; Placement; Exit; Multiple choice; Free response; Spanish version constructed specifically for Spanish speakers. Each of the two versions consists of levels (K-2, 3-5, 6-8, 9-12) Spanish version parallels the English version, but is not a translation.	K-12 Test levels not equated	English & Spanish	Individual/group; 5-40 minutes; Oral writing; marking, pointing, Hand/machine scored	New York City Board of Education Test Administration - LAB Office of Research, Evaluation, and Assessment 49 Flatbush Avenue Extension Brooklyn, New York 11201 (718) 935-3964
Language Assessment Scales (LAS-O)	Proficiency; Screening; Placement; Exit; Formal observation; Spanish version	1-12	English and Spanish	Individual 5-25 minutes oral bilingual examiner recommended Hand scored	CTB/McGraw Hill p.o. bOX 150 Monterey, CA 93942-0150 1 (800) 538-9547

Name of Testing Instrument	Description	Grade Level(s)	Languages	Administration Method/Time	Publisher/ Distributor
Maculaitis Assessment of Competence (MAC)	Proficiency Relative proficiency placement Diagnosis Exit Multiple choice Formal observation Rating scale Writing sample Measures L/S/R/W; uses pictures; responses in speaking or writing	Prek -12 author cautions against making interpretations across grades	English	Individual/Group 15 min.-1hr.50min. Oral, writing, bubbling Bilingual examiner recommended Hand/Machine scored	Steck-Vaughn-Berrent Publications P.O. Box 26015 Austin, TX 78755 1 (800) 531-5015 1 (800) 74-LEARN
Test of Language Development Primary	Has seven subtests that measure different components of spoken language, assess the understanding and meaningful use of spoken words, assess differing aspects of grammar, measure the abilities to say words correctly and to distinguish between words that sound similar.	K - 6	English	Individual 40 minutes	PRO-ED 800 Shoal Creek Blvd. Austin, TX 78757 (512) 451-3246
Test of Language Development	Has five subtests that measure different components of spoken language GENERALS, MALAPROPISMS, and VOCABULARY assess the understanding and meaningful use of spoken words. SENTENCE COMBINING, WORD ORDERING, and GRAMMATIC COMPREHENSION assess differing aspects of grammar	8.6 -12.11	English	Individual 40 minutes	PRO-ED 8700 Shoal Creek Boulevard Austin, Texas 78757-6897 (512) 451-3246 Fax (512) 451-8542

TESOL ESL STANDARDS FOR PRE-K THROUGH GRADE 12 STUDENTS

Goal 1: To Use English to Communicate in Social Settings

Standard 1: Students will use English to participate in social interaction.

Standard 2: Students will interact in, through, and with spoken and written English for personal expression and enjoyment.

Standard 3: Students will use learning strategies to extend their communicative competence.

Goal 2: To Use English to Achieve Academically in All Content Areas

Standard 1: Students will use English to interact in the classroom.

Standard 2: Students will use English to obtain, process, construct, and provide subject matter information in spoken and written form.

Standard 3: Students will use appropriate learning strategies to construct and apply academic knowledge.

Goal 3: To Use English in Socially and Culturally Appropriate Ways

Standard 1: Students will use the appropriate language variety, register, and genre, according to audience, purpose, and setting.

Standard 2: Students will use non-verbal communication appropriate to audience, purpose, and setting.

Standard 3: Students will use appropriate learning strategies to extend their sociolinguistic and sociocultural competence.

ESOL Program

Initial Language Classification Assessment Form

Student's Name _____ _____ _____ Date _____
                    (Last)   (First)   (Middle)

DOB _____ SS #/FSI # _____

Home School _____ Home Language _____

Grade _____ Test Administered _____ Level _____

ENGLISH PROFICIENCY	Well	Speaks With Almost Native Fluency	Survival English/Speaks Mostly the Home Language	Not At All/Just A Few Words
How well does the student understand spoken English?				
How well does the student speak English?				

LANGUAGE DOMINANCE	English	Home Language	Both
Which language does the student understand better?			
Which language does the student speak better?			

INTERVIEW ON FREQUENCY OF LANGUAGE USAGE	English	Home Language	Both
What language do people usually speak at the student's home?			
What language does the student speak at his/her home?			
What language does the student usually speak with his/her best friend when he/she is not at school?			
What language does the student usually speak with his/her friends and classmates during lunch time, on the school bus, or at recess?			

Assessor's Signature _____ Initial Language Classification _____

Center Placement _____

A¹ = No English or minimal language

A² = Receptive English; communicates in English in one-word responses

B¹ = Survival English; speaks mostly the home language

B² = Intermediate English; speaks in English with almost native fluency

C¹ = Bilingual; reading/writing of English may not be comparable with native English-speaking counterparts

C² = Bilingual; reading/writing of English may be comparable with native English-speaking counterparts

D = Speaks English fluently; understands primary language

E = Monolingual English speaker

LEP CODE: ☐ LY ☐ LP ☐ ZZ

For Multicultural Education Department Use Only

Address _____

_____

Parent's Phone _____

White & Pink Copies - MED   Yellow Copy - ESOL Folder/Cum Folder   Gold Copy - Other

Form #2590E (Revised 3/94)

EASING THE PAPER LOAD:
10 Techniques of Responding to Writing*

Technique	Number of Items Scored per Paper	Description
1. Student Self-Evaluation	0	Student chooses a goal (e.g., eliminating run-on sentences) and evaluates his or her own progress.
2. Student Editors (Peer Conferences)	0	Students read or listen to each other's writing, making positive comments and suggestions.
3. Student-Teacher Five-Minute Conferences	0	While the class is writing, teacher quickly skims one student's work and makes a postive comment and a suggestion (e.g., *Could you add information to make this clearer?*). By talking with several students each writing period, teacher can talk with every student once every week or two.
4. Student Publishing	0	Students share their writing with audiences other than the teacher: display their work, read it aloud, mail letters, and so on. A publishing idea is provided in every Writing Process Lesson in WORLD OF LANGUAGE.
5. General Impression (Holistic Scoring)	1	A single score of 0–4 or 0–6, for example, is based on an overall, or "whole" impression from a quick reading. For example, a 0 paper does not address the assignment in any way (e.g., a short story was assigned; student wrote gibberish or wrote a rhyme). A 4 paper not only addresses the assignment but shows sparkle or originality.
6. Single Focus (Primary Trait) Scoring	1–2	A single trait (e.g., *Did student name a problem and suggest solutions?*) is commented on or scored 0–4 or 0–6. A related trait (e.g., persuasiveness) may also be considered. Students focus on and improve one skill at a time.
7. Focused Holistic Scoring	2–4	A cross between holistic and primary trait scoring. Both an overall (holistic) impression and one or several specific traits (e.g., *Purpose and audience addressed? Well organized?*) may be scored 0–4 or 0–6.
8. Yes/No (Dichotomous Scale Scoring)	4–10	A checklist of about 4–10 criteria is marked yes or no (e.g., *Correct time order used? yes/no*). A Revision Checklist, provided in each Writing Process Lesson in WORLD OF LANGUAGE, may be used for this kind of scoring.
9. Analytic Scoring	4–10	A list of about 4–10 traits (e.g., ideas, organization, word choice, grammar, spelling, mechanics) are commented on or scored high, middle, or low.
10. Traditional Grading	everything	All errors are marked. Students might select, revise, and polish a favorite composition to submit for traditional grading every month or two.

☐ NO GRADING   ☐ QUICK GRADING

*Betty G. Gray, author, WORLD OF LANGUAGE, Grades K-8
from the Professional Handbook

Developmental Reading Rubric

Emergent	• Pretends to read
	• Uses illustrations to tell a story
	• Participates in reading of familiar books
	• Knows some letter sounds
	• Recognizes names/words in context
	• Memorizes pattern books and familiar books
	• Rhymes and plays with words
Developing	• Sees self as reader
	• Reads books with word patterns
	• Knows most letter sounds
	• Retells main idea of text
	• Recognizes simple words
	• Relies on print and illustrations
Beginning	• Relies more on print than illustrations
	• Recognizes names/words by sight
	• Uses sentence structure clues
	• Uses phonetic clues
	• Retells beginning, middle, and end
	• Begins to read silently
	• Uses basic punctuation
Expanding	• Begins to read short stories and books
	• Reads and finishes a variety of materials with guidance
	• Uses reading strategies
	• Retells plot, characters, and events
	• Recognizes different types of books
	• Reads silently for short periods of time
Bridging	• Begins to read chapter books of moderate difficulty
	• Reads and finishes a variety of materials with guidance
	• Reads and understands most new words
	• Uses reference materials to locate information with guidance
	• Increases knowledge of literary elements and genres
	• Reads silently for extended periods
Fluent	• Reads most literature appropriate to grade-level
	• Selects, reads, and finishes a wide variety of materials
	• Uses reference materials independently
	• Recognizes and uses literary elements and genres
	• Begins to interpret and expand meaning from literature
	• Participates in literary discussions

Adapted from Hill and Ruptic (1994).

ESL Reading Rubric

Pre-Reader	• Listens to read-alouds • Repeats words and phrases • Uses pictures to comprehend text • May recognize some sound/symbol relationships
Emerging Reader	• Participates in choral reading • Begins to retell familiar, predictable text • Uses visuals to facilitate meaning • Uses phonics and word structure to decode
Developing Reader	• Begins to make predictions • Retells beginning, middle, and end of story • Recognizes plot, characters, and events • Begins to rely more on print than illustrations • May need assistance in choosing appropriate texts
Expanding Reader	• Begins to read independently • Responds to literature • Begins to use a variety of reading strategies • Usually chooses appropriate texts
Proficient Reader	• Reads independently • Relates reading to personal experience • Uses a wide variety of reading strategies • Recognizes literary elements and genres • Usually chooses appropriate texts
Independent Reader	• Reads for enjoyment • Reads and completes a wide variety of texts • Responds personally and critically to texts • Matches a wide variety of reading strategies to purpose • Chooses appropriate or challenging texts

Adapted from a draft compiled by the ESL Portfolio Teachers Group, Fairfax County Public Schools, Virginia (1995).

Summary Evaluation Guidelines

Student _____ Date _____

This Student:	Never	Sometimes	Often	Always
• identifies the topic	1	2	3	4
• identifies the main idea	1	2	3	4
• combines/chunks similar ideas	1	2	3	4
• paraphrases accurately	1	2	3	4
• deletes minor details	1	2	3	4
• reflects author's emphasis	1	2	3	4
• recognizes author's purpose	1	2	3	4
• stays within appropriate length	1	2	3	4

Comments

Adapted from Casazza (1992).

Holistic Oral Language Scoring Rubric

Rating	Description
6	• Communicates competently in social and classroom settings • Speaks fluently • Masters a variety of grammatical structures • Uses extensive vocabulary but may lag behind native-speaking peers • Understands classroom discussion without difficulty
5	• Speaks in social and classroom settings with sustained and connected discourse; any errors do not interfere with meaning • Speaks with near-native fluency; any hesitations do not interfere with communication • Uses a variety of structures with occasional grammatical errors • Uses varied vocabulary • Understands simple sentences in sustained conversation; requires repetition
4	• Initiates and sustains a conversation with descriptors and details; exhibits self-confidence in social situations; begins to communicate in classroom settings • Speaks with occasional hesitation • Uses some complex sentences; applies rules of grammar but lacks control of irregular forms (e.g., *runned, mans, not never, more higher*) • Uses adequate vocabulary; some word usage irregularities • Understands classroom discussions with repetition, rephrasing, and clarification
3	• Begins to initiate conversation; retells a story or experience; asks and responds to simple questions • Speaks hesitantly because of rephrasing and searching for words • Uses predominantly present tense verbs; demonstrates errors of omission (leaves words out, word endings off) • Uses limited vocabulary • Understands simple sentences in sustained conversation; requires repetition
2	• Begins to communicate personal and survival needs • Speaks in single-word utterances and short patterns • Uses functional vocabulary • Understands words and phrases; requires repetitions
1	• Begins to name concrete objects • Repeats words and phrases • Understands little or no English

Adapted from a rating scale developed by ESL teachers Portfolio Assessment Group (Grades 1-12), Fairfax County Public Schools, Virginia.

Analytic Oral Language Scoring Rubric

Focus/Rating:	1	2	3	4	5	6
Speaking	Begins to name concrete objects	Begins to communicate personal and survival needs	Begins to initiate conversation; retells a story or experience; asks and responds to simple questions	Initiates and sustains a conversation with descriptors and details; exhibits self-confidence in social situations; begins to communicate in classroom settings	Speaks in social and classroom settings with sustained and connected discourse; any errors do not interfere with meaning	Communicates competently in social and classroom settings
Fluency	Repeats words and phrases	Speaks in single-word utterances and short patterns	Speaks hesitantly because of rephrasing and searching for words	Speaks with occasional hesitation	Speaks with near-native fluency; any hesitations do not interfere with communication	Speaks fluently
Structure			Uses predominantly present tense verbs; demonstrates errors of omission (leaves words out, word endings off)	Uses some complex sentences; applies rules of grammar but lacks control of irregular forms (e.g., *runned, mans, not never, more higher*)	Uses a variety of structures with occasional grammatical errors	Masters a variety of grammatical structures
Vocabulary		Uses functional vocabulary	Uses limited vocabulary	Uses adequate vocabulary; some word usage irregularities	Uses varied vocabulary	Uses extensive vocabulary but may lag behind native-speaking peers
Listening	Understands little or no English	Understands words and phrases, requires repetition	Understands simple sentences in sustained conversation; requires repetition	Understands classroom discussions with repetition, rephrasing, and clarification	Understands most spoken language, including classroom discussion	Understands classroom discussion without difficulty

Adapted from a rating scale developed by ESL teachers Portfolio Assessment Group (Grades 1-12), Fairfax County Public Schools, Virginia.

Sample Parent Letter for Student's Portfolio

_____
(Date)

Dear Parents:

Your child, (_____), will be putting
(Student's Name)
together a portfolio this year. This portfolio will contain samples of his
or her work that show what he/she is learning. I will use the portfolio
to identify each student's strengths and weaknesses and to plan
appropriate instructional activities.

At various times throughout the year, I will be asking you to review
the portfolio and to comment on your child's work. After you have
reviewed your child's portfolio, please make comments on the Portfolio
Summary Sheet and initial it at the bottom. Please call me if you have
any questions or would like to come in for a parent-student portfolio
conference. I am looking forward to working closely with you.

Sincerely,

_____
(Teacher's Name)

_____
(Teacher's Telephone Number)

Adapted from De Fina (1992).

Elementary School Reading/Writing Portfolio Cover Sheet

Student _____ School Year _____

Teacher _____ Grade _____

Level _____ Base School _____

ESL Center _____

Required Contents	1st Quarter	2nd Quarter	3rd Quarter	4th Quarter
1. Oral summary				
2. Story summary (writing or drawing)				
3. Writing sample (teacher choice)				
4. Student choice of writing (any type)				
5. Student self-evaluation				

Optional Contents

1. List of books/stories read in class				
2. List of books/stories read independently				
3. Reading interest inventory				
4. Literacy development checklist				
5. Content-sample (e.g., reading comprehension sample, project, report)				
6. Student choice (any type)				

Test	Initial Testing			Final Testing		
IPT	_____ Date	_____ Score	_____ Level	_____ Date	_____ Score	_____ Level
Reading	_____ Date	_____ Score	_____ Level	_____ Date	_____ Score	_____ Level
Writing	_____ Date	_____ Score	_____ Level	_____ Date	_____ Score	_____ Level
Placement						

Comments

Developed by elementary school ESL teachers, Prince William County Public Schools, Virginia.

♦ © Addison-Wesley. *Authentic Assessment for English Language Learners.* O'Malley/Valdez Pierce. This page may be reproduced for classroom use.

Middle School Reading/Writing Portfolio Cover Sheet

Student _____ Grade _____

Teacher _____ School _____

Level _____ School Year _____

Required Contents	1st Quarter	2nd Quarter	3rd Quarter	4th Quarter
1. Cloze sample				
2. Writing sample				
3. Self-rating strategies checklist				
4. List of books read				
5. Reading passage with comprehension questions				

Optional Contents

1. Content area samples				
2. Audio/video performances				
3. Illustrations				
4. Other				

Teacher Observations

1st Quarter	2nd Quarter	3rd Quarter	4th Quarter

Parent Comments

Signature	Signature	Signature	Signature

Developed by middle school ESL teachers, Prince William County Public Schools, Virginia.

High School Reading/Writing Portfolio Cover Sheet

Student _____ Grade _____

Teacher _____ School _____

Level _____ School Year _____

Date of Entry _____

Required Contents	1st Quarter	2nd Quarter	3rd Quarter	4th Quarter
1. Reading passage with comprehension questions				
2. Cloze sample				
3. Writing sample				
4. Written response to oral stimulus				
5. Written response to prompt/literature				
6. Self-rating strategies checklist				
7. Student choice				

Optional Contents

	1st Quarter	2nd Quarter	3rd Quarter	4th Quarter
1. Content area samples				
2. Audio performances				
3. List readings with short synopsis				
4. Oral language sample (including native language)				
5. Other				

1st Quarter	2nd Quarter	3rd Quarter	4th Quarter
Test scores LPT _____			
_____ Signature	_____ Signature	_____ Signature	_____ Signature

Developed by high school ESL teachers, Prince William County Public Schools, Virginia.

Portfolio Evaluation Summary

Student _____ Grade _____ Date _____

Teacher _____ School _____

First Language (L1) _____ Second Language (L2) _____

Directions: Circle L1 or L2 to indicate if student meets the standard.

Curriculum/ Assessment Area	Does Not Meet Standards		Meets Standards		Exceeds Standards	
Oral Language	L1	L2	L1	L2	L1	L2
Written Language	L1	L2	L1	L2	L1	L2
Reading	L1	L2	L1	L2	L1	L2
Overall Summary	L1	L2	L1	L2	L1	L2

Comments

Adapted from M. Gottlieb in Valdez Pierce and Gottlieb (1994).

Self-Assessment of Oral Language

Name _____ Date _____

Check (√) the box that shows what you can do. Add comments.

What Can You Do in English?	Difficulty Level				Comments
	Not Very Well	Okay	Well	Very well	
1. I can ask questions in class.					
2. I can understand others when working in a group.					
3. I can understand television shows.					
4. I can speak with native speakers outside of school.					
5. I can talk on the phone.					
6. I can ask for an explanation.					

Adapted from Bachman and Palmer (1989).

Self-Assessment of Academic Language Functions

Name _____ Date _____

Check (√) the box that best describes how well you can use English. Add comments.

Task	Not Very Well	Okay	Well	Very Well	Comments
1. I can describe objects and people.					
2. I can describe past events.					
3. I can listen to and understand radio programs.					
4. I can listen to and understand video and television.					
5. I can state an opinion.					
6. I can agree and disagree.					
7. I can summarize a story.					
8. I can give an oral report.					

Self-Assessment of Communication Strategies in Oral Language

Name _____ Date _____

Circle the answer that shows how often you do the following things.

When I have problems talking in English, I:

1. use my native language	Never	Sometimes	Often
2. ask for help.	Never	Sometimes	Often
3. use gestures or facial expressions.	Never	Sometimes	Often
4. avoid communication totally or partially.	Never	Sometimes	Often
5. use a synonym or a description.	Never	Sometimes	Often
6. make up new words.	Never	Sometimes	Often
7. simplify what I want to say.	Never	Sometimes	Often

Adapted from a form developed by ESL teacher S. Copley (1994)

Self-Assessment of Speaking Ability

Name_____ Date_____

Part 1: Place an X on each line to show how much you agree or disagree.

This week I used English to talk with_____ .

1. I think that I was successful.   Disagree ├──────┼──────┼──────┤ Agree

2. The person I spoke to understood me.   Disagree ├──────┼──────┼──────┤ Agree

3. I felt comfortable speaking with another
    person in English.   Disagree ├──────┼──────┼──────┤ Agree

4. I understood everything that this person
    said to me.   Disagree ├──────┼──────┼──────┤ Agree

5. I could do this again with no problem.   Disagree ├──────┼──────┼──────┤ Agree

Part 2: Complete the sentences below.

6. When someone doesn't understand me, I_____.____

7. When I don't understand someone, I_____.____

8. Now I know_____.____

Adapted from a form developed by ESL teacher M. Crossman (1994).

Addison-Wesley: *Authentic Assessment for English Language Learners*. O'Malley/Valdez Pierce. This page may be reproduced for classroom use.

Self-Assessment of Reading Strategies

Name _____ Date _____

Check (√) the box that indicates how you read.

Reading Strategies	Often	Sometimes	Almost Never
1. I think about what I already know on the topic.			
2. I make predictions and read to find out if I was right.			
3. I reread the sentences before and after a word I do not know.			
4. I ask another student for help.			
5. I look for the main idea.			
6. I take notes.			
7. I discuss what I read with others.			
8. I stop and summarize.			
9. I choose books from the library on my own.			
10. I make outlines of what I read.			

Adapted from Applebee, Langer, and Jullis (1988) and Rhodes (1993).

High-Stakes Assessment for ELL's

Information provided by state education agencies and compiled in a report by Dennis Holmes to NCBE.

	Mandatory Assessment(s)	Grades Tested	Subjects Tested	ELLs exempt from mainstream test	Alternative assessment for ELLs	Accommodations*	Graduation/Promotion at stake?
California	STAR	2-11	English Language Arts, Math	only if dictated by Individual Evaluation Plan	SABE/2 taken by Spanish-speaking ELLs in state less than 1–2 years, in addition to mainstream tests	None, unless dictated by Individual Evaluation Plan	No. In 2003–04, must pass state language arts & math assessments for H.S. graduation
	Stanford 9 (SAT-9)	2-8	Reading, Writing, Spelling, Math				
		9-11	Reading, Writing, Math, Science, Social Studies				
District of Columbia	Stanford 9	1-11	Reading, Math	if less than 3 yrs. English instruction with appropriate LAS score and principal's permission	None	Yes; must align with classroom instructional accommodations	H.S. Graduation. Requires passing SAT-9 or new reading and math test
Florida	High School Competency Test (HSCT)	11	Communication skills, Math	if receiving ESOL services for 2 years or less	None	Yes	H.S. Graduation. All students must pass HSCT
Illinois	Illinois Standards Achievement Tests	3,4,5,7, 8,10,11	Illinois Learning Standards	if in transitional bilingual education or transitional program of instruction for less than 3 years	Illinois Measure of Annual Growth (IMAGE) measures English reading and writing development	None, unless dictated by Individual Evaluation Plan	Grade Promotion
Maryland	Maryland Functional Testing Program (MFTP)	High school	Reading, Writing, Math, Citizenship	within one calendar year from date of enrollment in Maryland schools	None	Yes; as determined by an ELL committee, with approval from Dept. of Ed & local accountability coordinator	H.S. Graduation
Minnesota	Statewide Accountability Test	3, 5, 8	Reading, Writing, Math	if less than 1 year in U.S.	None	Yes	No
	Basic Standards Test	High school	Reading, Writing, Math		Translation of math section into Spanish, Vietnamese, and Hmong	Yes	H.S. Graduation
	Mandatory Assessment(s)	Grades Tested	Subjects Tested	ELLs exempt from mainstream test	Alternative assessment for ELLs	Accommodations*	Graduation/Promotion at stake?

*Please see next document for a listing of the accommodations provided

National Clearinghouse for Bilingual Education

High-Stakes Assessment for ELL's (cont.)

Information provided by state education agencies and compiled in a report by Dennis Holmes to NCBE.

New Jersey	High School Proficiency Test (HSPT)	11	Reading, Writing, Math	if in bilingual or ESL program less than 2 years, attended U.S. school for less than 3 consecutive years, or score below cut-off level for language assessment battery; must take SRA	Special Review Assessment (SRA) available in Haitian-Creole, Gujarati, Korean, Polish, Spanish, Arabic, Chinese, Japanese, Portuguese, and Vietnamese	Yes, for HSPT only	H.S. Graduation
New York	Regents Examination	High school	Language Arts, Math, Social Studies, Science	if enter U.S. schools in grade 9 or later may take translated test	Translations of all sections (except English Language Arts) in Chinese, Haitian Creole, Korean, Russian, and Spanish	Yes	H.S. Graduation
North Carolina	North Carolina Statewide Testing Program	3-12	Reading, Writing, Math, Social Studies, Science (not all subjects tested in all grades)	Exemptions available for up to two years	None	Yes	H.S. Graduation, beginning with the graduating class of 2003
Texas	Texas Assessment of Academic Skills (TAAS)	10	Reading, Writing, Math	if less than 1 year in U.S., test can be postponed	End-of-course exams in Algebra I, English II, and either Biology I or U.S. History instead of the TAAS	Yes; if student receives accommodation during classroom instruction	H.S. Graduation
Virginia	Standards of Learning (SOL)	3,5,8,11	Language Arts, Math, Social Studies, Science	may be granted a one-time exemption in grade 3, 5, or 8	None	Yes	H.S. Graduation, beginning with 9th grade class of 2000

*Please see next document for a listing of the accommodations provided

National Clearinghouse for Bilingual Education

Types of Accommodations Provided, by State

	Extra time	Breaks/additional breaks	Time of day flexibility	English/home language dictionary	Exam administered by ESL or home language teacher	Teacher may clarify test directions in home language	Teacher reads test questions aloud	Simplification/repetition of instructions in English	Small group/individual testing	Written copies of orally presented materials	Direct marking of test booklet	Student responds verbally
California	ONLY IF DICTATED BY INDIVIDUAL EVALUATION PLAN											
District of Columbia	•	•	•					•	•			
Florida	•			•	•	•						
Illinois	ONLY IF DICTATED BY INDIVIDUAL EVALUATION PLAN											
Maryland	•	•	•	•		•		•	•	•		
Minnesota	•	•	•			•	•	•	•			
New York	•	•	•	•			•		•			
North Carolina	•			•			•		•		•	
Virginia	•	•	•				•	•	•			•

Information was not provided for New Jersey or Texas

National Clearinghouse for Bilingual Education

Glossary of Professional Terms

Allomorphs: a variant form of a morpheme /z/ ➤ /z/, /s/, /ɪz/

Audio-lingual Method: A method of foreign or second language teaching based on the notion that second language learning should be regarded as a mechanistic process of habit formation.

Automatic Processing: When a language learner demonstrates the abilities of expert learners who manage many types of information simultaneously, because certain sub-skills have become automatic to them.

Auxiliary Verb: A verb that precedes a regular or main verb; it is also called a helping verb (*Susan has left*).

BICS: An acronym for Basic Interpersonal Communicative Language, also known as social language.

Behaviorism: An empiricist position that focuses on human behavior that is determined by specific environmental factors. With respect to language, a child learns a language through a stimulus, response, and reinforcement chain.

Borrowing: Process by which a language adopts words or phrases from another language.

CALP: An acronym for Cognitive Academic Language Proficiency. Also known as academic language associated with formal schooling.

Categories: Words are organized into different groups according to their behavior.

Cognates: Words that are derived from the same source and typically have similar form and meaning.

Cognitive Academic Language Learning Approach (CALLA): An approach of learning English through a strategy that promotes the acquisition of academic language skills.

Cognitive Strategies: Direct strategies which learners apply to the language or the task itself, e.g., remembering more effectively or compensating for missing information.

Common Underlying Proficiency (CUP): In second language learning, Cummins assumes that content and skills learned in the primary language will transfer to the target language.

Communicative Competence: This term refers to learners' ability to understand what is being said and to use language appropriately in a variety of contexts. This requires competence in four areas: grammatical, sociolinguistic, discourse, and strategic competence.

Consonants: Sounds formed when airflow is partially or completely obstructed in the mouth by the placement of tongue and position of the lips.

Constituents: Building blocks of a sentence.

Context: The real world information that helps us fill in the details that are not available in the discourse, enabling us to interpret what is said. (See also *epistemic, linguistic, social* and *physical context* in Chapter 10.)

Controlled Processing: When a learner first learns a language, he/she is limited in the way he/she handles the basic elements of the language.

Derivational Morphemes: Morphemes that are formed from root words, usually through affixes, e.g., /dirt/, /dir*ty*/.

Developmental Errors: Errors naturally produced by children in the process of acquiring a language that fade away once speakers become more proficient in the language.

Dialect: A language variety defined by geographic location and social factors such as class, religion, or ethnicity.

Direct Method (DM): Direct Method focuses on the promotion of communication in the target language where students learning English as a second language or foreign language are not allowed to use their native language in their learning process.

Direct Speech Acts: Utterances that perform their functions in a direct and literal manner.

Discourse: A continuous stretch of speech or written text beyond the sentence level.

EFL: English as a Foreign Language: This term is widely employed when referring to English taught to speakers of other languages, yet when English is not used as the primary language for instruction.

When using this term a number of assumptions are made:

○ The learner's native language is not English.
○ The learner is in a school environment where a language other than English is the primary language of instruction.
○ Proficiency in English is necessary for success in this particular subject, but not for success in school or for upward mobility.
○ The majority language is not English.
○ The dominant language is not English.
○ The learner lives in a neighborhood where a language other than English is widely spoken.

ELLs: English Language Learners: This term is widely employed to refer to students who are in the process of acquiring English in schools where English is the primary language of instruction.

When employing this term, a number of assumptions are made:

○ The learner's native language is not English.
○ The learner is in a school environment where English is necessary for success and upward mobility.
○ Although the learner may live in a neighborhood where English is not widely spoken (enclave community), the majority language is English.
○ English is the dominant language.

ENL: English as a New Language: This term is found in the most recent literature when referring to students who are in the process of acquiring English in schools where English is the primary language of instruction. This term is synonymous to ELL. The same assumptions made for ELL are made for students who are identified as learning English as a new language.

ESL: English as a Second Language: This term is widely employed to refer to the teaching of the English language to speakers of other languages when English is the primary language of instruction.

When employing this term, a number of assumptions are made:

○ The learner's native language is not English.
○ The learner is in a school environment where English is necessary for success and upward mobility.
○ Although the learner may live in a neighborhood where English is not widely spoken, the "majority" language is English.
○ English is the dominant language.

ESOL: English for Speakers of Other Languages: This term is widely employed when referring to the teaching of the English language to non-native speakers of English. It is assumed that the "learner" hears and speaks a language other than English at home.

Global Errors: Errors produced by learners that interfere with communication. Global errors may involve substitution of incorrect sounds or words and jumbled up sentences.

Grammar Translation Method (GTM): A method of foreign and second language teaching that focuses on reading, writing, translation, and the conscious learning of grammatical rules; its primary goal is to develop a literary mastery of the target language.

Grice's Conversational Maxims: Conversational rules that regulate how speakers should comply with certain cooperative principles.

Homonyms: Different words with the same pronunciation and spelling but different meanings (such as *baseball bat* and *bat* the animal)

Implicatures: Inferences based on certain warranted conditions.

Indirect Speech Acts: Utterances that perform their functions in an indirect and non-literal manner.

Inflectional Morphemes: Modify a word's form to make it fit the grammatical category to which it belongs, e.g., /walk/$\succ$/walk*ed*/, present tense to past tense form.

Interlanguage: The dynamic language system that is unique to L2 learners as they go through a number of states of grammar along a continuum, starting with their native language and ultimately approaching the target language.

Intonation: Rising and falling pitch in a language that does not change word meaning, but changes the function of a sentence.

Language Minority Students: This term refers to (A) individuals who were not born in the United States or whose native language is a language other than English; (B) individuals who come from environments where a language other than English is dominant; and (C) individuals who are Native Americans or Alaskan natives who come from environments where a language other than English has had a significant impact on their level of English language proficiency and who have sufficient difficulty speaking, reading, writing, or understanding English that they would not have the opportunity to learn successfully in classrooms where the language of instruction is English, or to fully participate in our society.

Learning Styles: The way we learn things in general (see multiple intelligences and cognitive styles in Chapter 19).

LEP: Language Enriched Pupil: Term employed to refer to second/English language learners.

LEP: Limited English Proficient: This term is widely employed when referring to students whose native language is not English and who are acquiring English as a second language. Under the terms of the Florida Educational Equity Act of 1984, a limited English proficient student is defined as a student whose home language is other than English as determined by a home language survey and whose English aural comprehension, speaking, reading, or writing proficiency level is below that of English speaking students of the same age and grade level.

Point: Some professionals in the field of second language acquisition argue that this term has a negative connotation because students are referred to as "limited." These students normally can communicate (at least orally) in their native language; thus, the fact that they are acquiring a second language should be viewed as an asset, not as a limitation.

Counterpoint: Ignoring the fact that lack of English proficiency, in a country where English is the official language of instruction, is detrimental to students who need to understand the instruction they are given.

Lexical Ambiguity: A word that has two or more possible meanings.

Linearity: Words are strung together in a linear form, e.g., *she goes to work every day* instead of *goes she work to every day.*

Local Errors: Errors that do not hinder communication—incorrect inflections on nouns and verbs, incorrect use or omission of articles, and other errors that involve single elements of the sentence.

Metacognitive Strategies: Indirect strategies in which learners manage or control their own learning process, e.g., managing your emotions, organizing and evaluating your learning.

Minimal Pairs: Words that differ by one phoneme, e.g., /pin/ vs. /bin/.

Morphemes: Minimal meaningful units, e.g., /boy/ vs. /boys/

Morphology: The study of word formation that deals with the internal structure of words in a language.

Multiple Intelligence: Intelligence is not a single construct or static, but a set of distinct intelligences that can be developed over a lifetime. (Such as linguistic, bodily-kinesthetic, musical, logical/mathematical, spatial/visual, interpersonal, intrapersonal, and naturalist intelligences).

Nativism: Also known as the mentalist perspective. This position focuses on the fact that children acquire a language by constructing their own grammar through a process of hypothesis-testing and not purely imitating adults' speech.

Overgeneralizations: A term used to describe developmental errors attributed to an application of a rule in instances where the rule does not apply. *Overgeneralization* is a broader term than *narrowing*. (See first and second language acquisition in Chapter 15.)

Phonemes: Distinctive sound units that make a difference when sounds form words.

Phonemic Sequence: Permissible way in which phonemes can be combined in a language.

Phonology: The study of sound systems which deals with pronunciation rules in a language.

Pragmatics: The study of how the meaning of utterances depends on the context in which they are used (such as time, place, social relationship between speaker and listener, speaker's assumptions about listener's beliefs).

Silent Language: Meaning that is conveyed through gestures, eye contact, space, and touch.

Social Interactionist: A theoretical position that focuses on the critical role of caregivers in facilitating innate abilities for language acquisition.

Socio-affective Strategies: Strategies for mediating and interacting with others, also considered as communication strategies.

Speech Register: The various ways of speaking that are marked by degrees of formality. Also known as *speech style.*

Strategies: Specific "attack-skills" that learners employ in problem-solving, including both learning and communication strategies. Learning strategies are typically receptive strategies for processing linguistic input (see *metacognitive, cognitive, and social-affective strategies* in Chapter 19). Communication strategies perform an expressive function.

Structural Ambiguity: Sentences that contain two or more meanings.

TESOL: Teaching English to Speakers of Other Languages/Teachers of English to Speakers of Other Languages: This term is widely employed when referring to the teaching of English to non-native speakers of English or when referring to teachers who teach English to second language learners. The term TESOL is employed in a variety of other contexts as well, for example: *TESOL strategies*. In this context the term refers to strategies which teachers use when teaching English to speakers of other languages and to non-native speakers of English.

Vowels: Sounds formed when airflow in the mouth is not blocked.

World Englishes: The term refers to the use of English for international and intranational purposes and assumes that there are many varieties of English spoken by native and non-native speakers of English. These varieties, although based on a native speaker's model, have distinct and systematic features at various linguistic levels (syntactic, morphological, lexical, stylistic, and discoural) that reflect the sociolinguistic underpinnings of their use.

References

Absedi, J. "Inclusion of Students with Limited English Proficiency." In *NAEP: Classification and Measurement Issues: CSE Report 629, Graduate School of Education and Information Studies*. Los Angeles, CA: University of California, 2004.

Ali, Ahmed. "Twilight in Delhi," in Kachru, Braj, "Non-native Literatures in English as a Resource for Language Teaching." In *Literature and Language Teaching*, Brumfit, C. J. & Carter, R. A. (Eds.). Oxford: Oxford University Press, 1991.

American Educational Research Association. *English Language Learners: Boosting Academic Achievement. Essential Information for Education Policy*, 2 (1). Washington, D.C.: Author, 2004.

Ariza Whelan, E. "The Immigrant in the United States: Socialization Processes and Reactions to Cultural Entry." Unpublished comprehensive exam paper, University of Massachusetts at Amherst, 1991.

August, D. "Literacy for English-Language Learners: Four Key Issues." Presented at the U.S. Department of Education's First Annual Summit on English Language Acquisition, Washington, D.C., November 2002.

August, D. & Hakuta, K. (1997). Cited in James Crawford (2004). *No Child Left Behind: Misguided Approach to School Accountability for English Language Learners*. Retrieved (2005) from www.NABE.org.

August, D. & Hakuta, K., eds. (1997a) *Improving Schooling for Language-Minority Children: A Research Agenda*. Washington, D.C.: National Academy Press.

Australian English Glossary from A to Zed. http://www.uta.fi/FAST/US1/REF/aust-eng.html.

Backes, J. "The American Indian High School Dropout Rate: A matter of style?" *Journal of American Indian Education* (May): 16–29 (1993).

Baker, C. *The Care and Education of Young Bilinguals. An Introduction for Professionals*. Multilingual Matters, Ltd., 2000.

Bear, D., Invernizzi, M., Templeton, S., & Johnston, F. *Words Their Way* (3rd Ed.). Upper Saddle River, NJ: Prentice Hall, 2004.

Bickner, R. & Peyasantiwong, P. "Cultural Variation in Reflective Writing." In A. Purves (Ed.). *Writing Across Languages and Cultures: Issues in Contrastive Rhetoric*, pp. 275–304. Newbury Park, CA: Sage Publishers, 1988.

Blevins, W. *Phonemic Awareness Activities for Early Reading Success*. New York: Scholastic Professional Books, 1997.

Bronley, K. "Buddy Journals Make the Reading-Writing Connection." *The Reading Teacher* 43 (2): 122–129 (1989).

Bronley, K. "Buddy Journals for ESL and Native-English Speaking Students." *TESOL Journal* 4 (3): 7–11 (1995).

Brown, H. & Douglas, D. *A Practical Guide to Language Learning: A Fifteen-Week Program of Strategies and Success*. New York: McGraw-Hill, 1989.

Brown, D. *Principles of Language Learning and Teaching*. Upper Saddle River, NJ: Prentice Hall, 1994.

Caine, G. & Caine, R. *Making Connections: Teaching and the Human Brain*. Alexandria, VA: Association of Supervision and Curriculum Development, 1991.

———. *Mind/Brain Learning Principles*. http://www.newhorizons.orgofc_21clicaine.html. (1997).

California State Department of Education, SOLOM (Student Oral Language Observation Matrix). Sacramento, CA: Bilingual Education Office.

Canadian English Glossary: www.//canadian.demon.co.uk/lang.htm.

Canale, M. "From Communicative Competence to Communicative Language Pedagogy." In J. Richards and Schmidt (Eds.), *Language and Communication*. New York: Longman, 1983.

Canale, M. & Swain, M. "Theoretical Bases of Communicative Approaches to Second Language Teaching and Testing." *Applied Linguistics* 1: 1–47, 1980.

Cardenas, J.A., Montecel, M. R., Supik, J. D., & Harris, R. J. "The Coca-Cola Valued Youth Program. Dropout Prevention Strategies for At-Risk Students." *Texas Researcher* 3: 111–130, 1992.

Cazden, C. "ESL Teachers as Language Advocates for Children." In *Children and ESL: Integrating Perspectives.* Washington, D.C.: TESOL Publications, pp. 7–22, 1986.

Chambers, J. & Parish, T. *Meeting the Challenge of Diversity: An Evaluation of Programs for Pupils with Limited Proficiency in English.* Vol. IV, *Cost of Programs and Services for LEP Students.* Berkeley, CA: BW Associates, 1992.

Chamot, A. U. & O'Malley, J. M. *A Cognitive Academic Language Learning Approach: An ESL Content-Based Curriculum.* Washington, D.C.: National Clearinghouse for Bilingual Education, 1986.

Chamot, A. U. & O'Malley, J. M. *The CALLA Handbook: Implementing the Cognitive Academic Language Learning Approach.* Reading, MA: Addison-Wesley, 1994.

Chamot, A. U. & O'Malley, J. M. "Instructional Approaches and Teaching Procedures." In K. Spangenberg-Urbschat and R. Pritchard (Eds.) *Kids Come in All Languages: Reading Instruction for ESL Students* (82–107). Newark, DE: International Reading Association, 1994.

Chittendon, L. "Teaching Writing to Elementary Children." Speech presented at the Bay Area Writing Project Workshop, University of California, Berkeley, 1994.

Clay, M. *The Early Detection of Reading Difficulties.* Auckland, New Zealand: Heinemann, 1979.

Clay, M. "Concepts about Print: In English and Other Languages." *The Reading Teacher* 42, (4): 268–277, 1989.

Cohen, A. D. *Second Language Learning: Insights for Learners, Teachers, and Researchers.* New York: Harper and Row, 1990.

———. Second language learning and use strategies: clarifying the issues. http://www.carla.umn.edu:16080/strategies/resources/SBlclarify.pdf (1996a).

———. The impact of strategies-based instructions on speaking a foreign language. http://www.carla.umn.edu/about/profiles/CohenPapers/SBlimpact.pdf (1996b).

Collier, V. P. & Thomas, W. P. "Program Models in Language-Minority Education in the United States." *NABE NEWS* 33–35, (May, 1996).

Coltrane, B. "English Language Learners and High-Stakes Tests: An Overview of the Issues." ERIC Document Reproduction Service No. EDO-FL-02-07. (November, 2002).

Comrie, B., Matthews, S., & Polinsky, M. (Eds.) *The Atlas of Languages: The Origins and Development of Languages Throughout the World.* London: Quatro Publishing PLC, 1996.

Connor, U. "Argumentative Patterns in Student Essays: Cross-Cultural Differences." In *Writing Across Languages: Analysis of L2 Text,* Ulla Connor and Robert B. Kaplan (Eds.). Reading, MA: Addison-Wesley Publishing Co., 1987.

Cortez, A. "The Emerging Majority: The Growth of the Latino Population and Latino Student Enrollments." *Intercultural Development Research Association Newsletter* (2003). Retrieved (2005), from http://www.idra.org/Newsltr/2003/Jan/Albert.htm.

Crago, M. D. "Development of Communicative Competence in Inuit Children: Implications for Speech-Language Pathology." *Journal of Childhood Communication Disorders* 13 (1):73–83, 1990.

Crawford, J. "Ten Common Fallacies about Bilingual Education." ERIC DIGEST. (On-line document). Available: Internet: http://www.cal.org/ericcll/diget/crawford01.html. (November, 1998).

Crawford, J. (2004) "No Child Left Behind: Misguided Approach to School Accountability for English Language Learners, Forum on Ideas to Improve the NCLB Accountability Provisions for Students with Disabilities and English Language Learners, Center for Education Policy, National Association for Bilingual Education. Retrieved (2005) from www.NCTE.org.

Cummins, J. "The Role of Primary Language Development in Promoting Educational Success for Language Minority Students." In California State Department of Education (Ed.), *Schooling and Language Minority Students: A Theoretical Framework* (pp. 3–49). Los Angeles: Evaluation, Dissemination and Assessment Center, California State University, 1981.

Cummins, J. *Tests, Achievement and Bilingual Students.* Wheaton, MD: National Clearinghouse for Bilingual Education, 1982.

Cunningham, P. *Phonics They Use: Words for Reading and Writing.* New York: Longman, 1995.

DeGeorge, G. P. "Assessment and Placement of Language Minority Students: Procedures for Mainstreaming." *Equity and Excellence* 23 (4):44–56, 1988.

Diaz-Rico, L. T. & Weed, K. Z. *The Crosscultural Language and Academic Development Handbook: A Complete K–12 Reference Guide.* Massachusetts: Allyn and Bacon, 1995.

DiCerbo, P. A. "Common Practices for Uncommon Learners: Addressing Linguistic and Cultural Diversity." In *Framing Effective Practice: Topics and Issues in Educating English Language Learners.* Washington, D.C.: U.S. Dept. of Ed. Office of Bilingual Ed. and Minority Languages Affairs, 2000.

Dörnyei, Z. "On the Teachability of Communication Strategies." *TESOL Quarterly* 29 (1):55–85 (1995).

Dulay, H., Burt, M., Krashen, S. *Language Two.* New York: Oxford University Press, 1982.

Dunn, R. "Learning Style and its Relation to Exceptionality at Both Ends of the Spectrum." *Exceptional Children* 49:496–506 (1983).

———. "Learning Style: State of the Scene." *Theory into Practice* 23:10–19 (1984).

Dutcher, N. In "A Global Perspective on Bilingualism and Bilingual Education." (1999) ERIC DIGEST (Online document). Available: Internet: http://www.cal.org/ericcll/digest/digestglobal.html. (1994).

Eggington, W. G. "Written Academic Discourse in Korean: Implications for Effective Communication." In *Writing Across Languages: Analysis of L2 Text*, Ulla Connor and Robert B. Kaplan (Eds.). Reading, MA: Addison-Wesley Publishing Co., 1987.

Erickson, J. & Omark, D. Eds. *Communication Assessment of the Bilingual, Bicultural Child.* Baltimore: University Park Press, 1981.

Fleishman, H. L. & Hopstock, P. J. "Descriptive Study of Services to Limited English Proficient Students." In *FORUM: The Changing Face of America* (Vol. 18, No. 4, Fall 1995). *Newsletter of the National Clearinghouse for Bilingual Education*, 1993.

Flemming, D. N., Germer, L. C., & Kelley, C. *All Things to All People: A Primer for K–12 ESL Teachers in Small Programs.* Alexandria, VA: TESOL, 1993.

Flexner, S. B. & Soukhanov, A. H. *Speaking Freely: A Guided Tour of American English.* New York: Oxford University Press, 1997.

Florida Board of Education. Multicultural, Education, Training, and Advocacy, Inc. (META Consent Decree) August 1990.

Florida Department of Education. Office of Multicultural Student Language Education (OMSLE). Fradd, S., Instructional Language Assessment CD.

Florida Department of Education. Office of Multicultural Student Language Education. (1990). Consent decree. (Online document) Available: Internet: http://www.firn.edu/doe/bin00011/restatem.htm.

Florida Department of Education. (1997–1998). LEP student countries of origin and languages. (Online document) Available: Internet: http://www.firn.edu/doe/bin00011/cnn19798.htm.

Freeman, D. & Freeman, Y. (2004). Three Types of English Language Learners, "School Talk." National Council of Teachers of English, July. Retrieved (2005) from www.NCTE.org.

Freeman, Y. & Freeman, D. *Whole Language for Second Language Learners.* Portsmouth, NH: Heinemann, 1992.

Fuey, V. "Teaching Language-Minority Students: Using Research to Inform Practice." *Equity & Excellence in Education* 30, (1):16–24, 1997.

Garcia, B. (1995). Florida Department of Education. "Issues Regarding the Education of LEP Students . . . A Restatement." (Online document) Available: Internet: http://www.firn.edu/doe/bin00011/restatem.htm.

Garcia, E. E. "Research and Review. The Education of Hispanics in Early Childhood: Of Roots and Wings." *Young Children* 52 (3):5–14, 1997.

Gardner, R. C. & Lambert, W. E. *Attitudes and Motivation in Second Language Learning.* Rowley, MA: Newbury House Publisher, 1972.

Gardner, H. *Frames of Mind: The Theory of Multiple Intelligences.* New York: Basic Books, Inc., 1983.

General Accounting Office. *Hispanics' Schooling. Risk Factors for Dropping Out and Barriers to Resuming Education.* Washington, D.C.: Author, 1994.

Ghrum, J. & Gilsan, E. *Teacher's Handbook: Contextualized Language Instruction.* Boston, MA: Hienle & Hienle, 1994.

Gibson, M. A. (2002) "Improving Graduation Outcomes for Migrant Students" ERIC Digest. Retrieved (2005) from http://www.ericdigest.org/2004-1/outcomes.htm.

Glover, J. A., Ronning, R. R., & Bruning, R. H. *Cognitive Psychology for Teachers.* New York: Macmillan Publishing Co., 1990.

Gonzalez, A. "Teaching in Two or More Languages in the Philippine Context." In J. Cenoz and F. Genese (Eds.), *Beyond Bilingualism: Multilingualism and Multilingual Education* (pp. 192–205). Clenedon, UK: Multilingual Matters, 1998.

Gonzalez, R. & Padilla, A. M. The Academic Resilence of Mexican-American High School Students. *Hispanic Journal of Behavioral Sciences,* 19(3): xx, 1997.

Goodman, Y. M. & Burke, C. L. *Reading Miscue Inventory Manual: Procedures for Diagnosis and Evaluation.* New York: Macmillan, 1972.

Goodman, K. S. *Miscue Analysis: Application to Reading Instruction.* Urbana, IL: National Council of Teachers of English, 1973.

Goodman, K. S., Goodman, Y. M., & Hood, W. J. *The Whole Language Evaluation Book.* Portsmouth, NH: Heinemann Educational Books, Inc., 1989.

Graham, C. R. "Beyond Integrative Motivation: The Development and Influence of Assimilative Motivation." Paper presented at the TESOL Convention, Houston, TX. (March, 1984).

Grice, H. P. "Logic and Conversation." In Jannedy et al., (Eds.) *Language Files.* Columbus, OH: Ohio State University Press, 1994: 236–238.

Hakuta, K. *Mirror of Language: The Debate on Bilingualism.* New York: Basic Books, 1986.

Hakuta, K. (2001). The Education of Language Minority Students. Testimony to the U.S. Commission on Civil Rights. April 13, 2001. Retrieved (2005) from www.stanford.edu/~hakuta/Docs/CivilRightsCommission.htm.

Harste, J., Burke, C., & Wood, V. *Language Stories and Literacy Lessons.* Portsmouth, NH: Heinemann, 1984.

Hoffman, L. (2005) "Overview of Public Elementary and Secondary Schools and Districts, 2001–2002." Retrieved (2005) from http://nces.ed.gov/pubs2003/overview03.

Holmes, D., Hedlund, P., & Nickerson, B. *Accommodating ELLs in State and Local Assessments.* Washington, DC: National Clearinghouse for Bilingual Education, 2000.

Hopstock, P. J. & Stephenson, T. (2003) "Report from the U.S. Department of Education, Office of English Language Enhancement, and Academic Achievement for Limited English Proficient Students, OELA." Retrieved (2005) from http://www.ncela.gwu.edu/stats/2_nation.htm.

Horbury, A. & Cotrell, K. "Cultural Factors Affecting the Acquisition of Reading Strategies in Bilingual Children." *Education 3 to 13* 24–26 (March, 1997).

Hudelsohn, S. "ESL Children's Writing: What We've Learned, What We're Learning." In *Children and ESL: Integrating Perspectives.* Washington, DC: TESOL Publications, 1986 pp. 23–54.

Hymes, D. *Directions in Sociolinguistics.* Philadelphia: University of Pennsylvania Press, 1974.

Indrasutra, C. "Narrative Styles in the Writing of Thai and American Students." In A. Purves (Ed.). *Writing Across Languages and Cultures: Issues in Contrastive Rhetoric,* pp. 275–304. Newbury Park, CA: Sage Publishers, 1988.

Jamieson, A., Curry, A., & Martinez, G. (2001) Cited in Diane August, "Literacy for English-Language Learners: Four Key Issues." Presented at the U.S. Department of Education's First-Annual Summit on English Language Acquisition, Washington, D.C., November 2002.

Jannedy, S., Poletto, R., & Wendon T. L. (Eds.) *Language Files.* Columbus, OH: Ohio University Press, 1994.

Johnson, L. "Success for Second Language Learners." *Learning* 50–52 (November/December, 1991).

Kachru, B. Literature and Language Teaching, Brumfit, C. J. and Carter R. A., (Eds.). Oxford, UK: Oxford University Press, 1991.

Kachru, B. Non-Native Literatures in English as a Resource for Language Teaching. *Literature and Language Teaching,* edited by R. Carter and C. Brumfit. London: Oxford University Press. pp. 140–149. (1991).

Kachru, B. *Standards, Codifications, and Sociolinguistic Realism: The English Language in the Outer Circle.* Cambridge: Cambridge University Press, 1985.

Kagan, J. "Reflection-Impulsivity and Reading Ability in Primary Grade Children." *Child Development* 36: 609–628 (1965).

Kaplan, R. B. "Cultural Thought Patterns in Intercultural Communication." *Language Learning* 16: 1–20 (1966).

———. "Contrastive Rhetoric and Second Language Learning: Notes Towards a Theory of Contrastive Rhetoric." In A. Purves (Ed.). *Writing Across Languages and Cultures: Issues in Contrastive Rhetoric*, pp. 275–304. Newbury Park, CA: Sage Publishers, 1988.

Kauchak, D., Eggen, P., & Carter, C. *Introduction to Teaching*. Upper Saddle River, NJ: Prentice-Hall, 2002.

Kindler, A. L. *Survey of the States' Limited English Proficient Students and Available Educational Programs and Services 2000–2001 Summary Report*. Washington, DC: U.S. Department of Education, Office of English Language Acquisition, Language Enhancement and Academic Achievement for Limited English Proficient Students, 2002. Retrieved (2005) from http://www.ncela.gwu.edu/states/reports/seareports/00012/sea0001.pdf.

Krashen, S., Long, M., & Scarcella, R. "Age, Rate, and Eventual Attainment in Second Language Acquisition." *TESOL Quarterly* 13(4):573–582 (1979).

Krashen, S. (1981). *Second Language Acquisition and Second Language Learning*. Oxford, UK: Pergamon Press.

Krashen, S. & Terrell, T. (1983). *The Natural Approach: Language Acquisition in the Classroom*. San Francisco: Alemany Press.

Kreeft, J. "Dialogue Writing-Bridge from Talk to Essay Writing." *Language Arts* 61: 141–150 (1983).

Lakoff, G. & Johnson, M. *Metaphors We Live By*. Chicago: University of Chicago Press, 1980.

Larsen-Freeman, D. *Techniques and Principles in Language Teaching*. Hong Kong: Oxford University Press, 1986.

Law, B. & Eckes, M. *The More-Than-Just-Surviving Handbook: ESL for Every Classroom Teacher*. Winnipeg: Peguis, 1990.

Lazear, D. *Seven Ways of Teaching*. Palatine, IL: IRI/Skylight Training and Publishing, 1991.

Leki, I. *Academic Writing: Exploring Processes and Strategies*. New York: St. Martin's Press, 1995.

Lennenberg, E. *Biological Foundations of Language*. New York: John Wiley & Sons, 1967.

Lightbown, P. & Spada, N. *How Languages are Learned*. Oxford, UK: Oxford University Press, 1993.

Martinez, Y., Scott, J., Cranston-Gingras, & Platt, F. "Voices from the Field: Interviews with Students from Migrant Farmworker Families." *The Journal of Educational Issues of Language Minority Students* 14 (Winter): 333–348 (1994). (Available online), http://www.ncbe.gwu.edu/miscpubs/jeilms/vol14/martinez.htm.

Maslow, A. *Motivation and Personality*. Second Ed. New York: Harper & Row, 1970.

McClelland, J. L., Rumelhart, D. E., & Hinton, G. E. "The Appeal of Parallel Distributed Processing." In D. E. Rumelhart, J. L. McClelland, and PDP Research Group (Eds.). *Parallel Distributed Processing: Explorations in the Microstructures of Cognition*. Vol. 1: Foundations (pp. 3–44). Cambridge, MA: MIT Press, 1986.

McDonough, S. H. *Strategy and Skill in Learning a Foreign Language*. London: Edward Arnold, 1995.

McLaughlin, B., T. Rossman, and B. McLeod (1983). Second language learning: An information-processing perspective. *Language Learning 33*, 135–158.

McLaughlin, B. *Theories of Second Language Learning*. London: Edward Arnold, 1987.

Meisels, S. *Using Work Sampling in Authentic Assessments*. Educational Leadership Vol. 54, No. 4: (1996/1997).

Menken, K. *What Are the Critical Issues in Wide-Scale Assessment of English Language Learners?* (Issue Brief No. 6). Washington, D.C.: National Clearinghouse for Bilingual Education, 2000.

Messick, S. & Associates (Eds.) *Individuality in Learning*. San Francisco: Jossey-Bass, 1976.

Mitchell, R., *Testing for Learning: How New Approaches to Evaluation Can Improve American Schools*. New York: Free Press, 1992.

National Clearinghouse for Bilingual Education. (1996). "Summary Report of the Survey of the States' Limited English Proficient Students and Available Educational Programs and Services 1994–1995." Retrieved from http://www.ncbe.gwu.edu/ncbepubs/seareports/94-95/enrollment.htm#public and http://www.ncbepubs/seareports/96-97//f3.htm.

National Clearinghouse for English Language Acquisition. *NCELA, 2002-2003 Report*. Retrieved from www.ncela.gwu.edu/policy/states/index.htm.

No Child Left Behind Act of 2001, Public Law 197-110. 107th Congress of the United States of America, 1st Session (January 8, 2002). Retrieved (2005) from http://www.ed.gov/legislation/ESEA02/107-110.pdf.

No Child Left Behind, NCLB. Retrieved from http://www.wrightslaw.com/news/2002nclb.sign.htm.

Nyikos, M. "Prioritizing Student Learning: A Guide for Teachers." *Focus on the Foreign Language Learner*. Lorraine Strasheim (Ed.), 25–39. Lincolnwood: NTC, 1991.

N.Z. English to U.S. English Dictionary. http://nz.com/NZ/Culture/NZDic.html.

Office of Educational Research and Improvement. (1993). "Reaching the goals. Goal 2: High school completion." In Vaznaugh, A. (1995, March). Dropout intervention and language minority youth. The Online ERIC DIGEST (online serial), 1. Available: Internet: http://www.cal.org/ericcll/digest/vaznau01.html.

O'Grady, W., Dobrovolsky, M., Aronoff, M. *Contemporary Linquistics: An Introduction*. New York: St. Martin's Press, 1989.

O'Malley, J. M. & Chamot, A. U. *Learning Strategies in Second Language Acquisition*. Cambridge, UK: Cambridge University Press, 1990.

O'Malley, J. M. & Valdez Pierce, L. *Authentic Assessment for English Language Learners: Practical Approaches for Teachers*. New York: Addison-Wesley, 1996.

Olsen, L. & Jaramillo, A. *Turning the Tides of Exclusion: A Guide for Educators and Advocates for Immigrant Students*. Oakland: CA, Tomorrow, 1999.

Osterman, K. F. "Students' Need for Belonging in the School Community." Review of Educational Research, 70(3): 323–367 (2000).

Ostler, S. "English in Parallels: A Comparison of English and Arabic Prose." In *Writing Across Languages: Analysis of L2 Text*, Ulla Connor and Robert B. Kaplan (Eds.) 169–185. Reading, MA: Addison-Wesley Publishing Co., 1987.

Oxford, R. L. *Language Learning Strategies: What Every Teacher Should Know*. Rowley, MA: Newbury House, 1990.

Pakir, A. "The Range and Depth of English-Knowing Bilinguals in Singapore." *World Englishes* 10: 167–180 (1991).

Parker, F. & Riley, K. *Linguistics for Non-Linguists: A Primer With Exercises*. Boston: Allyn and Bacon, 2000.

Paulson, F. et al. "What Makes a Portfolio a Portfolio?" *Educational Leadership* February: 60–63 (1992).

Peregoy, S. & Boyle, O. *Reading, Writing and Learning in ESL: A Resource Book for K–12 Teachers*, Fourth Edition. New York: Longman, 2005.

Perez, E. (1994). "Phonological Differences among Speakers of Spanish-Influenced English." In J. Vernthal & N. Bankson (Eds.) *Child Phonology: Characteristics, Assessment and Intervention with Special Populations*. (pp. 245–254). New York: Thieme, 1994.

Peyton, J. K., & Staton, J. *Resource Guide: A Dialogue Journal Bibliography*. Washington, D.C.: NCLE, 1993.

Pinell, G. & Fountas, I. *Word Matters: Teaching Phonics and Spelling in the Reading/Writing Classroom*. Porstmouth, NH: Heinemann, 1998.

Piper, T. *Language and Learning: The Home and School Years*. New Jersey: Merrill and Prentice Hall, 1998.

Platt, J. & Weber, H. *English in Singapore and Malaysia: Status: Features: Functions*. Kuala Lumpur: Oxford University Press, 1980.

Pugh, S. L., Hicks, J. W., Davis, M., & Venstra, T. *Bridging: A Teacher's Guide to Metaphorical Thinking*. Illinois: National Council of Teachers of English, 1992.

Quirk, R. *The English Language in a Global Context*. Cambridge: Cambridge University Press, 1985.

Reid, J. "The Learning Style Preferences of ESL Students." *TESOL Quarterly* 21.1 (March): 87–111 (1987).

———. *Teaching ESL Writing*. New Jersey: Prentice Hall Regents, 1993.

———. "Learning Styles." In P. Byrd and J. Reid (Eds.) *Grammar in the Composition Class*. Boston: Heinle and Heinle, 1998.

Reinart, H. "One Picture Is Worth a Thousand Words? Not Necessarily." *Modern Language Journal* 60:160–168 (1976).

Reppen, R. & Grabe, W. "Spanish Transfer Effects in the English Writing of Elementary Students." Lenguas Modernas 20, 113–128 (1993).

Rhodes, L. K. & Shanklin, N. *Windows Into Literacy*. Portsmouth, NH: Heinemann, 1992.

Roberge, M. M. "Generation 1.5 Immigrant Students: What Special Experiences, Characteristics and Educational Needs Do They Bring to Our English Classes?" Paper presented at the 37th Annual TESOL Convention, Baltimore, MD, 2003.

Romo, H. "Mexican Immigrants in High Schools: Meeting their Needs." ERIC DIGEST. ERIC/CRESS. Appalachia Educational Laboratory, Charleston, West Virginia. (ERIC Document Reproduction Service No. ED1.331/2:EDO-RC-92-8). (March, 1993).

Ross, L. "Connecting with Kids and Parents of Different Cultures: How to Develop Positive Relationships with Today's Diverse Families." *Instructor* (July/August) 51–53: (1995).

Rubin, J. "What the Good Language Learner Can Teach Us." *TESOL Quarterly* 9:41–51 (1975).

Ruiz de Velasco, J., Fix, M., & Chu Clewell, B. "Overlooked and Underserved Immigrant Students in U.S. Secondary Schools." Washington, D.C., The Urban Institute, 2000.

Sa'Adeddin, M. "Text Development and Arabic-English Negative Interference." *Applied Linguistics* 10:36–51 (1989).

Samovar, L. A. & Porter, R. E. *Communication Between Cultures.* (5th edition). Belmont, CA: Thomson/Wadsworth, 2004.

Schall, J. "Unbeatable Ways to Reach Your LEP Students." *Instructor* (July/August) 54–59 (1995).

Schmidt, R. "Deconstructing Consciousness in Search of Useful Definitions for Applied Linguistics." *AILA Review* Vol. 11: 11–16 (1994).

Schrank, J. "The Language of Advertising Claims." Retrieved on November 11, 2005 at http://sunset.backbone.olemiss.edu/~egjbp/comp/ad-claims.html.

Schumann, J. "Social and Psychological Factors in Second Language Acquisition." In J. Richards (Ed.) *Understanding Second and Foreign Language Learning: Issues and Approaches.* Rowley, MA: Newbury House, 1978.

Selvon, S. "A Brighter Sun." In Kachru, Braj. *Non-Native Literatures in English as a Resource for Language Teaching. Literature and Language Teaching.* Brumfit, C. J. and Carter, R. A. (Eds.). Oxford, UK: Oxford University Press, 1991.

Skinner, B. F. *Verbal Behavior.* New York: Appleton-Century-Crofts, 1957.

Smith, F. "Content Learning: A Third Reason for Using Literature in Teaching Reading." *Reading Research and Instruction* 32(3):64–71 (1993).

Smith, L. Fundamentals of Phonetics. A Practical Guide for Students. Boston: Allyn and Bacon, 2005.

Stephens, M. "Pop Goes the World." *Los Angeles Times Magazine*, pp. 22–26, 34. (January 17, 1993).

Stern, H. H. *Issues and Options in Language Teaching.* Oxford: OUP, 1992.

Tarone, E. "Some Thoughts on the Notion of Communication Strategy." *TESOL Quarterly* 15:285–295 (1981).

Teale, W. H. "Emergent Literacy: Reading and Writing Development in Early Childhood." In *Research in Literacy: Merging Perspectives.* Thirty-Sixth Yearbook of the National Reading Conference, edited by J. E. Readance and R. S. Baldwin. Rochester, NY: National Reading Conference, 1987.

TESOL. *ESL Standards for Pre K–12 Students.* Bloomington, IL: TESOL, Inc., 1997.

"The Bilingual Brain." *Discover*, 19.10:26 (1997).

Thomas, W. P. & Collier, V. *Improving Schools for English Language Learners.* Fairfax, VA: George Mason University Press, (2003).

Thomas, W. P. & Collier, V. (2001). "National Study of School Effectiveness for Language Minority Students' Long-term Academic Achievement." Retrieved 2005 from www.crede.ucsc.edu/research/llaa/1.1_final.htm.

Tongue, R. K. *The English of Singapore and Malaysia.* Singapore: Eastern University Press, 1974.

Tucker, R. G. "A Global Perspective on Bilingualism and Bilingual Education." ERIC DIGEST (available online), http://www.cal.org/ericcll/digestglobal.html. (August, 1991).

United States Census Bureau, 2000. "Brief: The Asian Population: 2000," U.S. Department of Commerce Economics and Statistics Adminstration. Retrieved (2005) from http://www.censusbureau.org.

United States Department of Education. (2005) Retrieved (2005) from http://www.ed.gov/nclb/accountability/index.htm.

United States Department of Education. *Descriptive Study of Services to Limited English Proficient Students.* Washington, D.C.: Planning and Evaluation Service, 1993.

United States Department of Education, Office of English Language Acquisition. "Language Enhancement and Academic Achievement for Limited English Proficient Students, OELA (1992–1993 to 2002–2003)." Retrieved (2005) from www.ncela.gwu.edu/policy/states/index.htm.

Varghese, M. (2005) "An Introduction to Meeting the Needs of English Language Learners." Retrieved (2005) from http://www.newhorizons.org/spneeds/ell/varghese.htm.

Ventriglia, L. *Conversations of Miguel and Maria: How Children Learn a Second Language*. MA: Addison-Wesley, 1982.

Violand-Sanchez, E. (2005). "Meeting the Instructional Needs of High School Language Learners." Retrieved (2005) from http://www.publishers.org/school/pdf/Dr.EmmaVioland-Sanchez.html.

Vygotsky, L. S. *Mind in Society: The Development of Higher Psychological Processes*. Cambridge, MA: Harvard University Press, 1978.

Walter, T. *Amazing English!* Boston, MA: Addison-Wesley, 1996.

Wenden, A. "Facilitating Learning Competence: Perspectives on an Expanded Role for Second Language Teachers." *Canadian Modern Language Review* 41:980–990 (1985).

Whorf, B. *Language, Thought and Reality: Selected Writings of Benjamin Lee Whorf*. Cambridge, MA: MIT Press, 1956.

Zarillo, J. J. *Ready for RICA: A Test Preparation Guide for California's Reading Instruction Competence Assessment*. Upper Saddle River, NJ: Prentice Hall, 2000.

Zelasko, N. & Antunez, B. *If Your Child Learns in Two Languages*. Washington, D.C.: National Clearing House for Bilingual Education, 2000. (Online document). Available: http://www.ncbe.gwu.edu/ncbepubs/parent/index.htm.

Zellermeyer, M. "An Analysis of Oral and Literate Texts: Two Types of Reader-Writer Relationships in Hebrew and English." In B. Rafoth and D. Rubin (Eds.) 287–303. *The Social Construction of Written Communication*. Norwood, NJ: Ablex, 1988.

Zgonc, Y. *Sounds in Action: Phonological Awareness Activities and Assessment*. Petersborough, NH: Crystal Springs Books, 2000.

Index